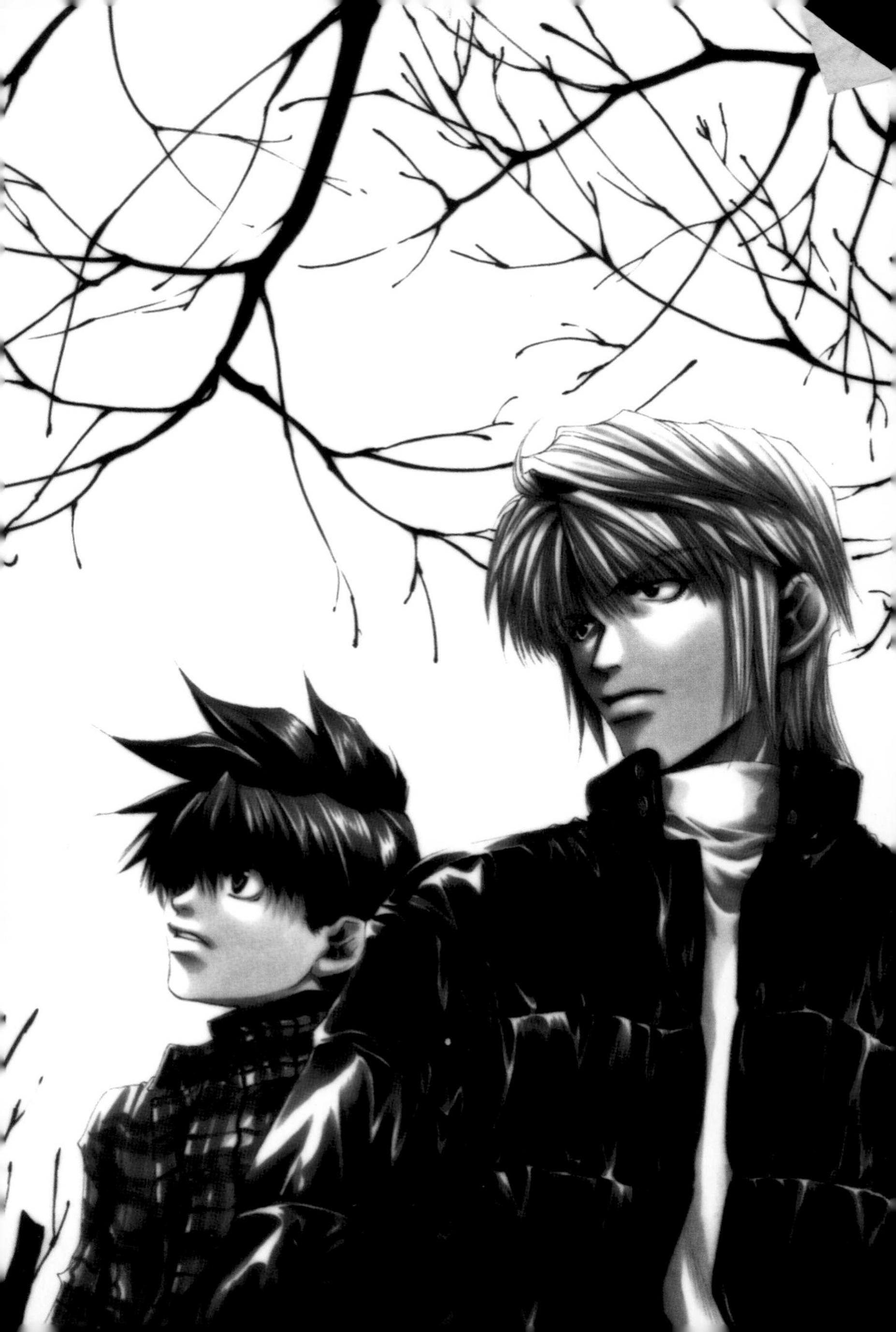

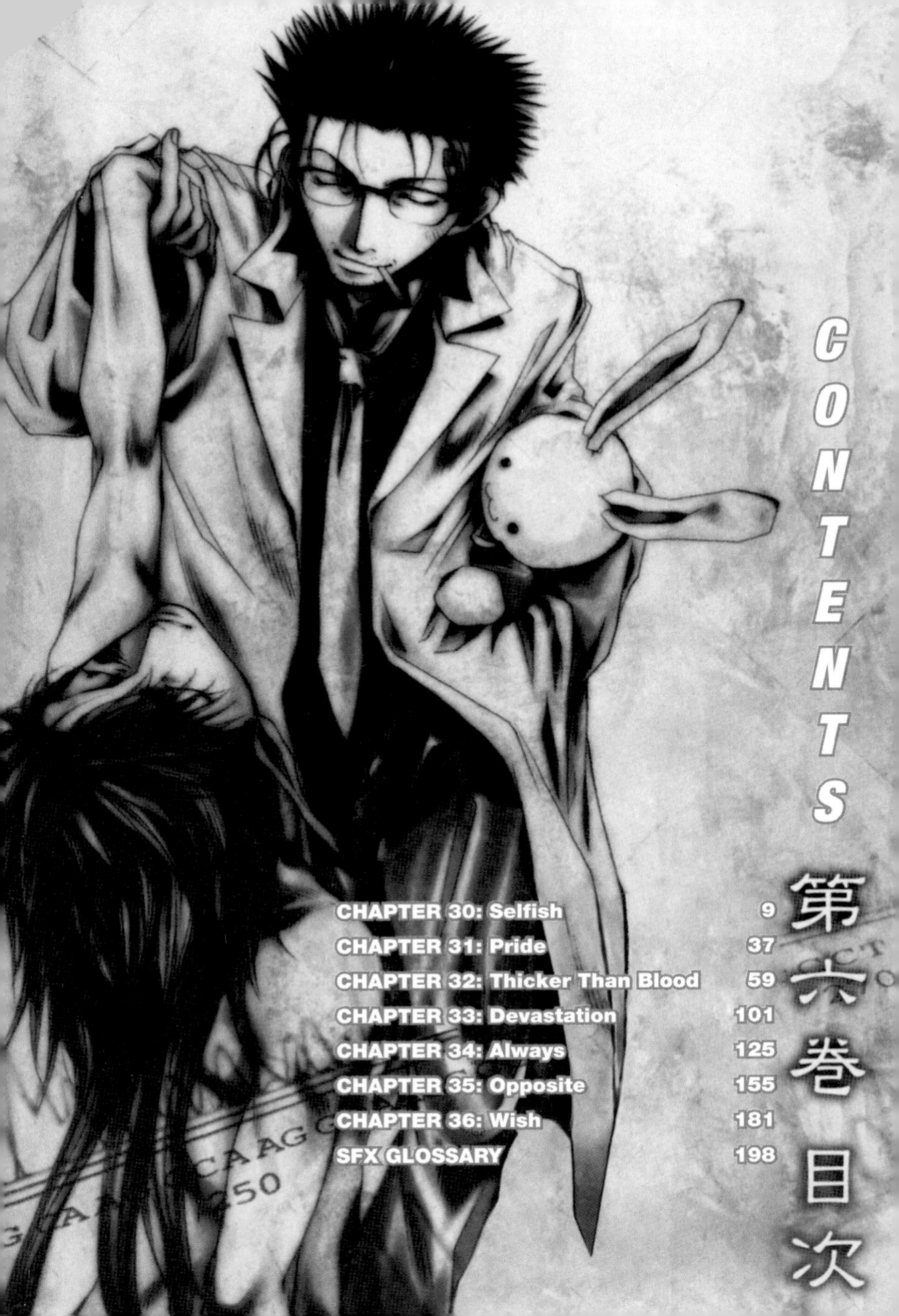

CONTENTS

CHAPTER 30: Selfish — 9

CHAPTER 31: Pride — 37

CHAPTER 32: Thicker Than Blood — 59

CHAPTER 33: Devastation — 101

CHAPTER 34: Always — 125

CHAPTER 35: Opposite — 155

CHAPTER 36: Wish — 181

SFX GLOSSARY — 198

第六巻 目次

最遊記

SAIYUKI

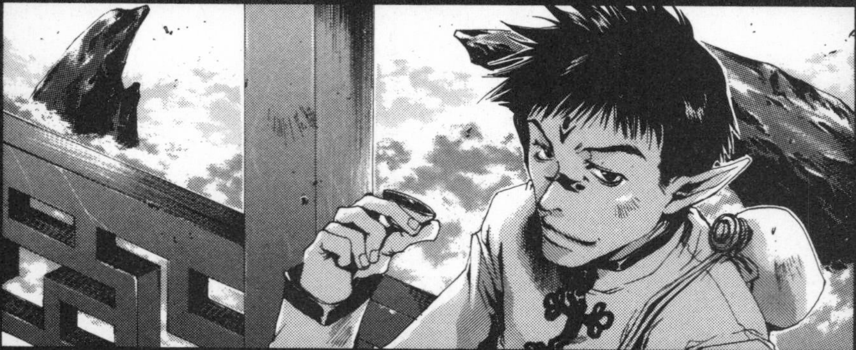

6

KAZUYA MINEKURA

SAIYUKI Vol. 6
Created by Kazuya Minekura

Translation - Athena Nibley and Alethea Nibley
Associate Editor - Peter Ahlstrom
English Adaptation - Lianne Sentar
Retouch and Lettering - Derron Bennet
Production Artist - Louis Csontos
Cover Layout - Anna Kernbaum

Editor - Lillian Diaz-Przybyl
Digital Imaging Manager - Chris Buford
Pre-Press Manager - Antonio DePietro
Production Managers - Jennifer Miller and Mutsumi Miyazaki
Art Director - Matt Alford
Managing Editor - Jill Freshney
VP of Production - Ron Klamert
Editor-in-Chief - Mike Kiley
President and C.O.O. - John Parker
Publisher and C.E.O. - Stuart Levy

A **TOKYOPOP** Manga

TOKYOPOP Inc.
5900 Wilshire Blvd. Suite 2000
Los Angeles, CA 90036

E-mail: info@TOKYOPOP.com
Come visit us online at www.TOKYOPOP.com

ISBN: 1-59532-431-3

First TOKYOPOP printing: January 2005
10 9 8 7 6 5 4 3 2 1
Printed in the USA

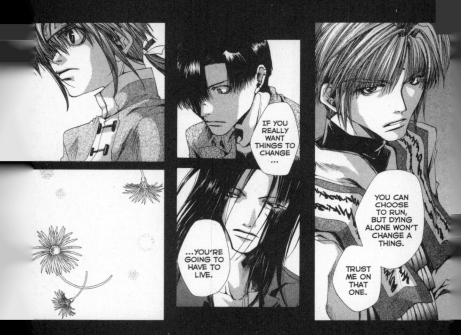

YOU CAN CHOOSE TO RUN, BUT DYING ALONE WON'T CHANGE A THING.
TRUST ME ON THAT ONE.
IF YOU REALLY WANT THINGS TO CHANGE ...
...YOU'RE GOING TO HAVE TO LIVE.

The Story So Far

Shangri-La lies in chaos. After the combination of science and youkai magic caused the Minus Wave--a force that drove all youkai in the land mad--Genjyo Sanzo, Sha Gojyo, Cho Hakkai, and Son Goku began their journey West to stop the revival of Gyumaoh and thus save the world. Nothing, however, can save the companions from feeling animosity toward each other for a good ninety percent of the journey.

After reflecting on how Hakkai's revenge in the past led to the first full meeting of the Sanzo Ikkou, our heroes traveled to the desert to seek the lost Tenchi Kaigen sutra of a murdered Sanzo. The youkai responsible for the priest's death resided in an underground fortress, but the fortress' dangerous entrance alone was enough to lead the Sanzo Ikkou into the youkai's clutches. Sanzo still managed to defeat the malicious youkai...but not before the youkai emptied a lethal amount of poison into the injured priest.

In the meantime, Kougaiji and Dokugakuji also set out into the desert to also seek the missing sutra. They discovered Jeep, but can't help but wonder what happened to his owners...

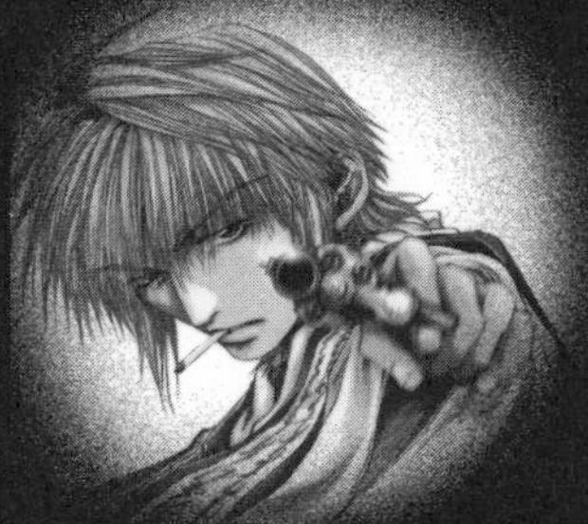

Genjyo Sanzo –

A very brutal, worldly priest. He drinks, smokes, gambles and even carries a gun. He's looking for the sacred scripture of his late master, Sanzo Houshi. He's egotistical, haughty and has zero sense of humor, but this handsome 23-year-old hero also has calm judgment and charisma. His favorite phrases are "Die" and "I'll kill you." His main weapons are the Maten Sutra, a handgun, and a paper fan for idiots. He's 177cm tall (approx. 5'10"), and is often noted for his drooping purple eyes.

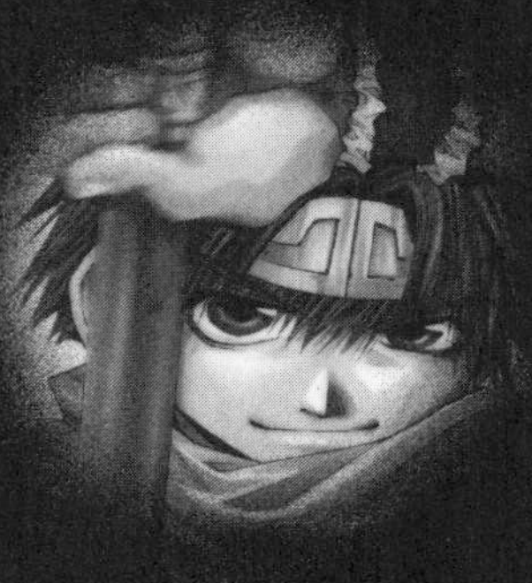

Son Goku –

The brave, cheerful Monkey King of legend; an unholy child born from the rocks where the aura of the Earth was gathered. His brain is full of thoughts of food and games. To pay for crimes he committed when he was young, he was imprisoned in the rocks for five hundred years without aging. Because of his optimistic personality, he's become the mascot character of the group; this 18-year-old of superior health is made fun of by Gojyo, yelled at by Sanzo and watched over by Hakkai. He's 162cm tall (approx. 5'4"). His main weapon is the Nyoi-Bo, a magical cudgel that can extend into a sansekkon staff.

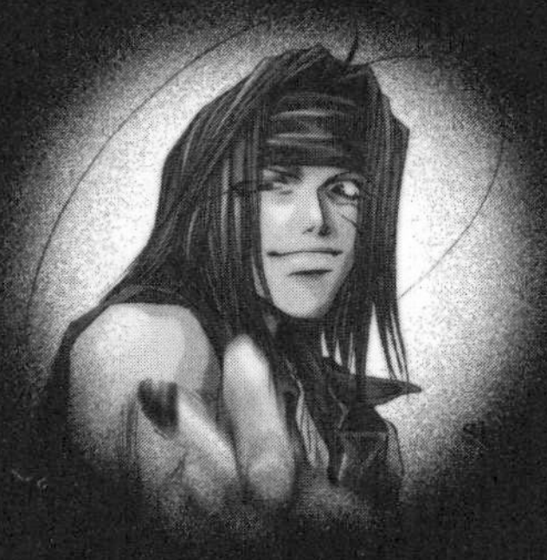

Sha Gojyo –

Gojyo is a lecherous kappa (water youkai). His behavior might seem vulgar and rough at first glance (and it is), but to his friends he's like a dependable older brother. He and Goku are sparring partners, he and Hakkai are best friends, and he and Sanzo are bad friends (ha ha!). Sometimes his love for the ladies gets him into trouble. Because of his unusual heritage, he doesn't need a limiter to blend in with the humans. His favorite way of fighting is to use a shakujou, a staff with a crescent-shaped blade connected by a chain; it's quite messy. He's 184cm tall (approx. 6'), has scarlet hair and eyes, and is a 22-year-old chain smoker.

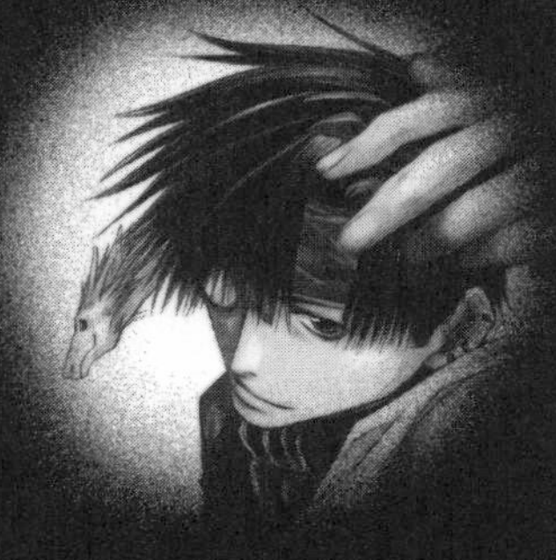

Cho Hakkai –

A pleasant, rather absent-minded young man with a kind smile that suits him nicely. It's sometimes hard to tell whether he's serious or laughing to himself at his friends' expense. His darker side comes through from time to time in the form of a sharp, penetrating gaze, a symbol of a dark past. As he's Hakuryu's (the white dragon) owner, he gets to drive the Jeep. Because he uses kikou jutsu (Chi manipulation) in battle, his "weapon" is his smile (ha ha!). He's 22 years old, 181cm tall (approx. 5'11") and his eyes are deep green (his right eye is nearly blind). The cuffs he wears on his left ear are Youkai power limiters.

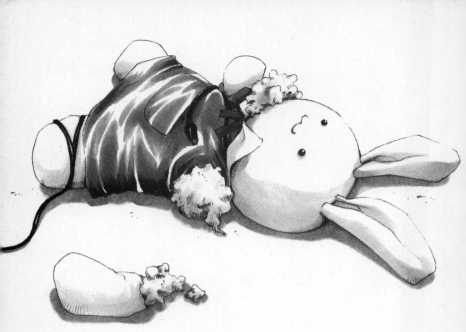

EVEN IF THERE'S NO
MEANING IN THIS LIFE...

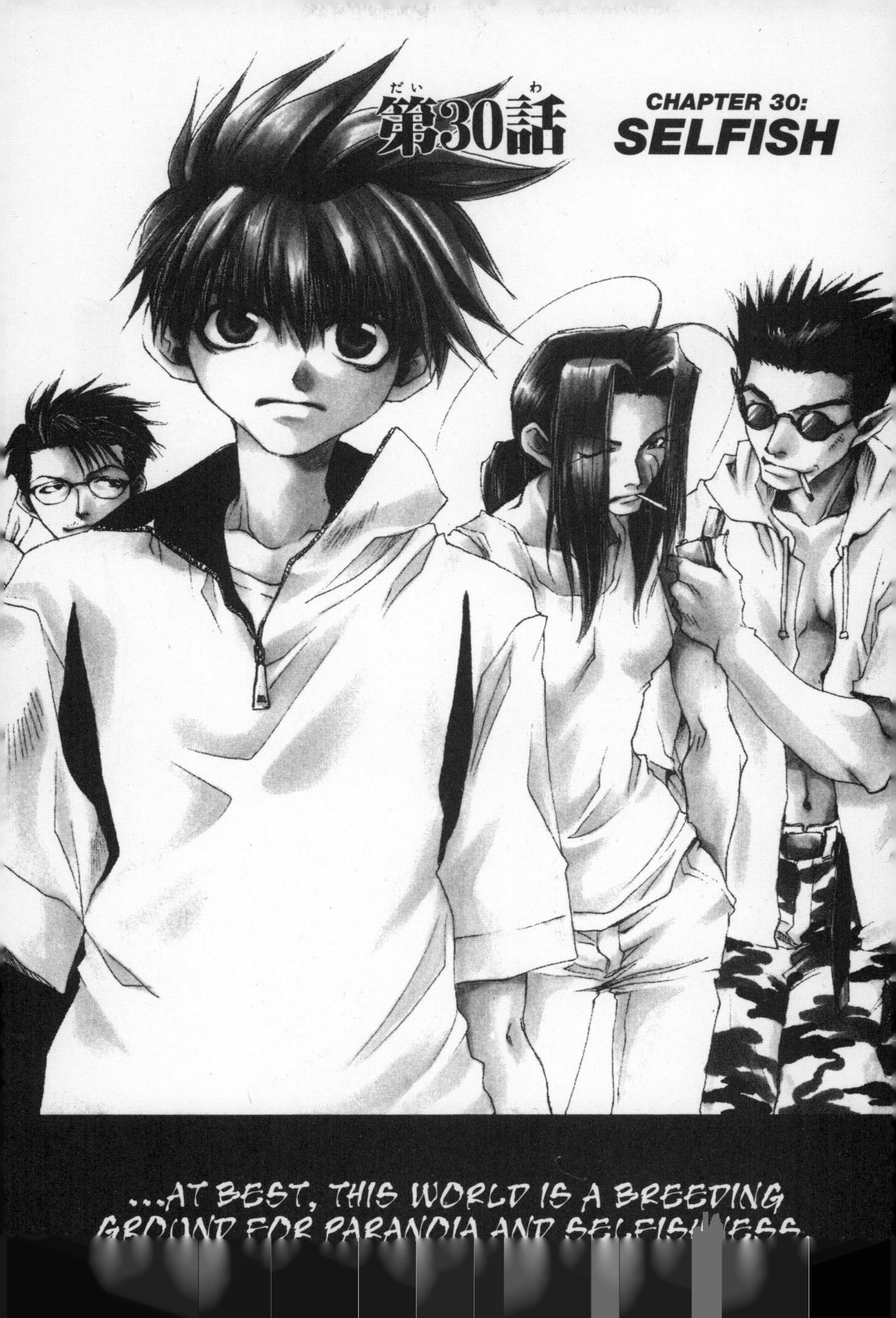
第30話
だい わ
CHAPTER 30:
SELFISH
...AT BEST, THIS WORLD IS A BREEDING
GROUND FOR PARANOIA AND SELFISHNESS.

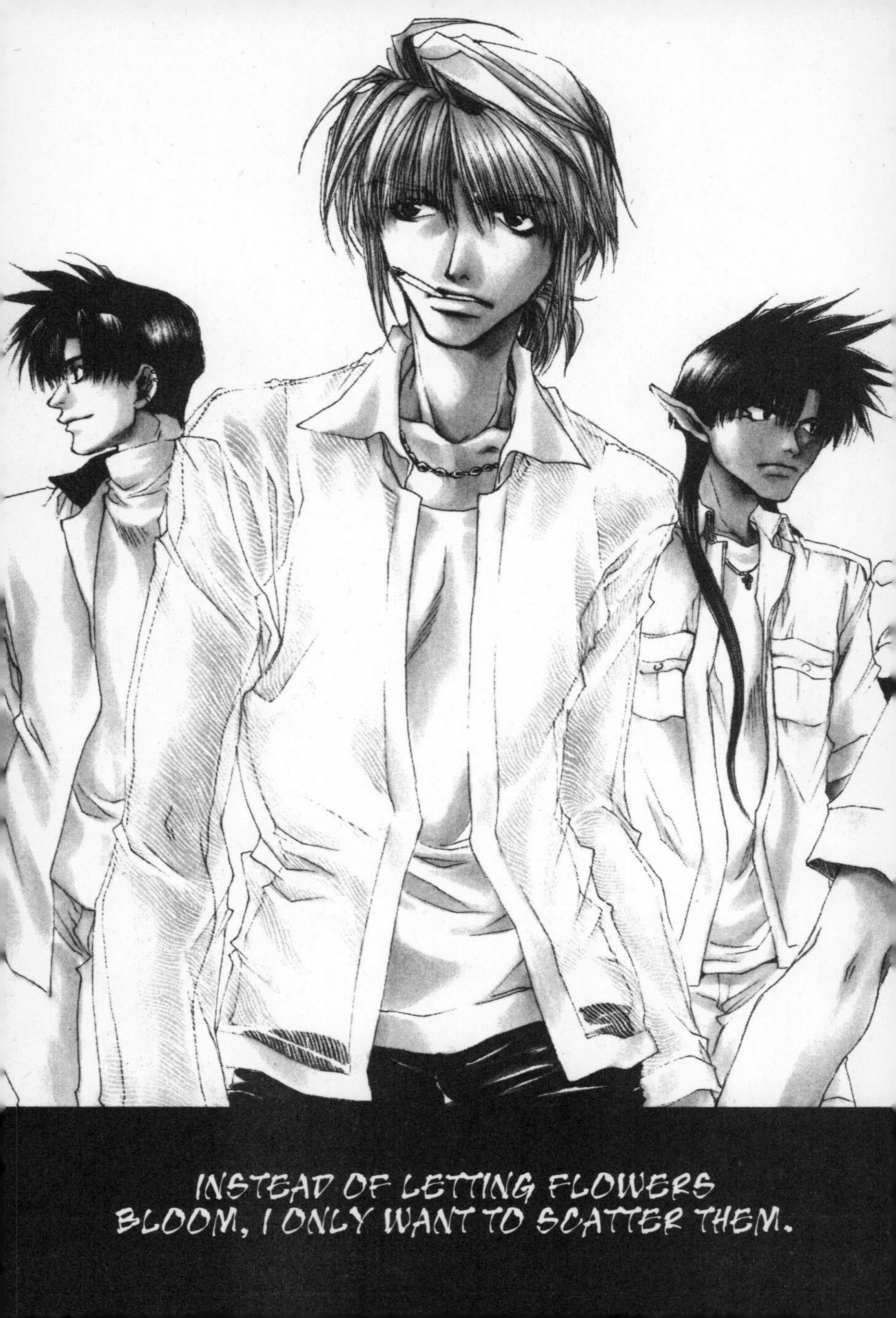

INSTEAD OF LETTING FLOWERS
BLOOM, I ONLY WANT TO SCATTER THEM.

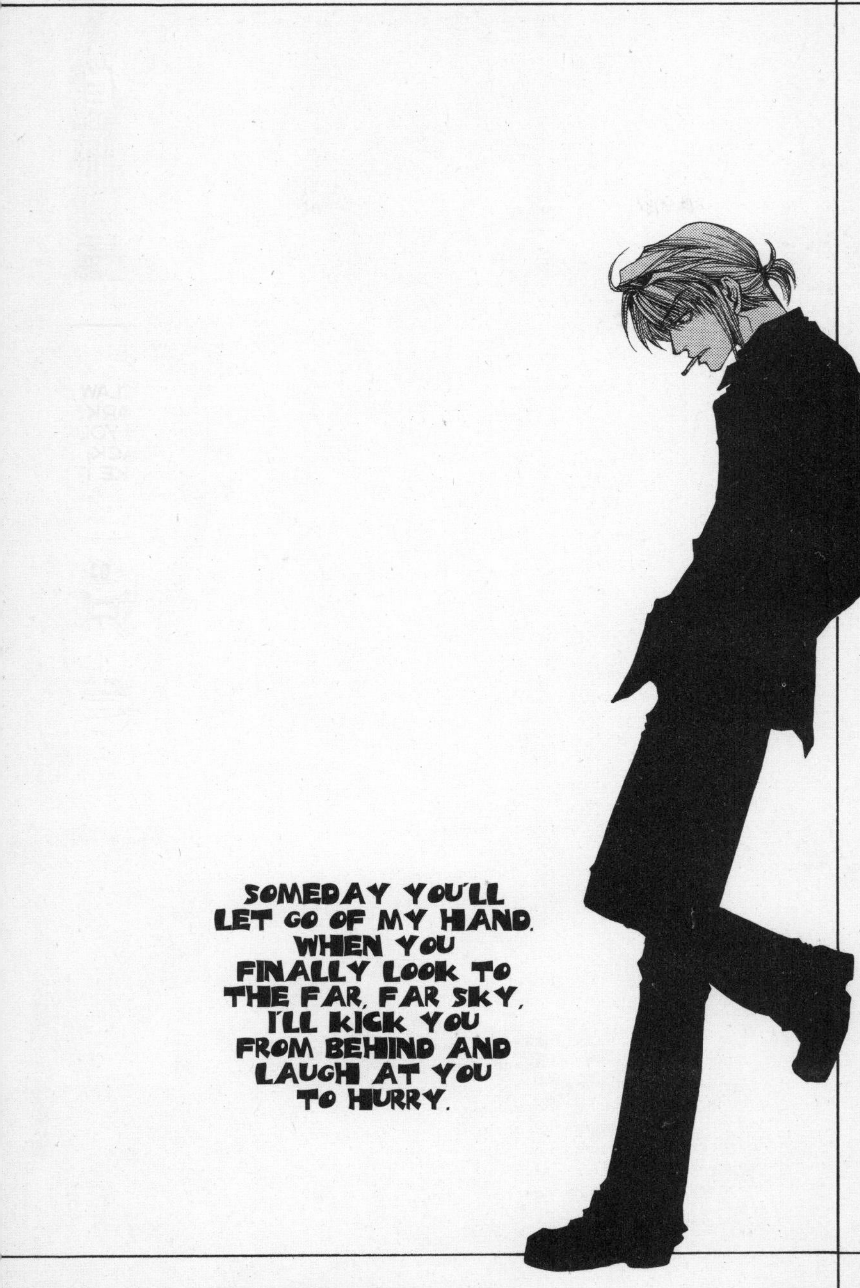
SOMEDAY YOU'LL LET GO OF MY HAND. WHEN YOU FINALLY LOOK TO THE FAR, FAR SKY, I'LL KICK YOU FROM BEHIND AND LAUGH AT YOU TO HURRY.

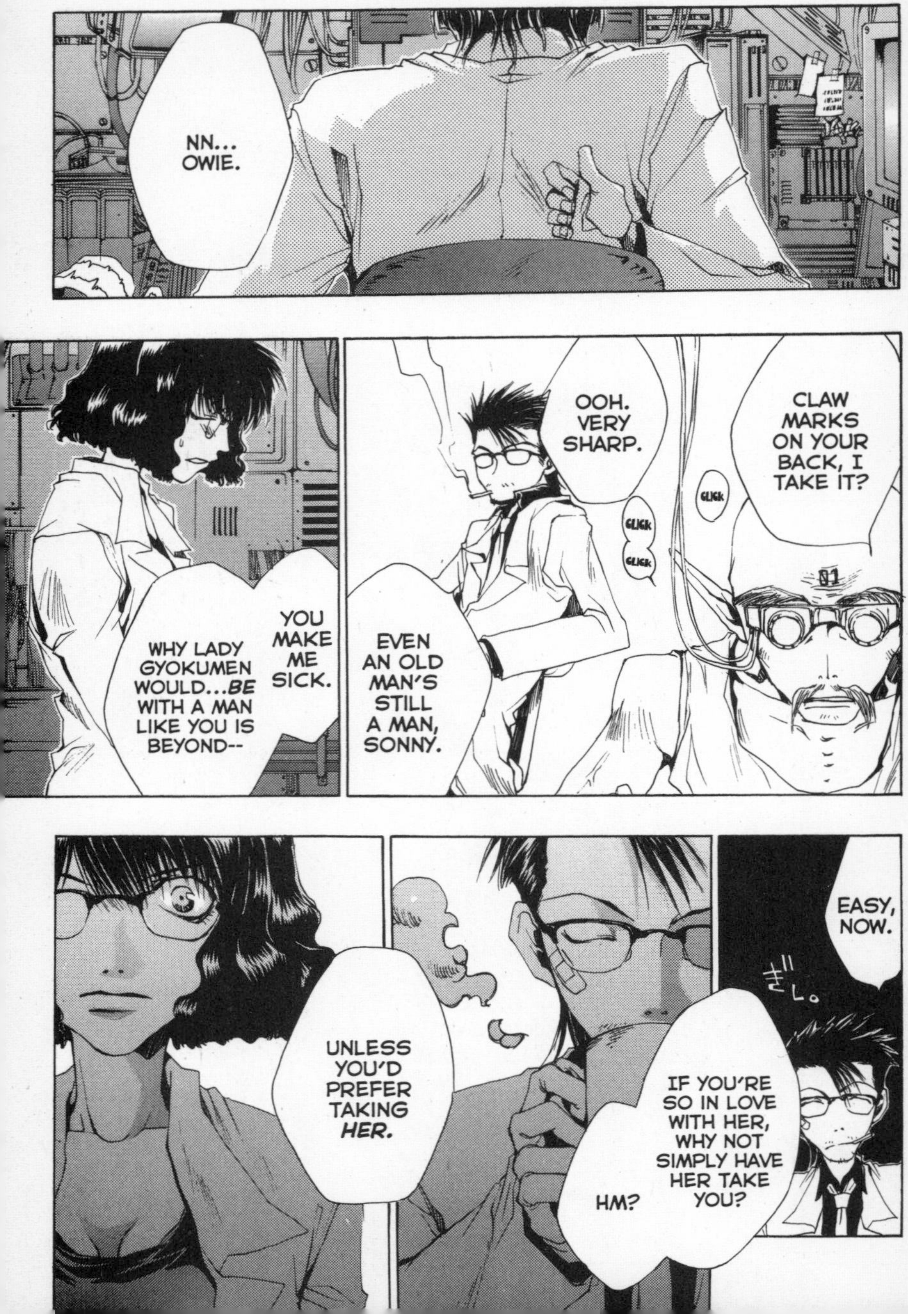
NN... OWIE.
CLAW MARKS ON YOUR BACK, I TAKE IT?
OOH. VERY SHARP.
GLICK
GLICK
GLICK
EVEN AN OLD MAN'S STILL A MAN, SONNY.
YOU MAKE ME SICK.
WHY LADY GYOKUMEN WOULD...*BE* WITH A MAN LIKE YOU IS BEYOND--
EASY, NOW.
ぎし。
IF YOU'RE SO IN LOVE WITH HER, WHY NOT SIMPLY HAVE HER TAKE YOU?
HM?
UNLESS YOU'D PREFER TAKING ***HER.***

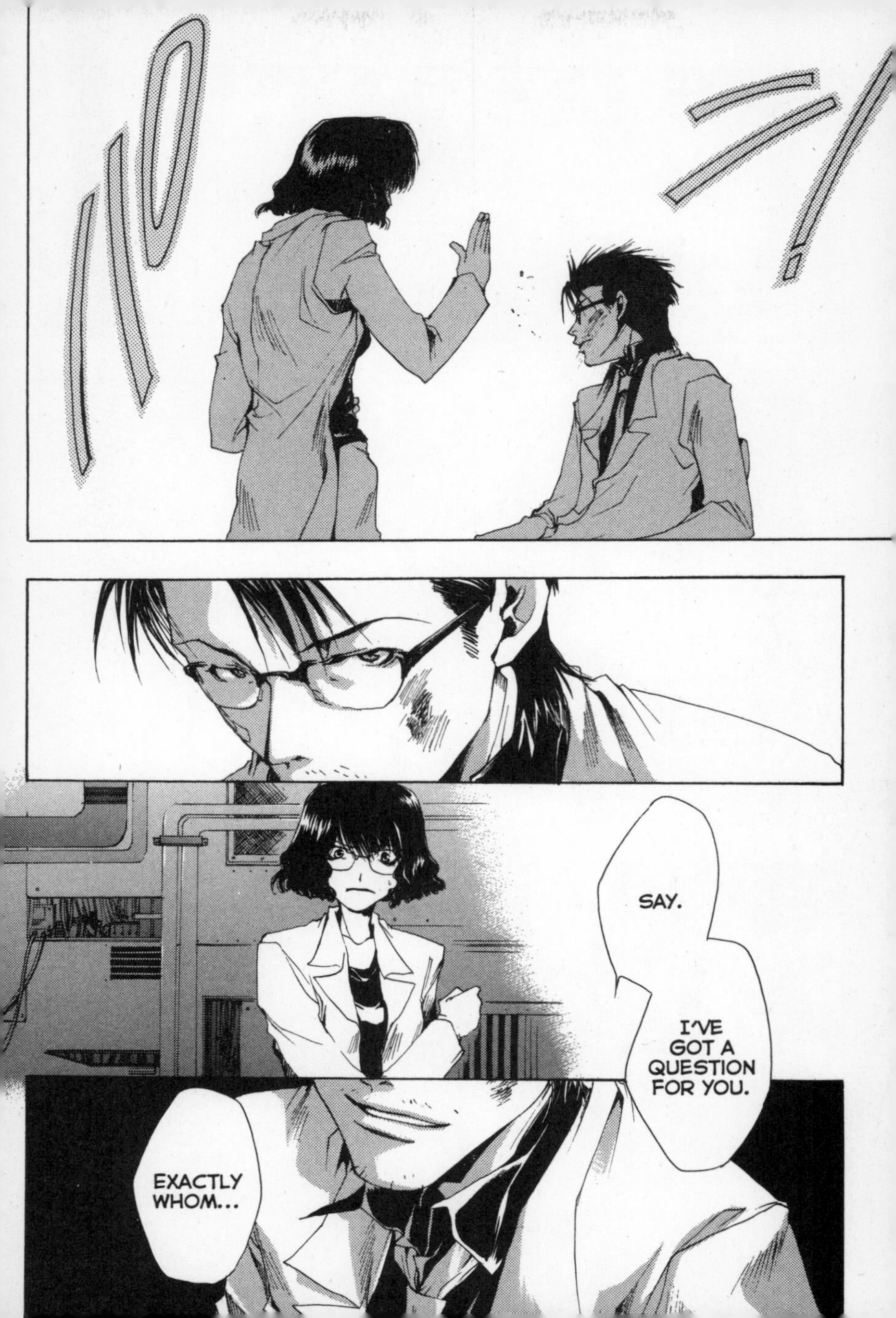
SAY.
I'VE GOT A QUESTION FOR YOU.
EXACTLY WHOM...

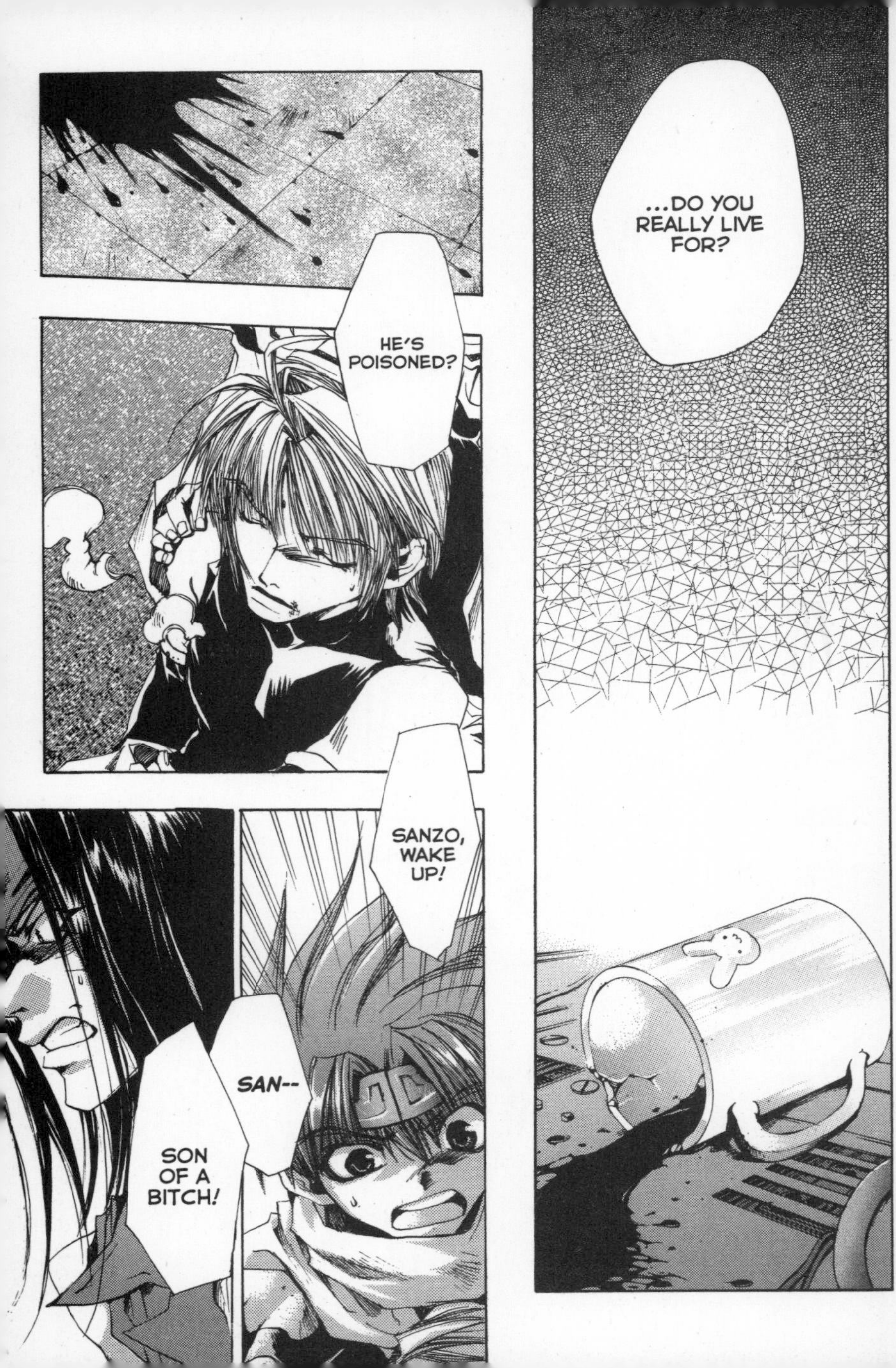
...DO YOU REALLY LIVE FOR?
HE'S POISONED?
SANZO, WAKE UP!
SAN--
SON OF A BITCH!

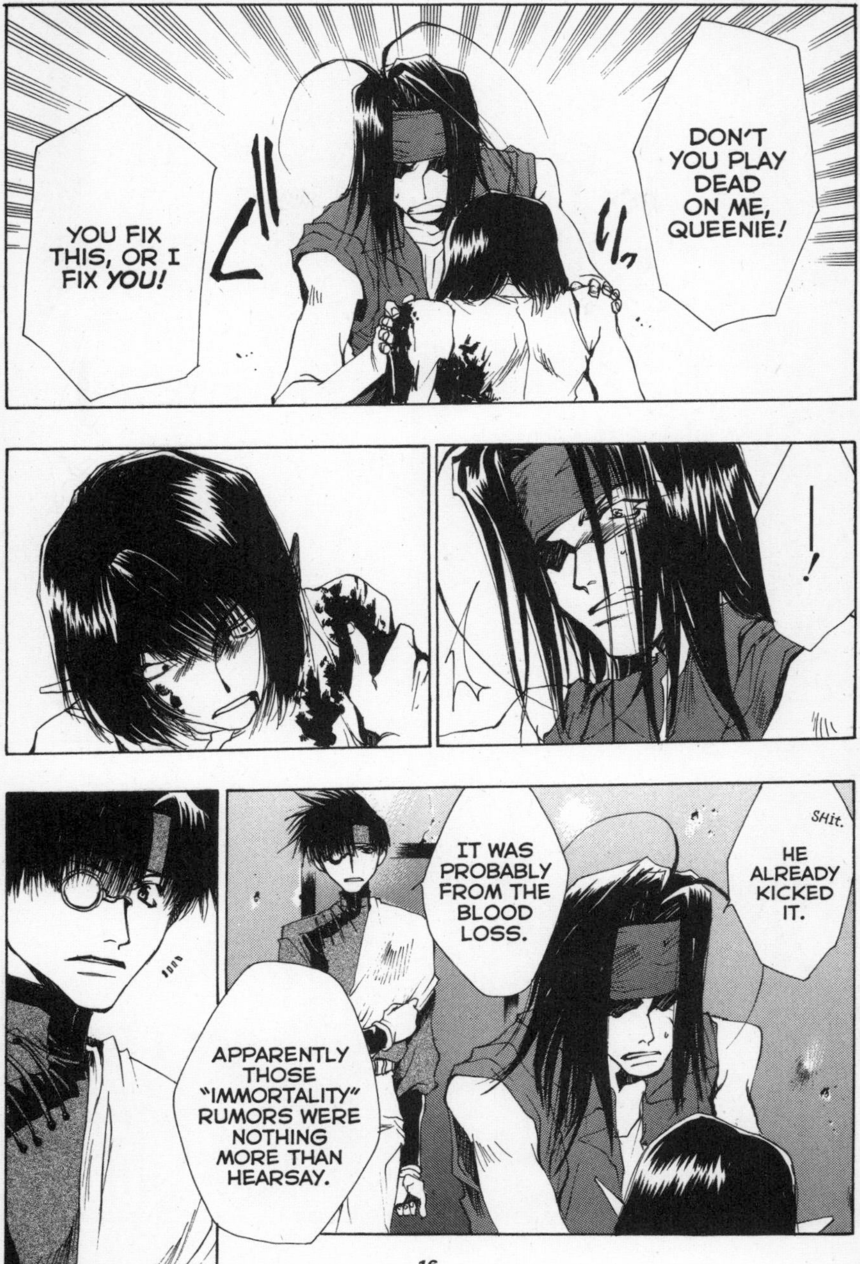
DON'T YOU PLAY DEAD ON ME, QUEENIE!
YOU FIX THIS, OR I FIX YOU!
!
SHit.
HE ALREADY KICKED IT.
IT WAS PROBABLY FROM THE BLOOD LOSS.
APPARENTLY THOSE "IMMORTALITY" RUMORS WERE NOTHING MORE THAN HEARSAY.

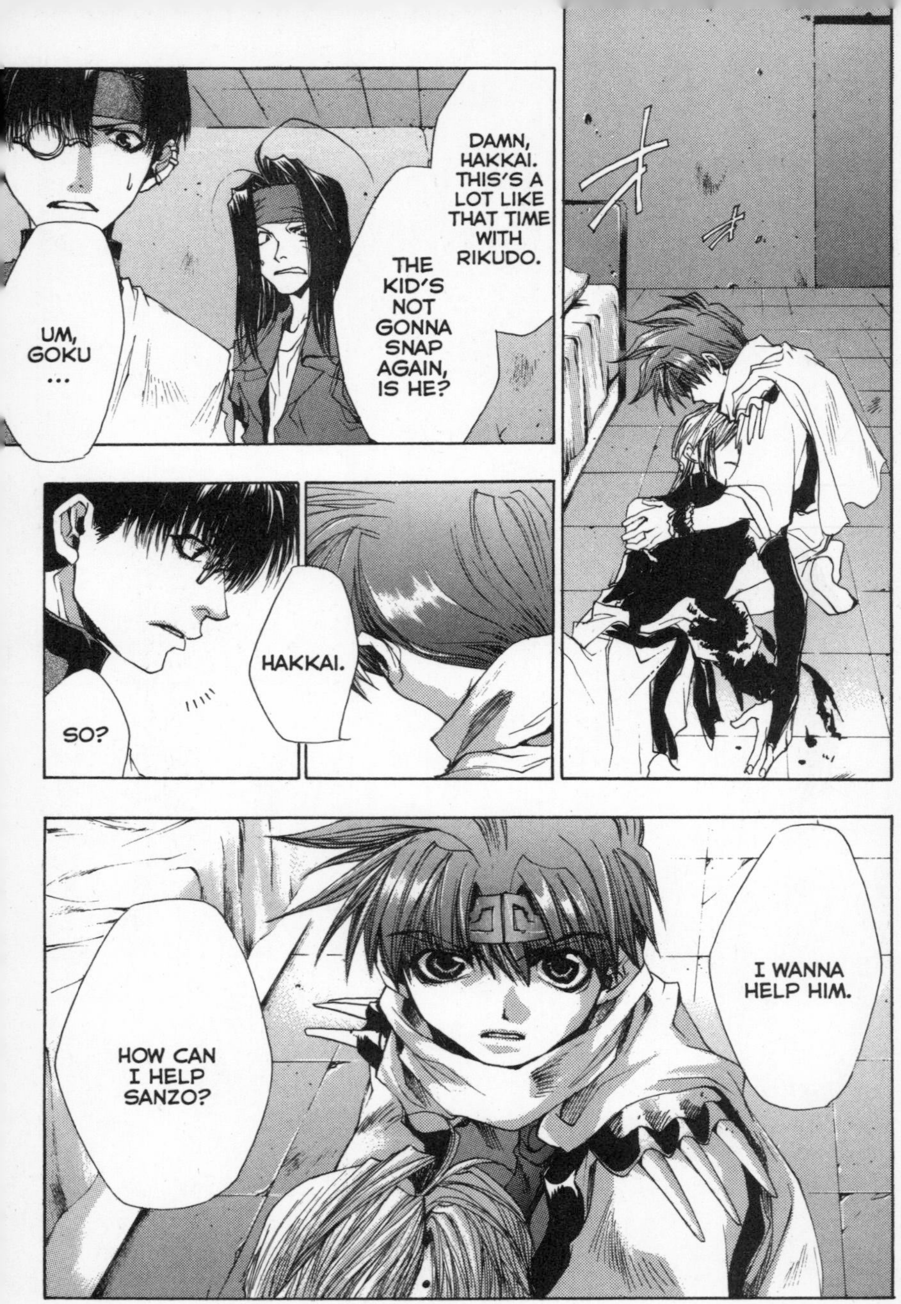
DAMN, HAKKAI. THIS'S A LOT LIKE THAT TIME WITH RIKUDO.
THE KID'S NOT GONNA SNAP AGAIN, IS HE?
UM, GOKU ...
HAKKAI.
SO?
I WANNA HELP HIM.
HOW CAN I HELP SANZO?

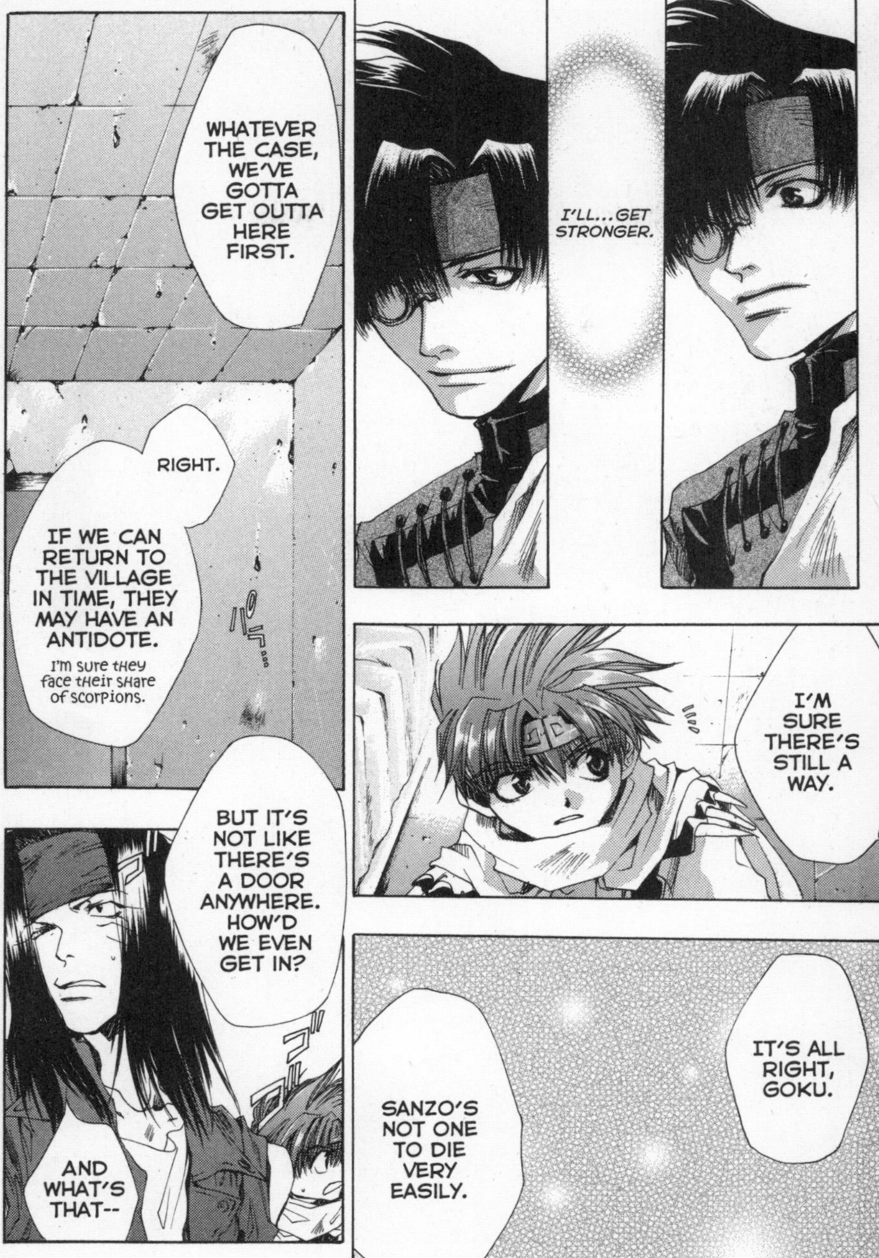
I'LL...GET STRONGER.
I'M SURE THERE'S STILL A WAY.
WHATEVER THE CASE, WE'VE GOTTA GET OUTTA HERE FIRST.
RIGHT.
IF WE CAN RETURN TO THE VILLAGE IN TIME, THEY MAY HAVE AN ANTIDOTE.
I'm sure they face their share of scorpions.
IT'S ALL RIGHT, GOKU.
SANZO'S NOT ONE TO DIE VERY EASILY.
BUT IT'S NOT LIKE THERE'S A DOOR ANYWHERE. HOW'D WE EVEN GET IN?
AND WHAT'S THAT--

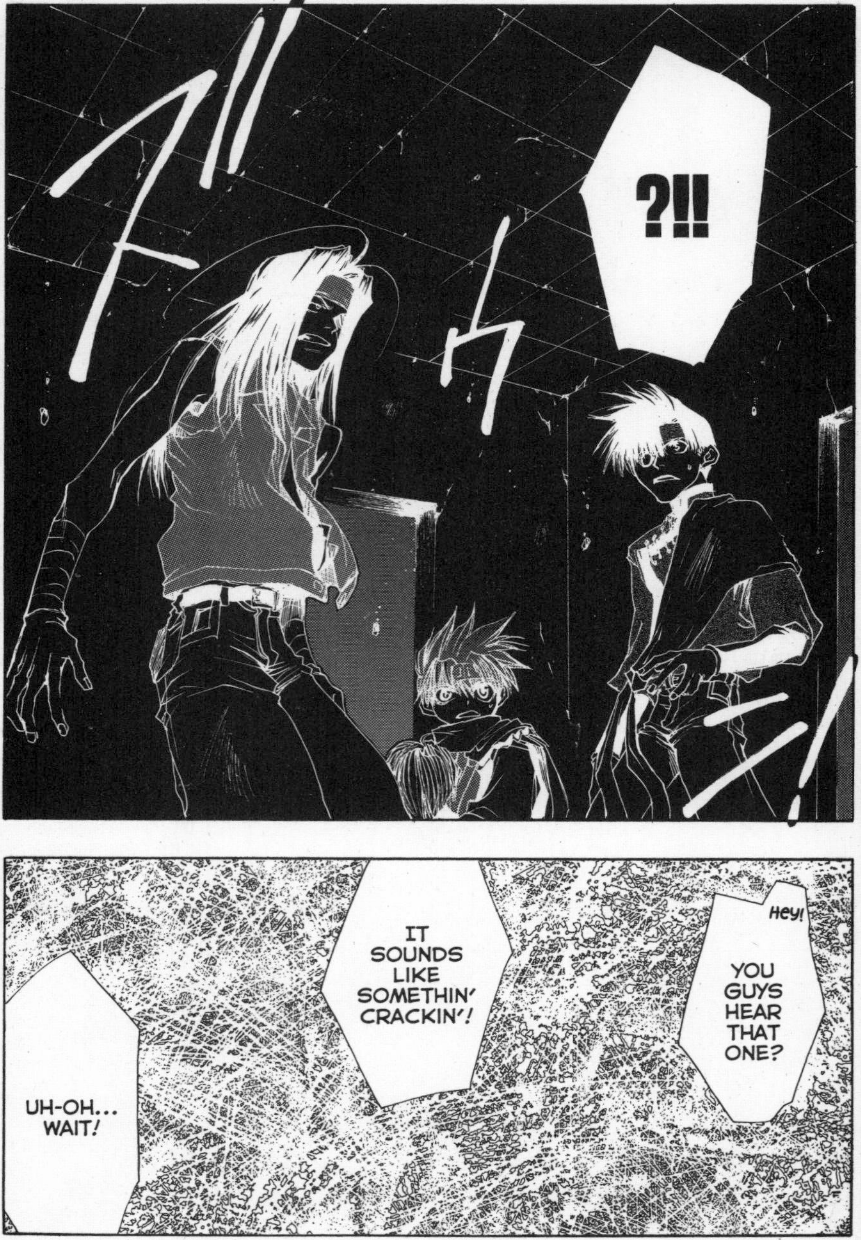
?!!
HEY!
YOU GUYS HEAR THAT ONE?
IT SOUNDS LIKE SOMETHIN' CRACKIN'!
UH-OH... WAIT!

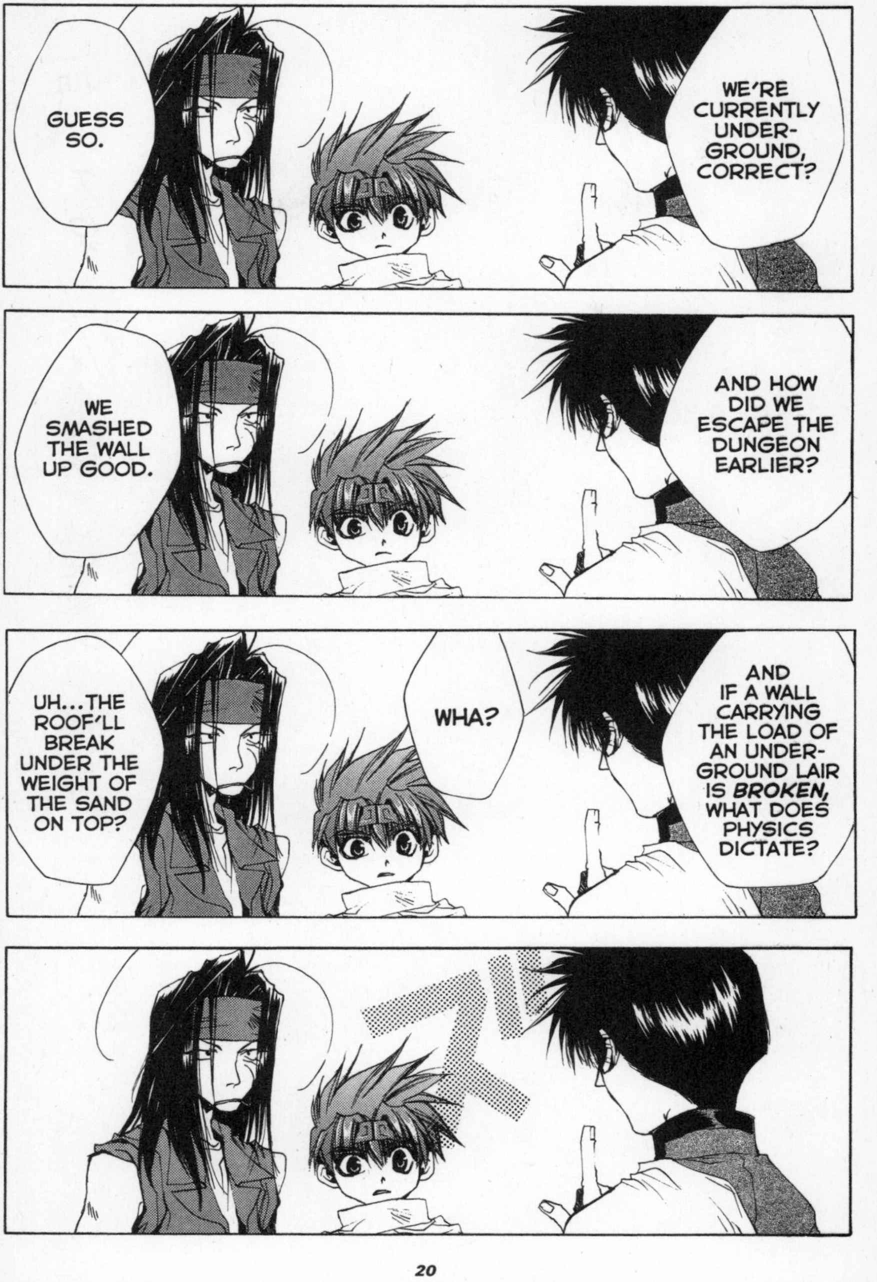
WE'RE CURRENTLY UNDER-GROUND, CORRECT?
GUESS SO.
AND HOW DID WE ESCAPE THE DUNGEON EARLIER?
WE SMASHED THE WALL UP GOOD.
AND IF A WALL CARRYING THE LOAD OF AN UNDER-GROUND LAIR IS *BROKEN*, WHAT DOES PHYSICS DICTATE?
WHA?
UH...THE ROOF'LL BREAK UNDER THE WEIGHT OF THE SAND ON TOP?

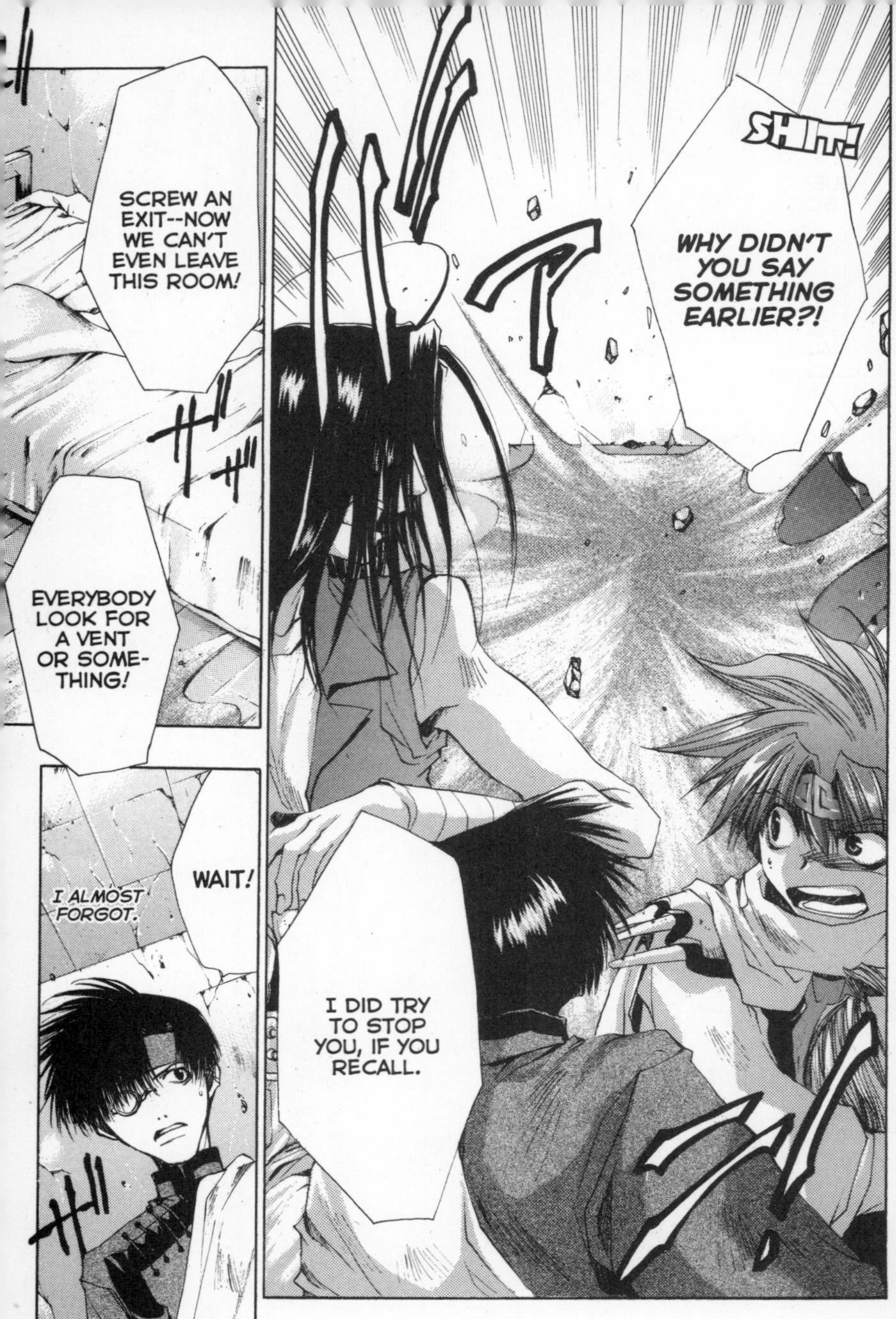
SHIT!
WHY DIDN'T YOU SAY SOMETHING EARLIER?!
I DID TRY TO STOP YOU, IF YOU RECALL.
SCREW AN EXIT--NOW WE CAN'T EVEN LEAVE THIS ROOM!
EVERYBODY LOOK FOR A VENT OR SOME-THING!
WAIT!
I ALMOST FORGOT.

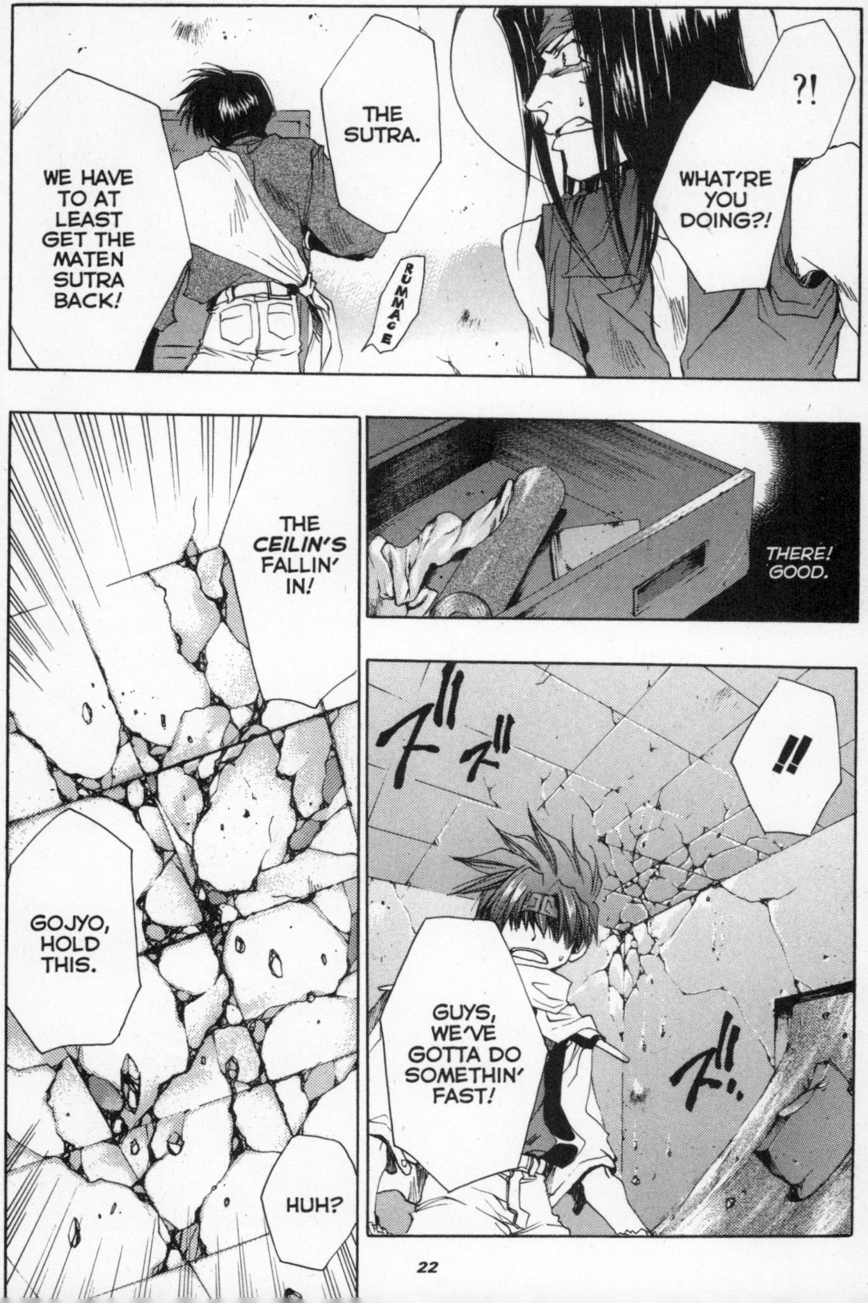
?!
WHAT'RE YOU DOING?!
THE SUTRA.
RUMMAGE
WE HAVE TO AT LEAST GET THE MATEN SUTRA BACK!
THERE! GOOD.
!!
GUYS, WE'VE GOTTA DO SOMETHIN' FAST!
THE *CEILIN'S* FALLIN' IN!
GOJYO, HOLD THIS.
HUH?

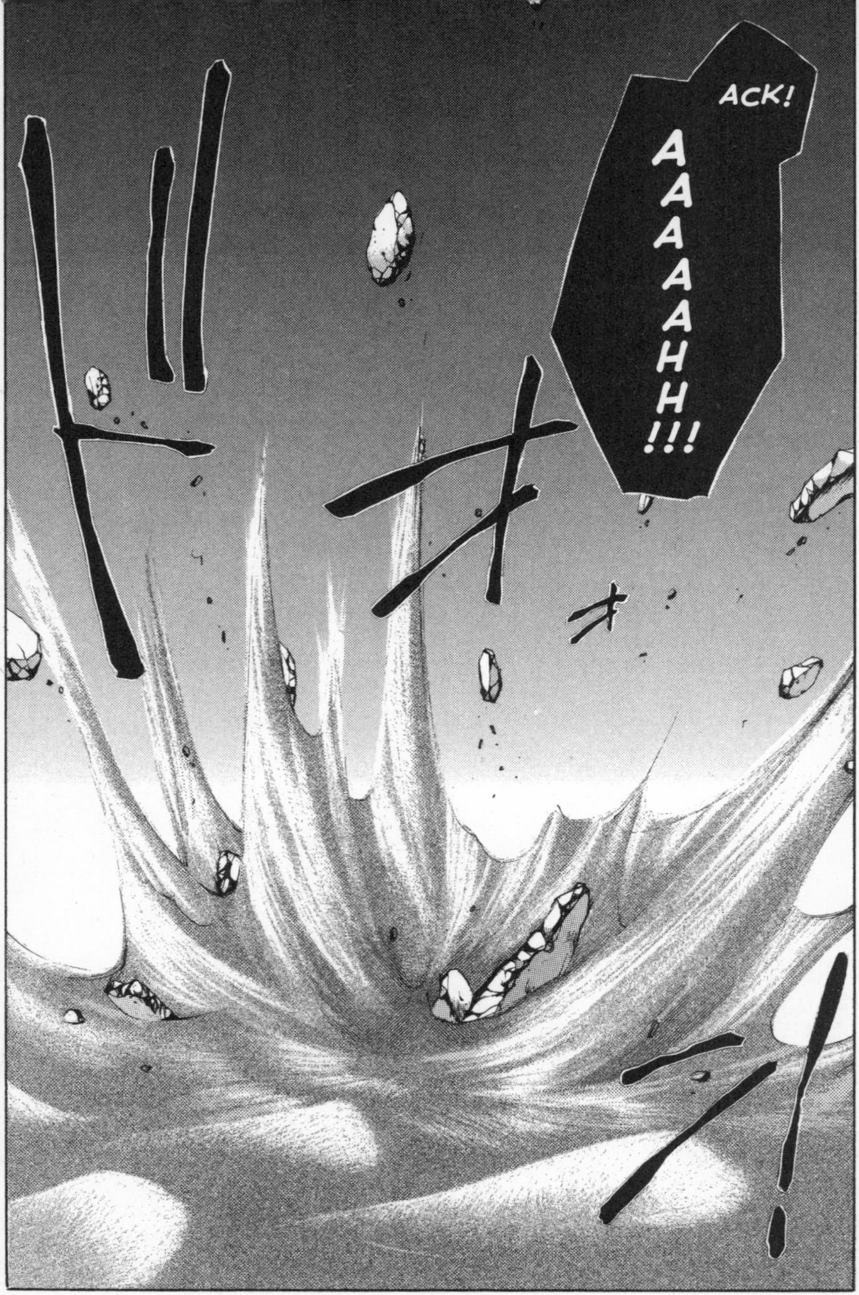
ACK!
AAAAAAHH!!!

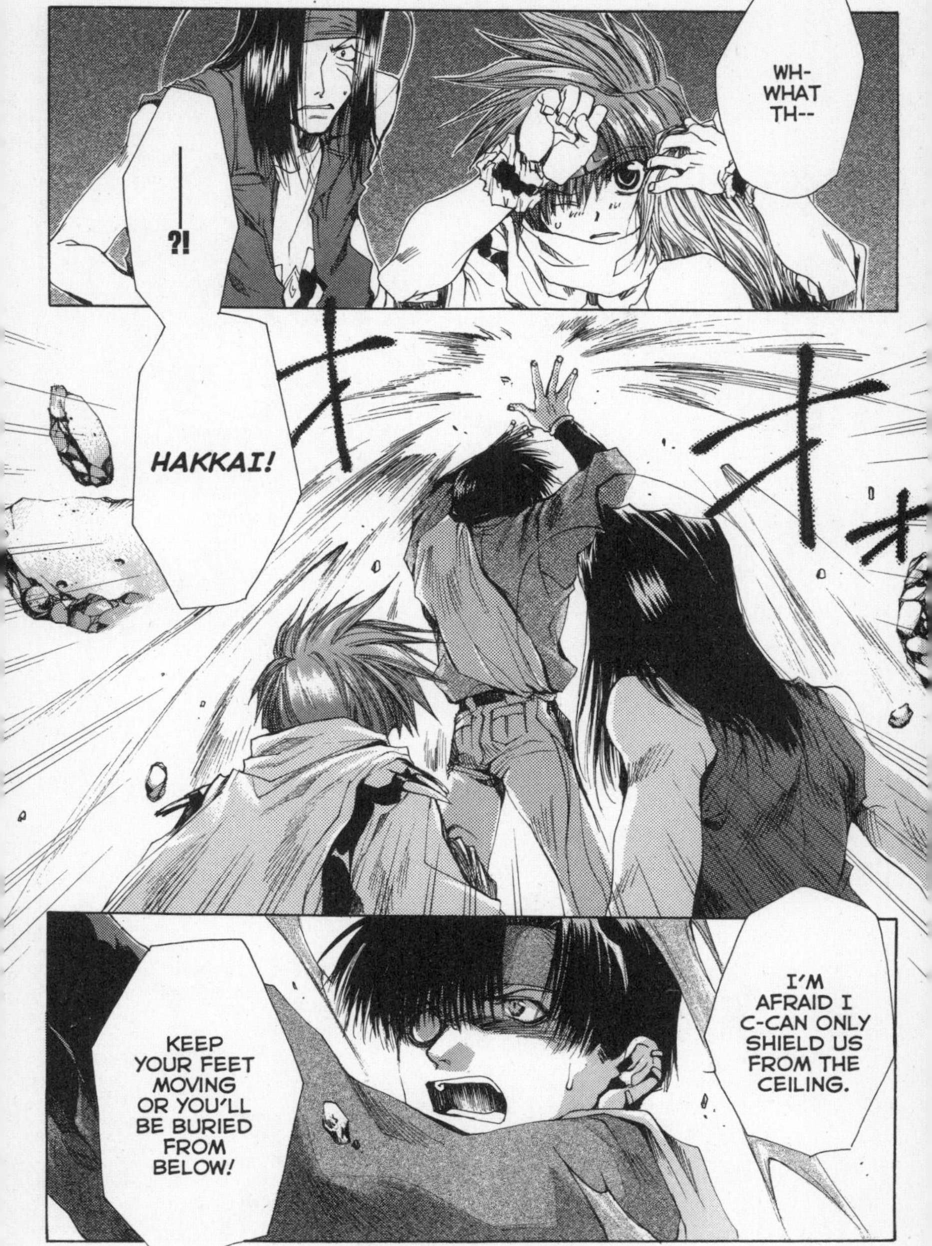
WH- WHAT TH--
——?!
オオォ
HAKKAI!
I'M AFRAID I C-CAN ONLY SHIELD US FROM THE CEILING.
KEEP YOUR FEET MOVING OR YOU'LL BE BURIED FROM BELOW!

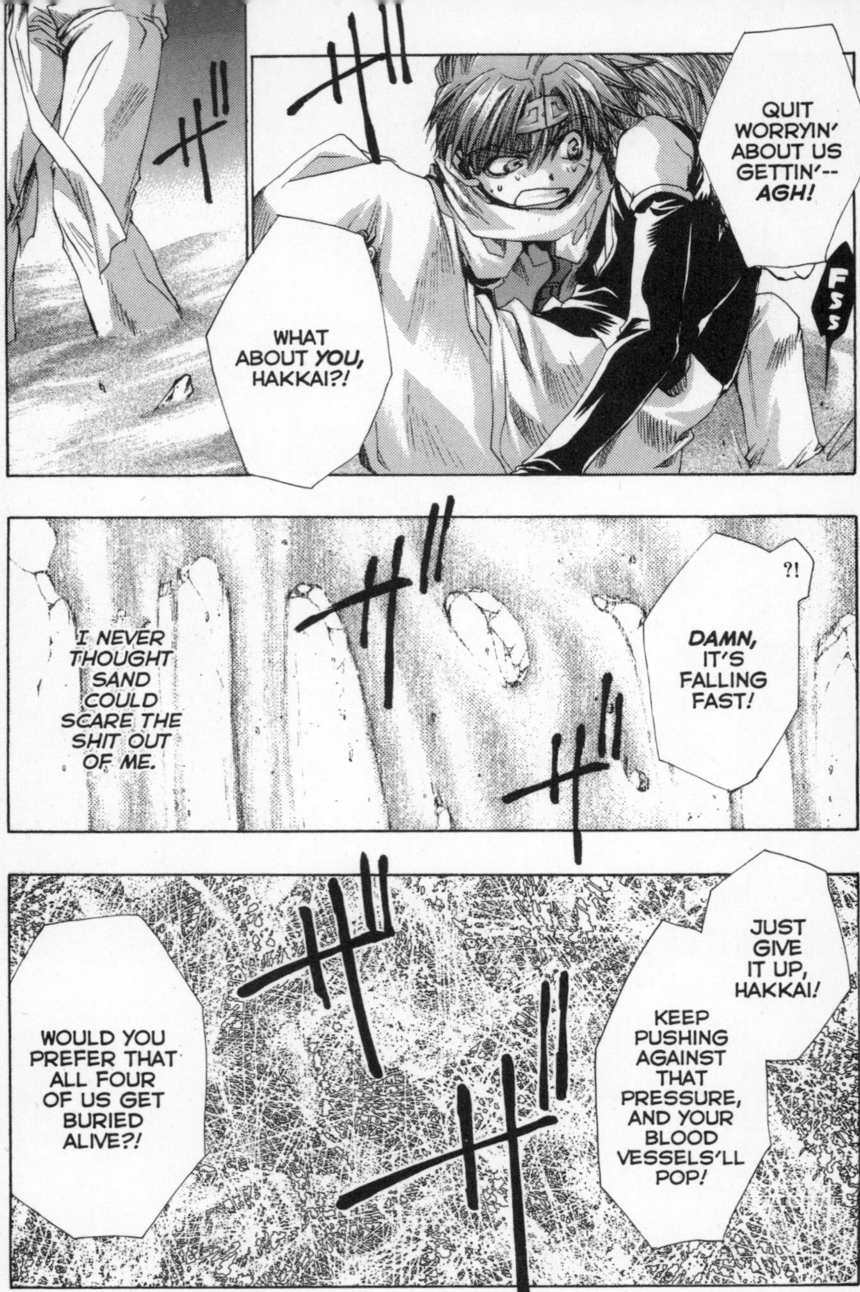
QUIT WORRYIN' ABOUT US GETTIN'-- *AGH!*
FSS
WHAT ABOUT *YOU*, HAKKAI?!
?!
DAMN, IT'S FALLING FAST!
I NEVER THOUGHT SAND COULD SCARE THE SHIT OUT OF ME.
JUST GIVE IT UP, HAKKAI!
KEEP PUSHING AGAINST THAT PRESSURE, AND YOUR BLOOD VESSELS'LL POP!
WOULD YOU PREFER THAT ALL FOUR OF US GET BURIED ALIVE?!

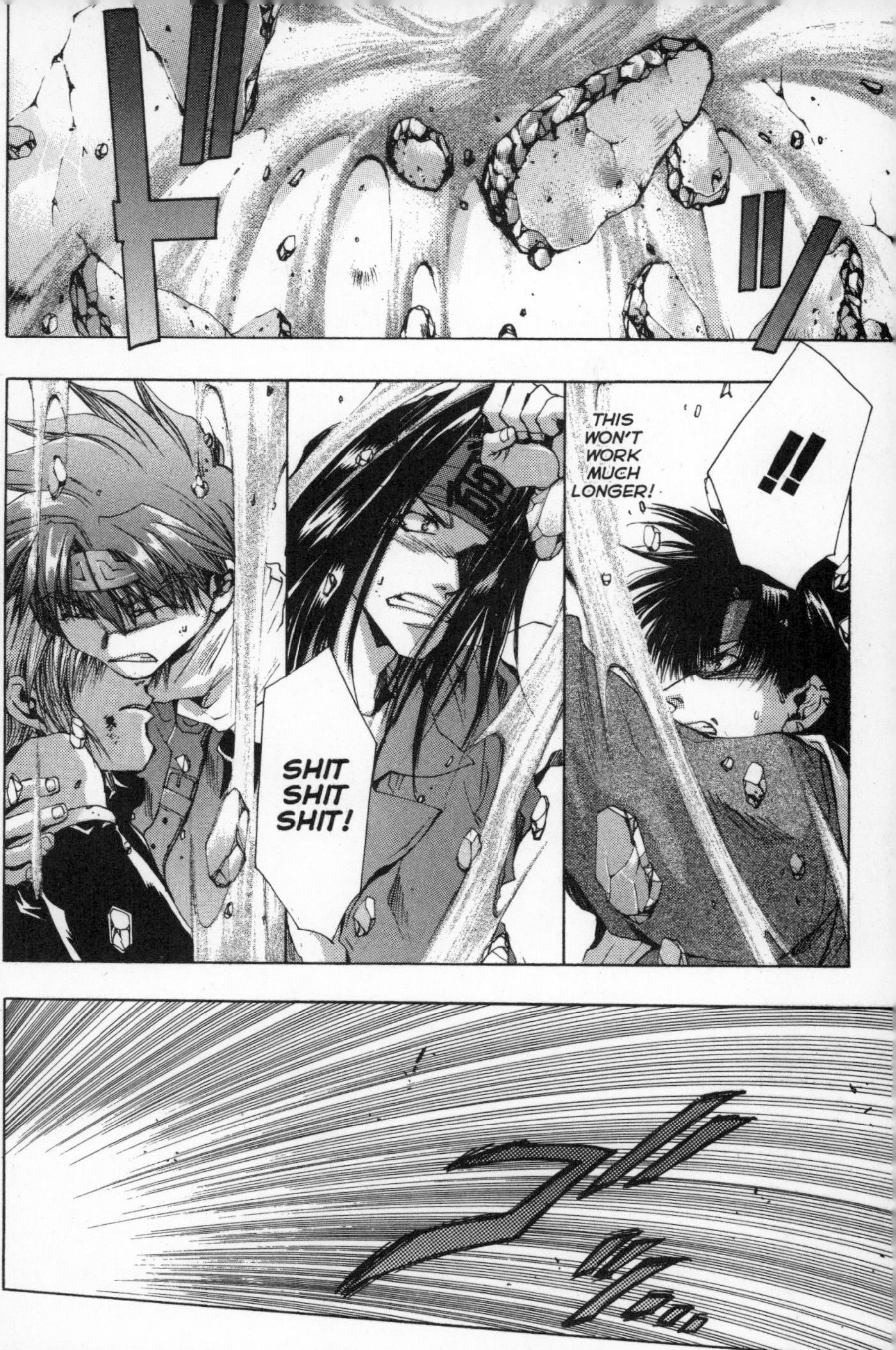
!!
THIS WON'T WORK MUCH LONGER!
SHIT SHIT SHIT!

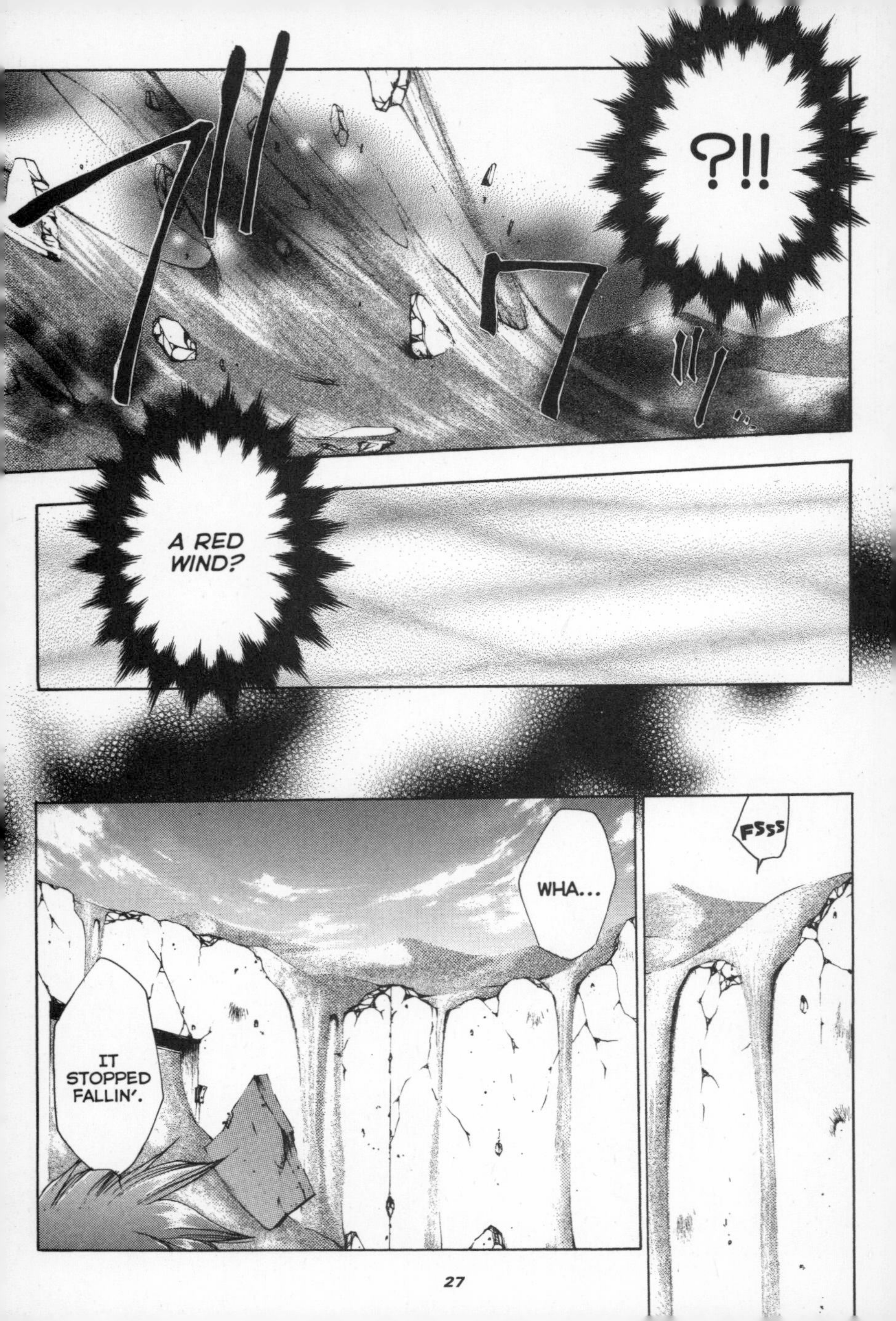
?!!
A RED WIND?
FSSS
WHA...
IT STOPPED FALLIN'.

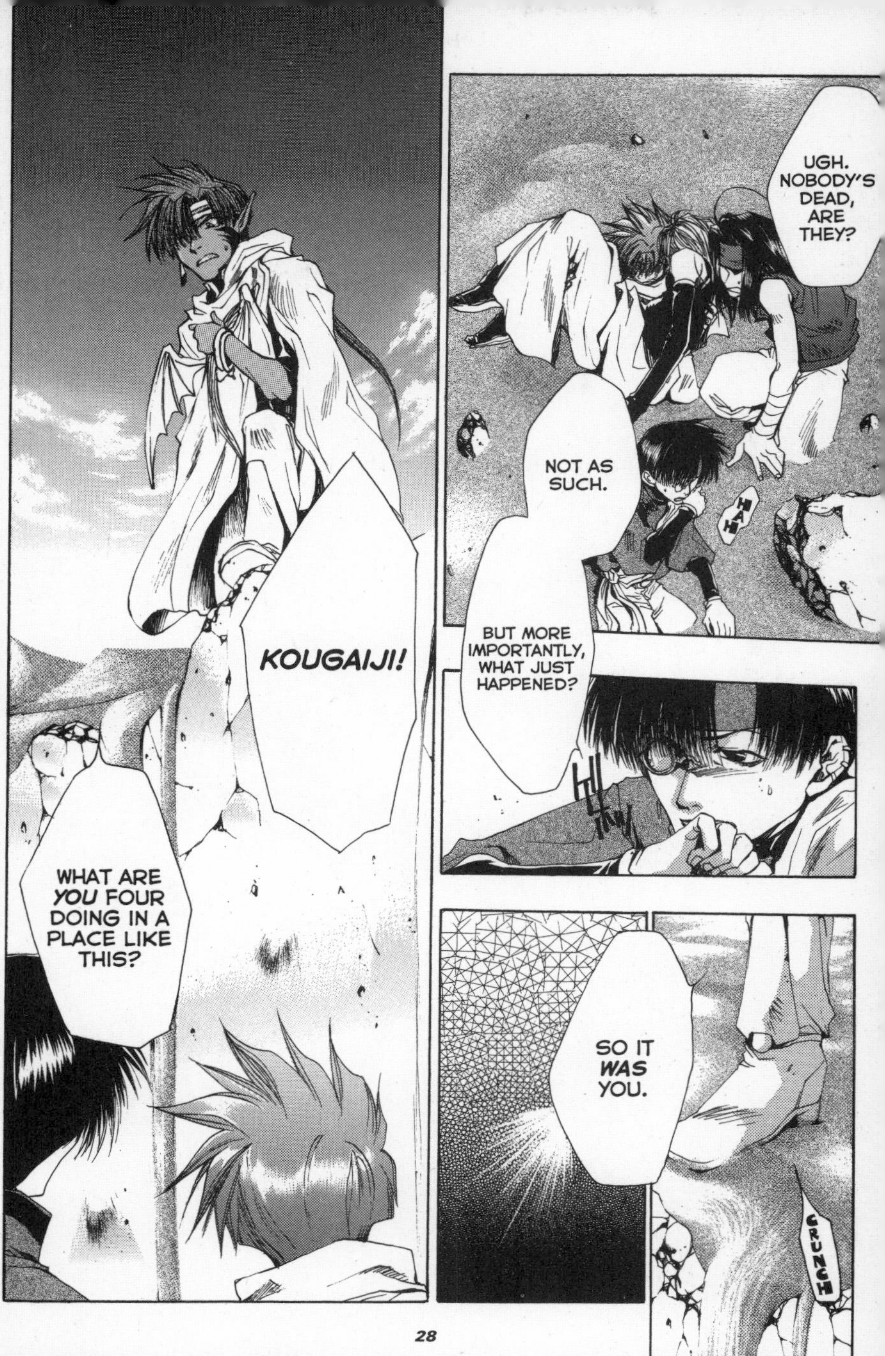
UGH. NOBODY'S DEAD, ARE THEY?
NOT AS SUCH.
HAH
BUT MORE IMPORTANTLY, WHAT JUST HAPPENED?
SO IT WAS YOU.
CRUNCH
KOUGAIJI!
WHAT ARE YOU FOUR DOING IN A PLACE LIKE THIS?

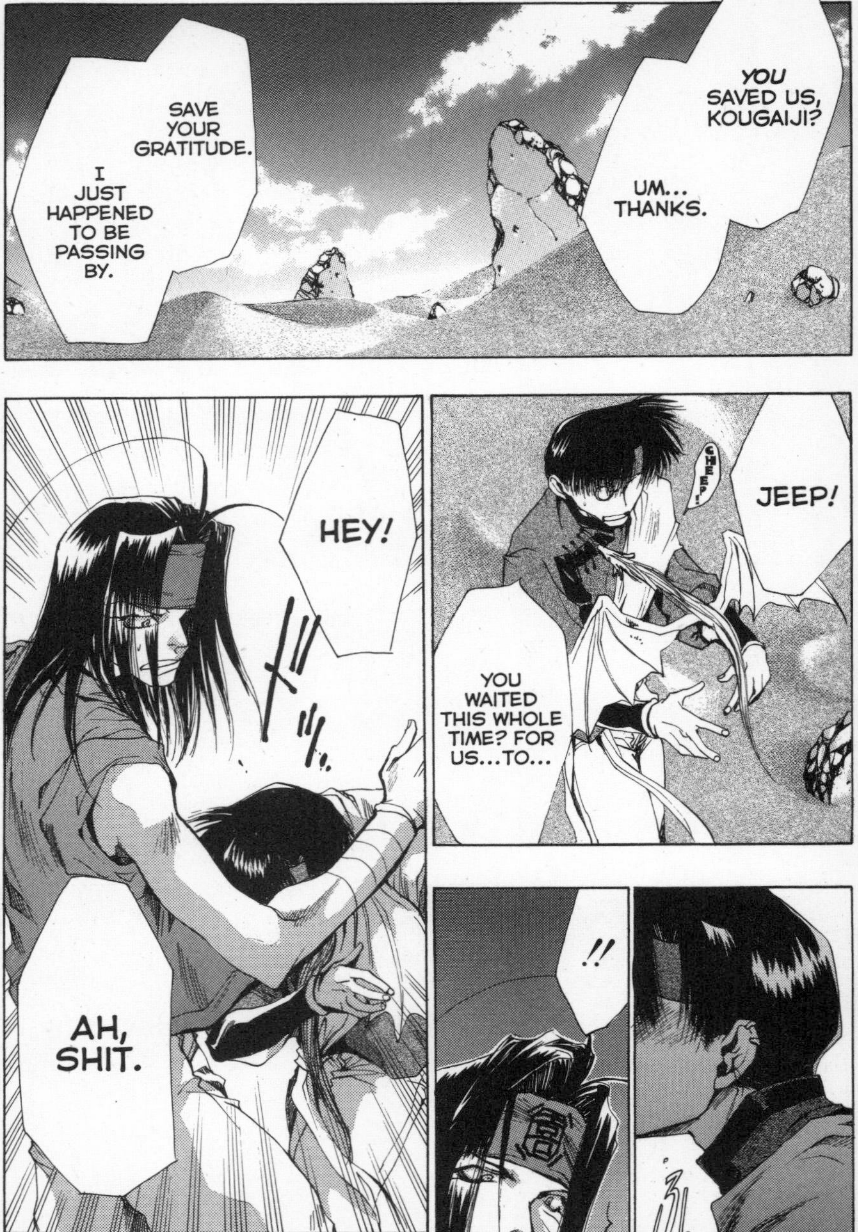
YOU SAVED US, KOUGAIJI?
UM... THANKS.
SAVE YOUR GRATITUDE.
I JUST HAPPENED TO BE PASSING BY.
CHEEP!
JEEP!
YOU WAITED THIS WHOLE TIME? FOR US...TO...
!!
HEY!
AH, SHIT.

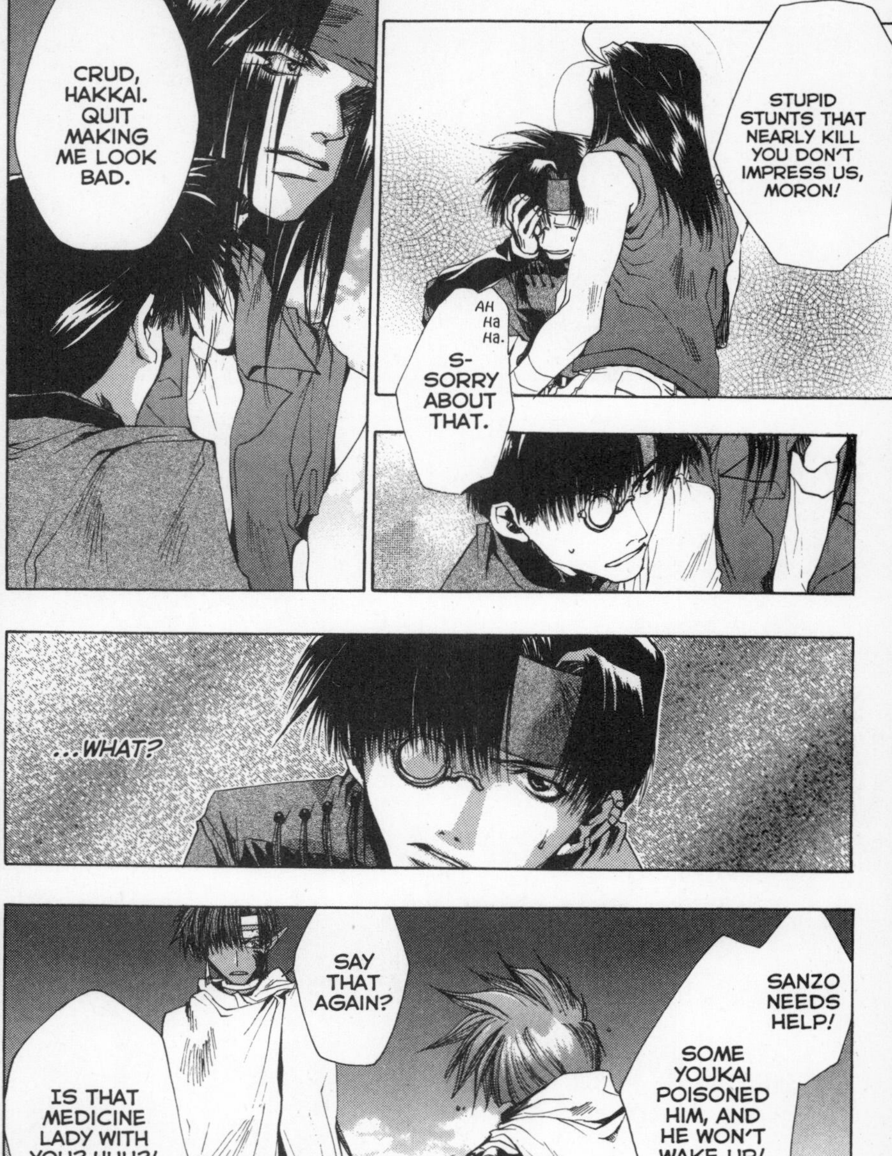
STUPID STUNTS THAT NEARLY KILL YOU DON'T IMPRESS US, MORON!
AH Ha Ha.
S-SORRY ABOUT THAT.
CRUD, HAKKAI. QUIT MAKING ME LOOK BAD.
...WHAT?
SANZO NEEDS HELP!
SOME YOUKAI POISONED HIM, AND HE WON'T WAKE UP!
SAY THAT AGAIN?
IS THAT MEDICINE LADY WITH YOU? HUH?!

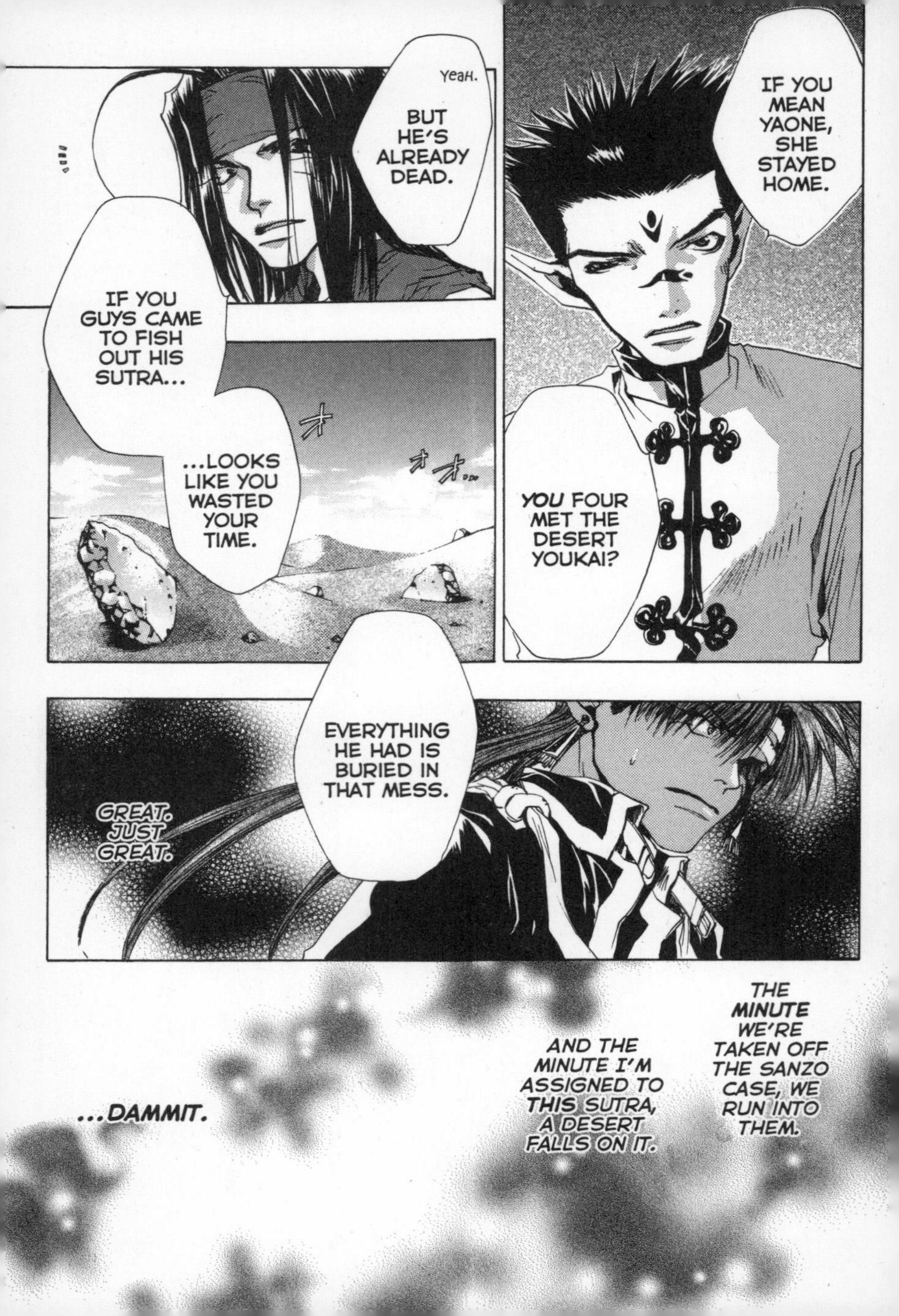
IF YOU MEAN YAONE, SHE STAYED HOME.
YOU FOUR MET THE DESERT YOUKAI?
Yeah.
BUT HE'S ALREADY DEAD.
IF YOU GUYS CAME TO FISH OUT HIS SUTRA...
...LOOKS LIKE YOU WASTED YOUR TIME.
EVERYTHING HE HAD IS BURIED IN THAT MESS.
GREAT. JUST GREAT.
THE MINUTE WE'RE TAKEN OFF THE SANZO CASE, WE RUN INTO THEM.
AND THE MINUTE I'M ASSIGNED TO THIS SUTRA, A DESERT FALLS ON IT.
...DAMMIT.

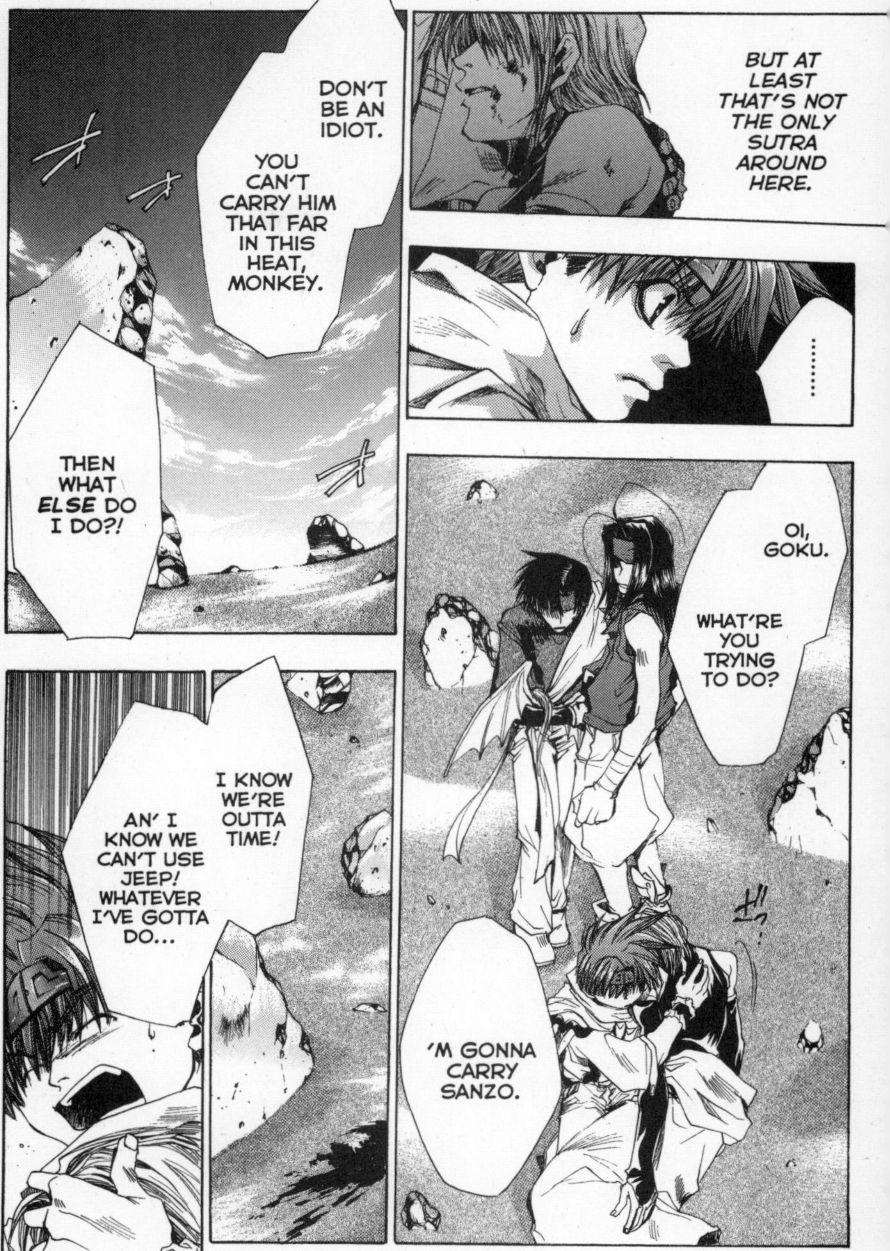
BUT AT LEAST THAT'S NOT THE ONLY SUTRA AROUND HERE.
......
OI, GOKU.
WHAT'RE YOU TRYING TO DO?
'M GONNA CARRY SANZO.
DON'T BE AN IDIOT.
YOU CAN'T CARRY HIM THAT FAR IN THIS HEAT, MONKEY.
THEN WHAT *ELSE* DO I DO?!
I KNOW WE'RE OUTTA TIME!
AN' I KNOW WE CAN'T USE JEEP! WHATEVER I'VE GOTTA DO...

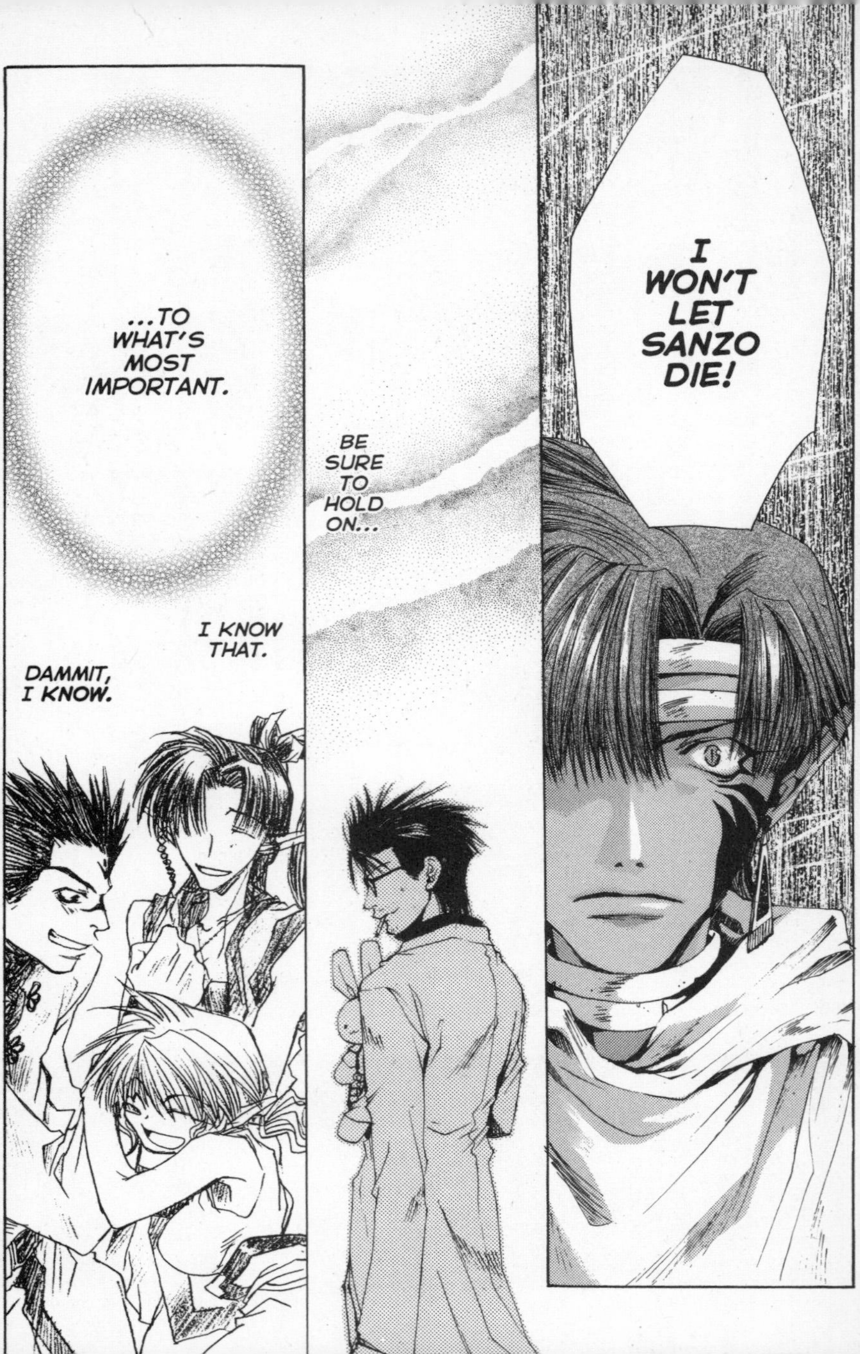
I WON'T LET SANZO DIE!
BE SURE TO HOLD ON...
...TO WHAT'S MOST IMPORTANT.
I KNOW THAT.
DAMMIT, I KNOW.

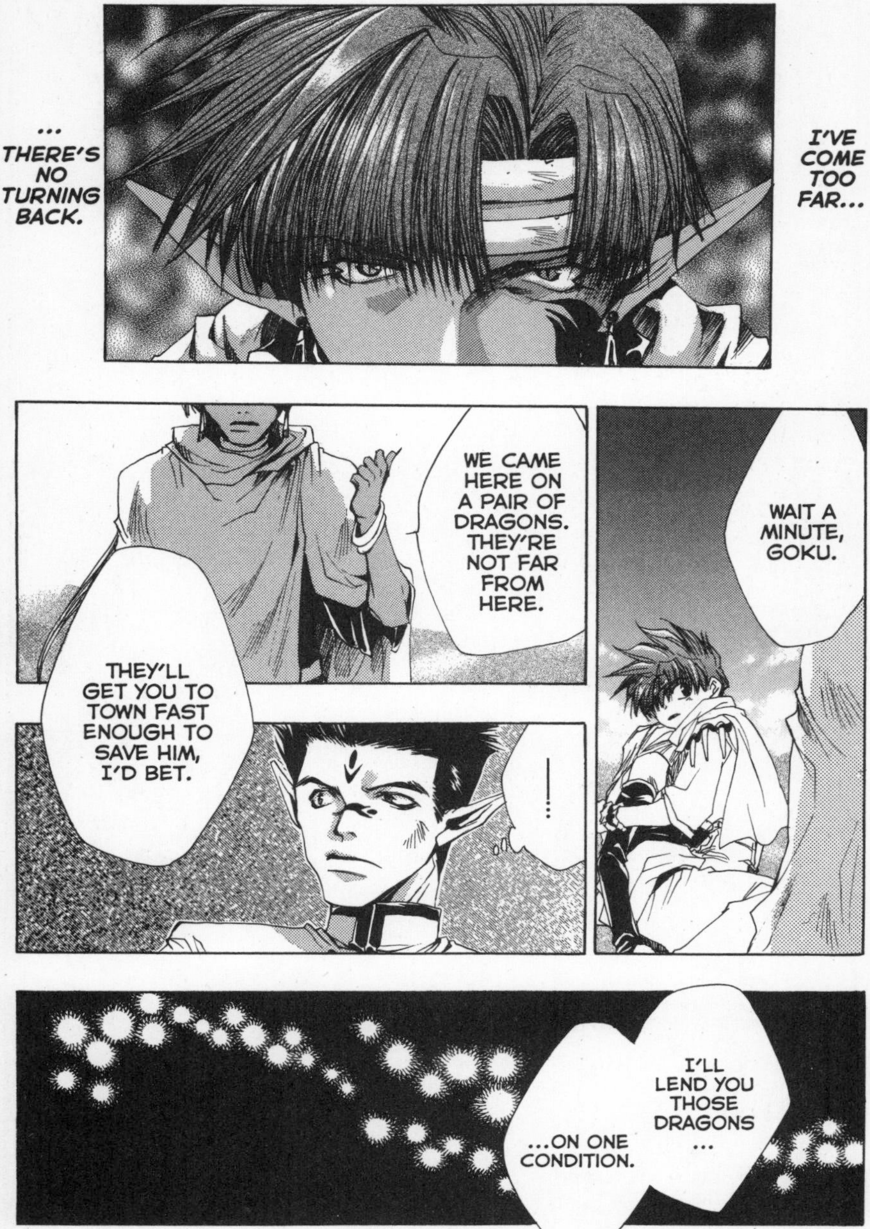
I'VE COME TOO FAR...
...THERE'S NO TURNING BACK.
WAIT A MINUTE, GOKU.
WE CAME HERE ON A PAIR OF DRAGONS. THEY'RE NOT FAR FROM HERE.
THEY'LL GET YOU TO TOWN FAST ENOUGH TO SAVE HIM, I'D BET.
...!
I'LL LEND YOU THOSE DRAGONS...
...ON ONE CONDITION.

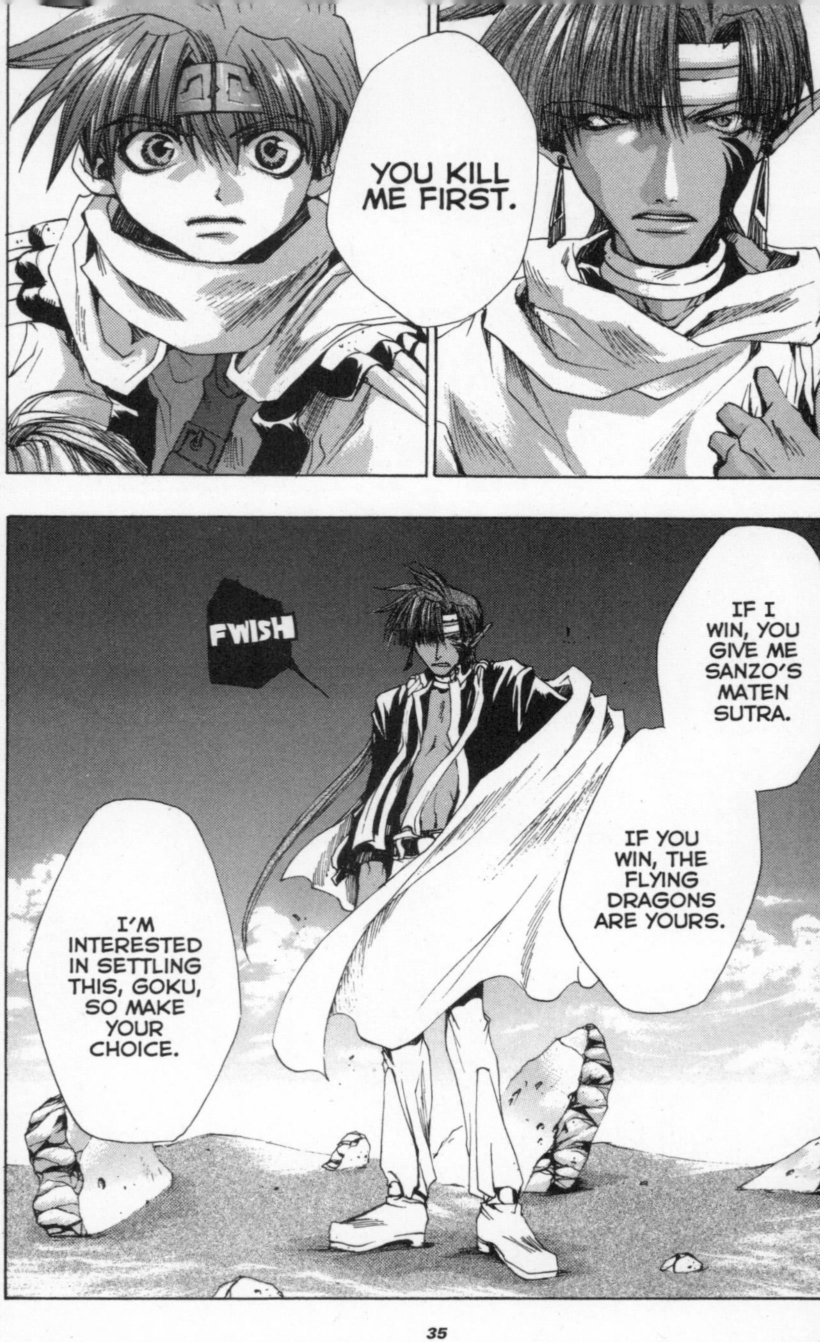
YOU KILL ME FIRST.
IF I WIN, YOU GIVE ME SANZO'S MATEN SUTRA.
FWISH
IF YOU WIN, THE FLYING DRAGONS ARE YOURS.
I'M INTERESTED IN SETTLING THIS, GOKU, SO MAKE YOUR CHOICE.

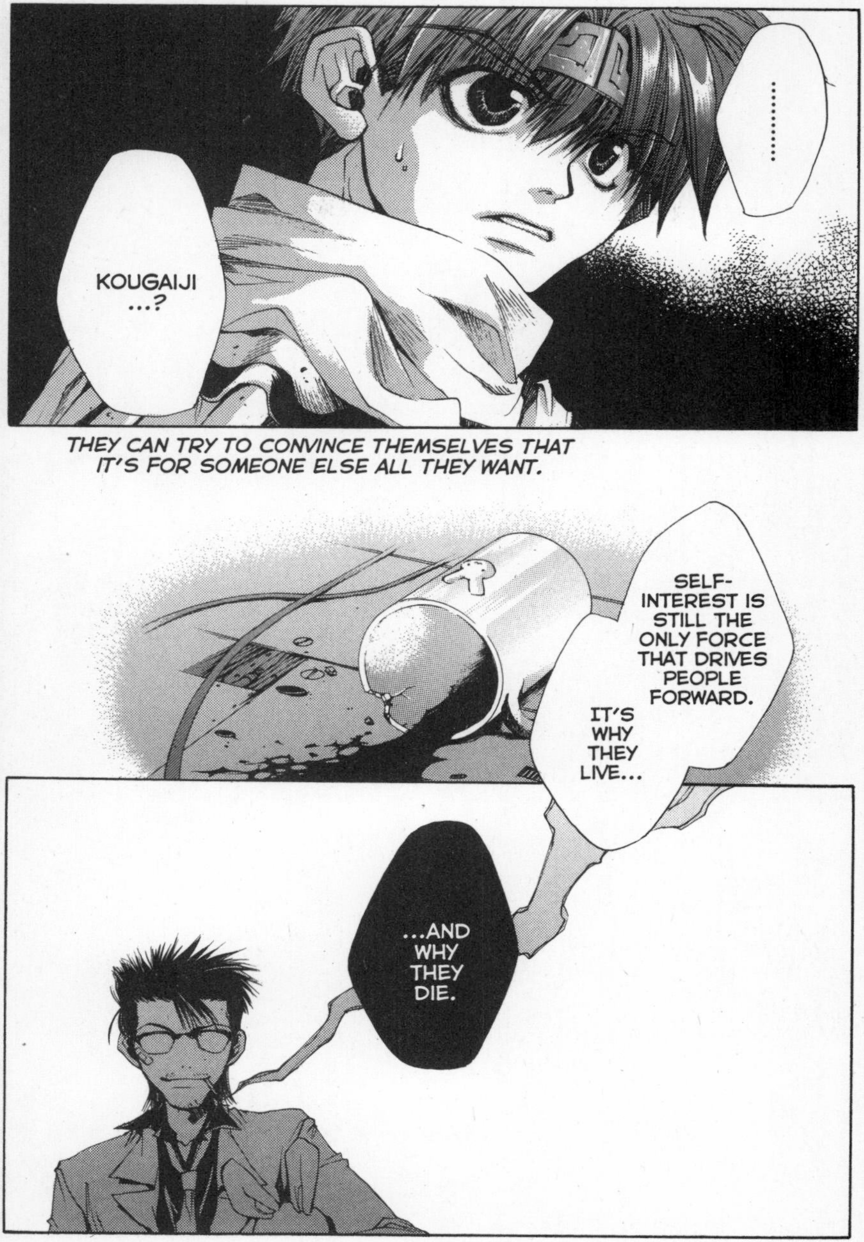
....
KOUGAIJI ...?
THEY CAN TRY TO CONVINCE THEMSELVES THAT IT'S FOR SOMEONE ELSE ALL THEY WANT.
SELF-INTEREST IS STILL THE ONLY FORCE THAT DRIVES PEOPLE FORWARD.
IT'S WHY THEY LIVE...
...AND WHY THEY DIE.

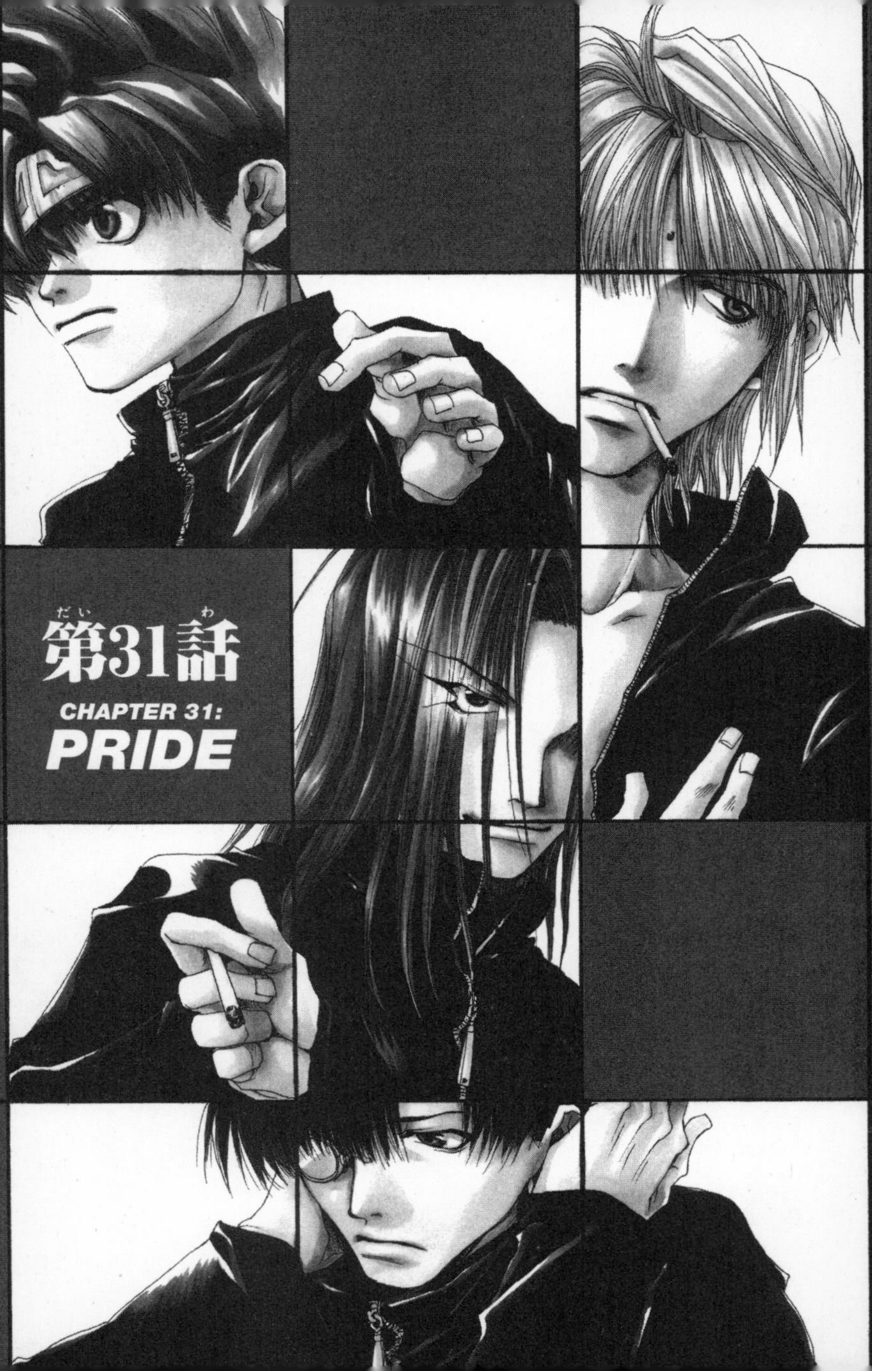

だい わ
第31話
CHAPTER 31:
PRIDE

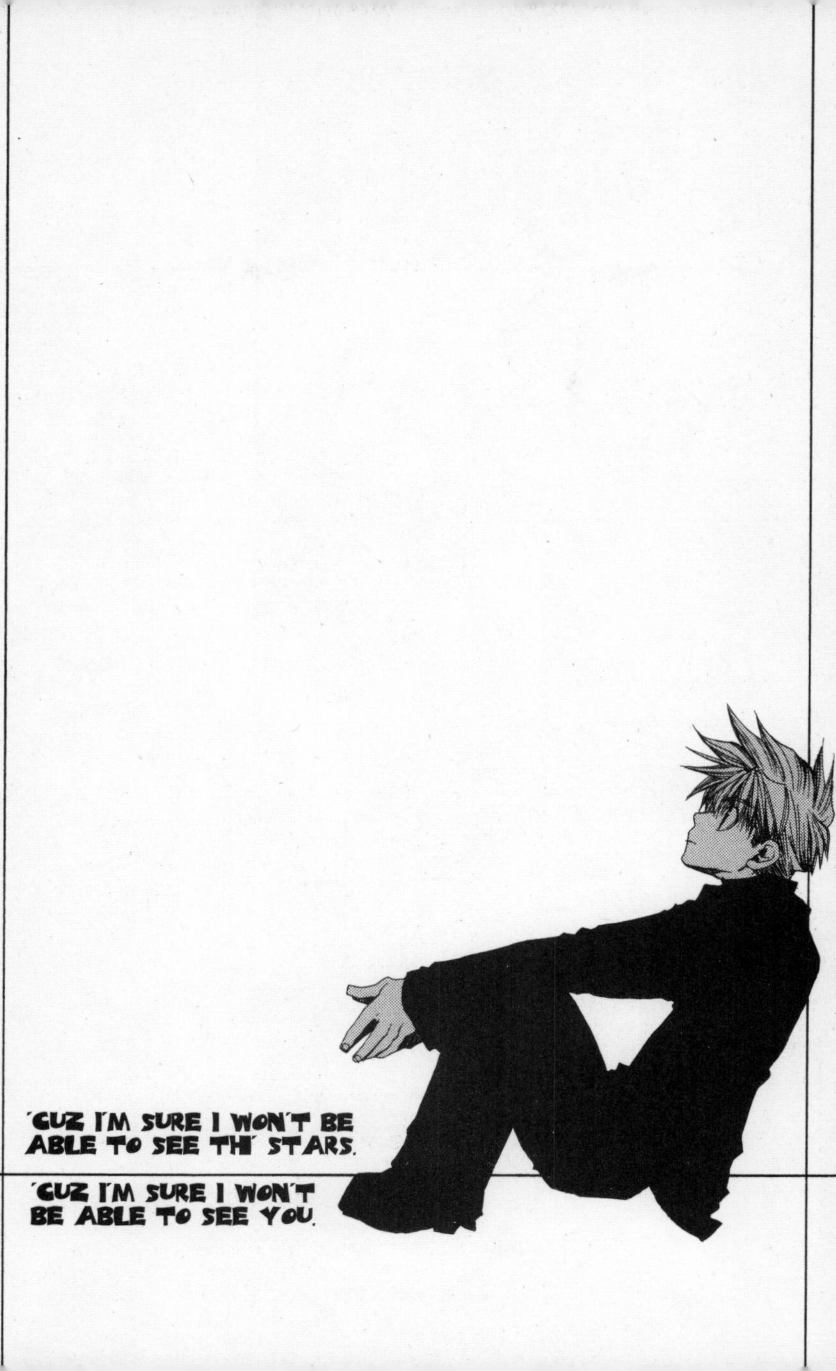
'CUZ I'M SURE I WON'T BE ABLE TO SEE TH' STARS.
'CUZ I'M SURE I WON'T BE ABLE TO SEE YOU.

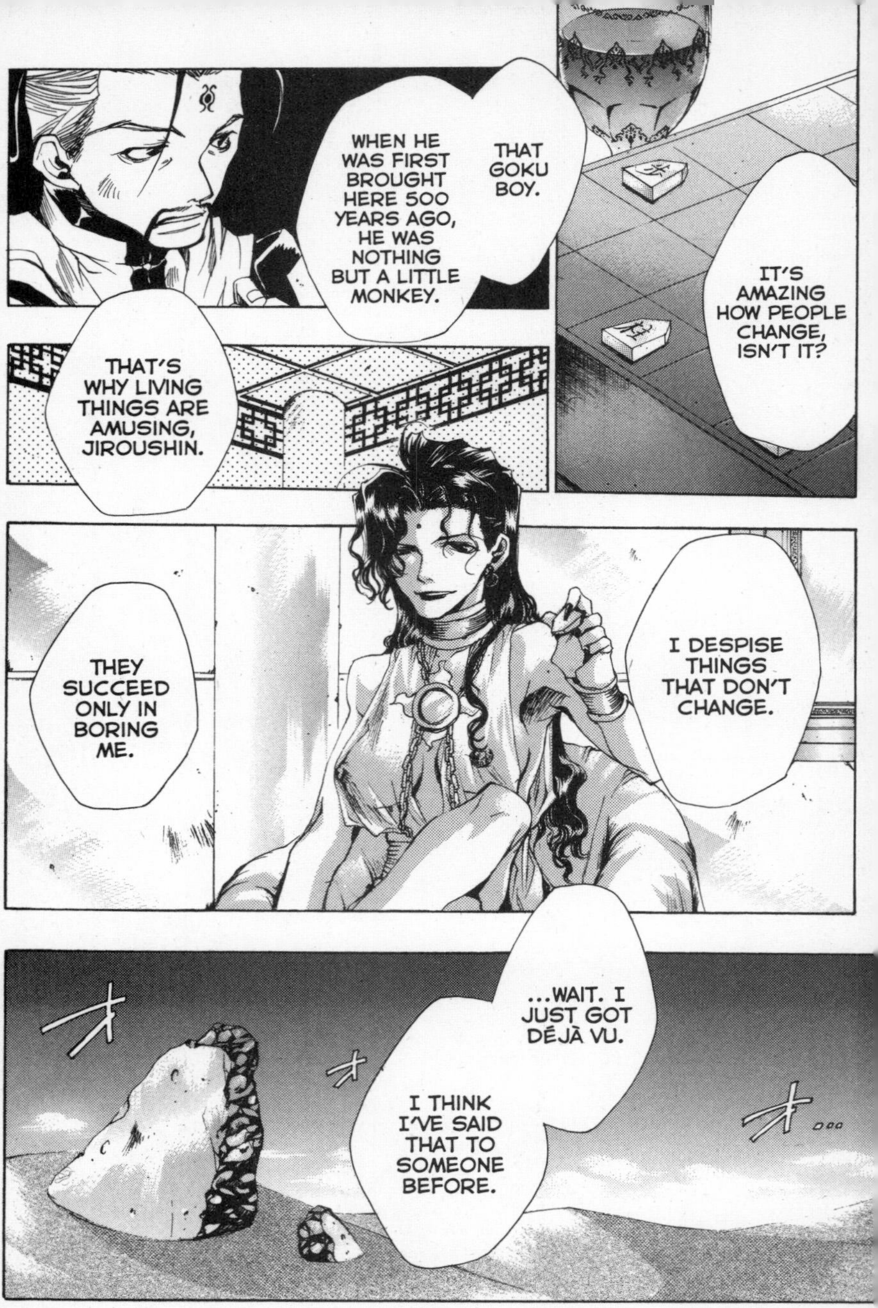
THAT GOKU BOY.
WHEN HE WAS FIRST BROUGHT HERE 500 YEARS AGO, HE WAS NOTHING BUT A LITTLE MONKEY.
IT'S AMAZING HOW PEOPLE CHANGE, ISN'T IT?
THAT'S WHY LIVING THINGS ARE AMUSING, JIROUSHIN.
I DESPISE THINGS THAT DON'T CHANGE.
THEY SUCCEED ONLY IN BORING ME.
...WAIT. I JUST GOT DÉJÀ VU.
I THINK I'VE SAID THAT TO SOMEONE BEFORE.

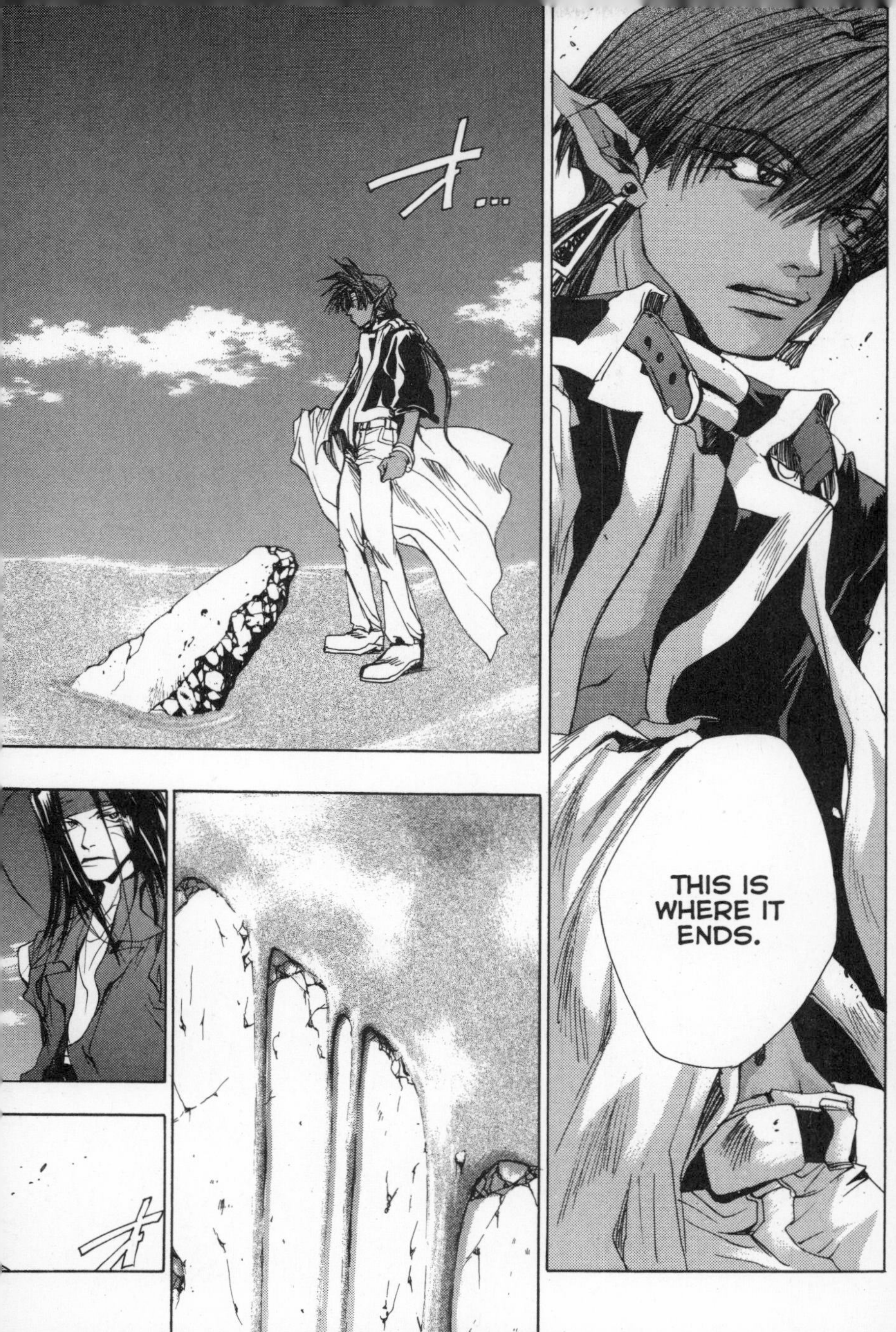
THIS IS WHERE IT ENDS.
オ...
オ

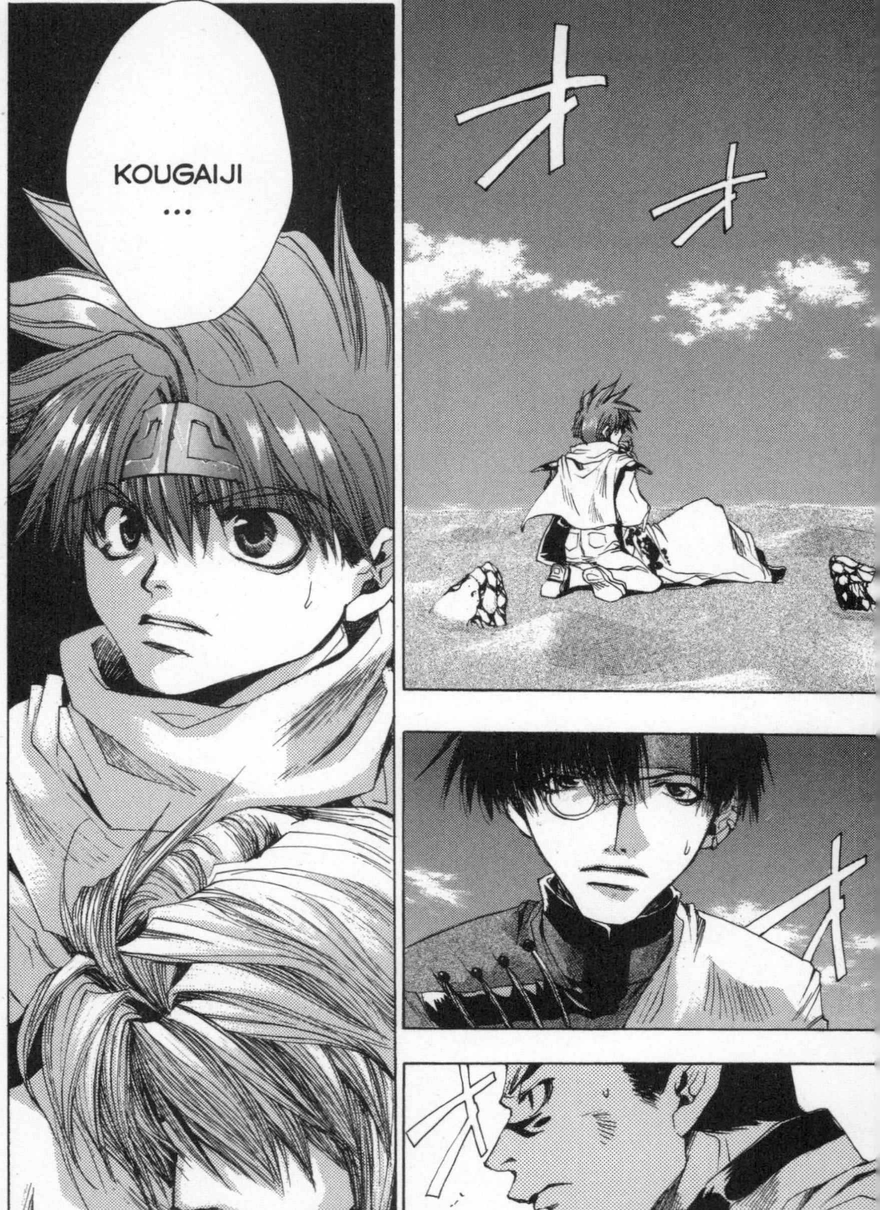

オ
ォ
オ
オ
KOUGAIJI
...

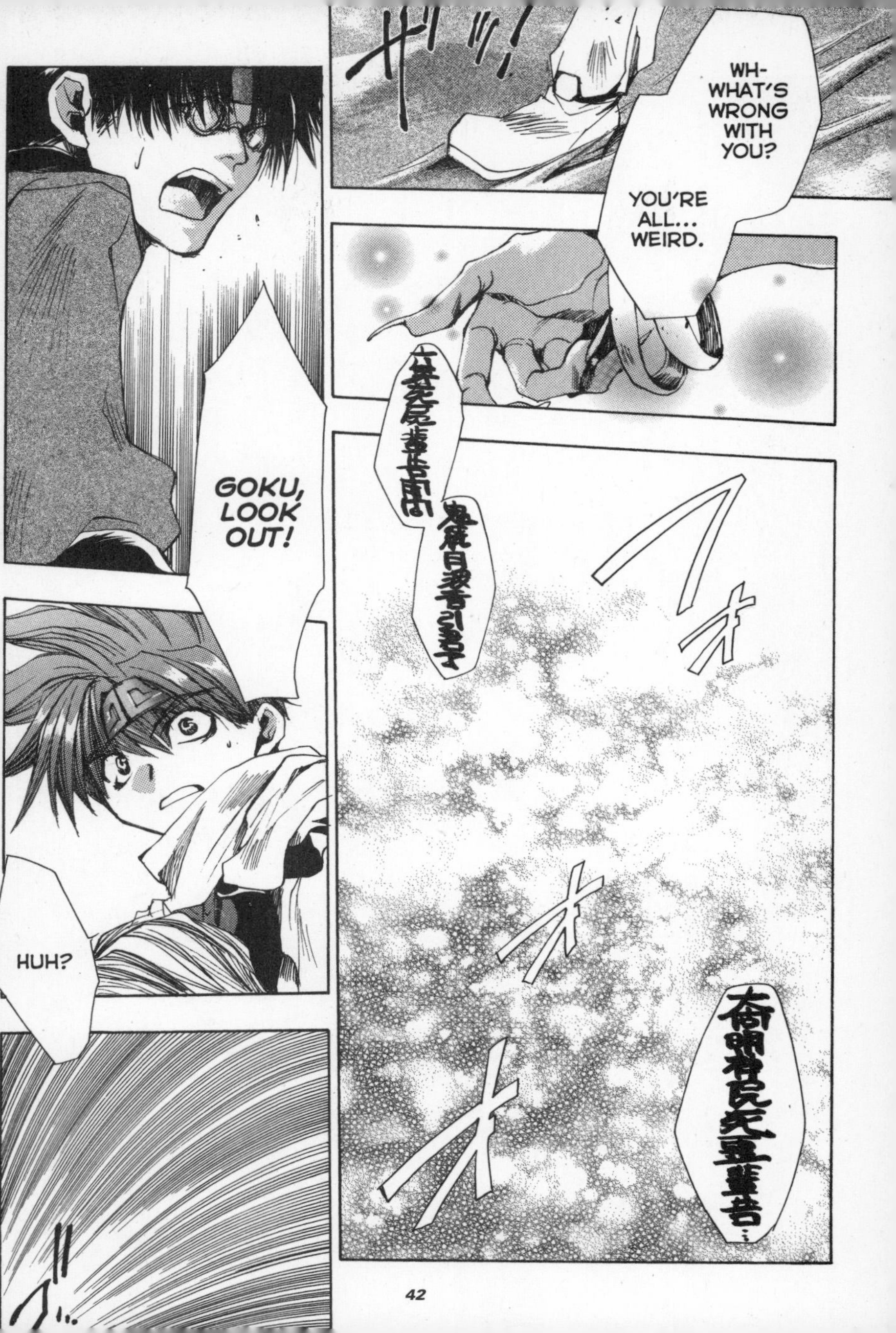
ザッ！
WH-WHAT'S WRONG WITH YOU?
YOU'RE ALL... WEIRD.
GOKU, LOOK OUT!
オオオ
HUH?

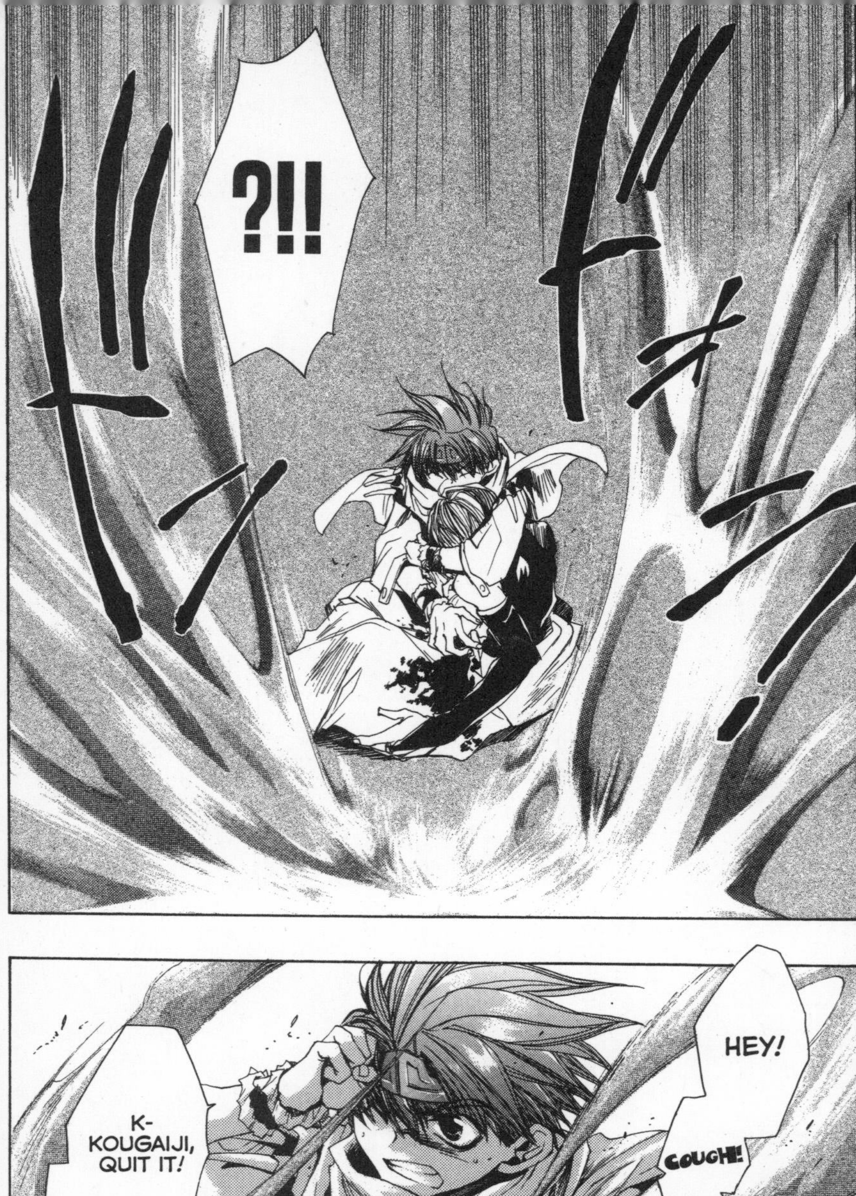
?!!
HEY!
COUGH!
COUGH!
K-KOUGAIJI, QUIT IT!
NNGH!

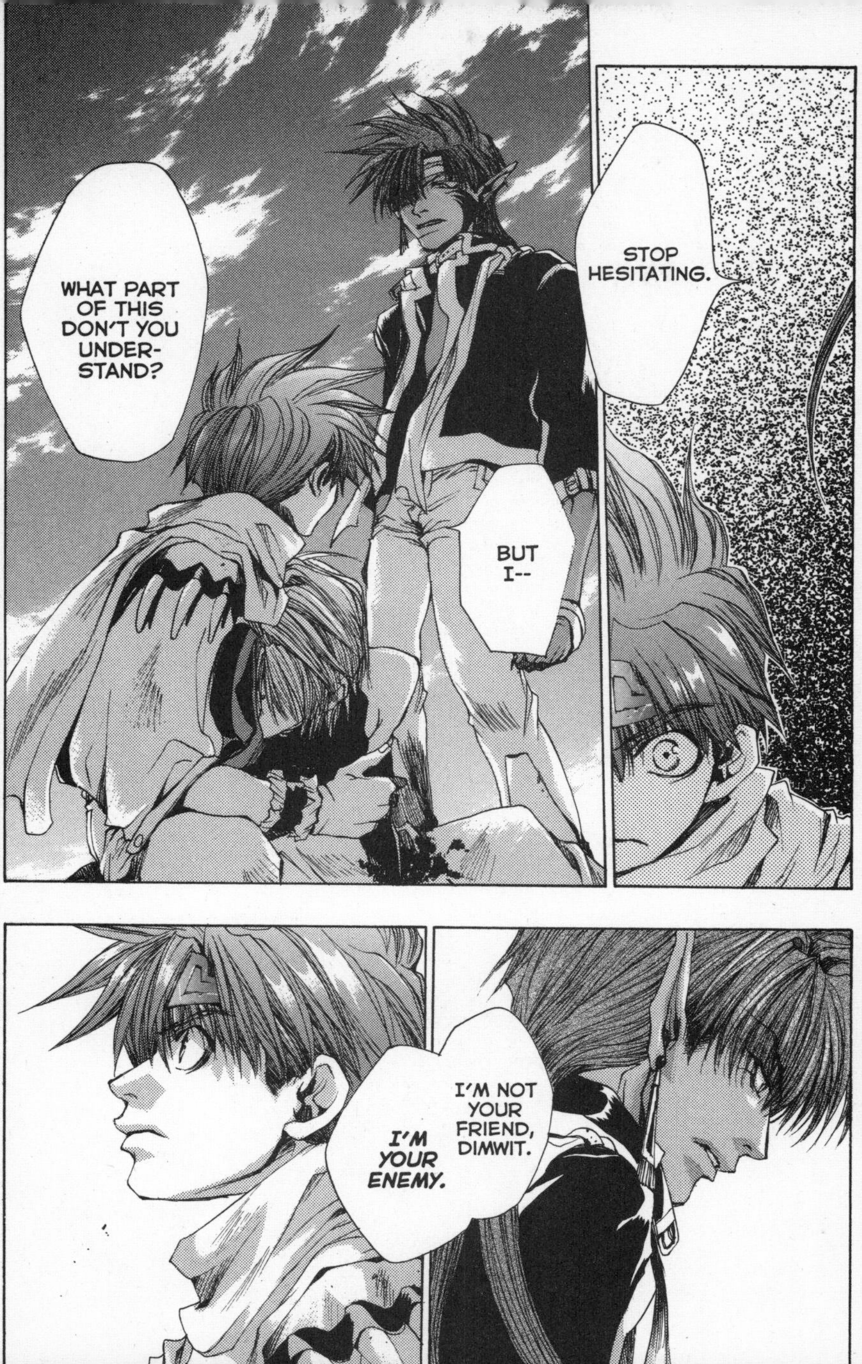
STOP HESITATING.
WHAT PART OF THIS DON'T YOU UNDER-STAND?
BUT I--
I'M NOT YOUR FRIEND, DIMWIT.
I'M YOUR ENEMY.

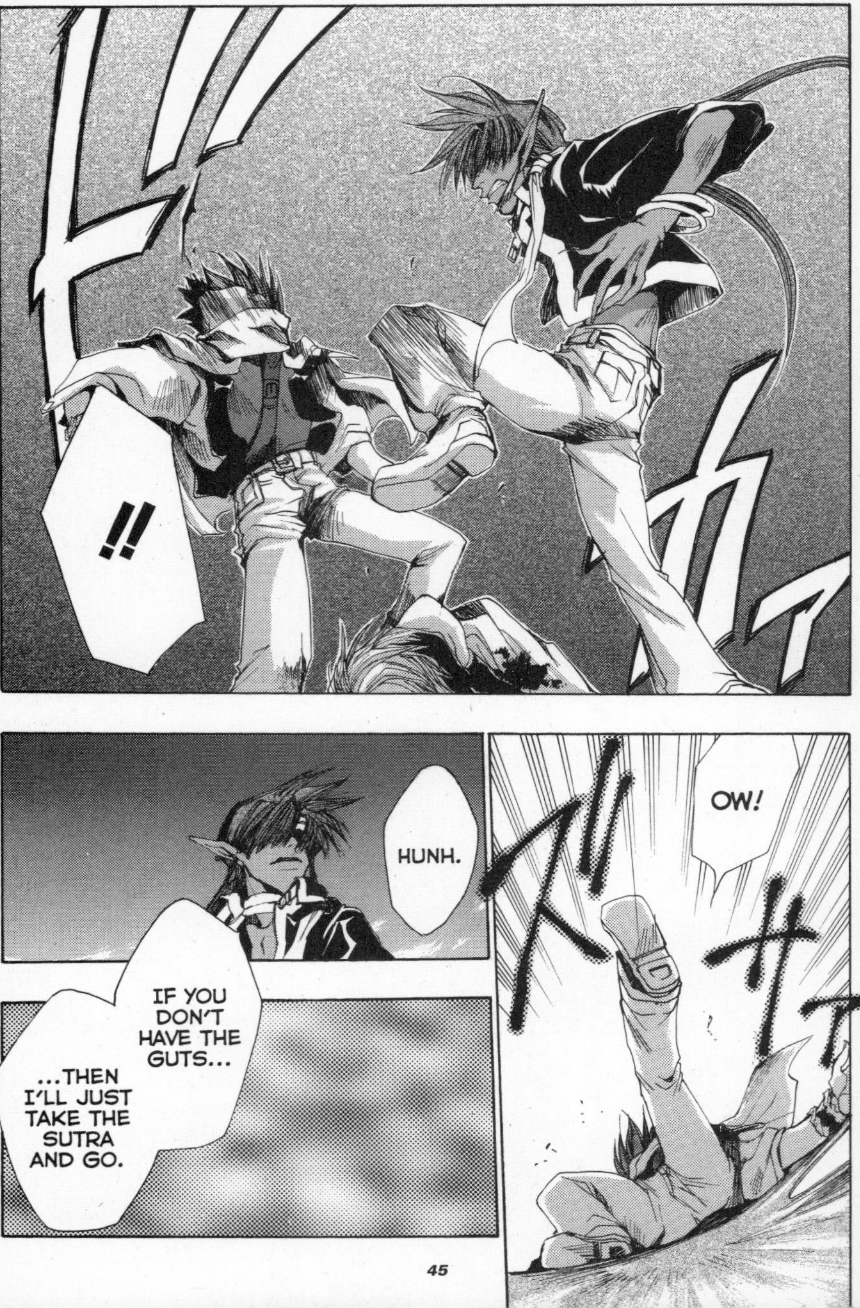
!!
OW!
HUNH.
IF YOU DON'T HAVE THE GUTS...
...THEN I'LL JUST TAKE THE SUTRA AND GO.

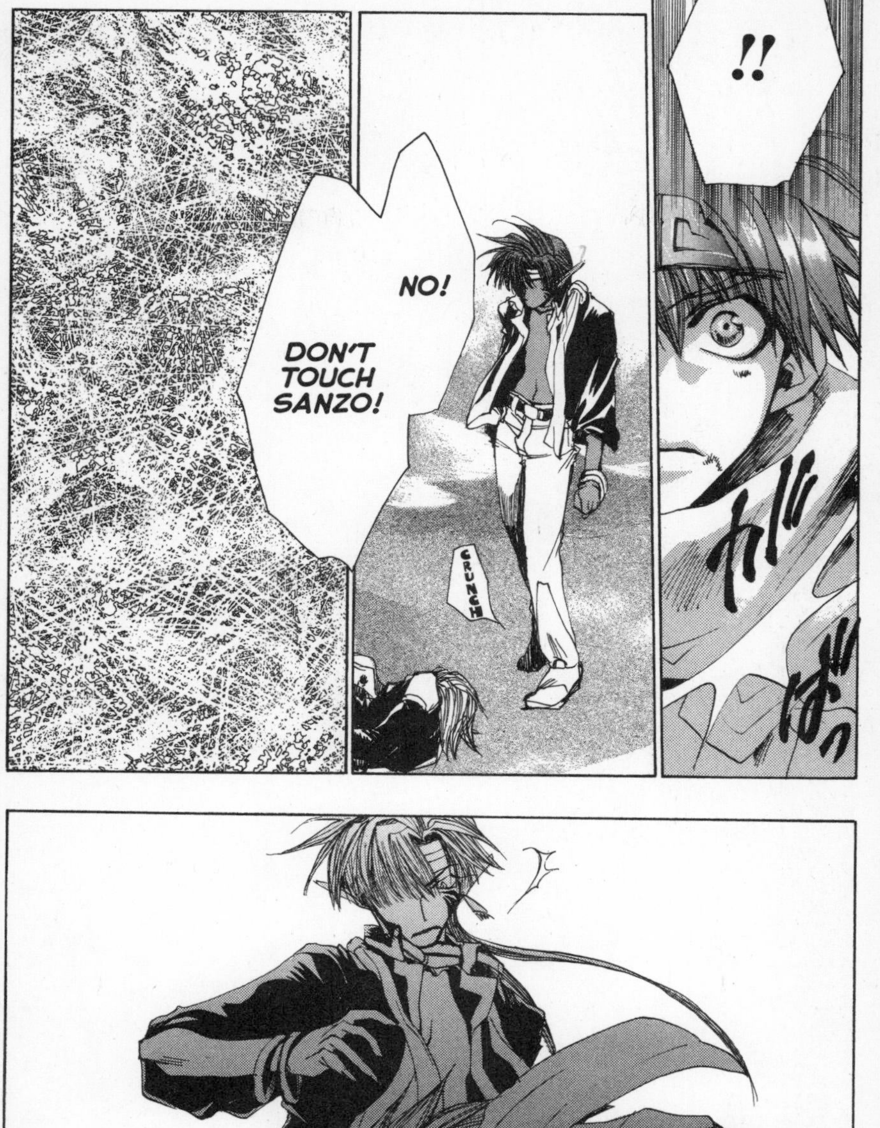
!!
NO!
DON'T TOUCH SANZO!
CRUNCH

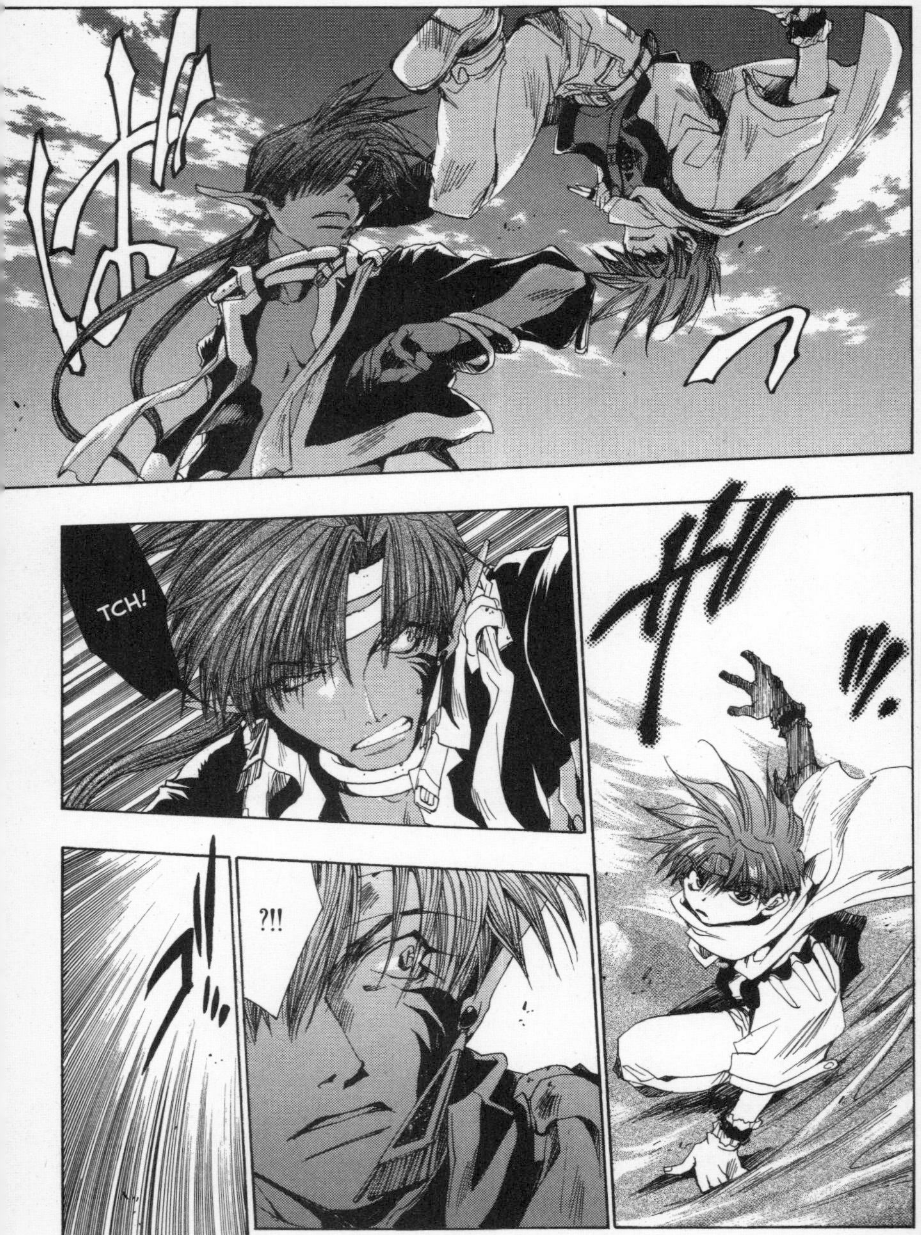
TCH!
?!!

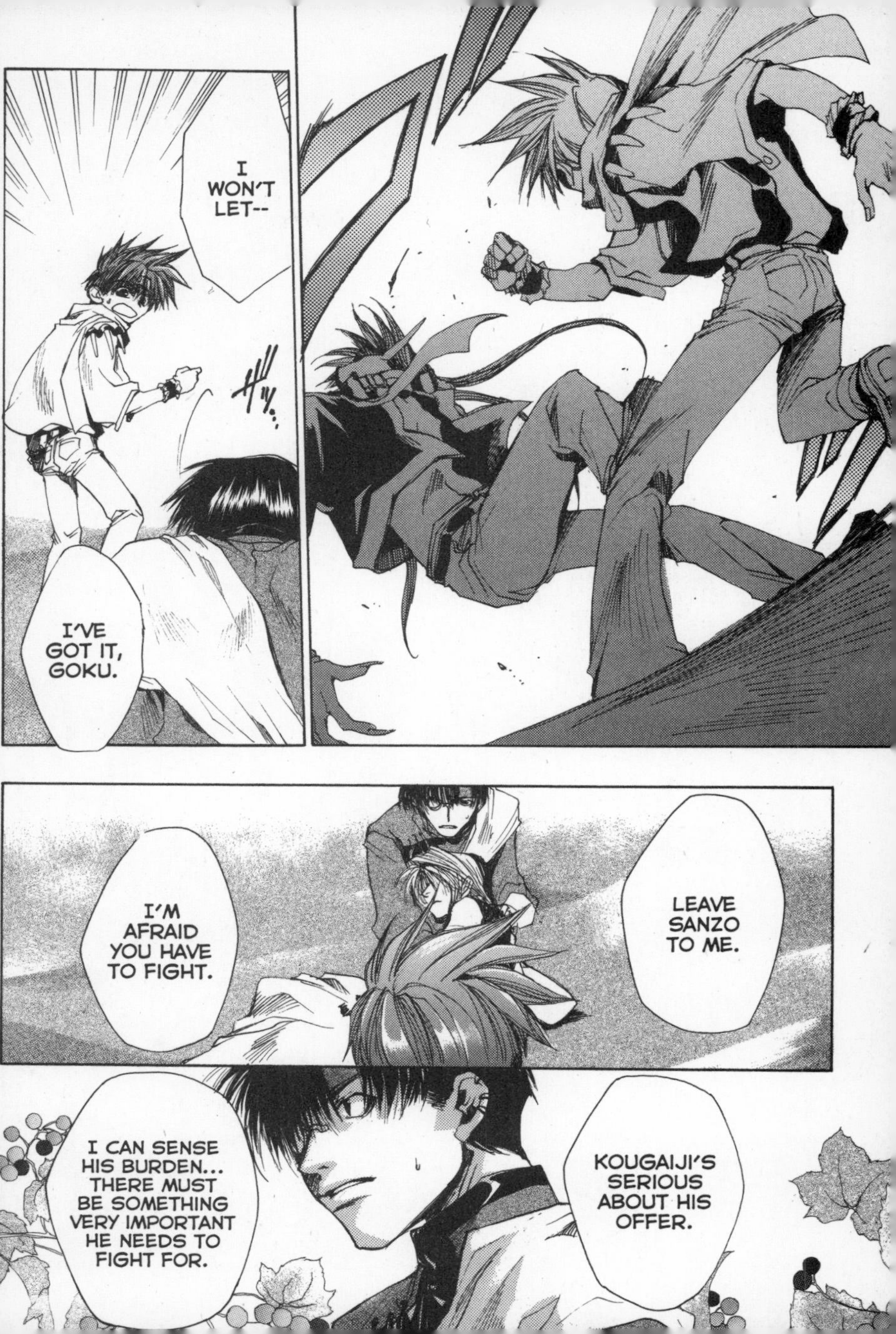
I WON'T LET--
I'VE GOT IT, GOKU.
LEAVE SANZO TO ME.
I'M AFRAID YOU HAVE TO FIGHT.
KOUGAIJI'S SERIOUS ABOUT HIS OFFER.
I CAN SENSE HIS BURDEN... THERE MUST BE SOMETHING VERY IMPORTANT HE NEEDS TO FIGHT FOR.

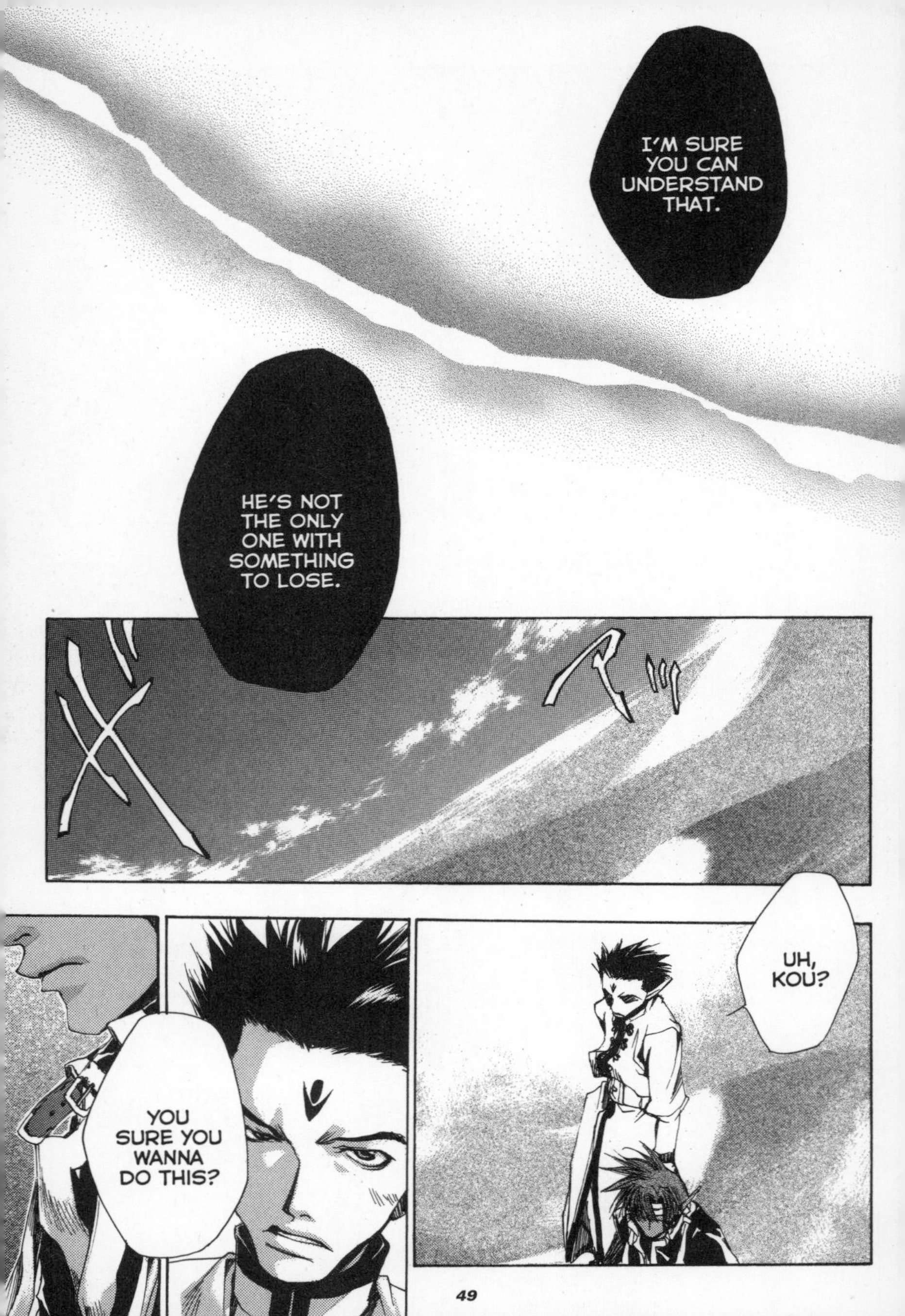
I'M SURE YOU CAN UNDERSTAND THAT.
HE'S NOT THE ONLY ONE WITH SOMETHING TO LOSE.
UH, KOU?
YOU SURE YOU WANNA DO THIS?

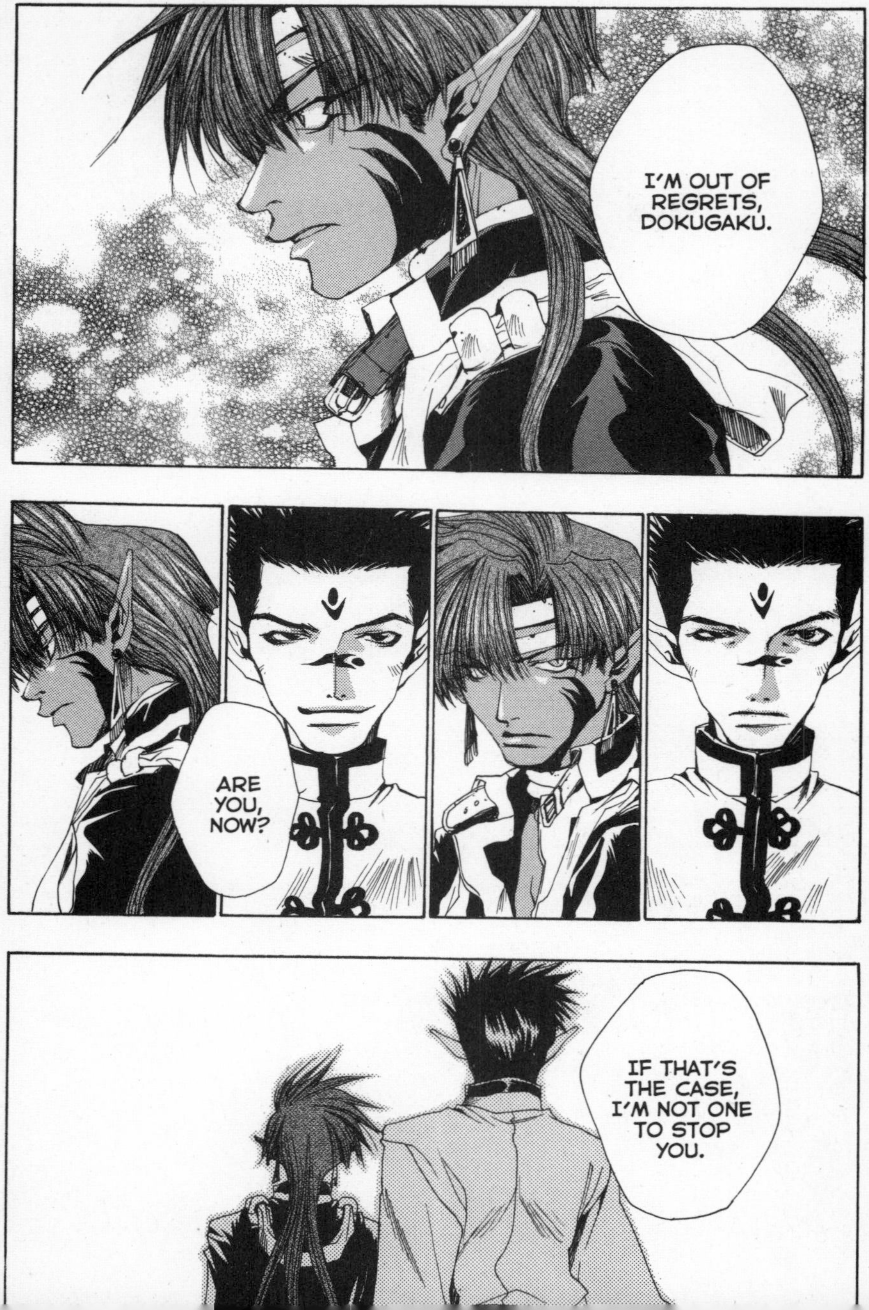
I'M OUT OF REGRETS, DOKUGAKU.
ARE YOU, NOW?
IF THAT'S THE CASE, I'M NOT ONE TO STOP YOU.

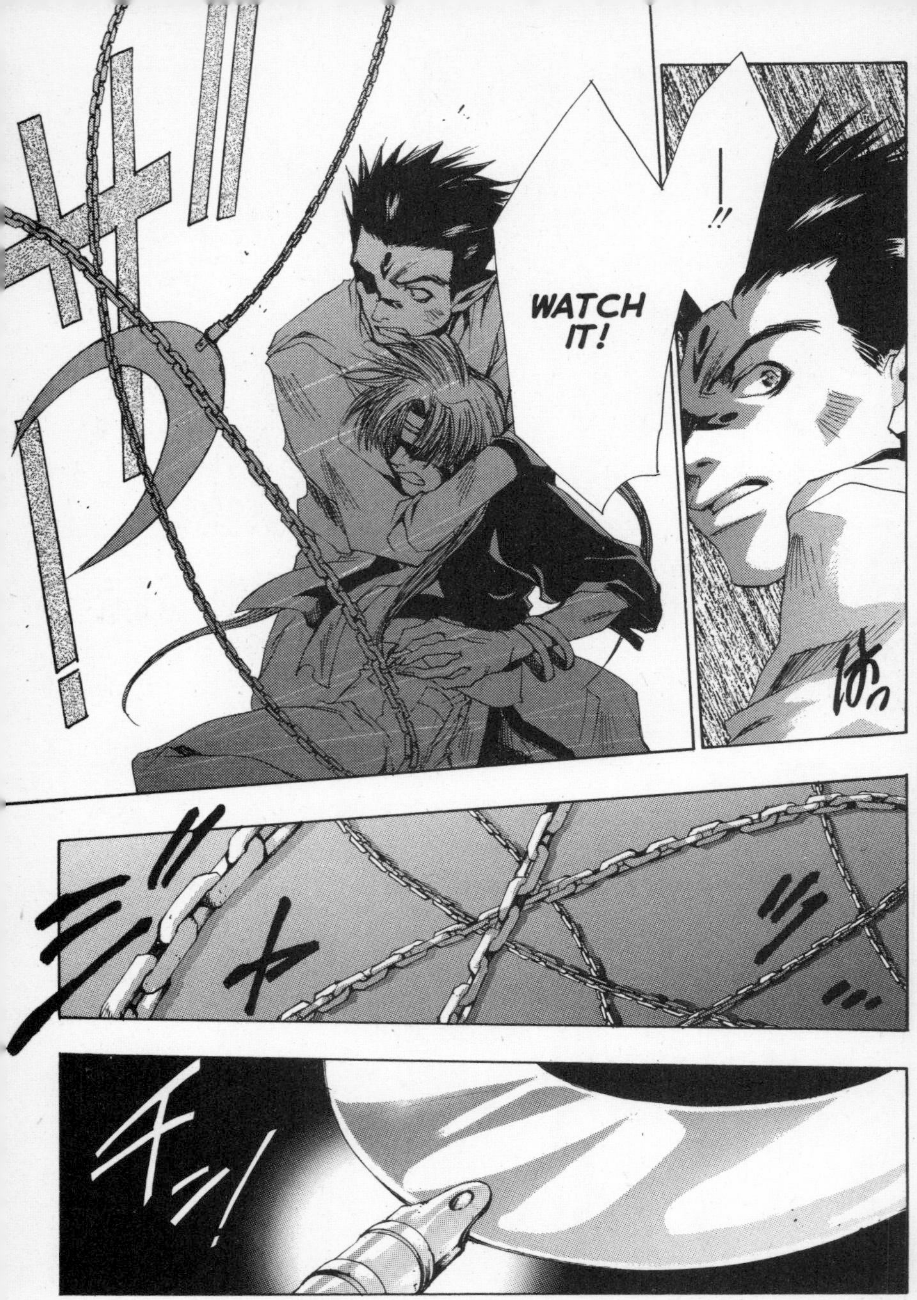
!!
はっ
WATCH IT!

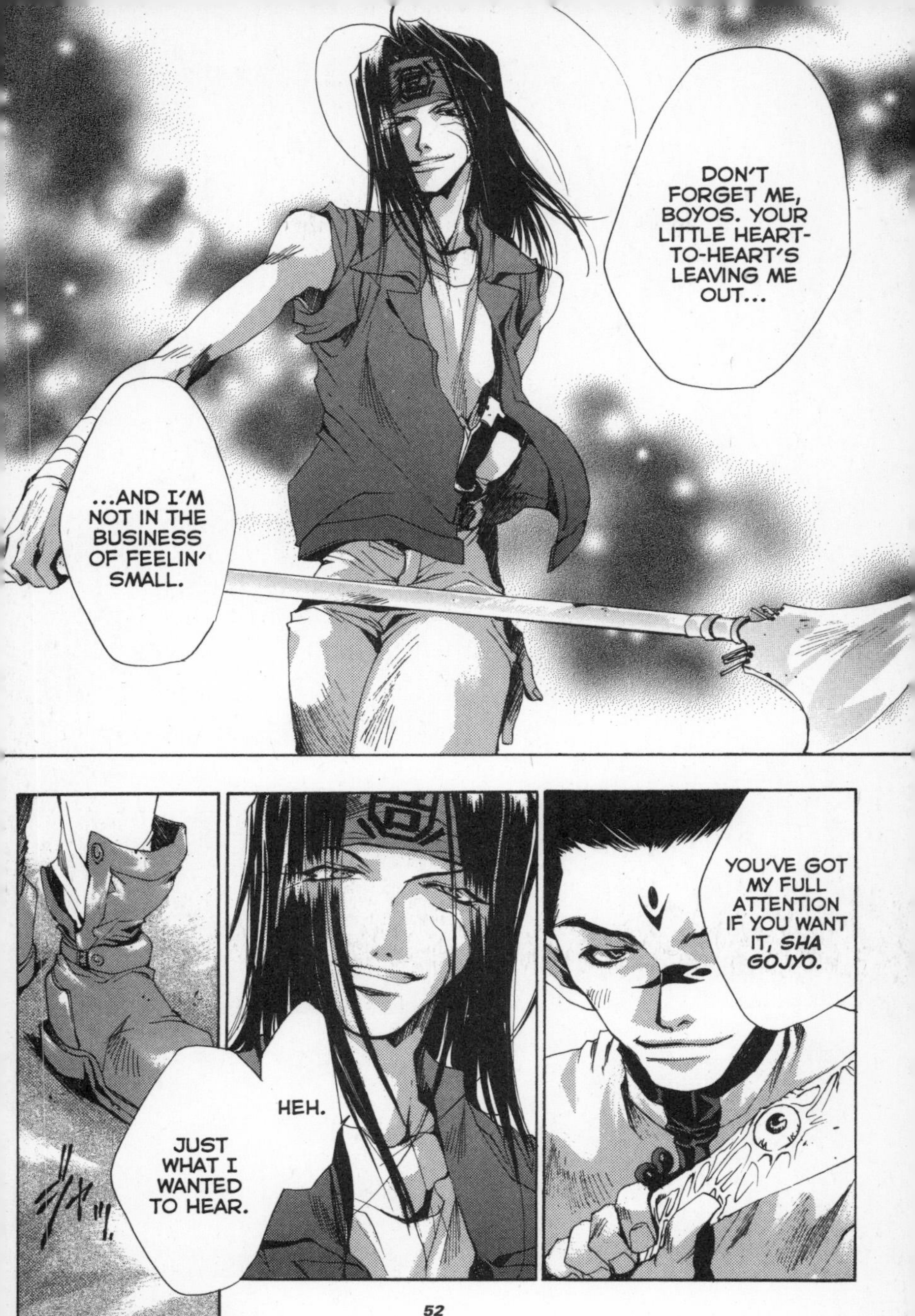
DON'T FORGET ME, BOYOS. YOUR LITTLE HEART-TO-HEART'S LEAVING ME OUT...
...AND I'M NOT IN THE BUSINESS OF FEELIN' SMALL.
YOU'VE GOT MY FULL ATTENTION IF YOU WANT IT, *SHA GOJYO.*
HEH.
JUST WHAT I WANTED TO HEAR.

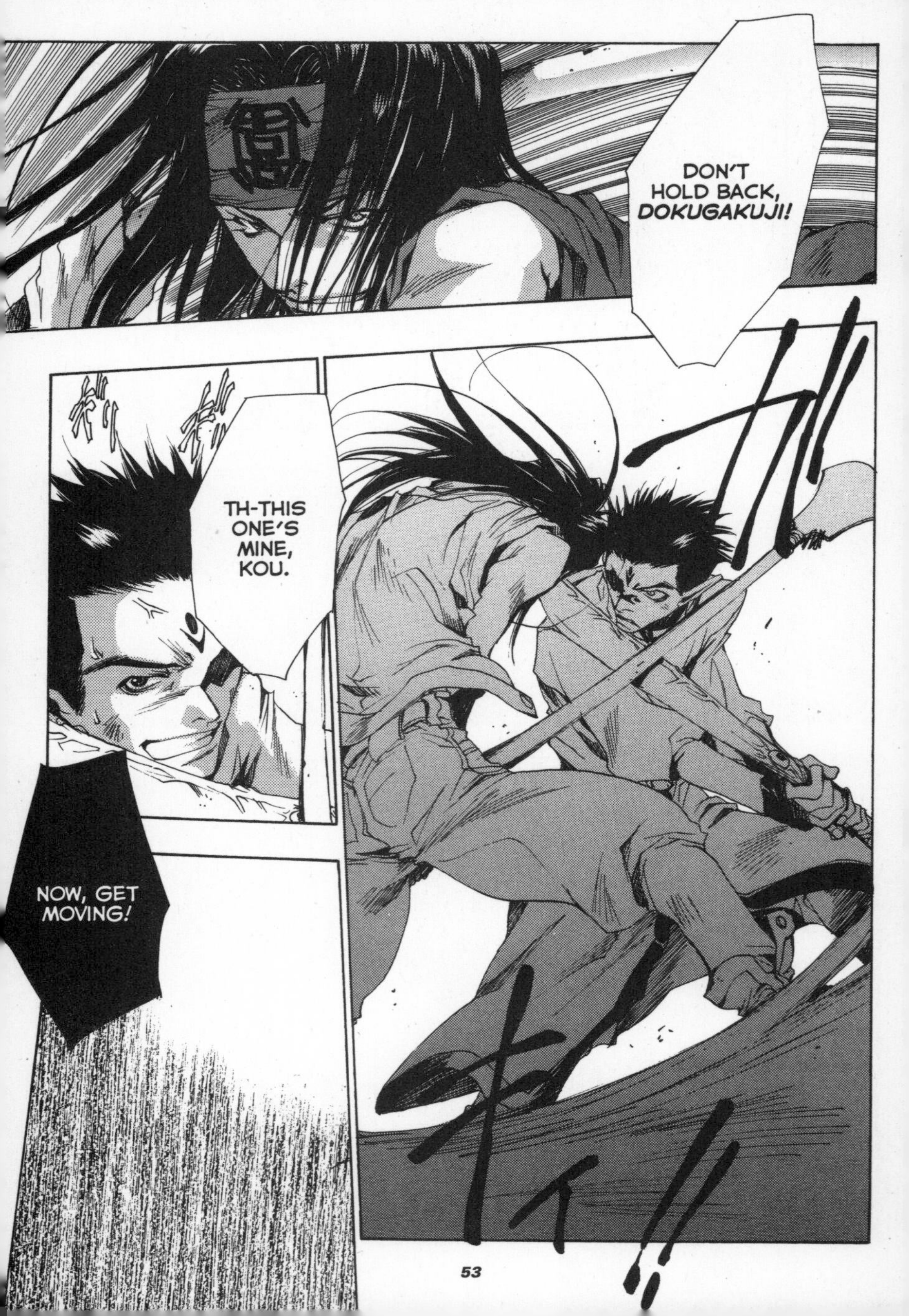
DON'T HOLD BACK, DOKUGAKUJI!
TH-THIS ONE'S MINE, KOU.
NOW, GET MOVING!

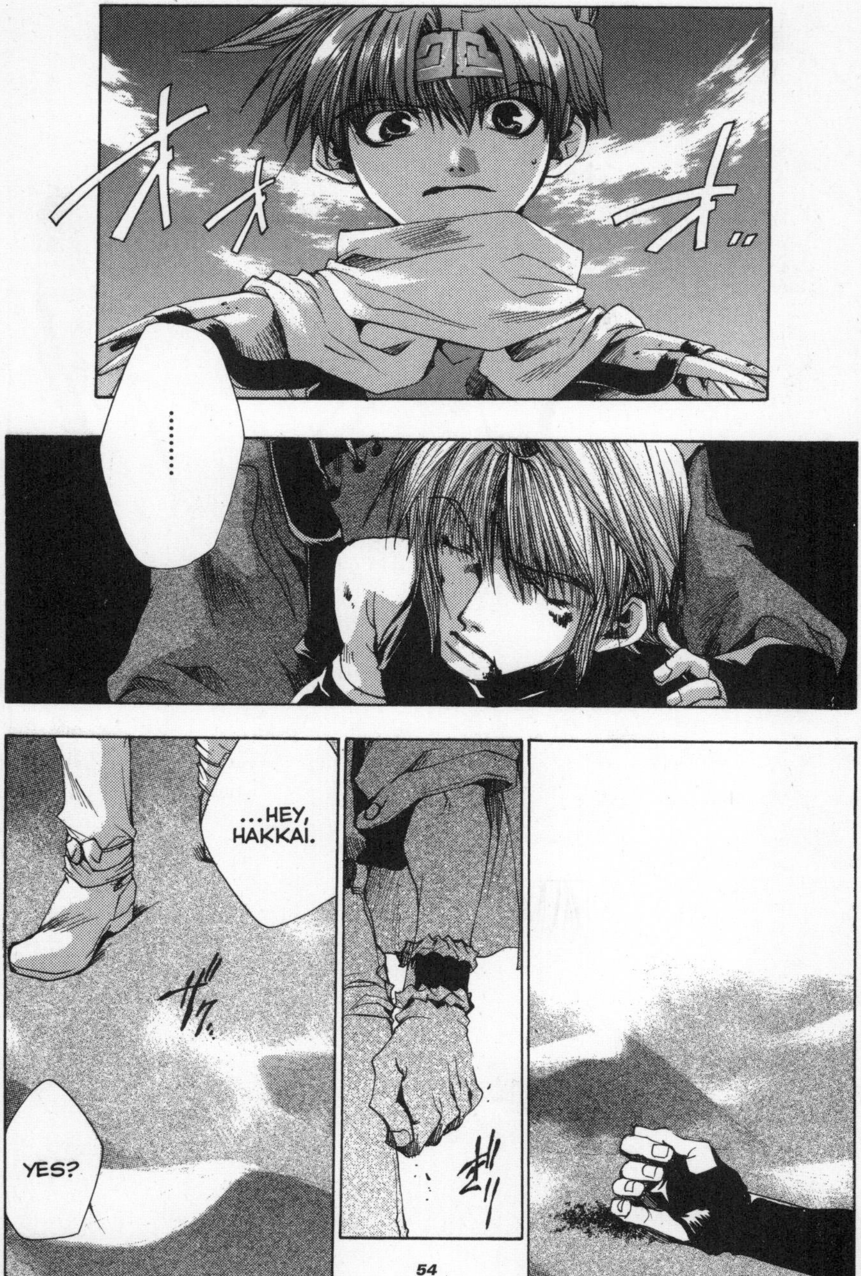
......
...HEY, HAKKAI.
YES?

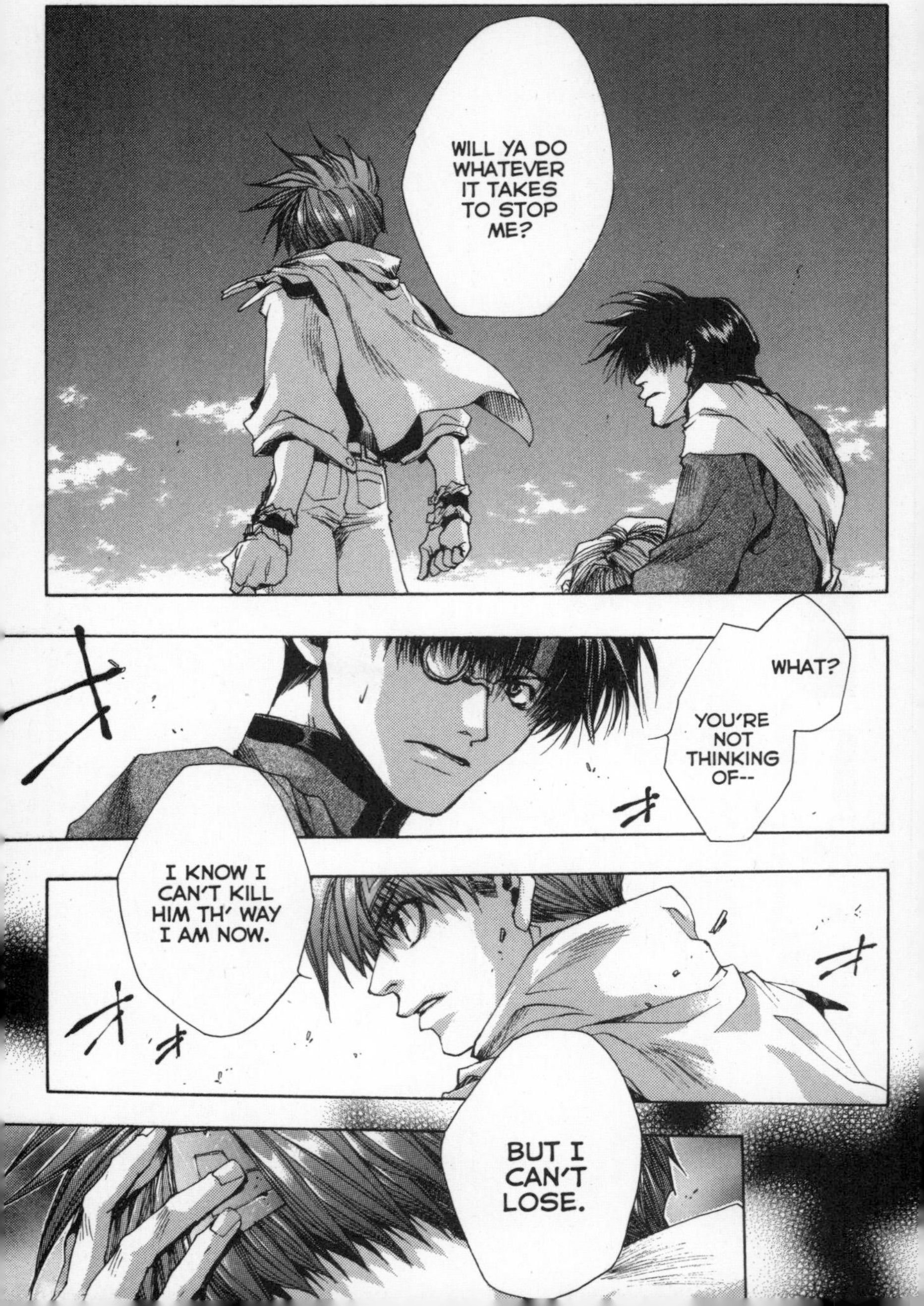
WILL YA DO WHATEVER IT TAKES TO STOP ME?
WHAT?
YOU'RE NOT THINKING OF--
I KNOW I CAN'T KILL HIM TH' WAY I AM NOW.
BUT I CAN'T LOSE.

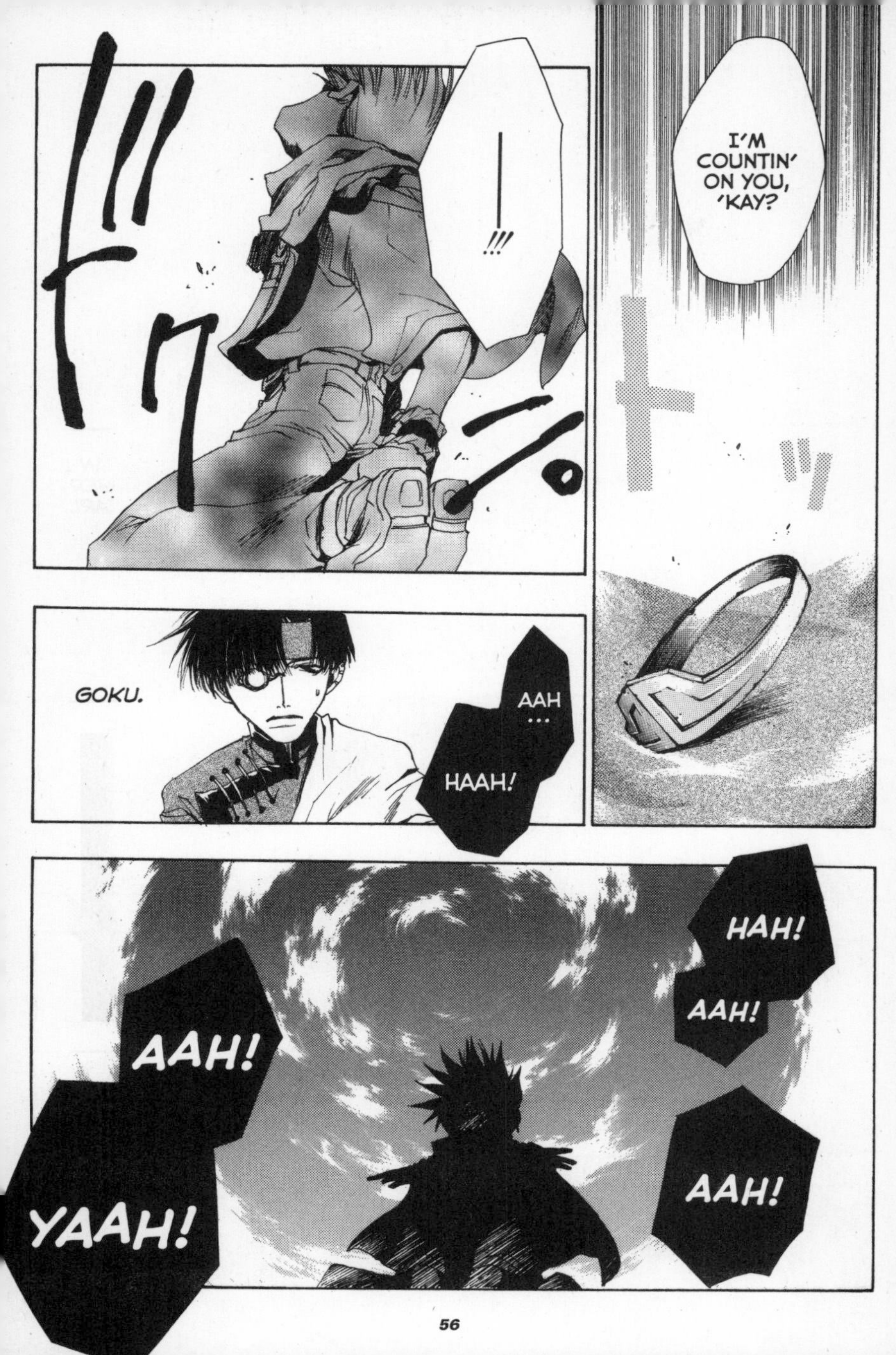
I'M COUNTIN' ON YOU, 'KAY?
—!!!
AAH...
HAAH!
GOKU.
HAH!
AAH!
AAH!
AAH!
YAAH!

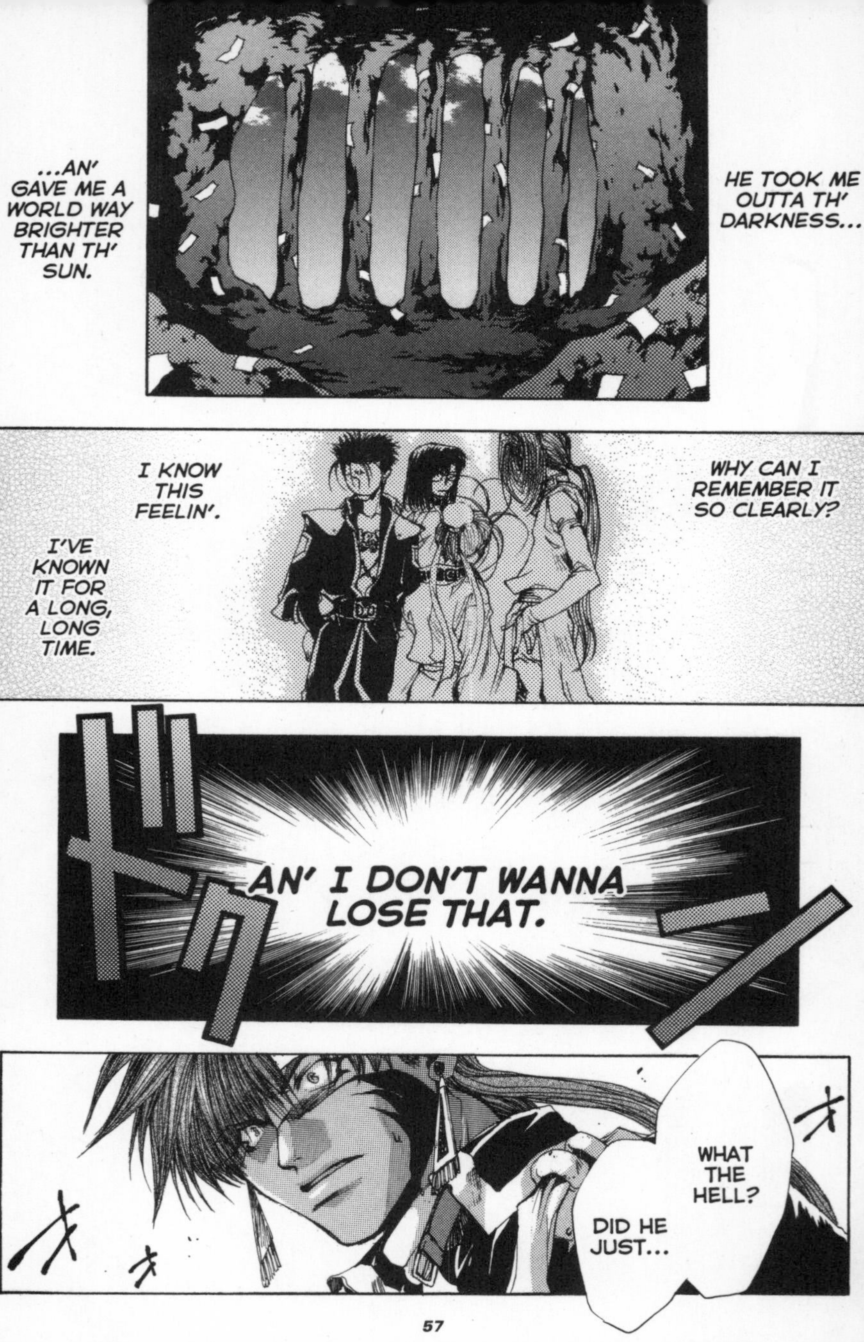
HE TOOK ME OUTTA TH' DARKNESS...
...AN' GAVE ME A WORLD WAY BRIGHTER THAN TH' SUN.
WHY CAN I REMEMBER IT SO CLEARLY?
I KNOW THIS FEELIN'.
I'VE KNOWN IT FOR A LONG, LONG TIME.
AN' I DON'T WANNA LOSE THAT.
WHAT THE HELL?
DID HE JUST...

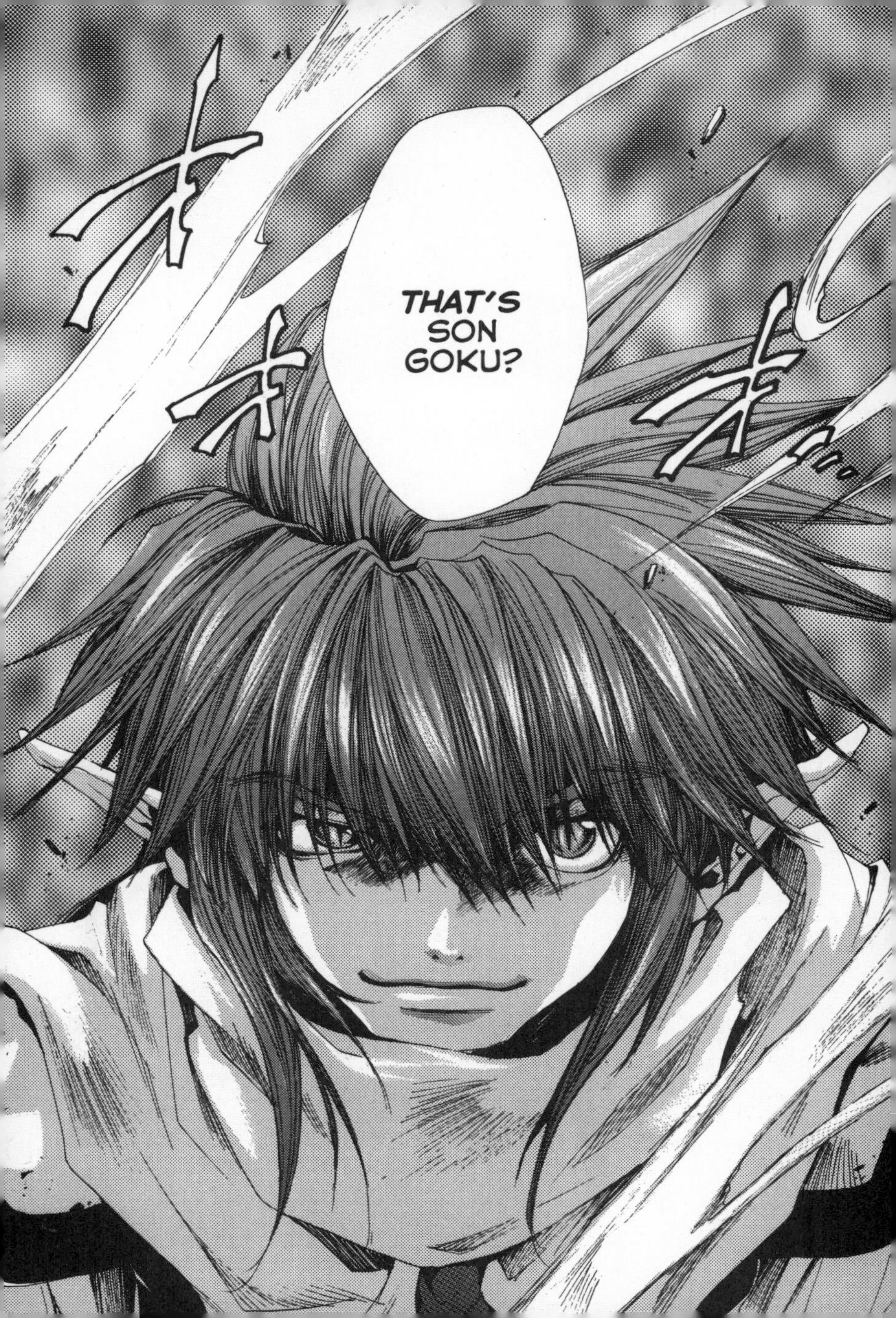
THAT'S SON GOKU?

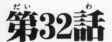

第32話

CHAPTER 32:
THICKER THAN BLOOD

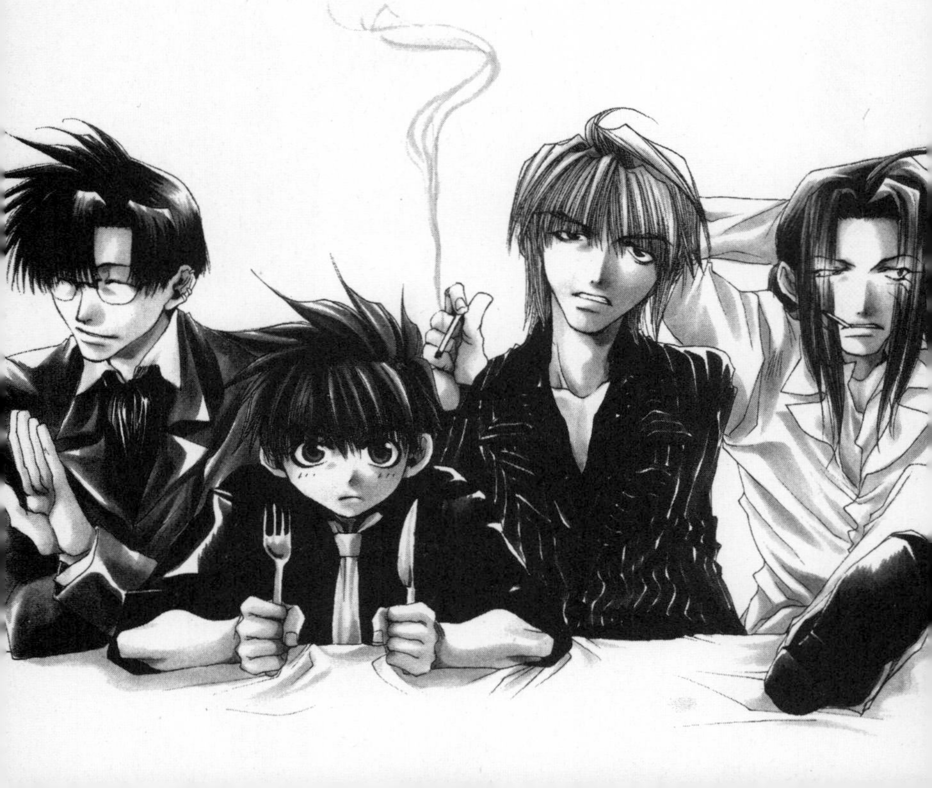

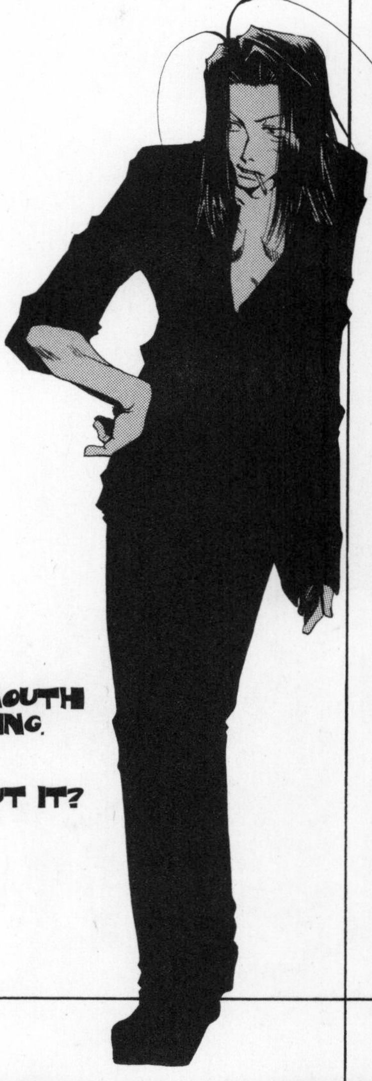

EXPLAIN TO ME, WITH THAT MOUTH OF YOURS, THIS BITTER FEELING.

WHERE DO YOU WANT ME TO PUT IT?

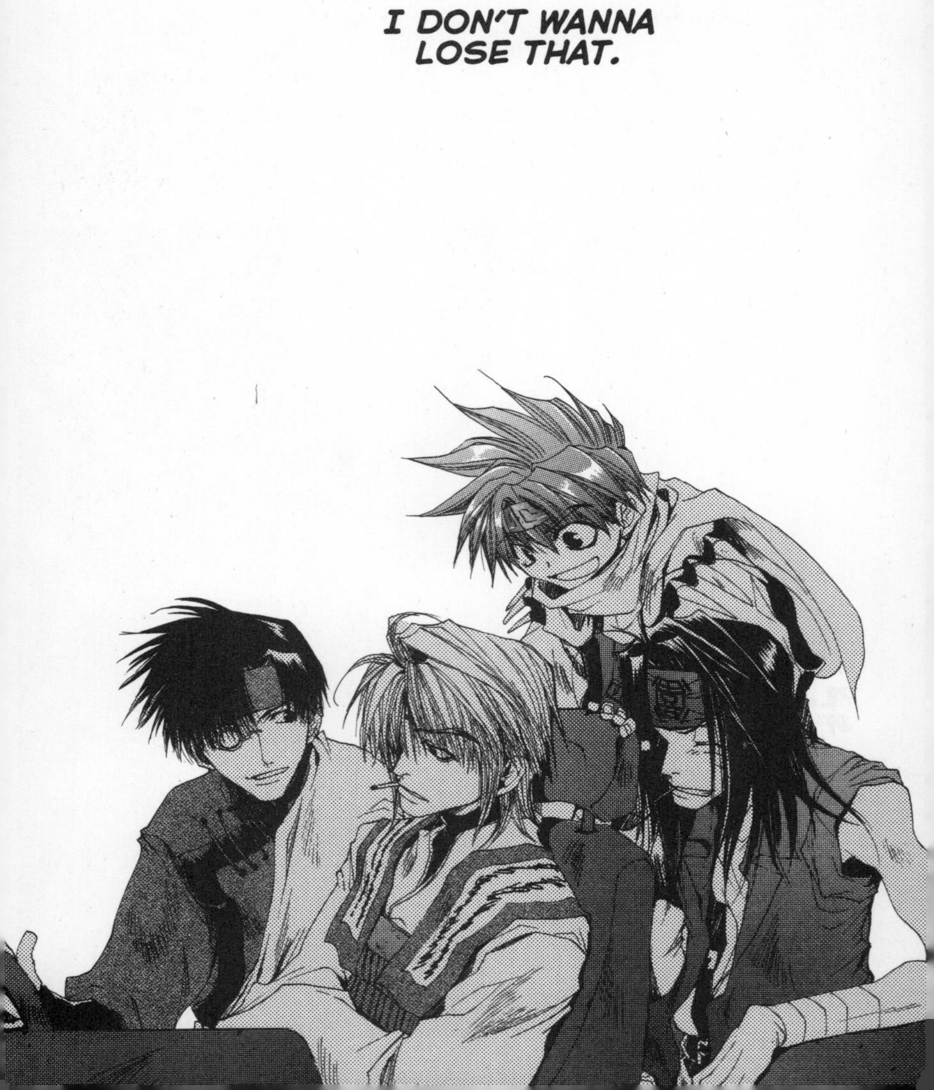
I DON'T WANNA LOSE THAT.

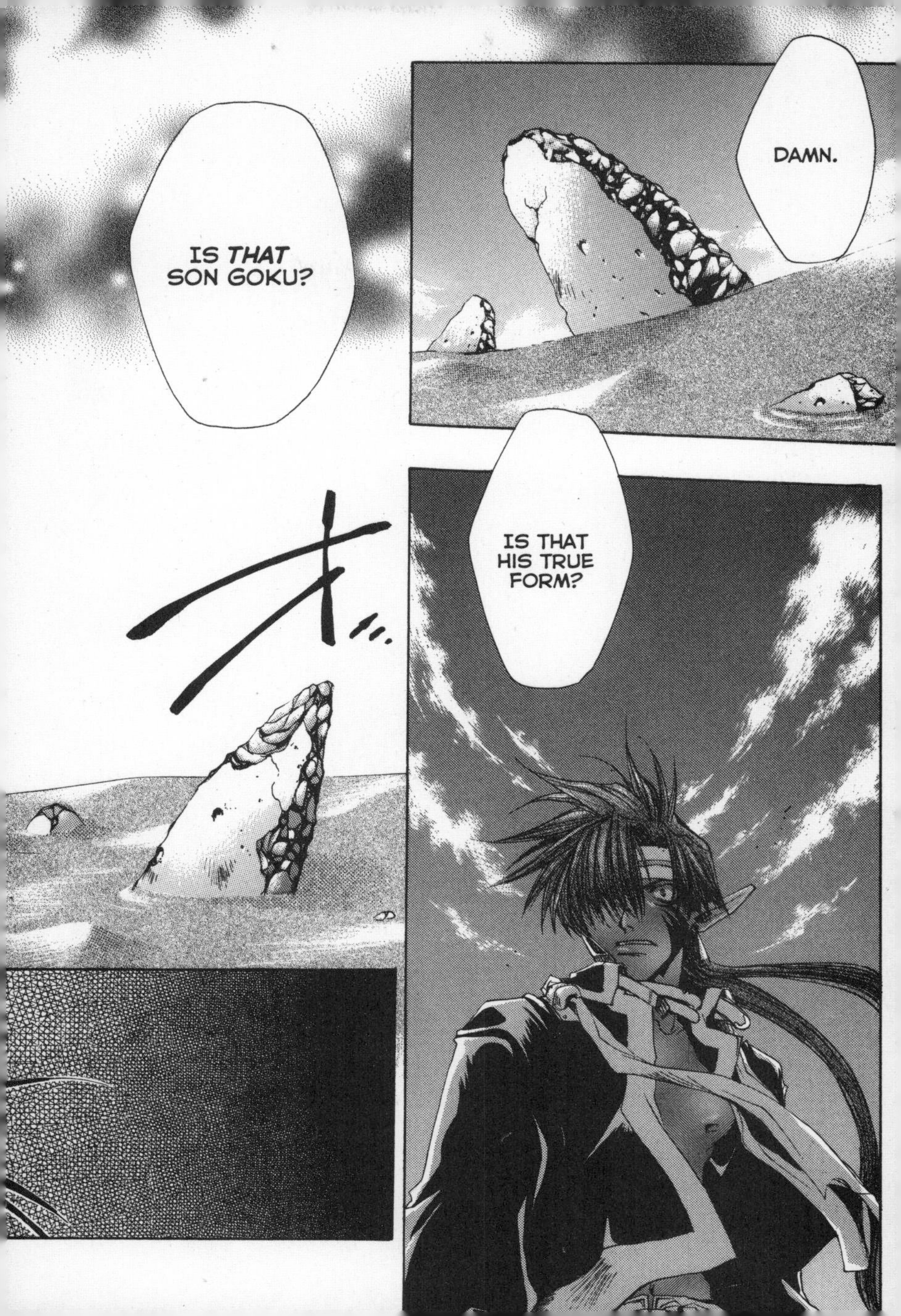
DAMN.
IS *THAT* SON GOKU?
IS THAT HIS TRUE FORM?

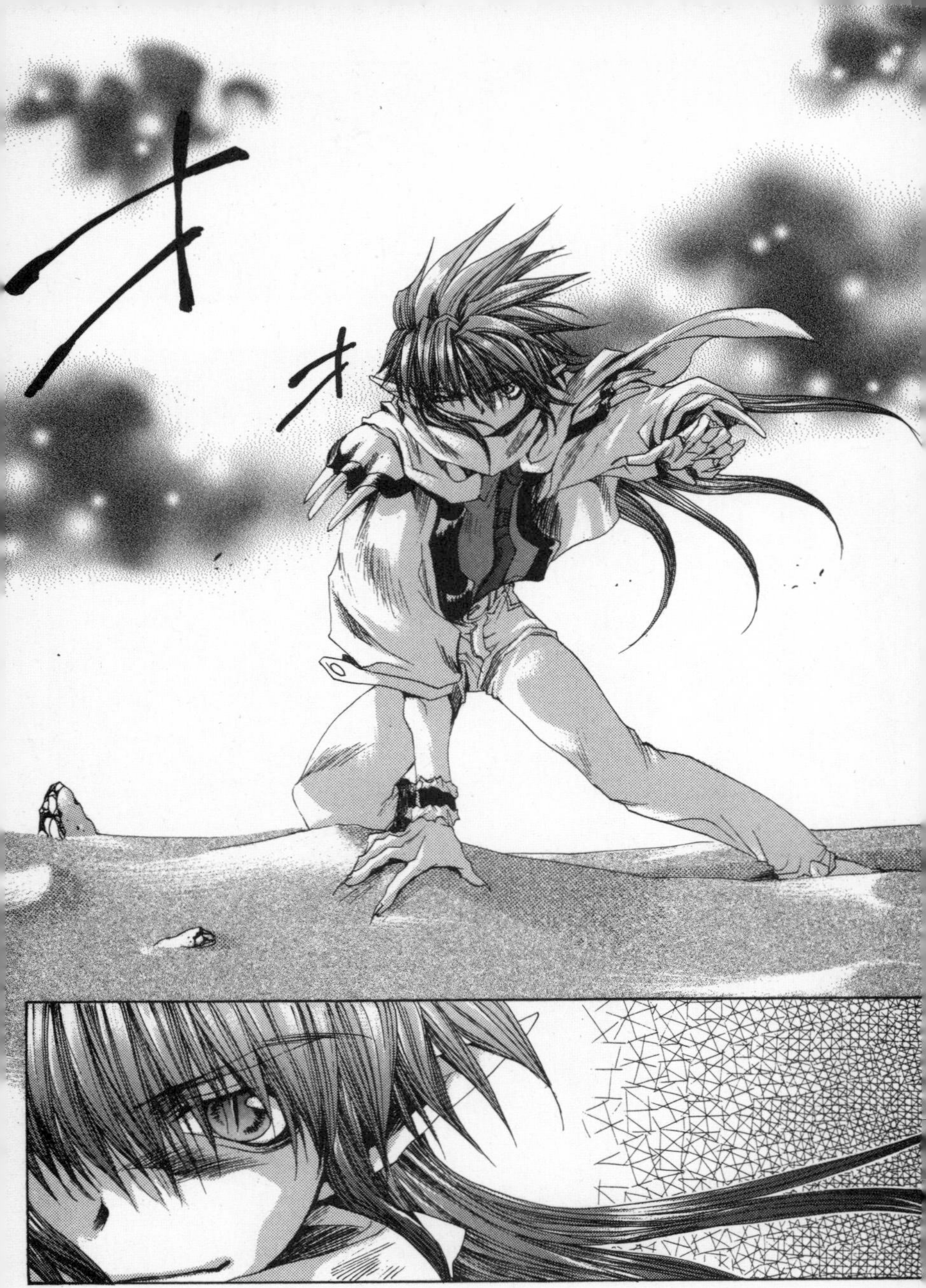
オォ

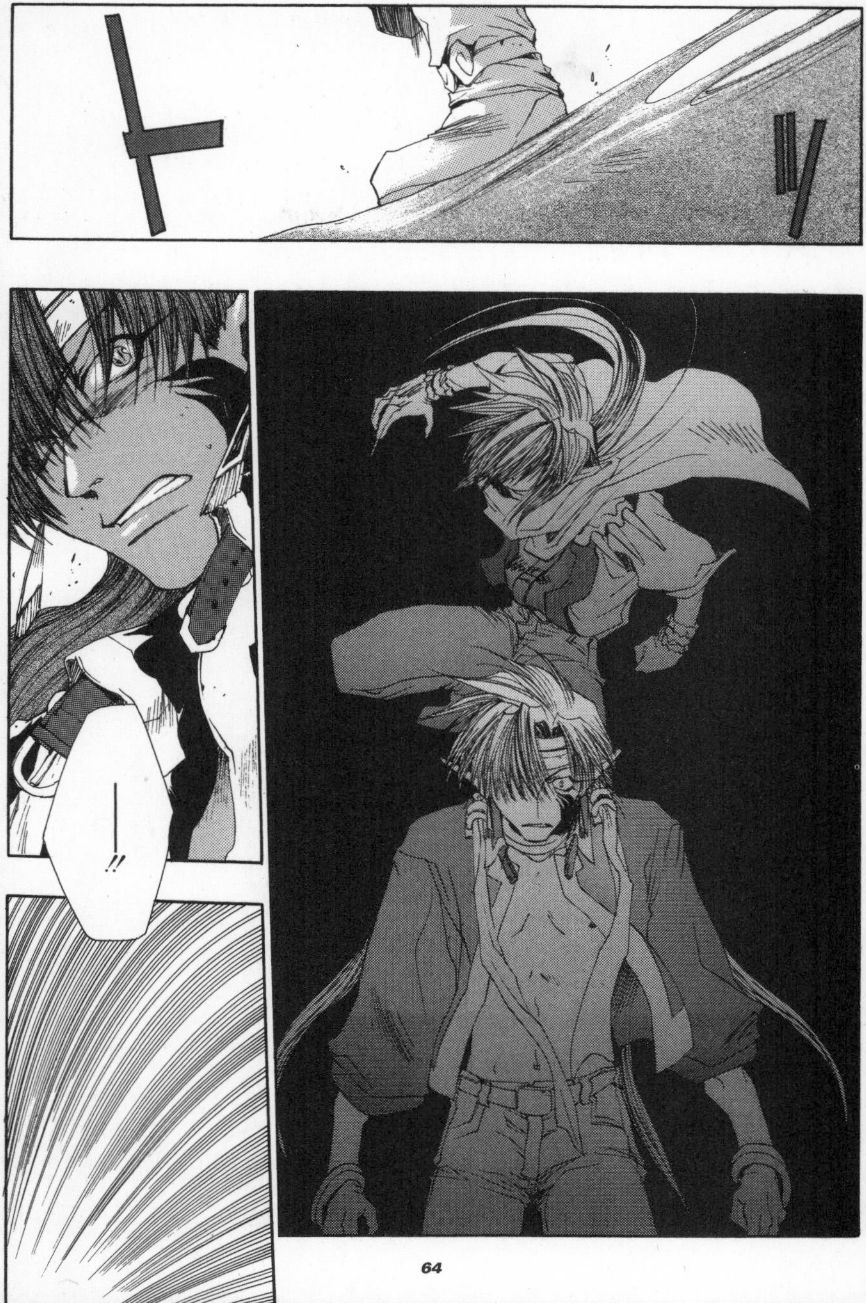
—!!

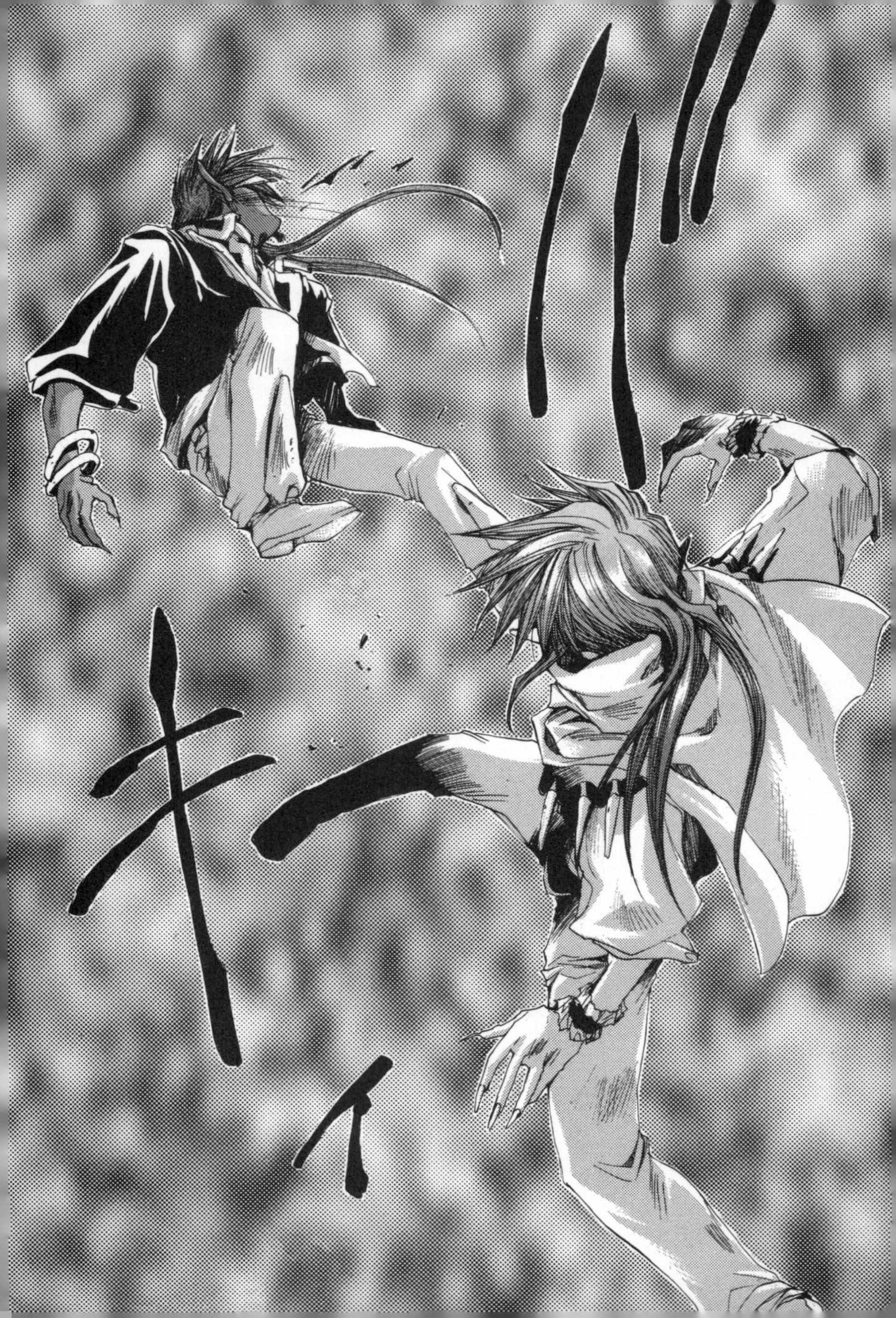
キィ

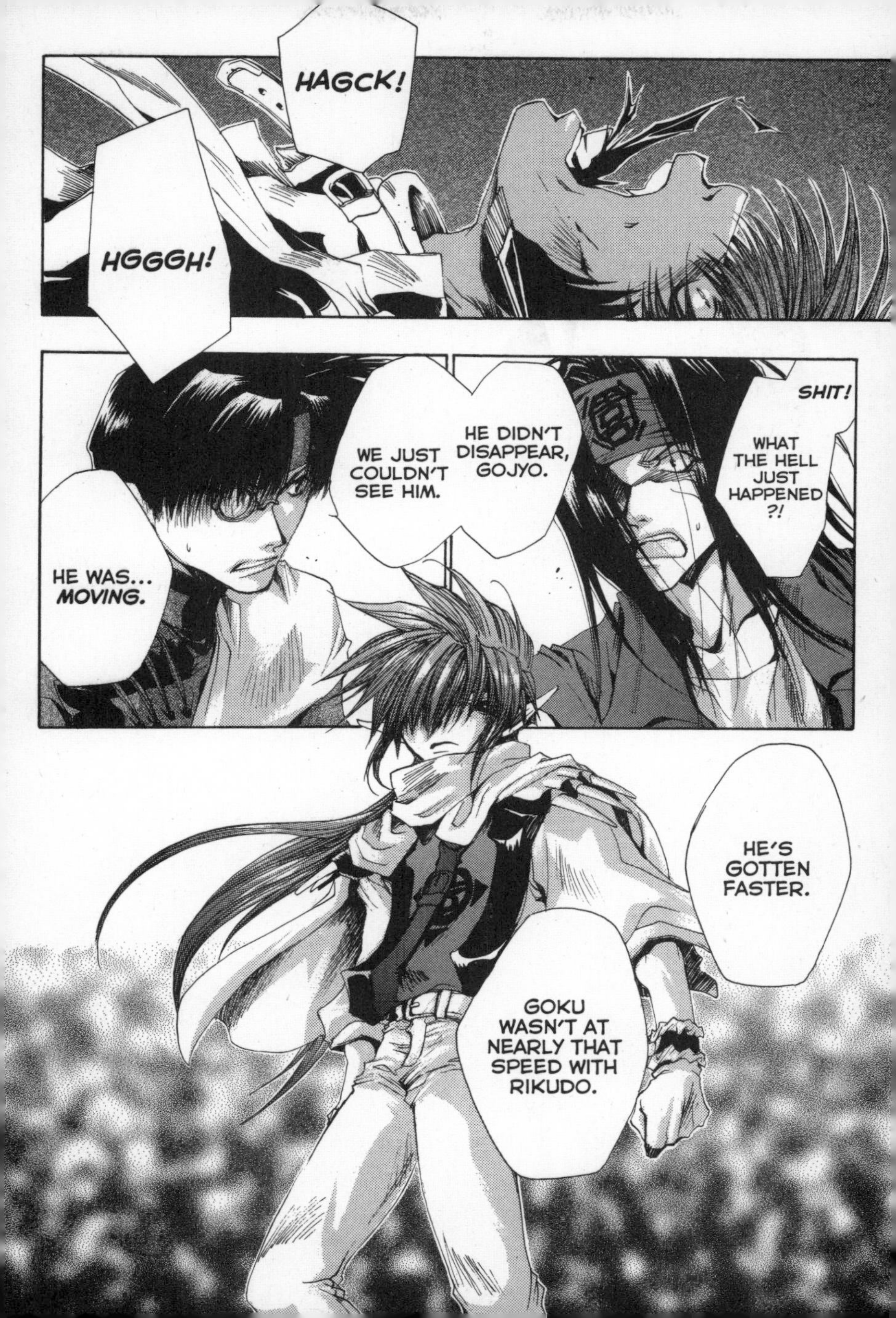
HAGCK!
HGGGH!
SHIT!
WHAT THE HELL JUST HAPPENED?!
HE DIDN'T DISAPPEAR, GOJYO.
WE JUST COULDN'T SEE HIM.
HE WAS... MOVING.
HE'S GOTTEN FASTER.
GOKU WASN'T AT NEARLY THAT SPEED WITH RIKUDO.

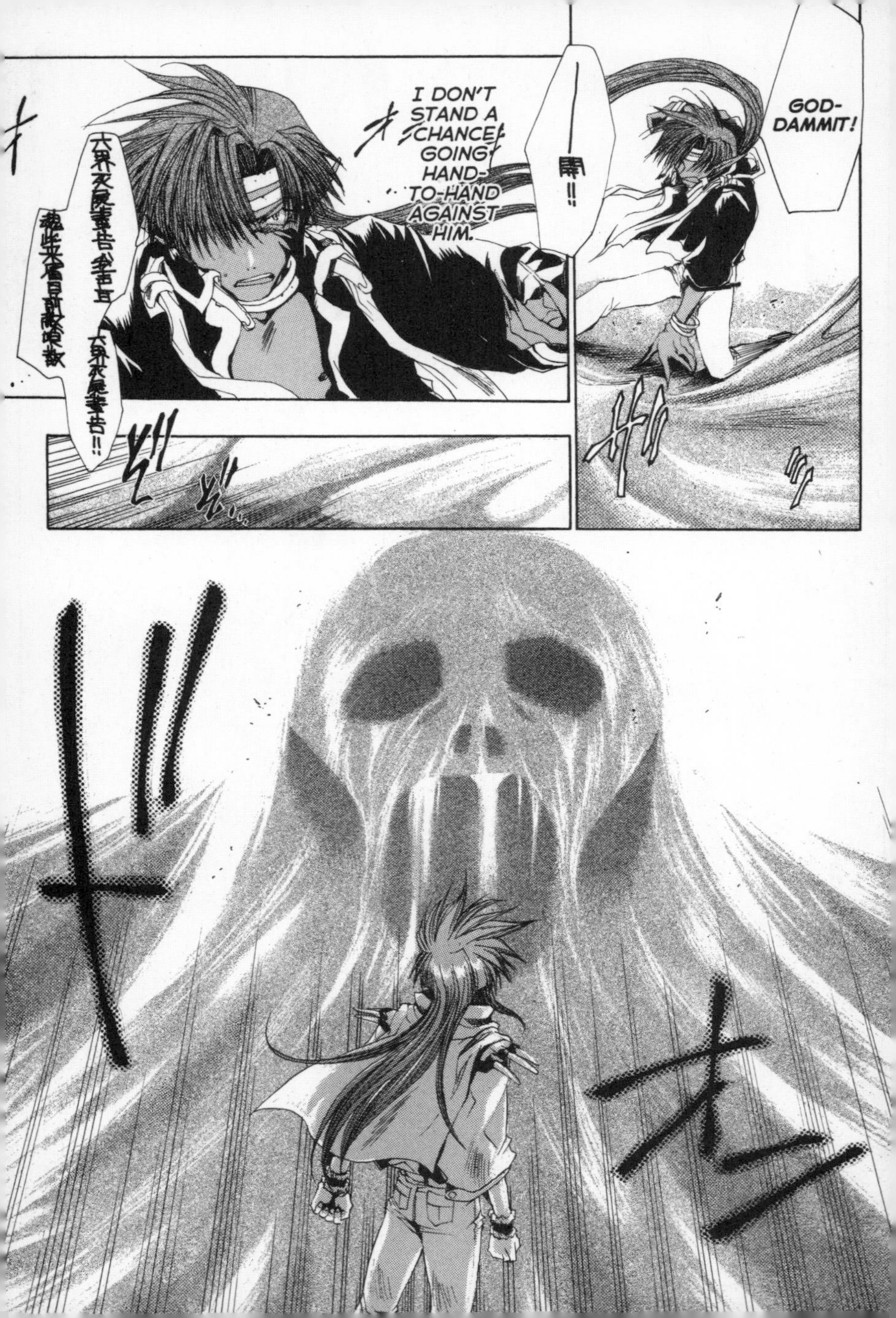
GOD-DAMMIT!
I DON'T STAND A CHANCE GOING HAND-TO-HAND AGAINST HIM.

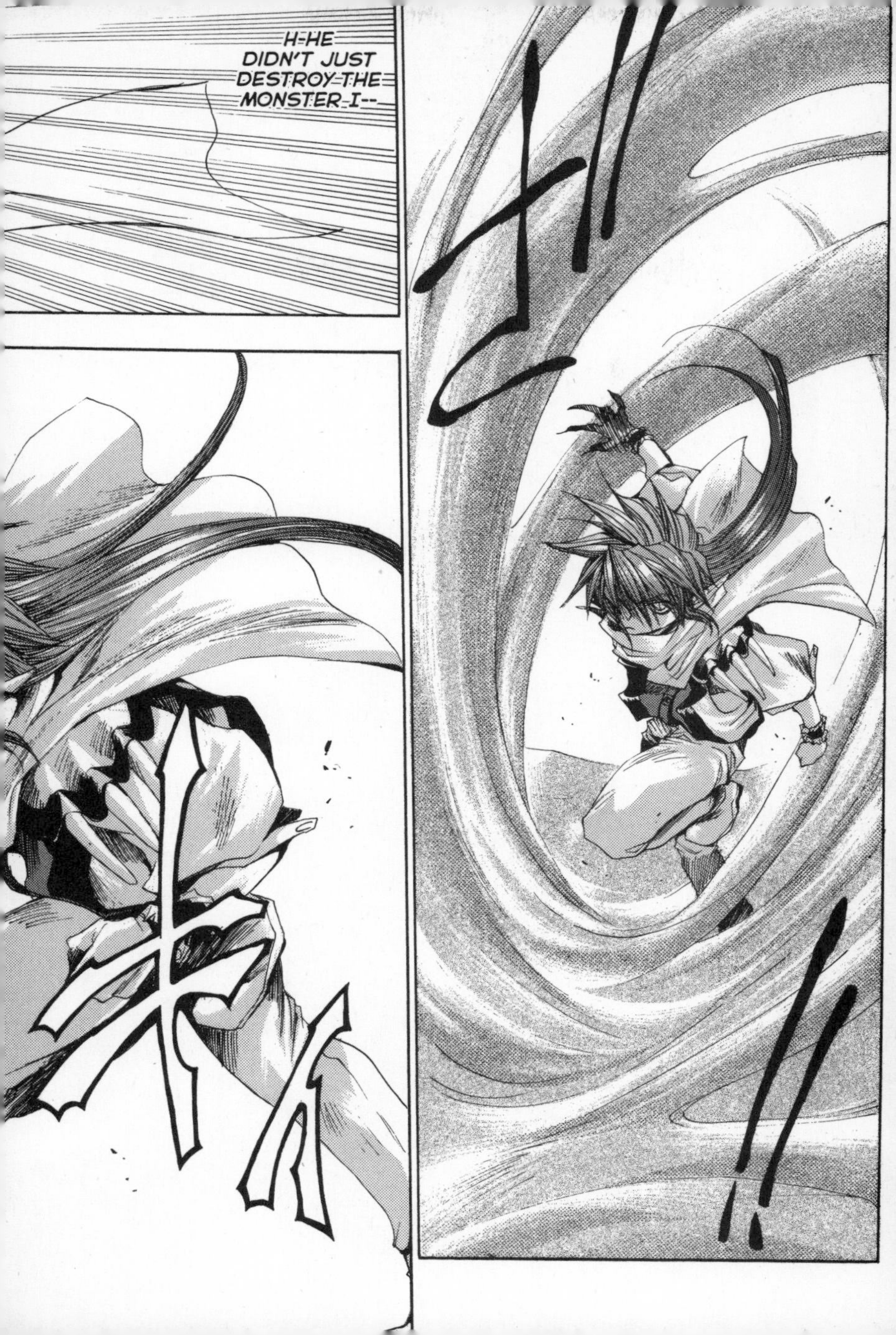
H-HE DIDN'T JUST DESTROY THE MONSTER I--

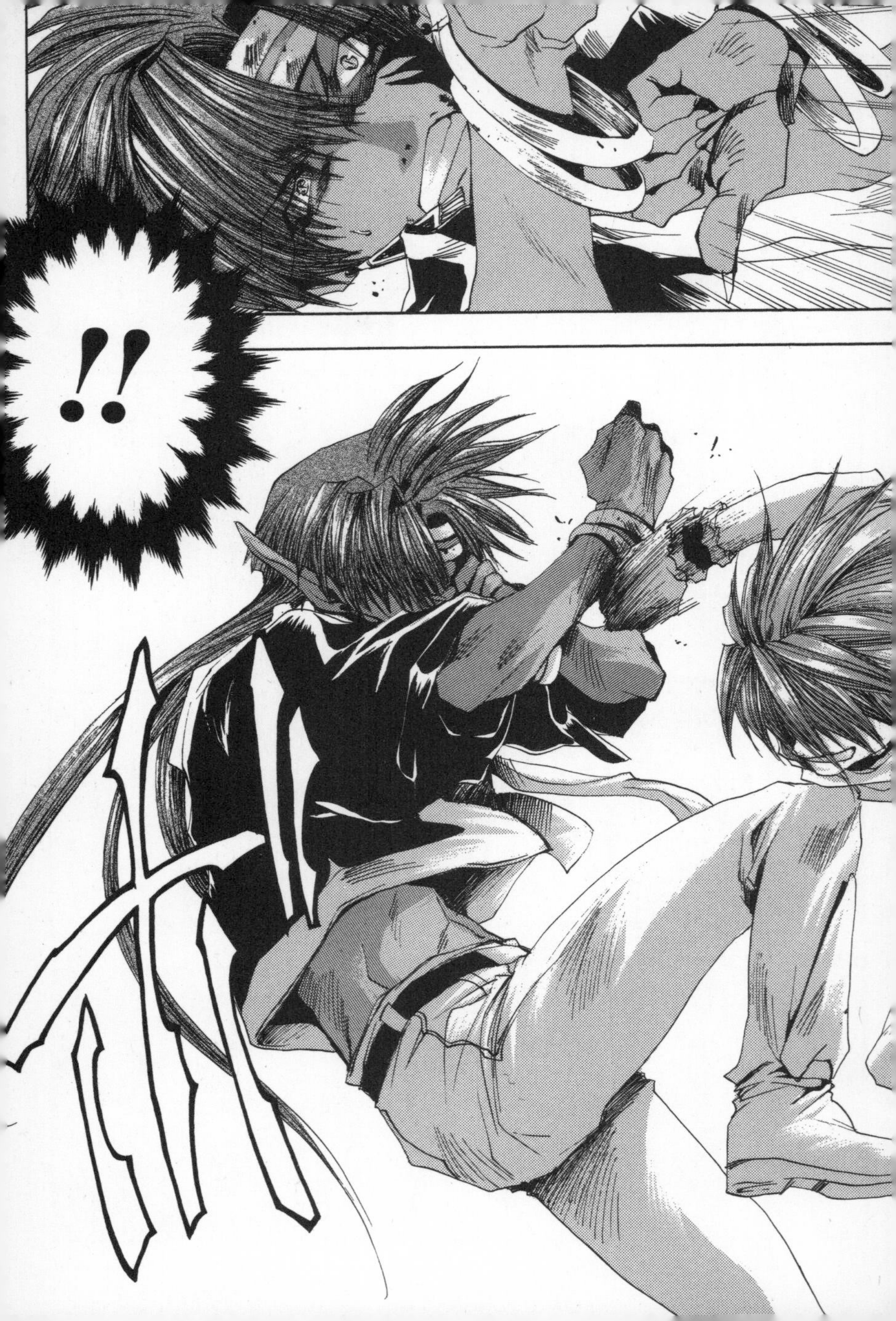
!!

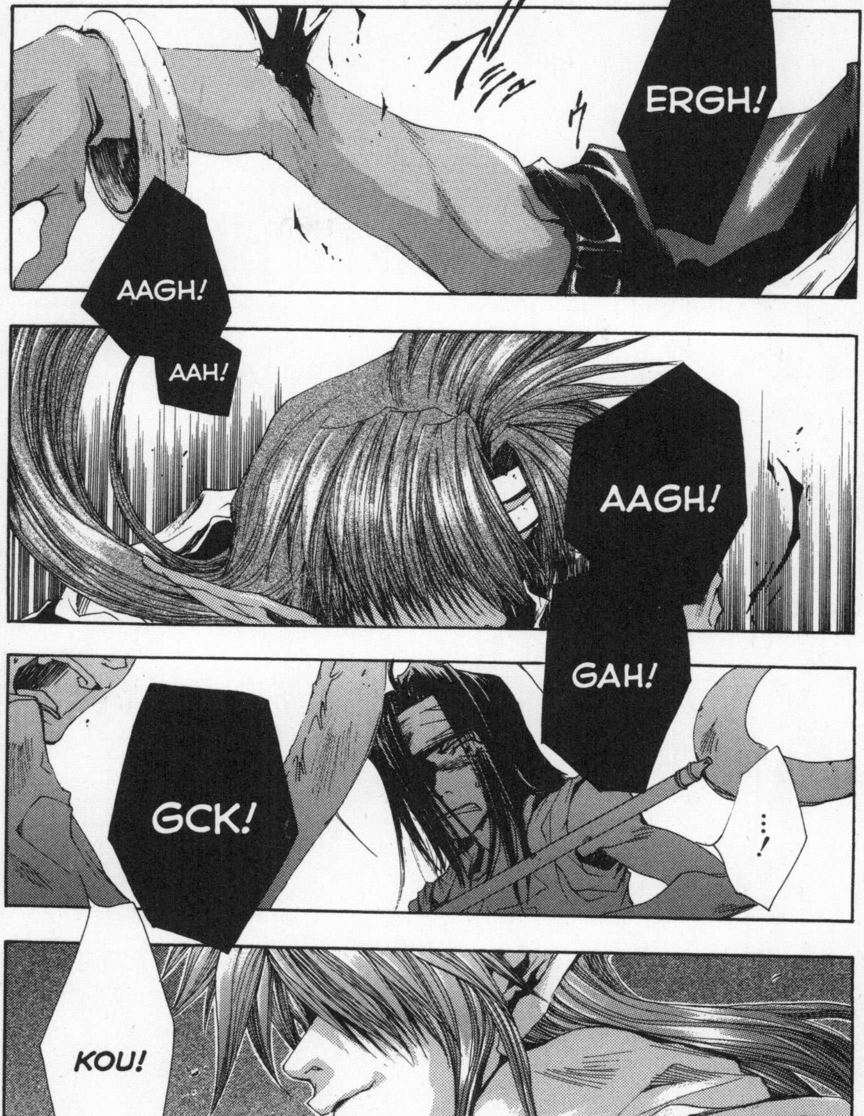
ERGH!
AAGH!
AAGH!
AAH!
GAH!
...!
GCK!
KOU!

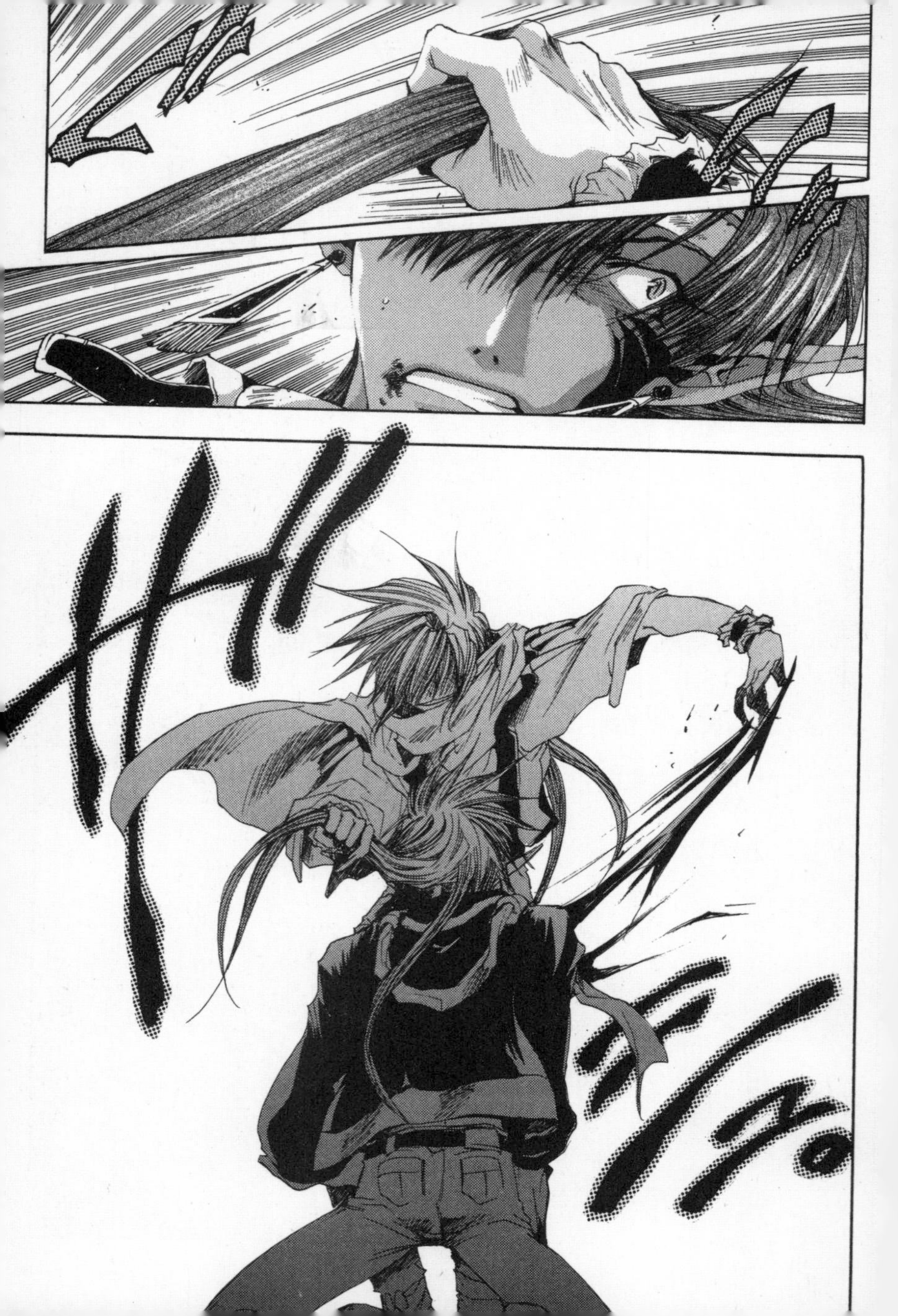

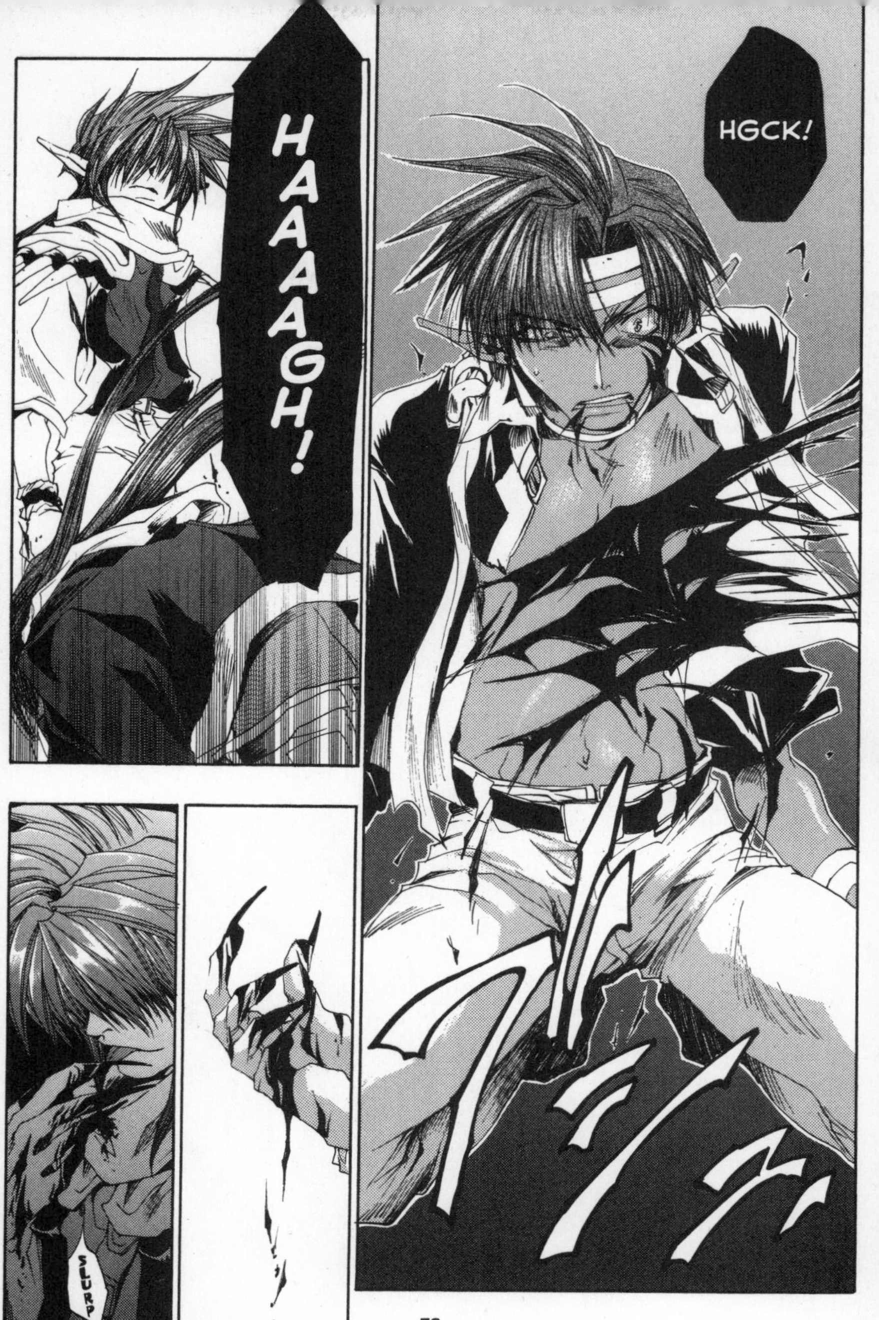
HGCK!
HAAAAGH!
SLURP

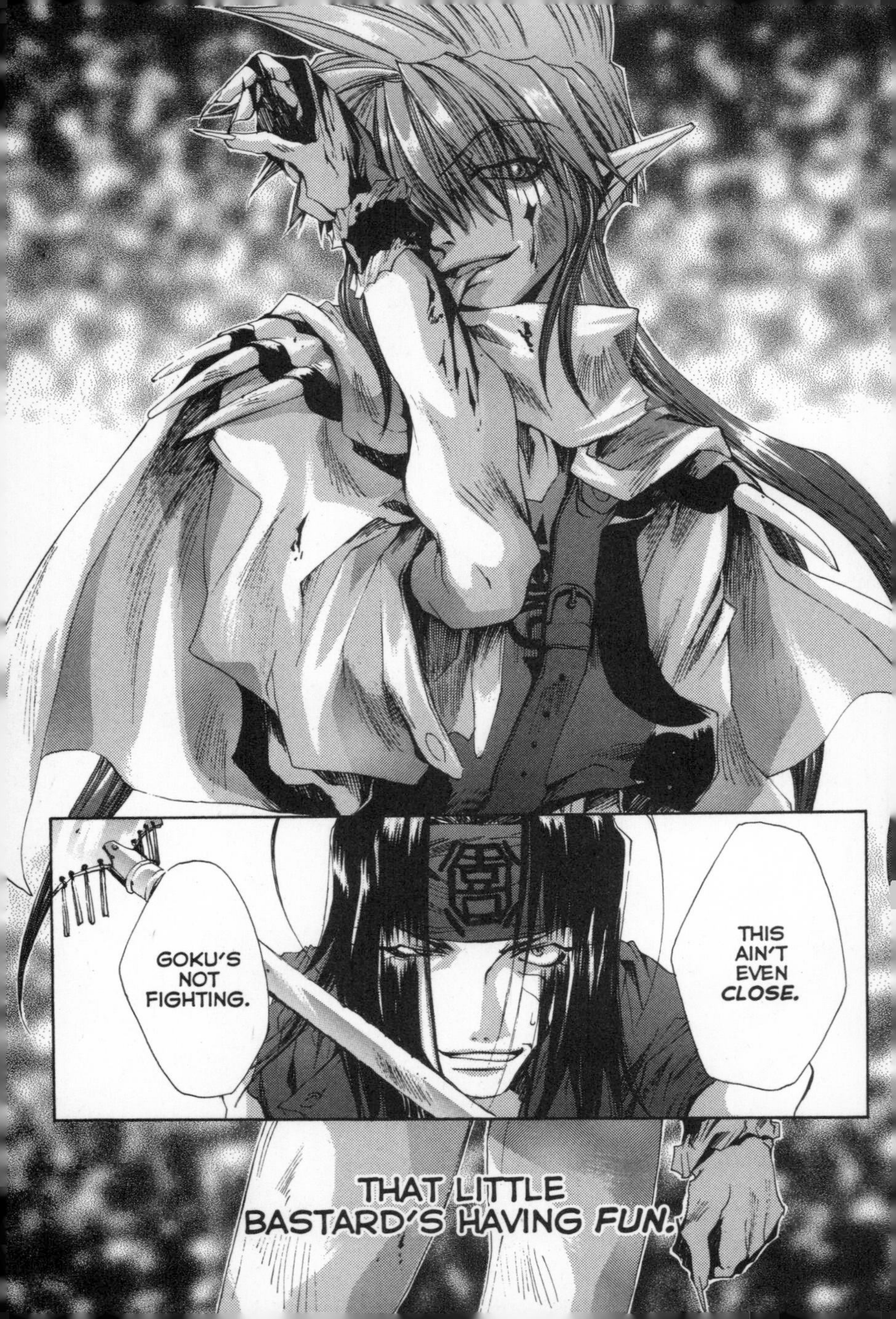
THIS AIN'T EVEN CLOSE.
GOKU'S NOT FIGHTING.
THAT LITTLE BASTARD'S HAVING FUN.

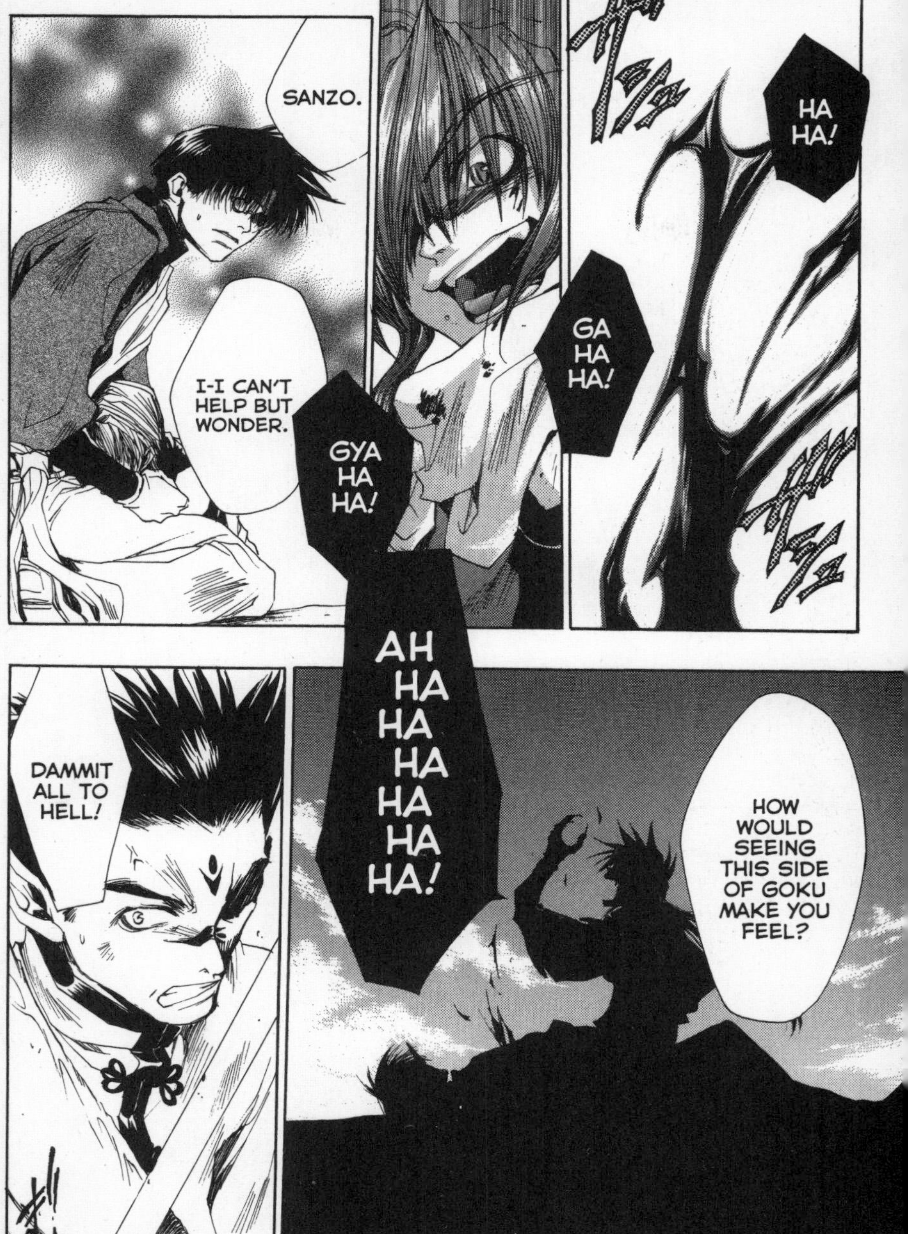
HA HA!
GA HA HA!
GYA HA HA!
SANZO.
I-I CAN'T HELP BUT WONDER.
AH HA HA HA HA HA HA HA!
HOW WOULD SEEING THIS SIDE OF GOKU MAKE YOU FEEL?
DAMMIT ALL TO HELL!

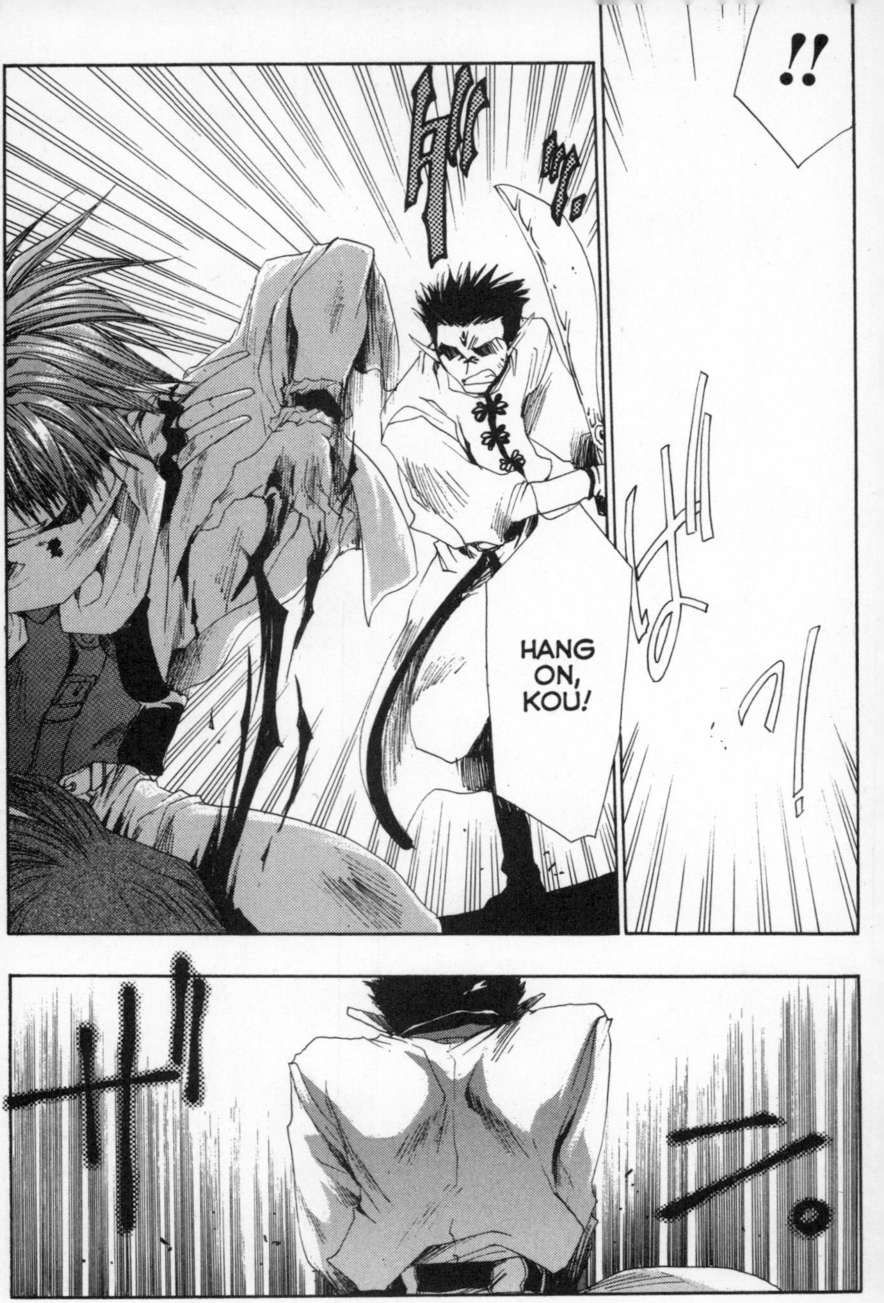
!!
HANG ON, KOU!

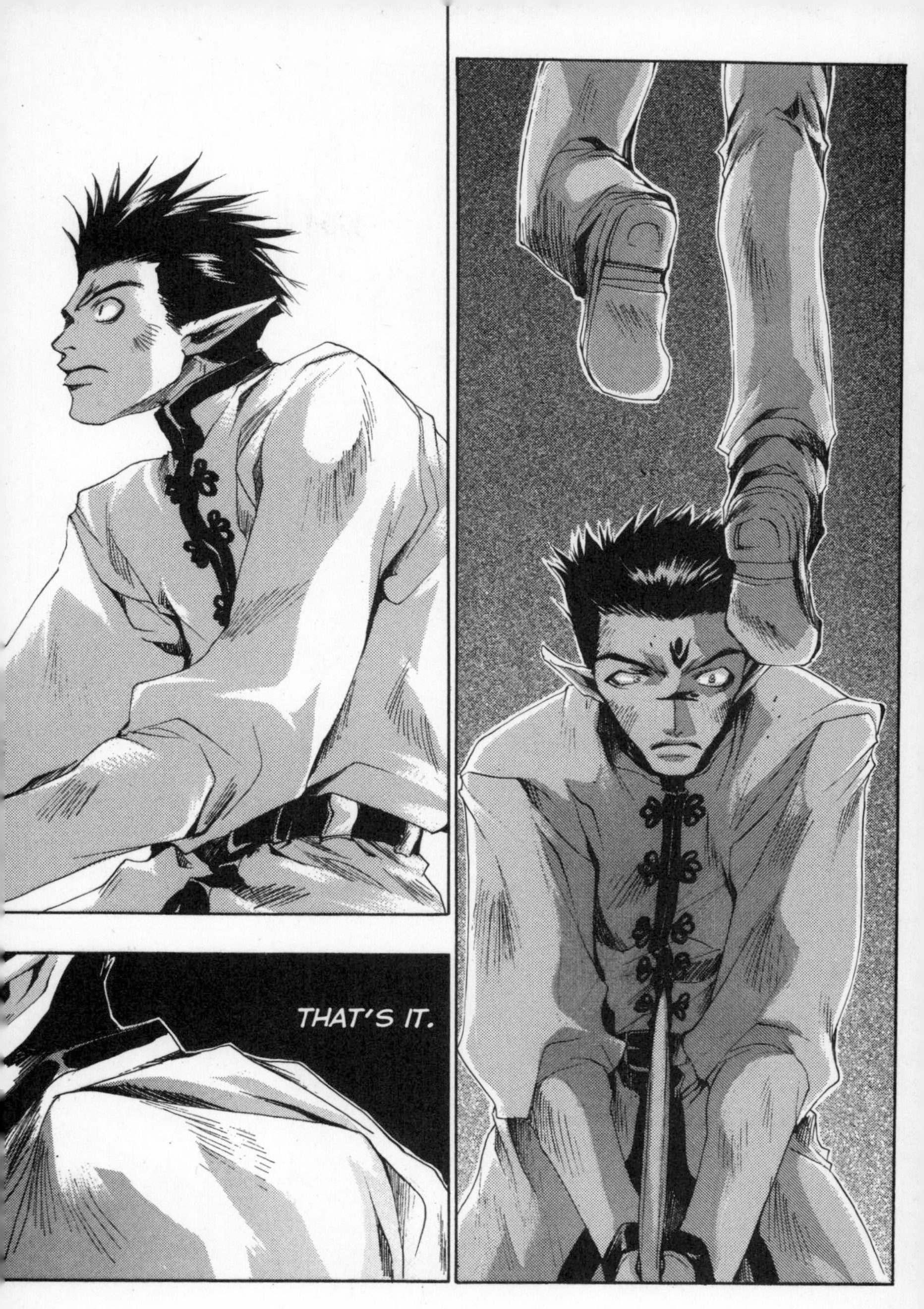
THAT'S IT.

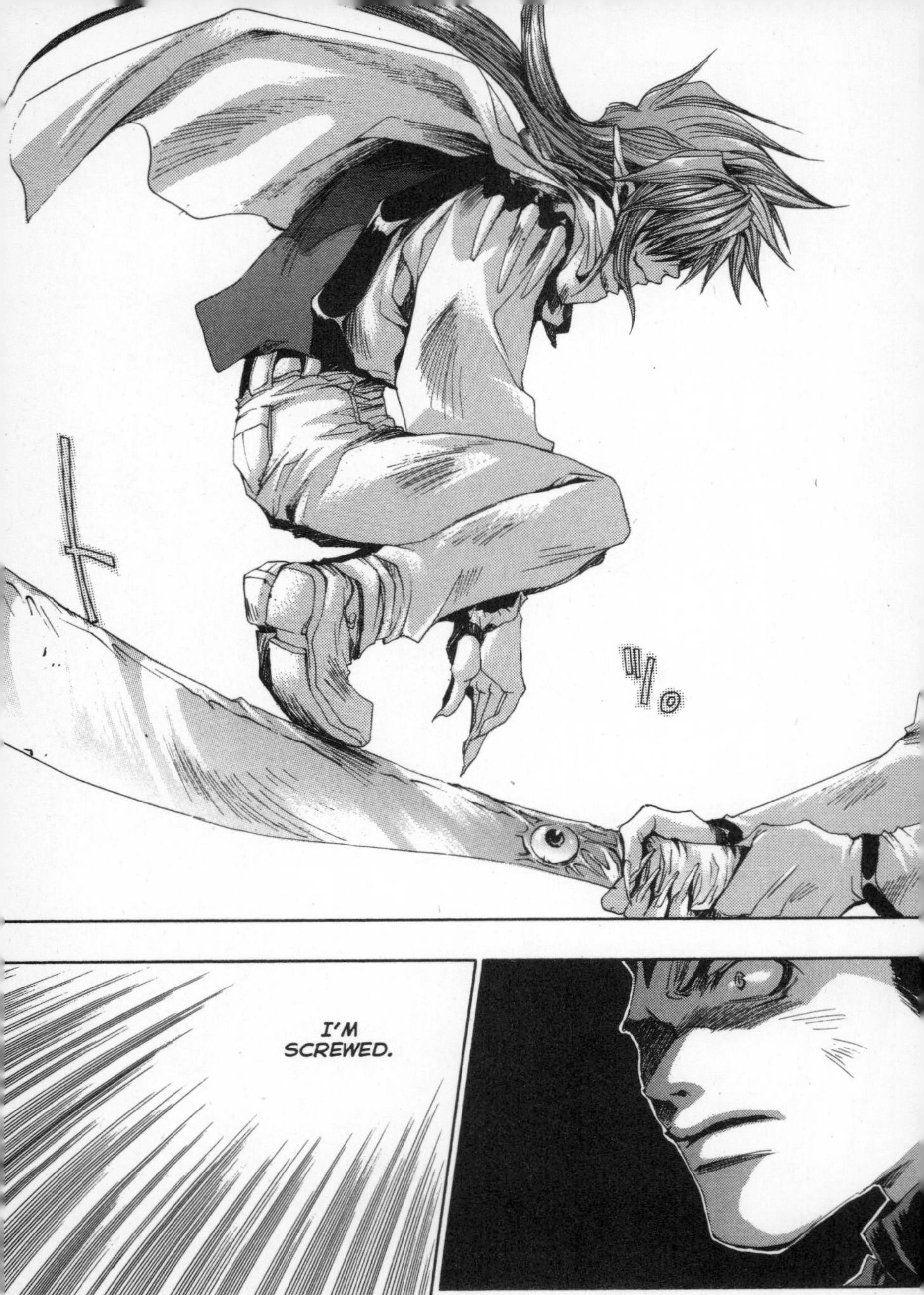
I'M SCREWED.

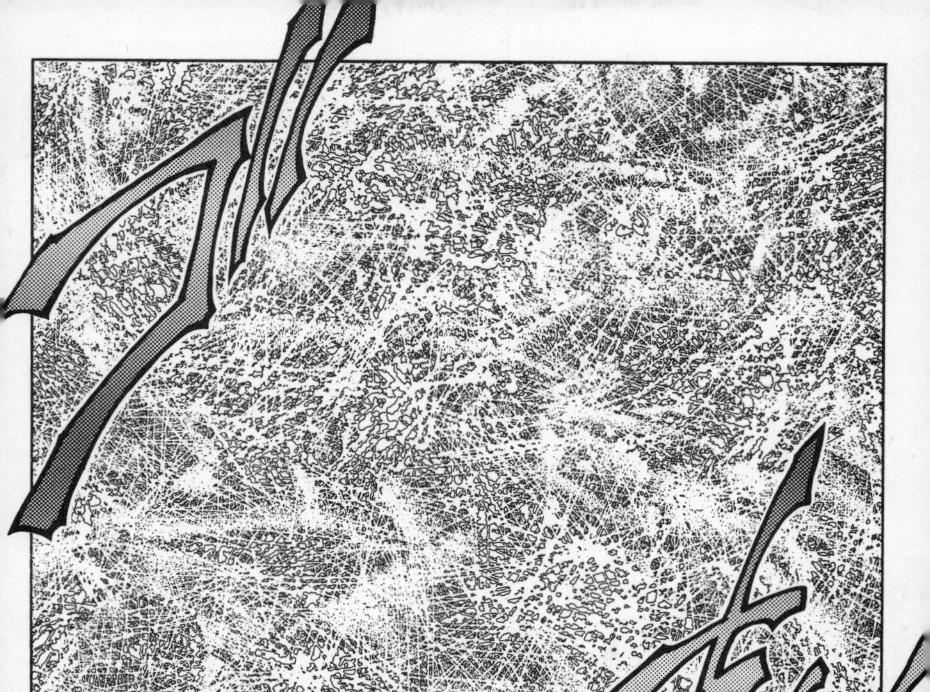

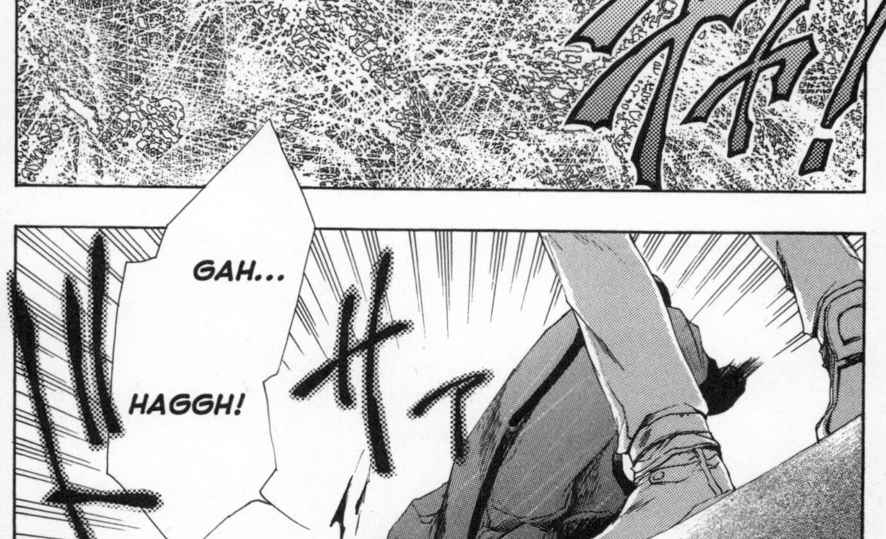
GAH...
HAGGH!

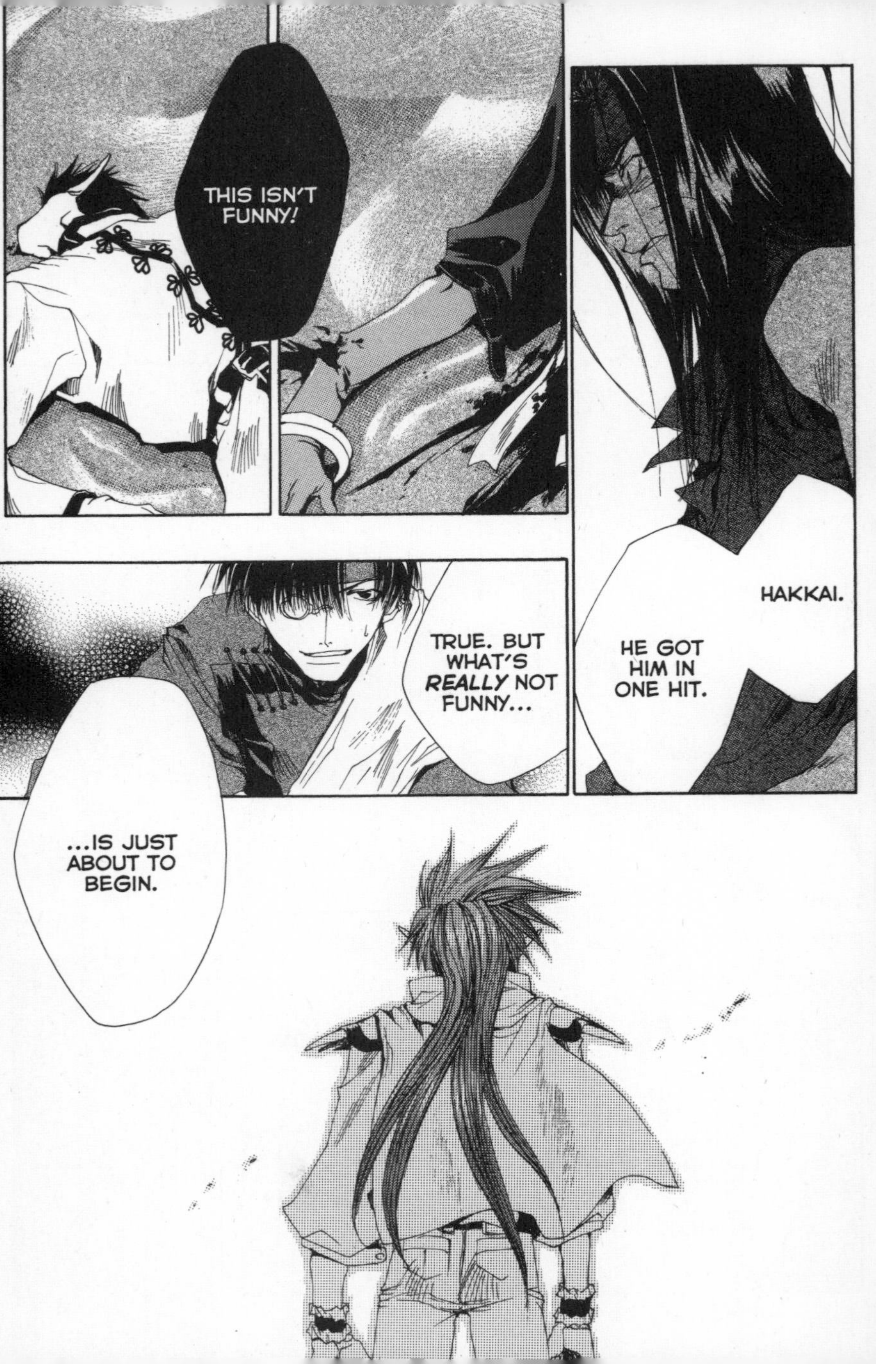
HAKKAI.
HE GOT HIM IN ONE HIT.
THIS ISN'T FUNNY!
TRUE. BUT WHAT'S *REALLY* NOT FUNNY...
...IS JUST ABOUT TO BEGIN.

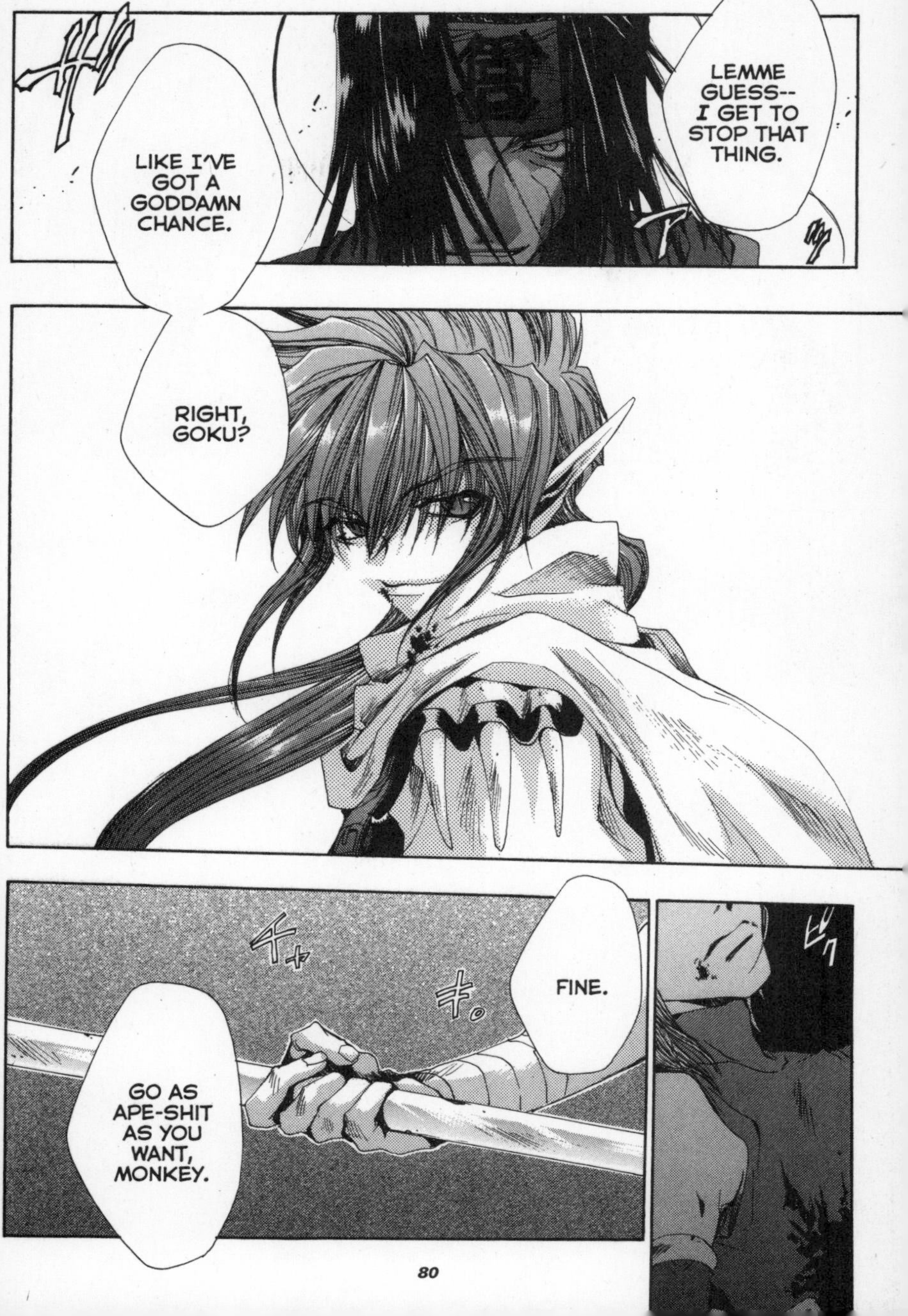
LEMME GUESS-- *I* GET TO STOP THAT THING.
LIKE I'VE GOT A GODDAMN CHANCE.
RIGHT, GOKU?
FINE.
GO AS APE-SHIT AS YOU WANT, MONKEY.

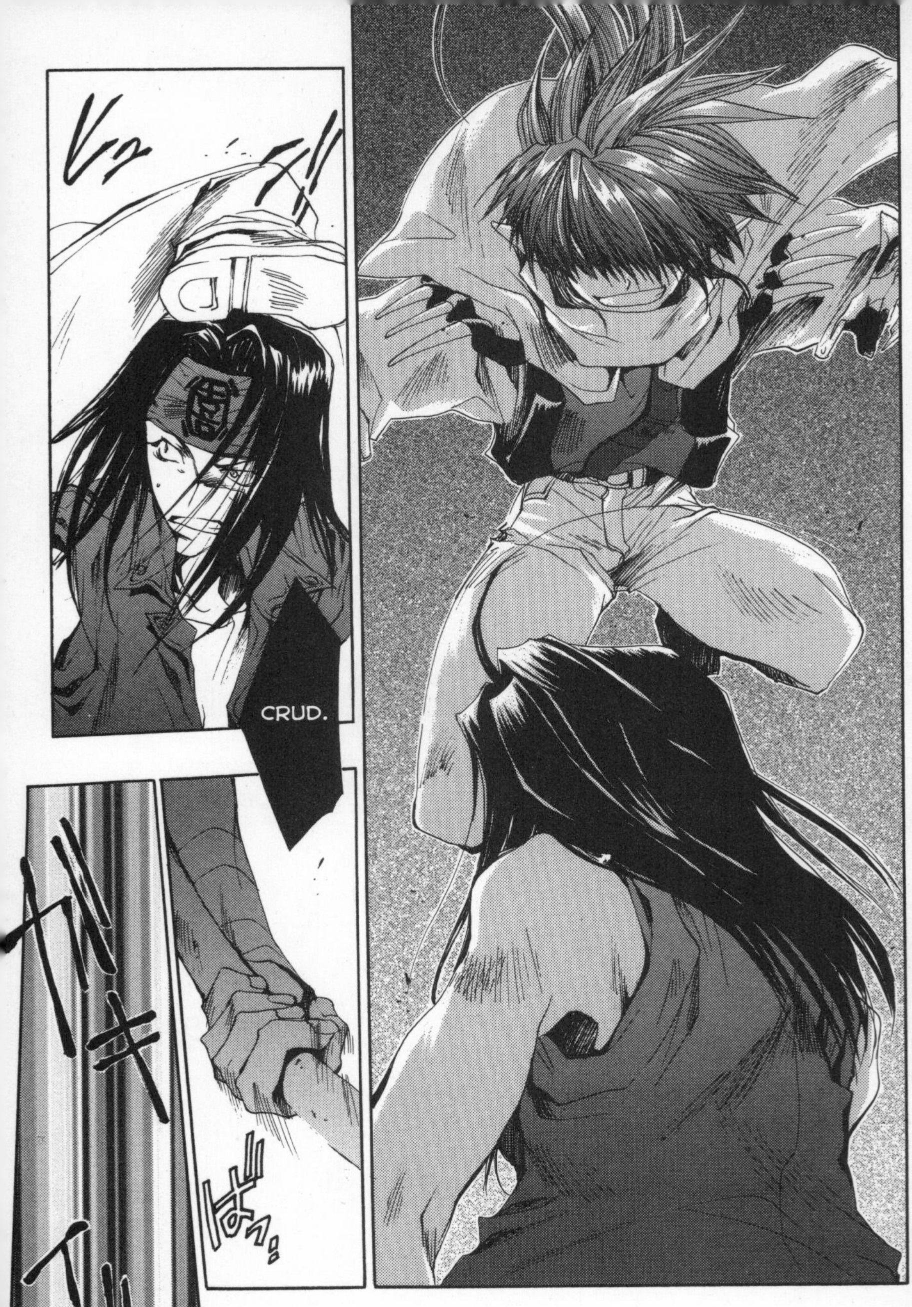
CRUD.

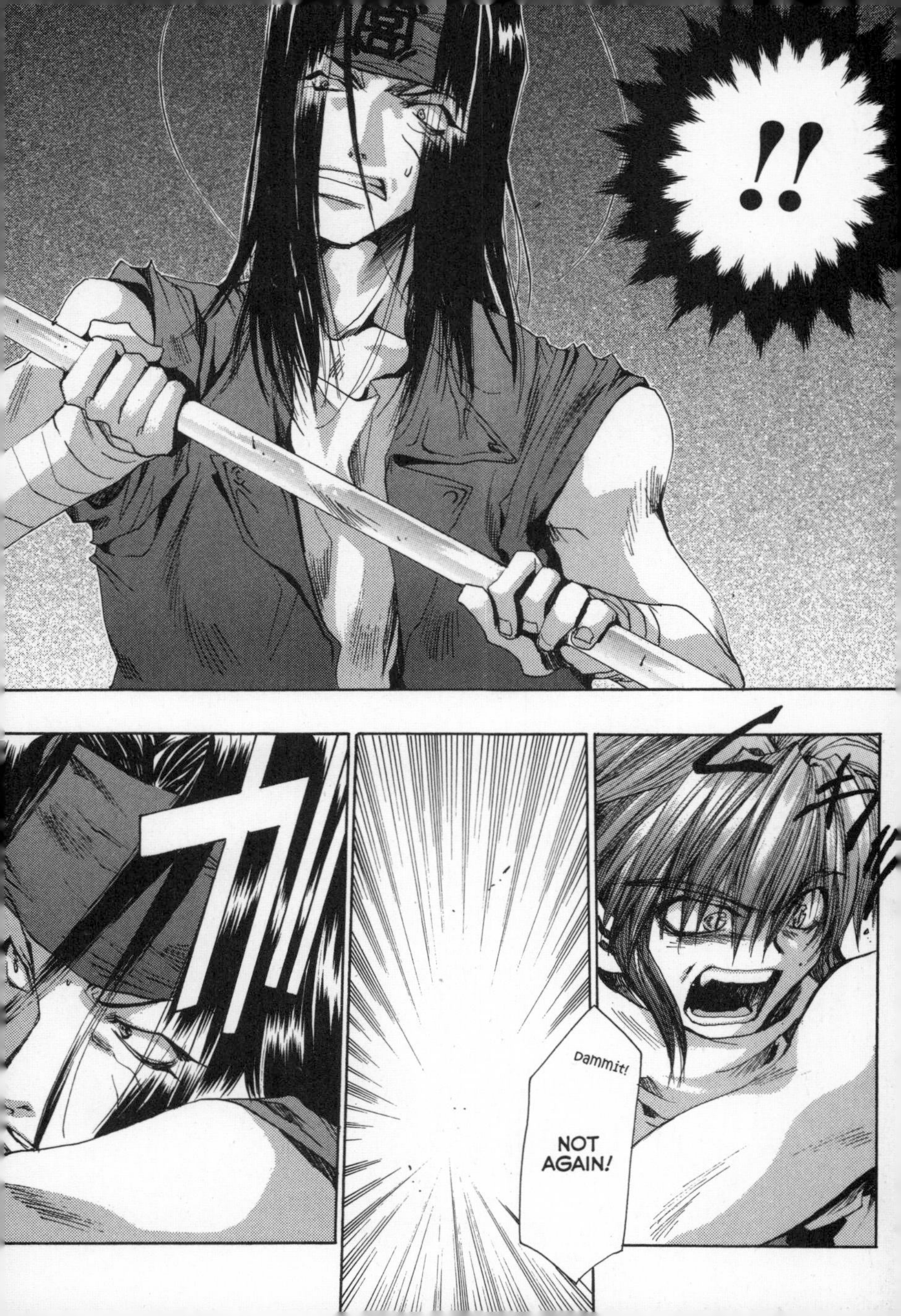
!!
Dammit!
NOT AGAIN!

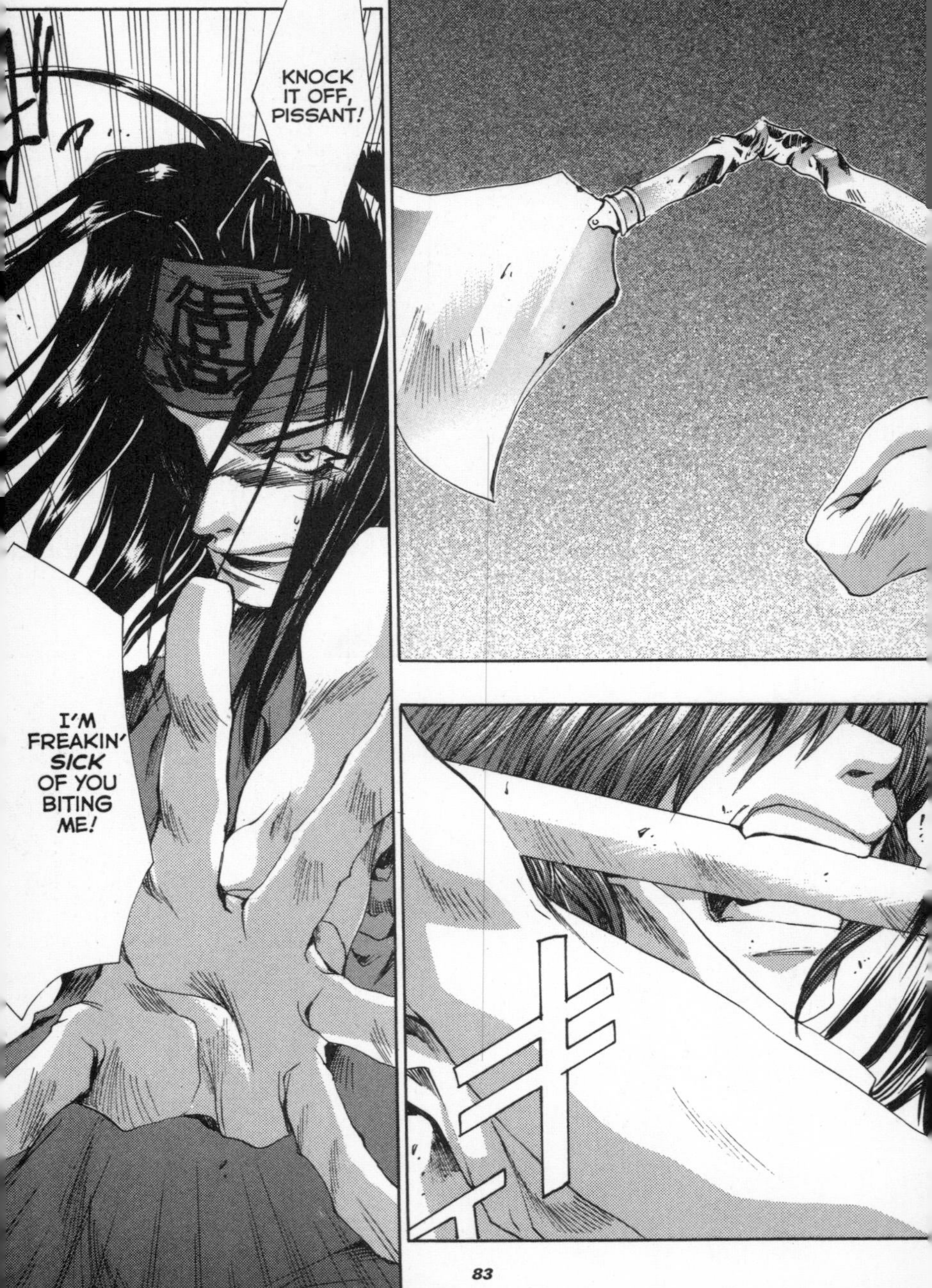
KNOCK IT OFF, PISSANT!
I'M FREAKIN' *SICK* OF YOU BITING ME!

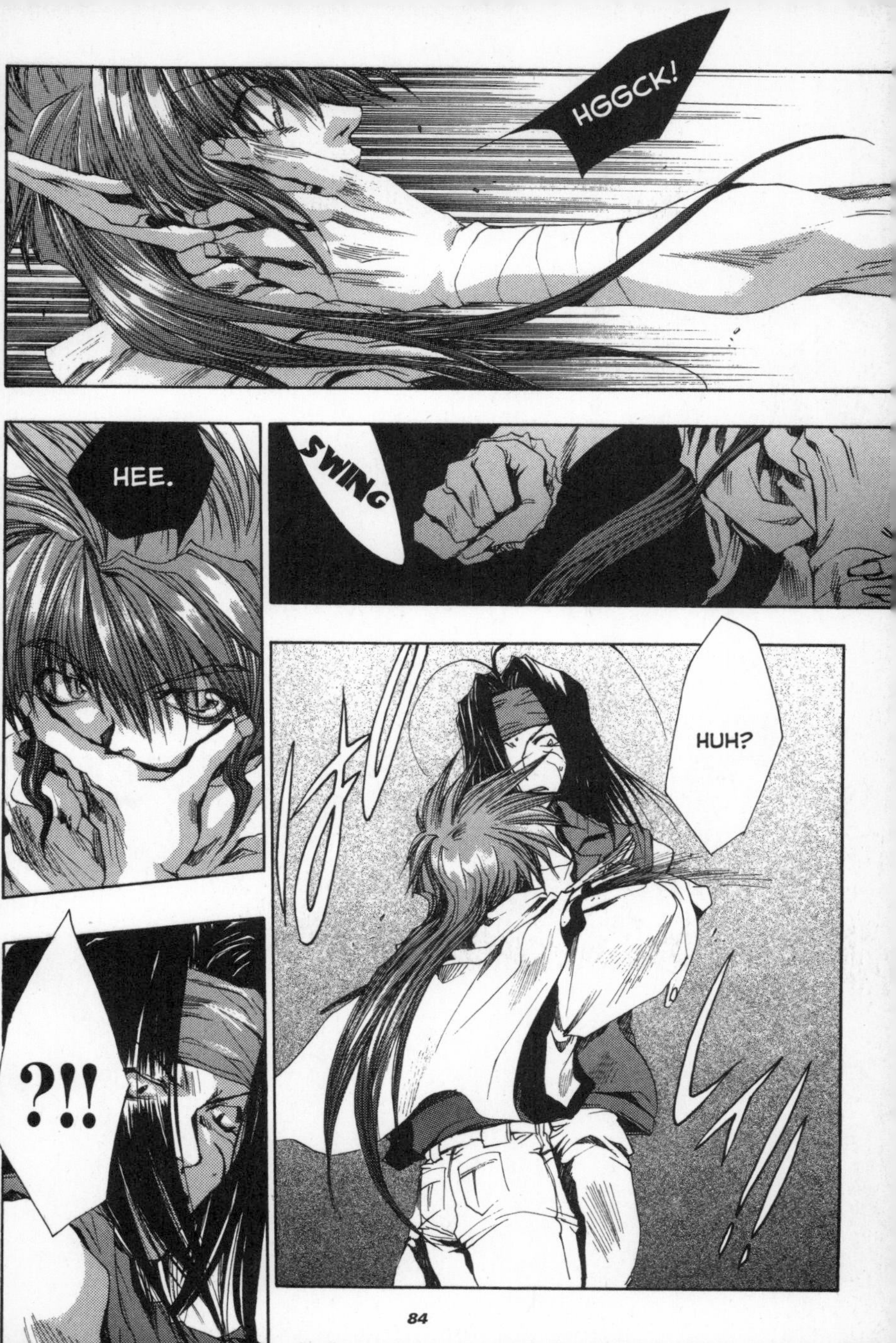
HGGCK!
SWING
HEE.
HUH?
?!!

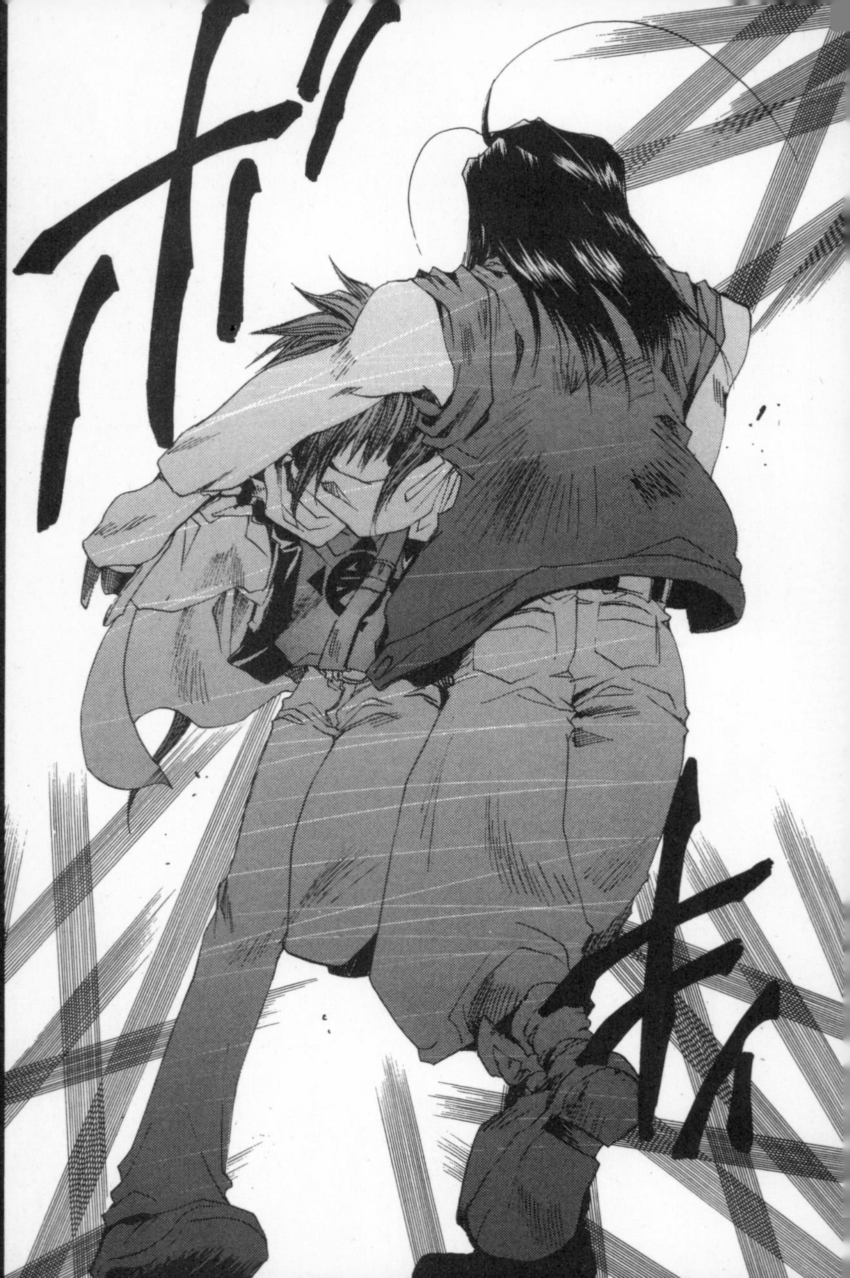
ザ

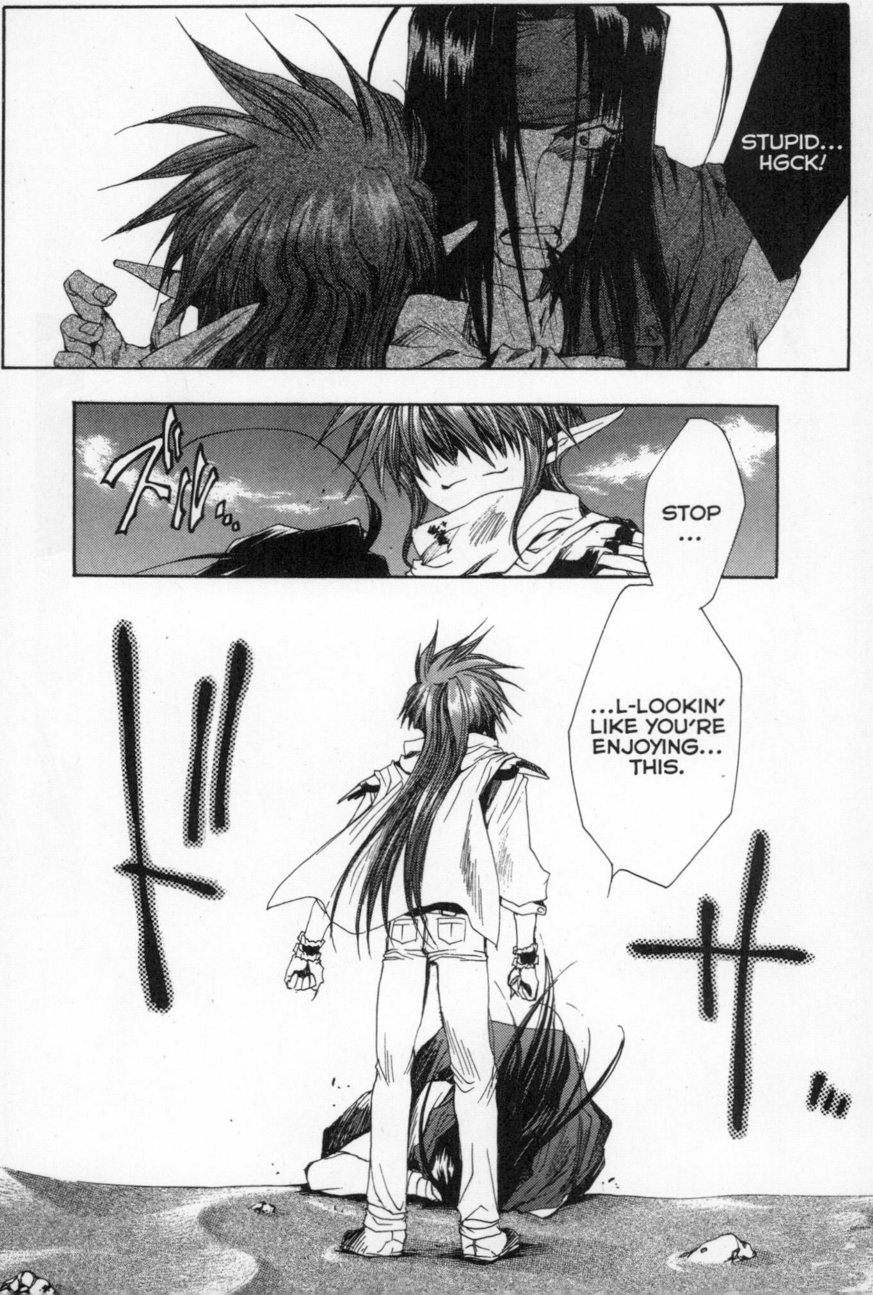
STUPID... HGCK!
ズル
STOP ...
...L-LOOKIN' LIKE YOU'RE ENJOYING... THIS.
ドサ

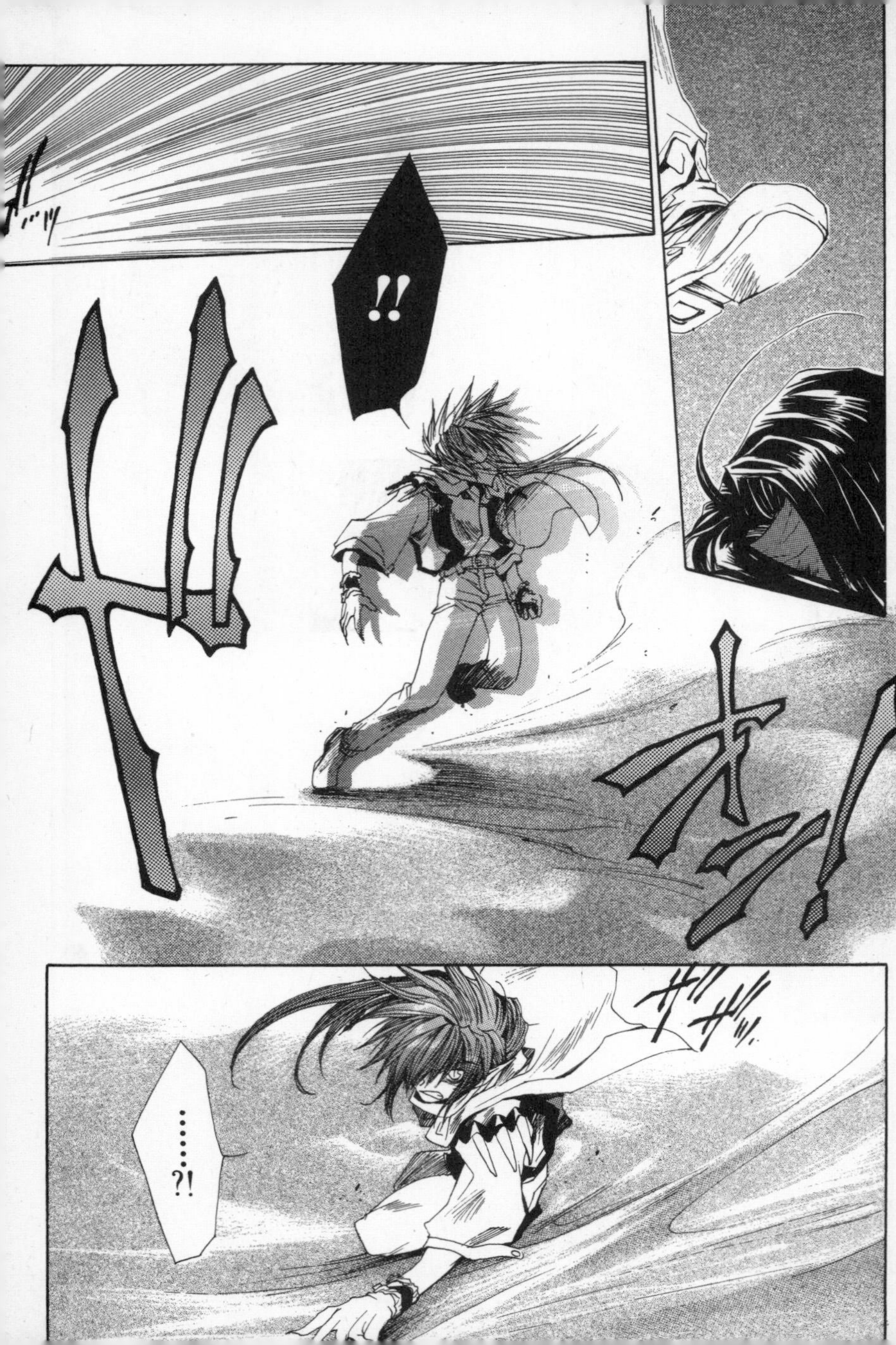
!!
......?!

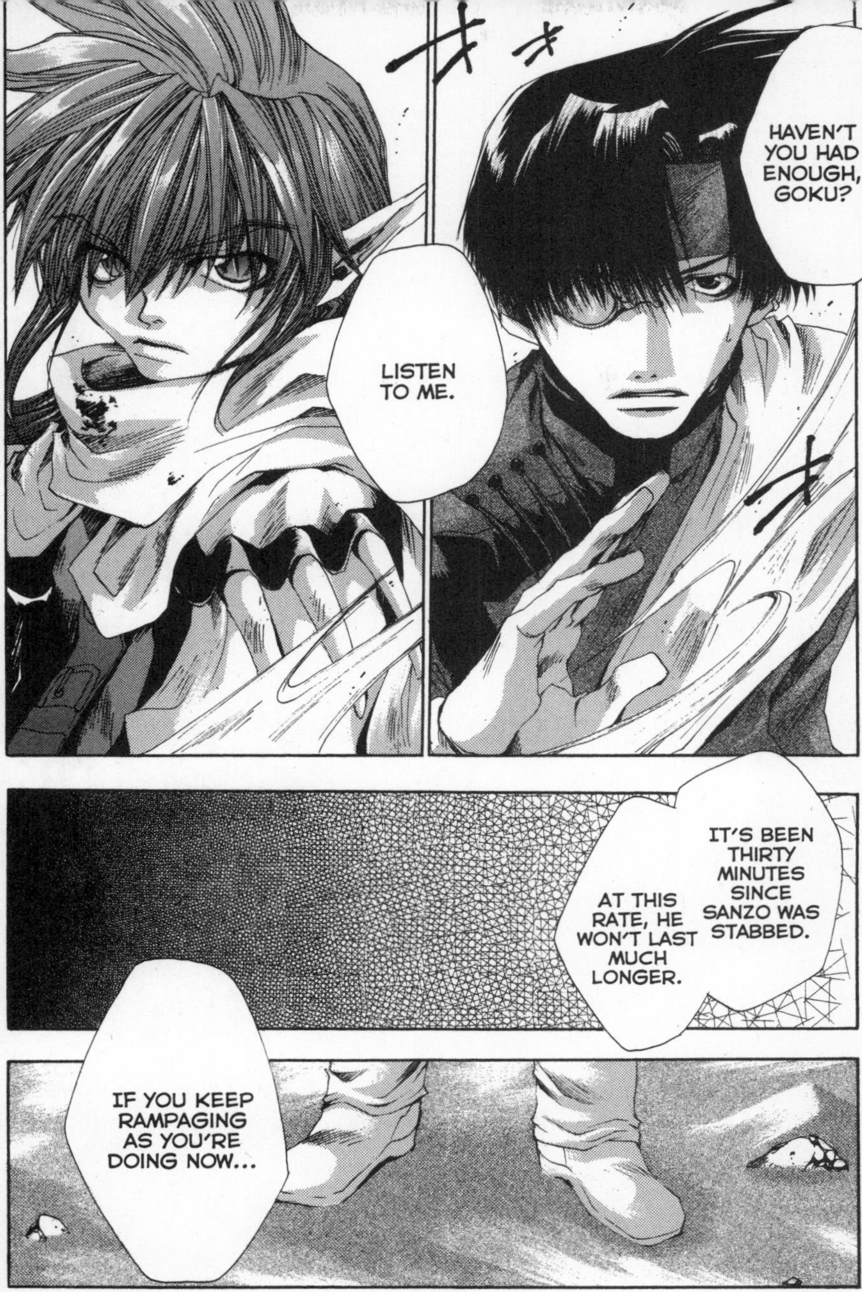
HAVEN'T YOU HAD ENOUGH, GOKU?
LISTEN TO ME.
IT'S BEEN THIRTY MINUTES SINCE SANZO WAS STABBED.
AT THIS RATE, HE WON'T LAST MUCH LONGER.
IF YOU KEEP RAMPAGING AS YOU'RE DOING NOW...

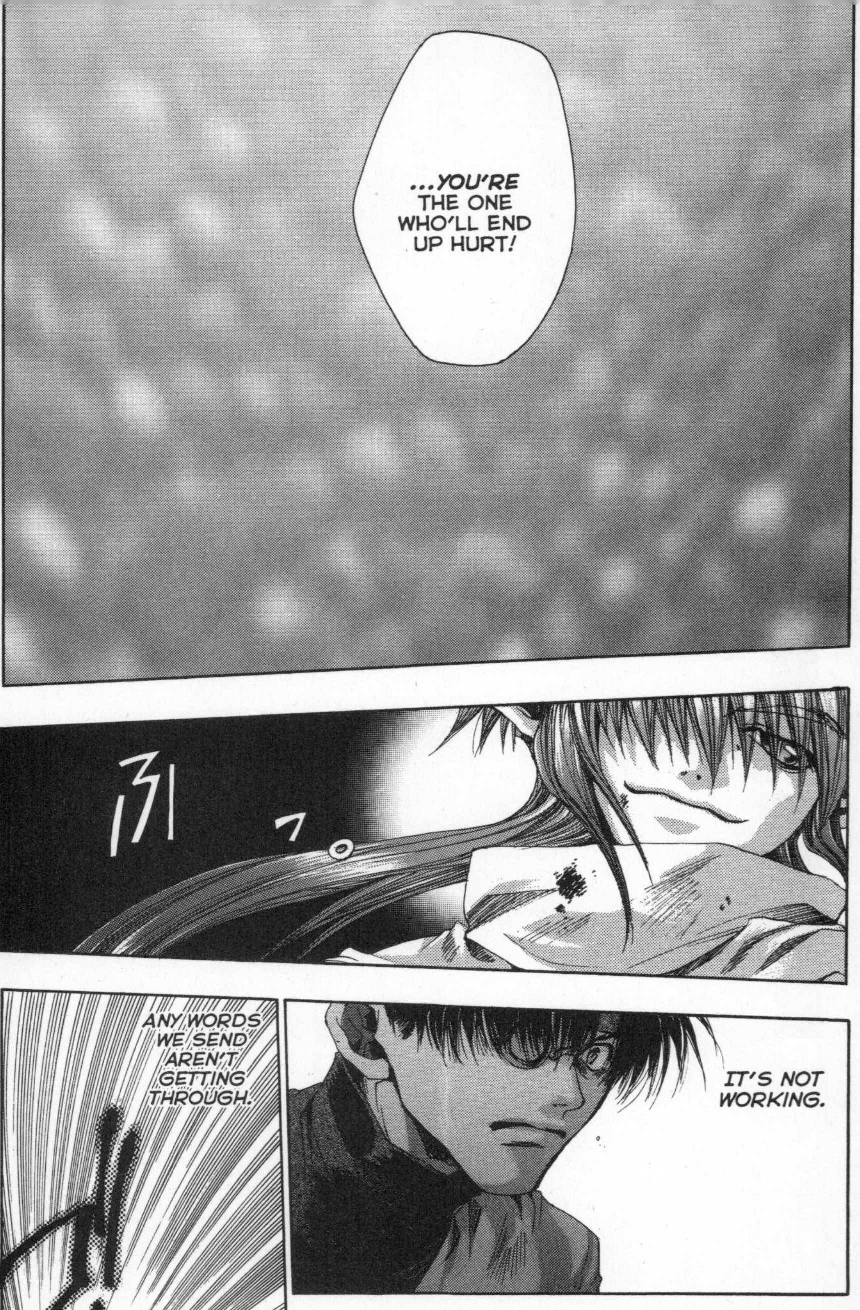
...YOU'RE THE ONE WHO'LL END UP HURT!
IT'S NOT WORKING.
ANY WORDS WE SEND AREN'T GETTING THROUGH.

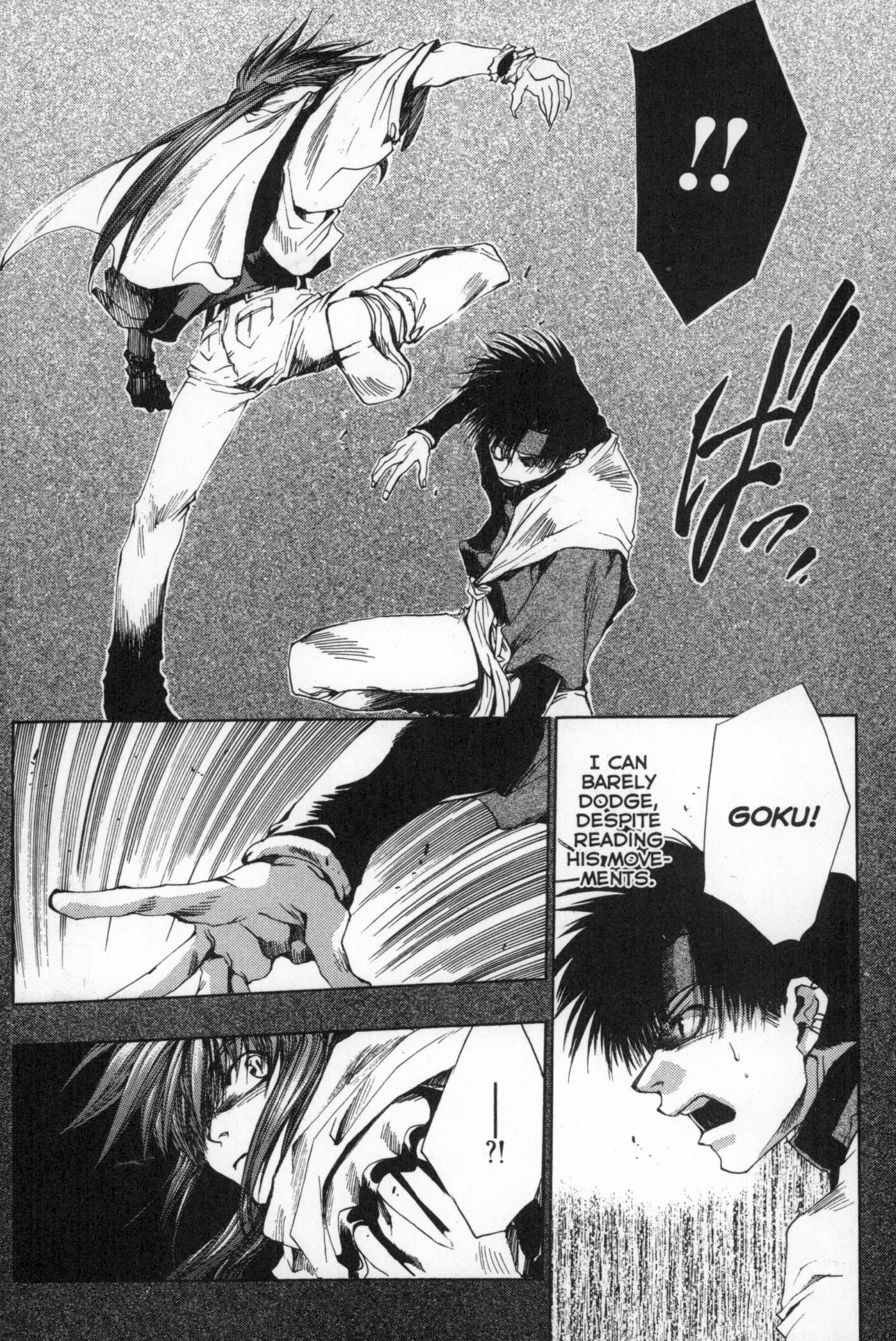

!!
GOKU!
I CAN BARELY DODGE, DESPITE READING HIS MOVEMENTS.
—?!

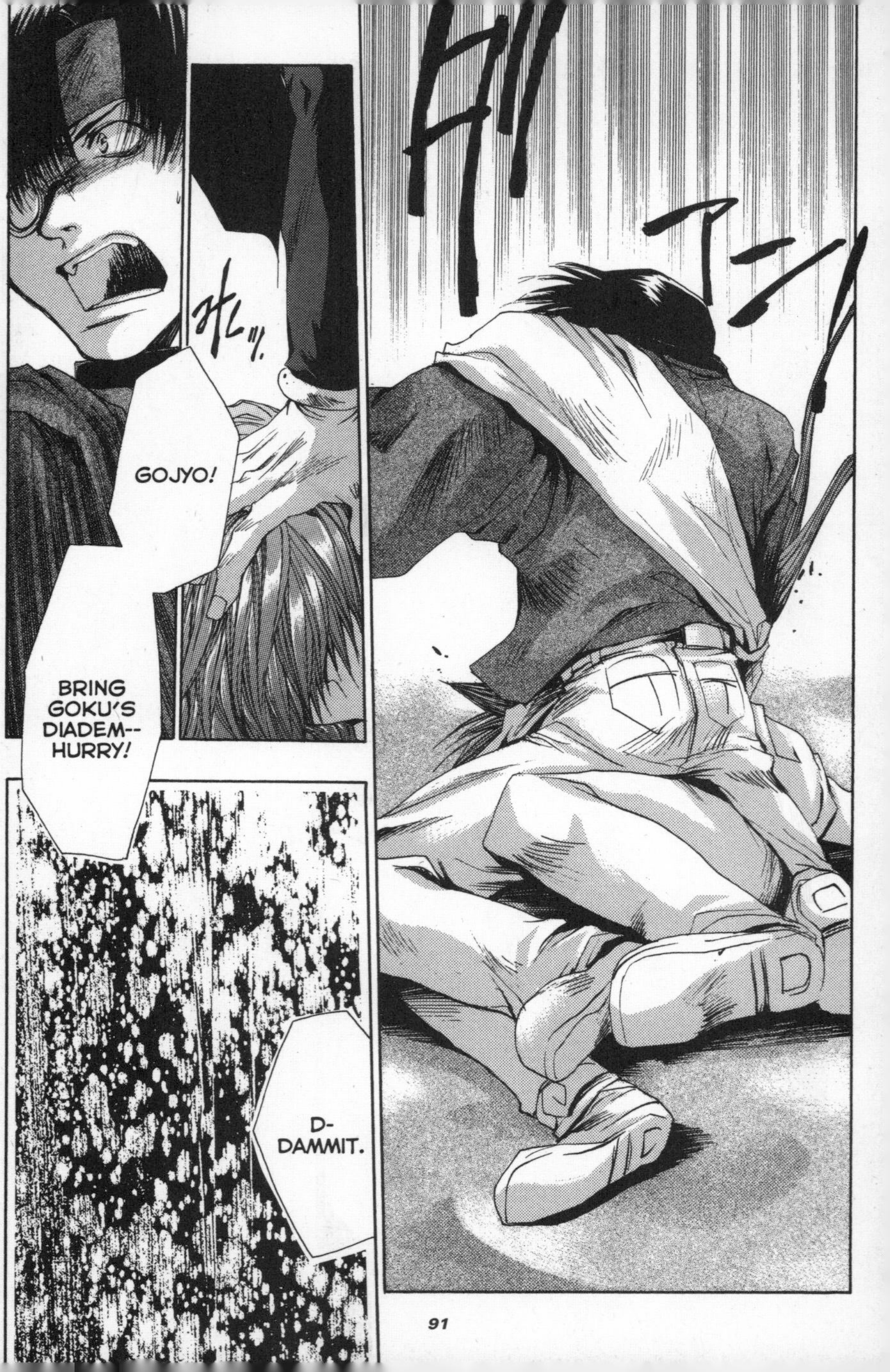
GOJYO!
BRING GOKU'S DIADEM--HURRY!
D-DAMMIT.

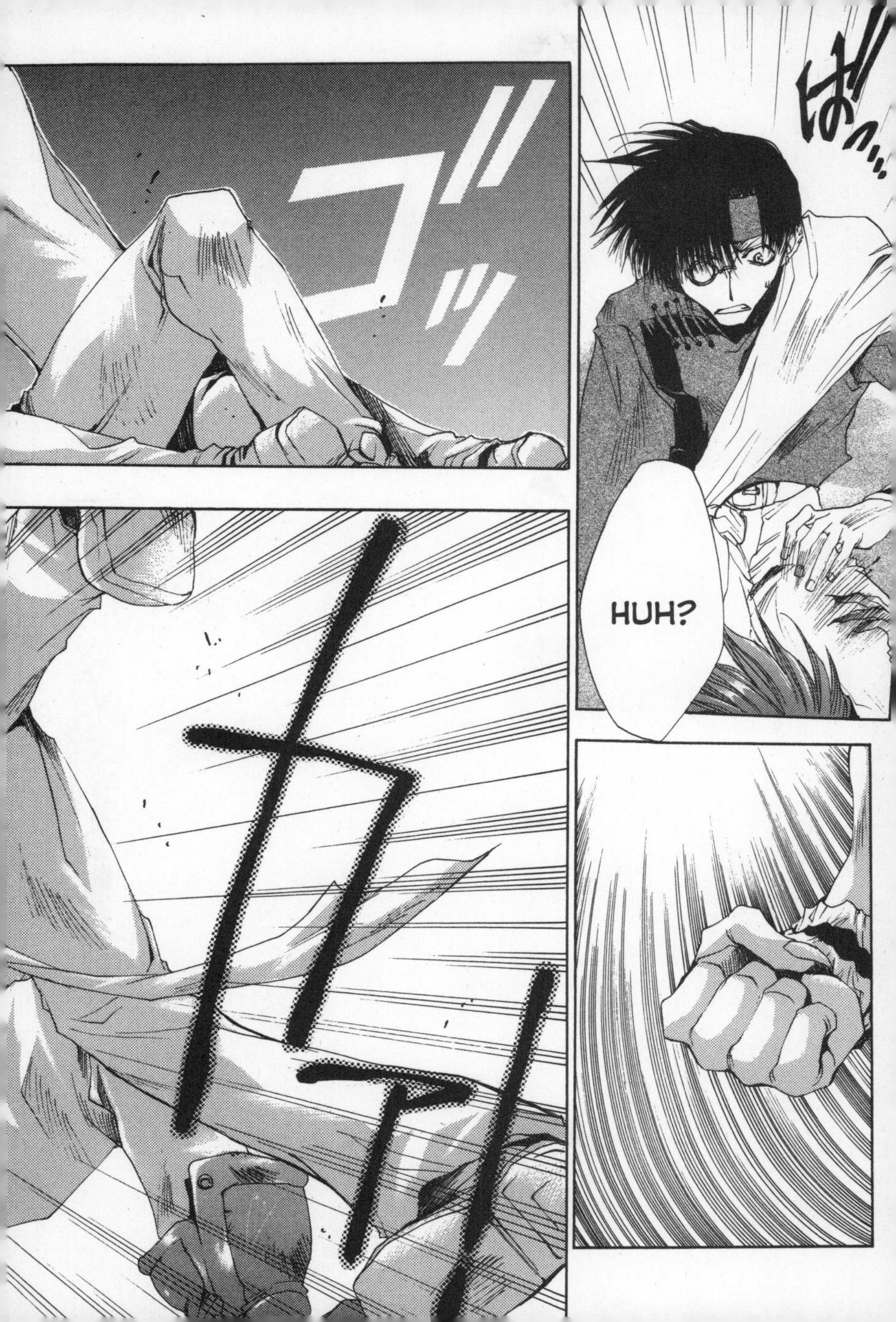
HUH?
ゴッ

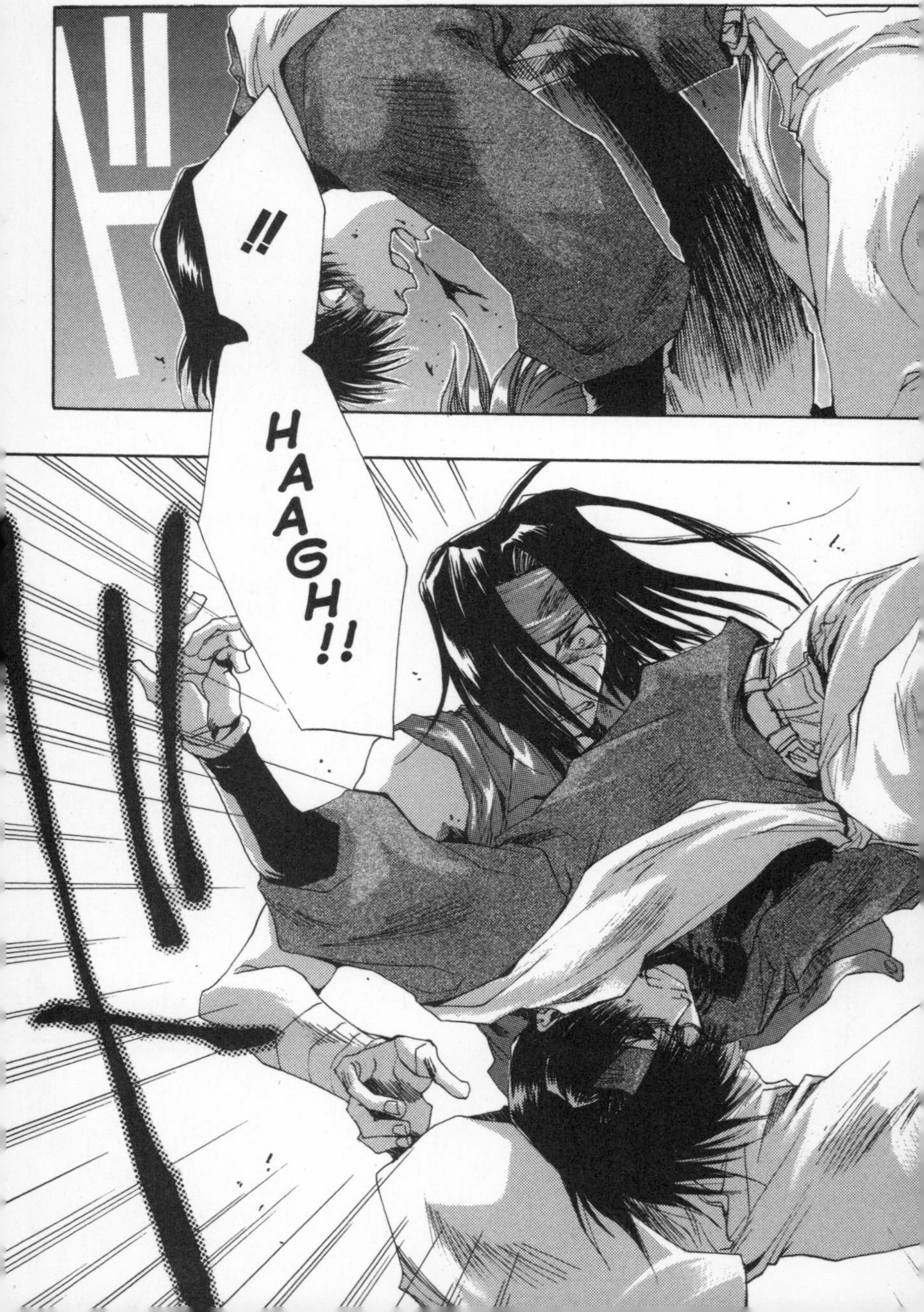
!!
HAAGH!!

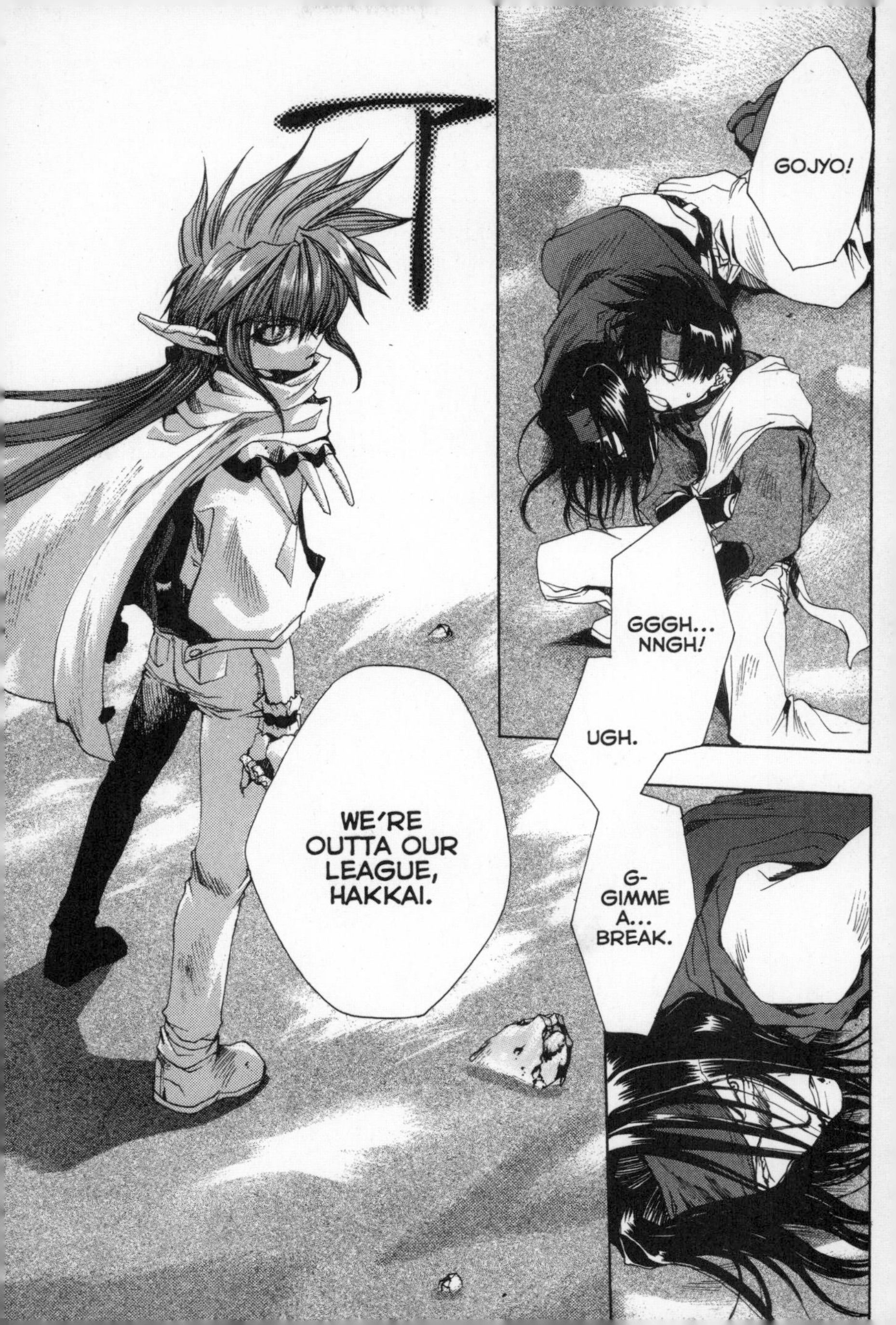
GOJYO!
GGGH... NNGH!
UGH.
G-GIMME A... BREAK.
WE'RE OUTTA OUR LEAGUE, HAKKAI.

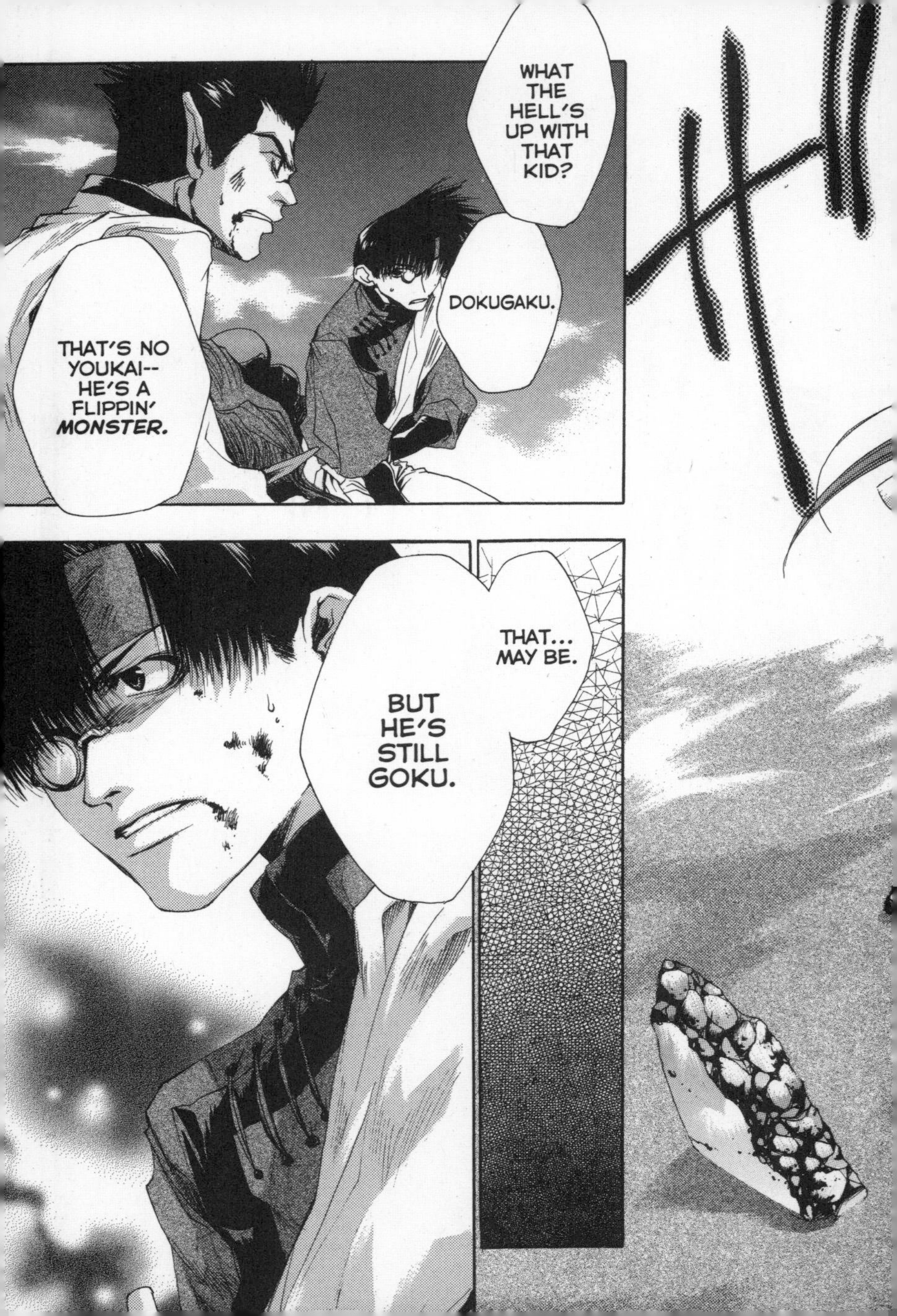
WHAT THE HELL'S UP WITH THAT KID?
DOKUGAKU.
THAT'S NO YOUKAI-- HE'S A FLIPPIN' *MONSTER.*
THAT... MAY BE.
BUT HE'S STILL GOKU.

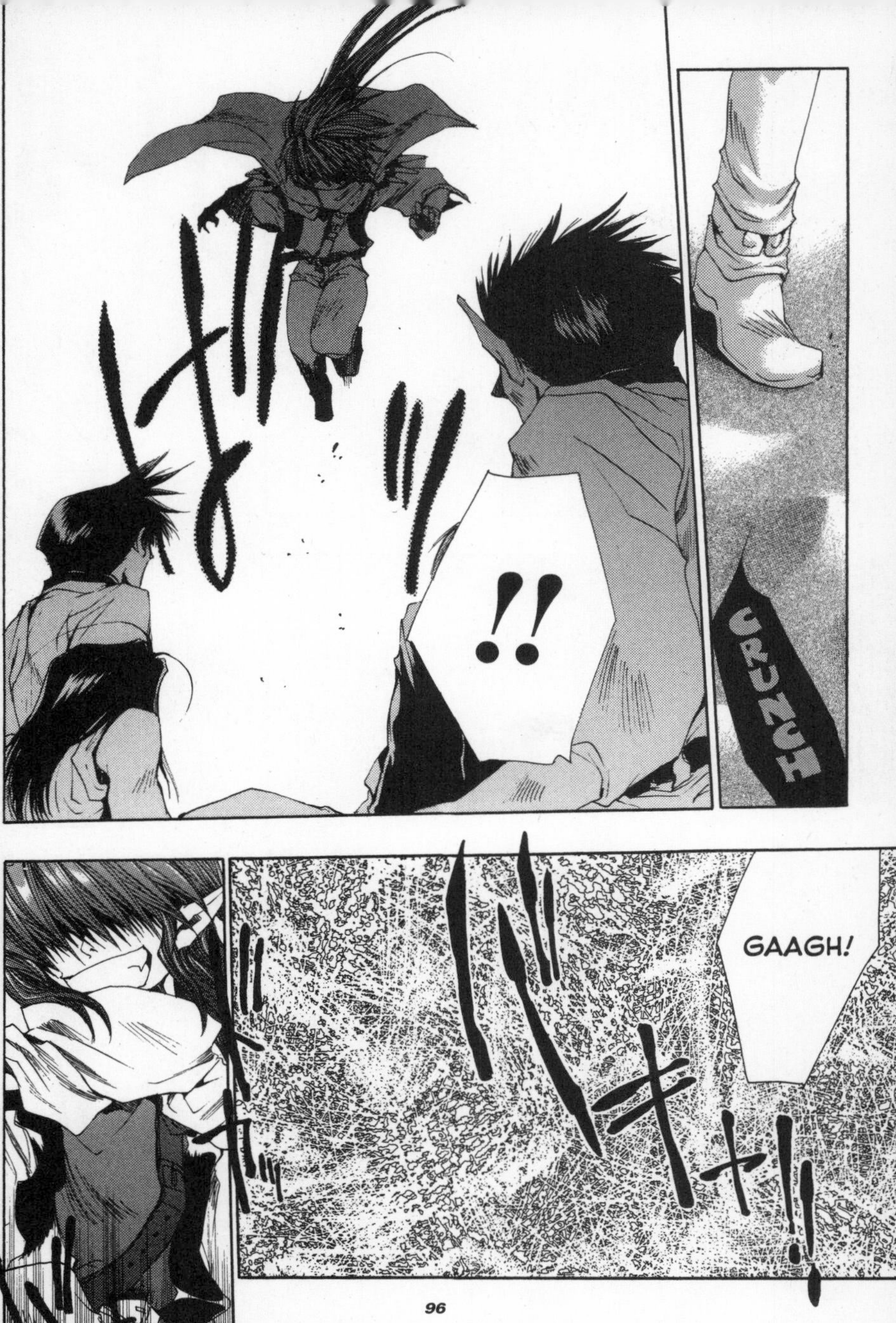
CRUNCH
!!
GAAGH!

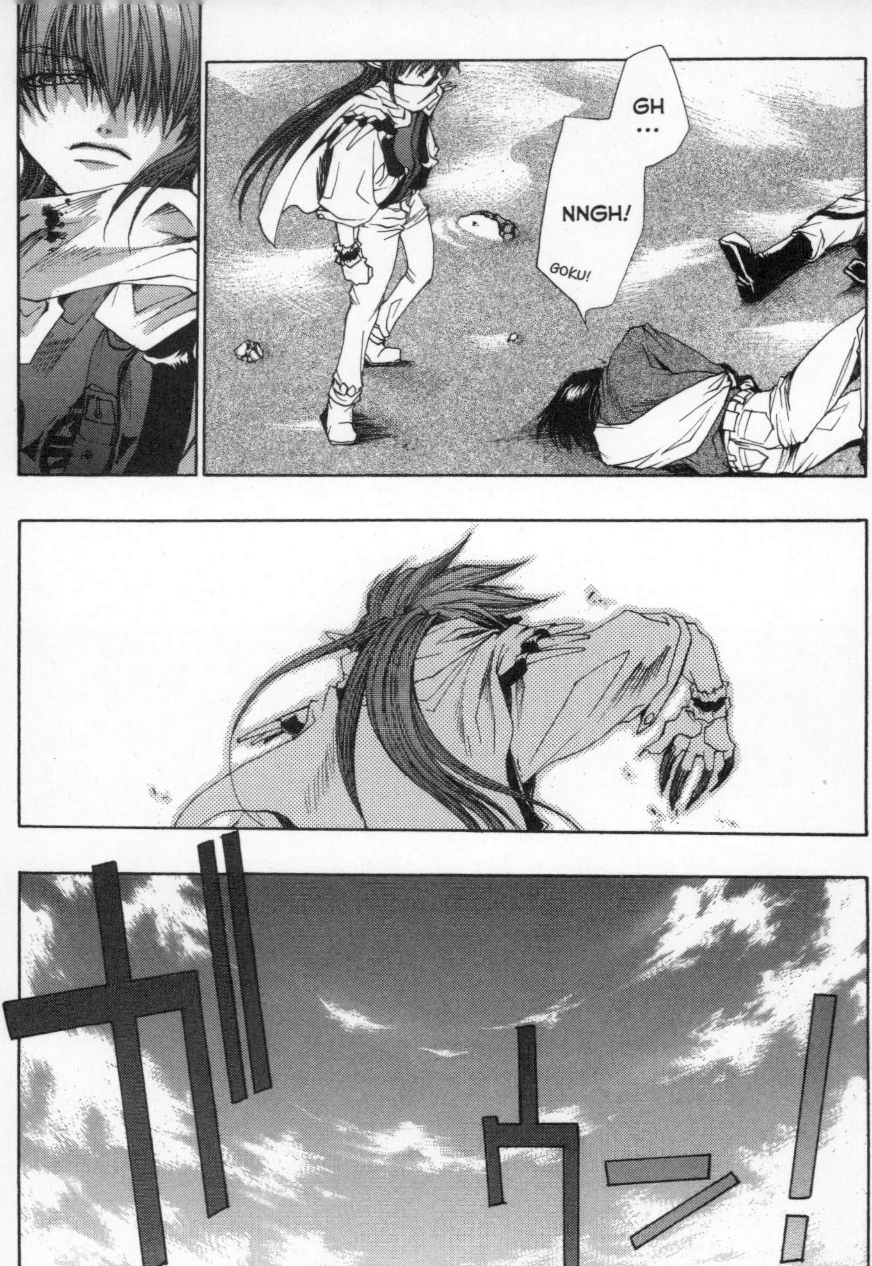
GH ...
NNGH!
GOKU!

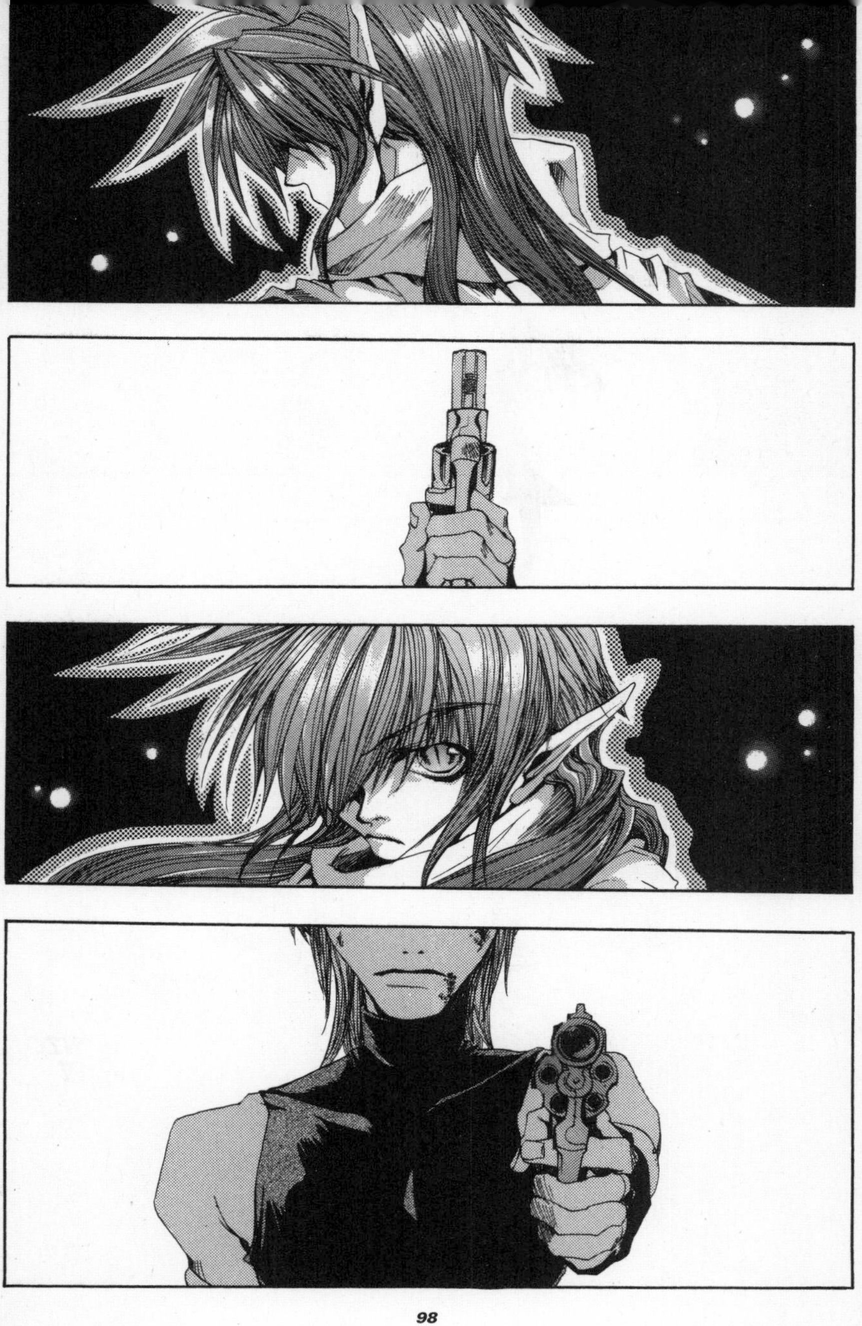

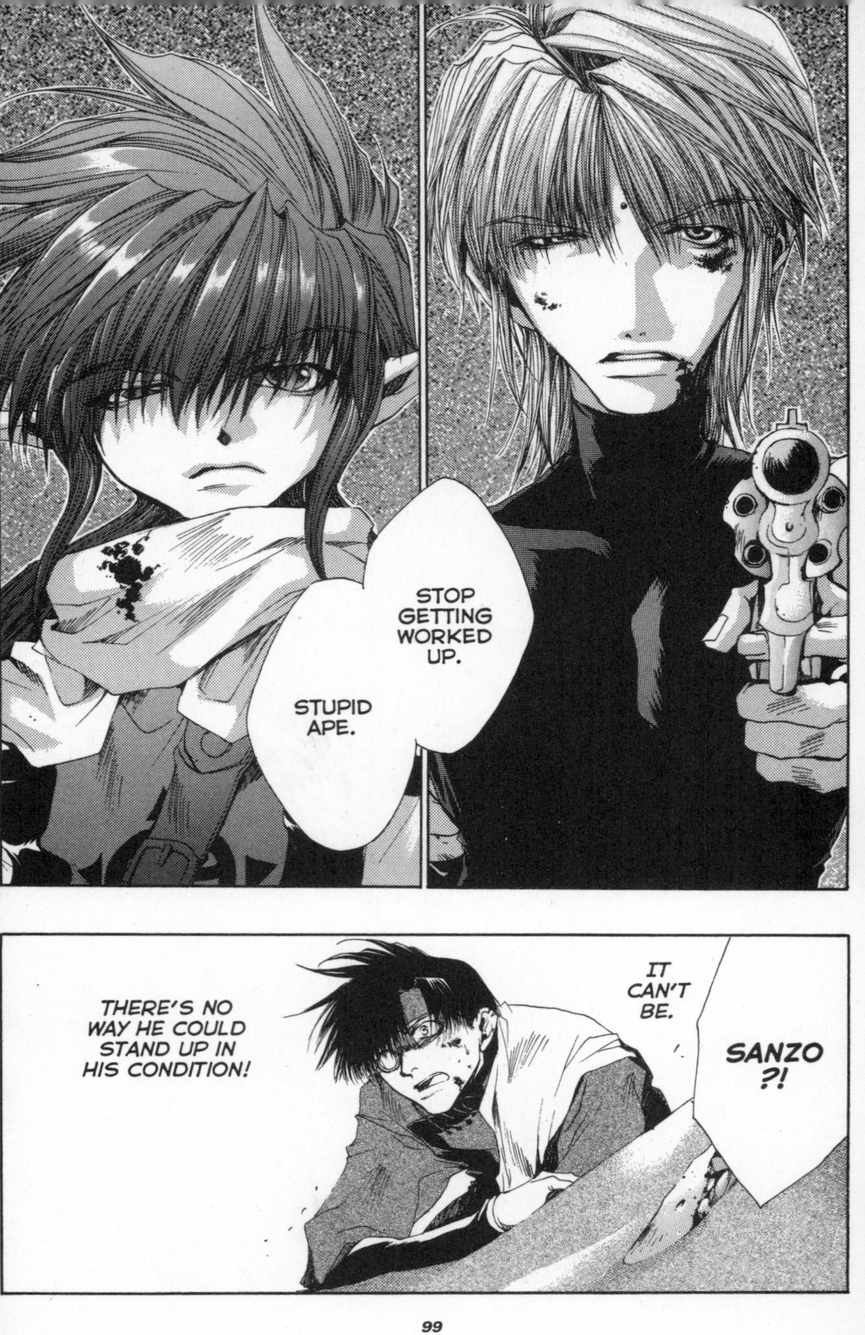
STOP GETTING WORKED UP.
STUPID APE.
SANZO ?!
IT CAN'T BE.
THERE'S NO WAY HE COULD STAND UP IN HIS CONDITION!

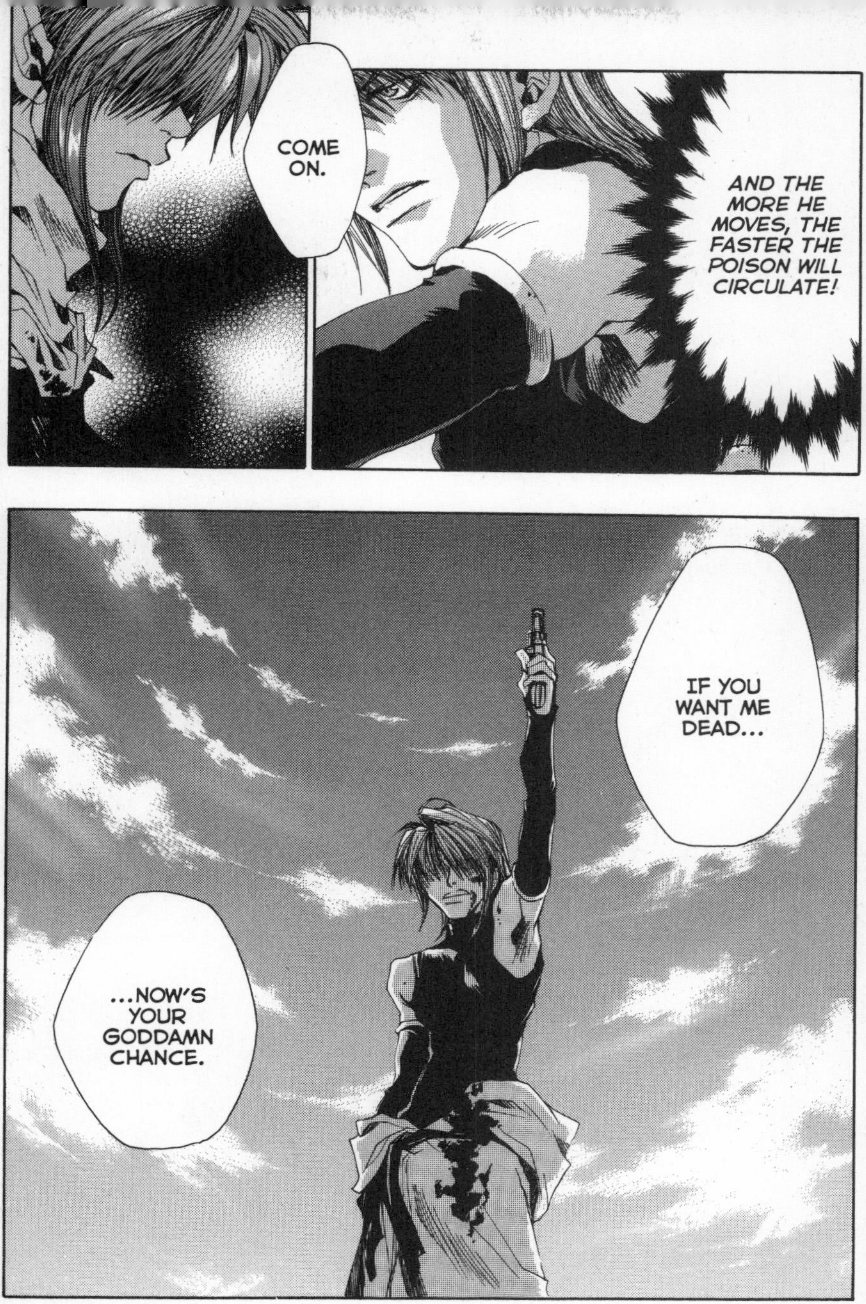

COME ON.
AND THE MORE HE MOVES, THE FASTER THE POISON WILL CIRCULATE!
IF YOU WANT ME DEAD...
...NOW'S YOUR GODDAMN CHANCE.

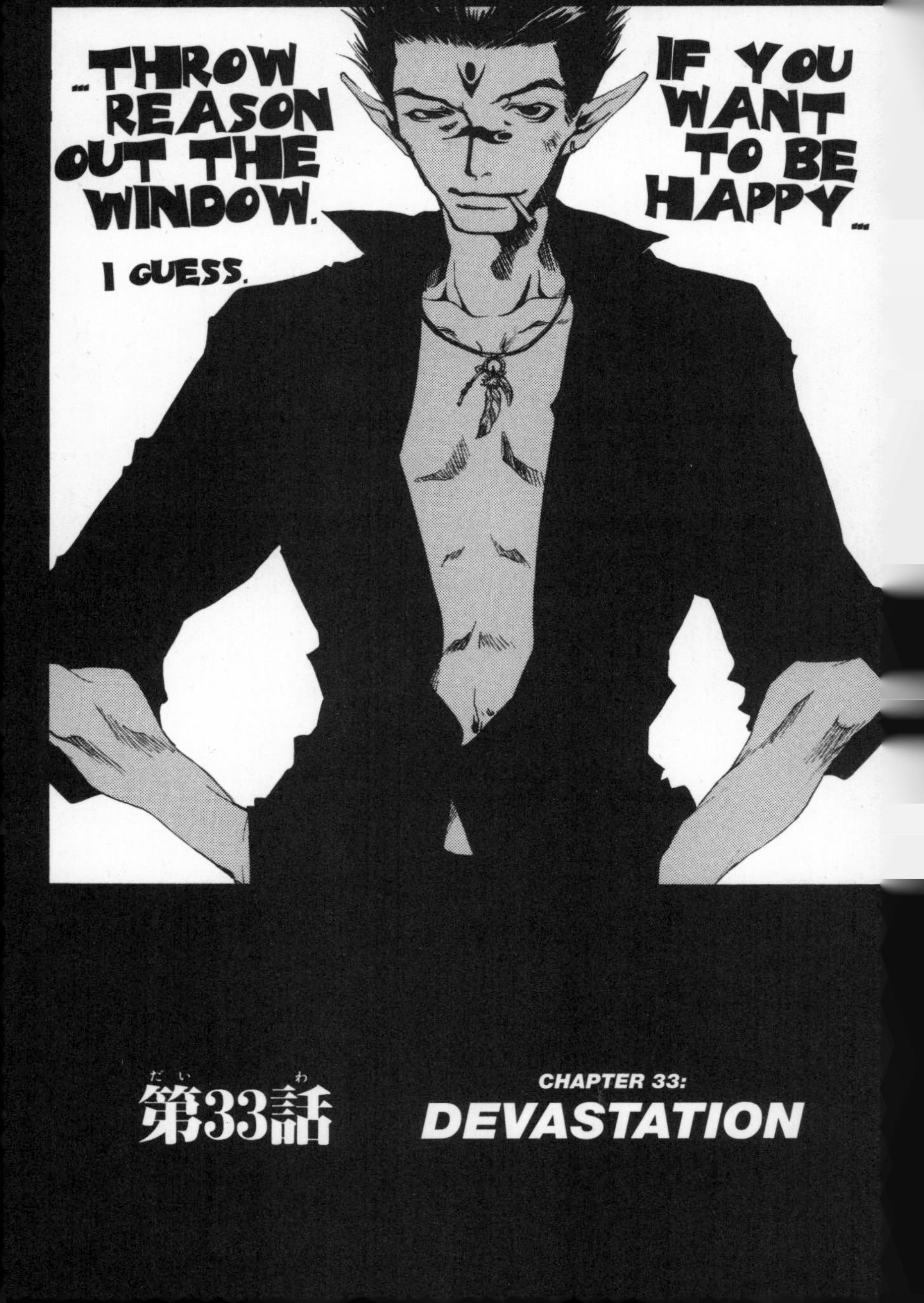
IF YOU WANT TO BE HAPPY...
...THROW REASON OUT THE WINDOW.
I GUESS.

第33話 CHAPTER 33: DEVASTATION

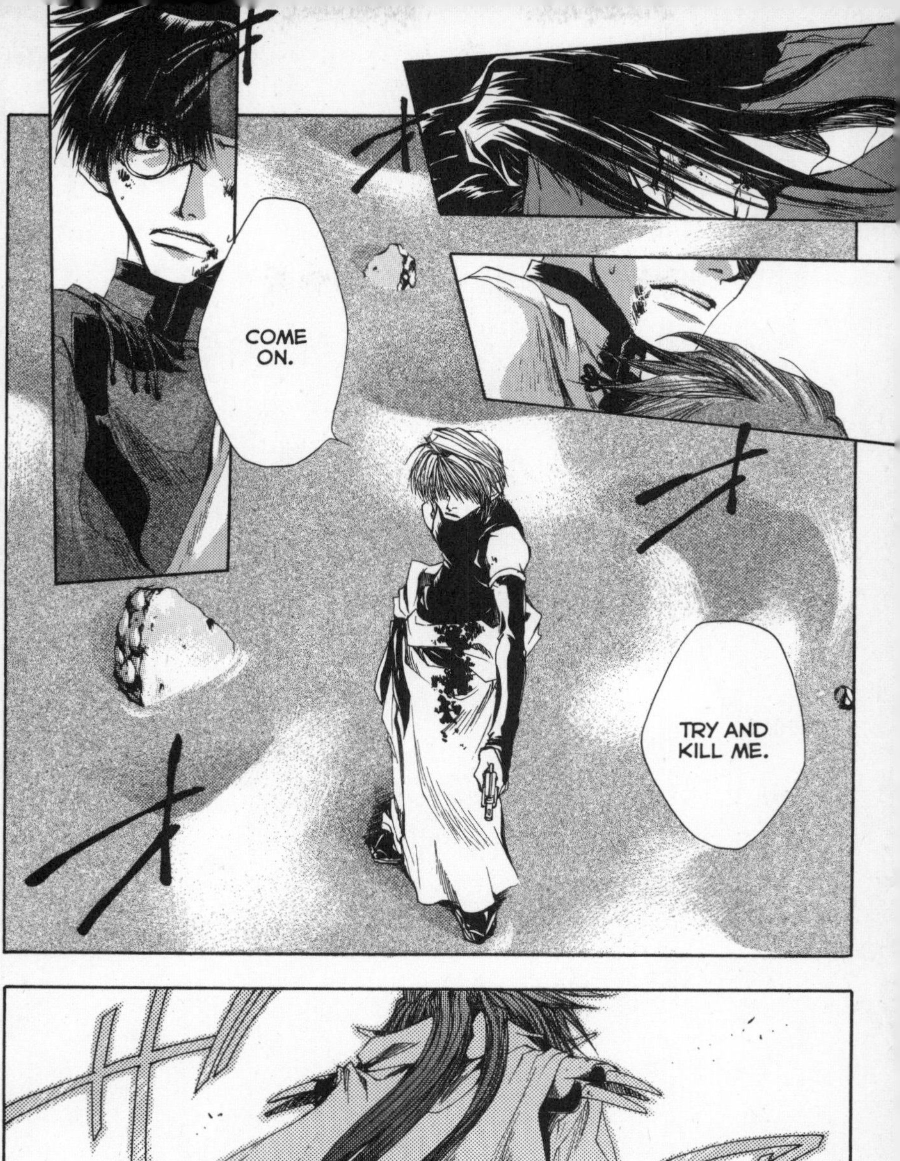
COME ON.
TRY AND KILL ME.

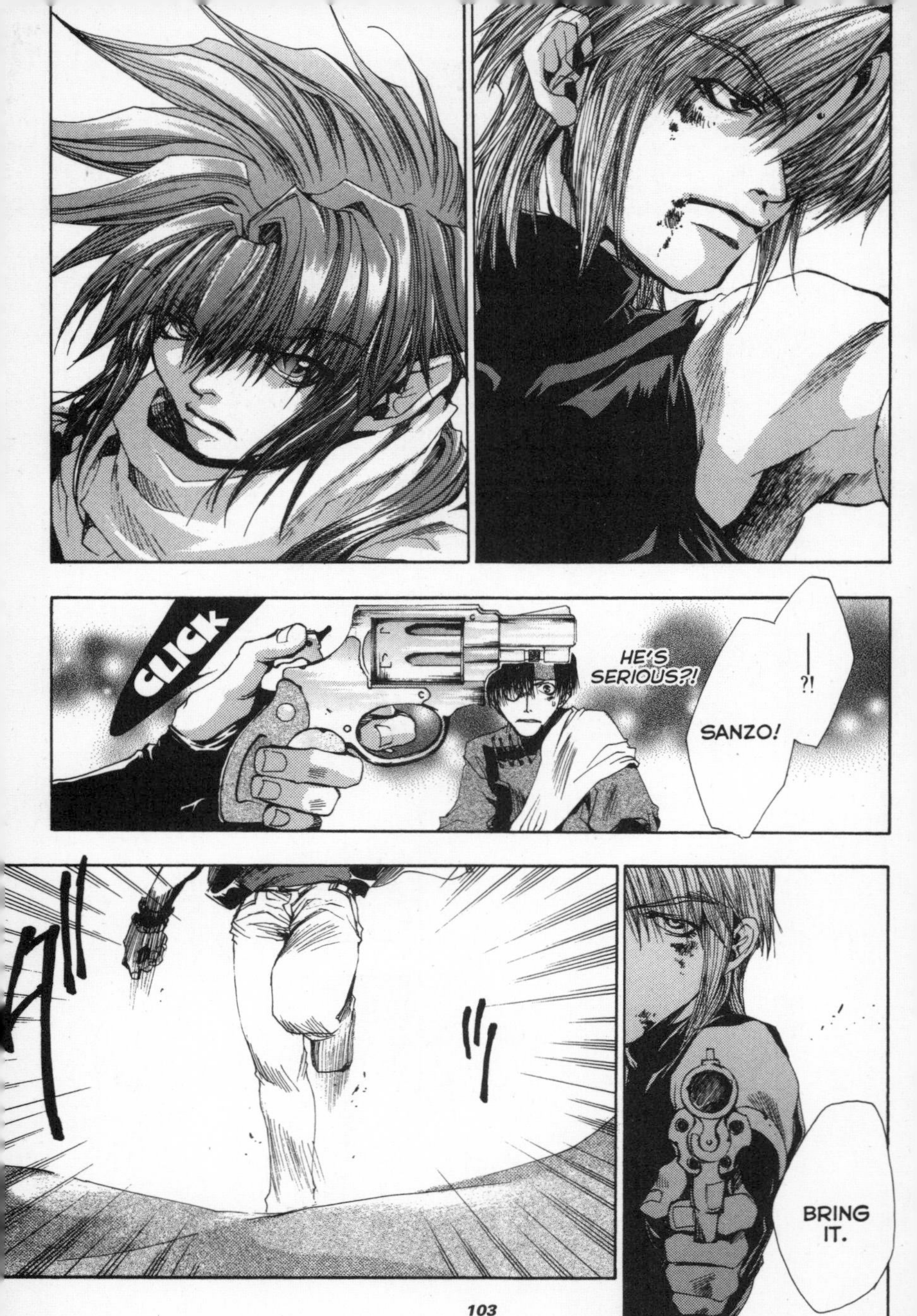
—?!
SANZO!
HE'S SERIOUS?!
CLICK
...!
BRING IT.

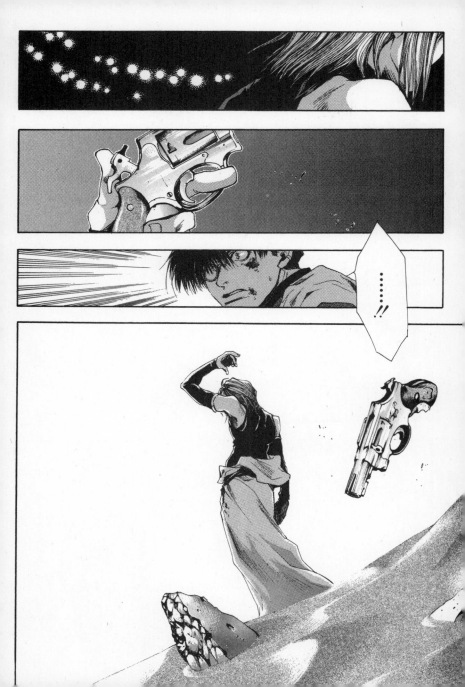

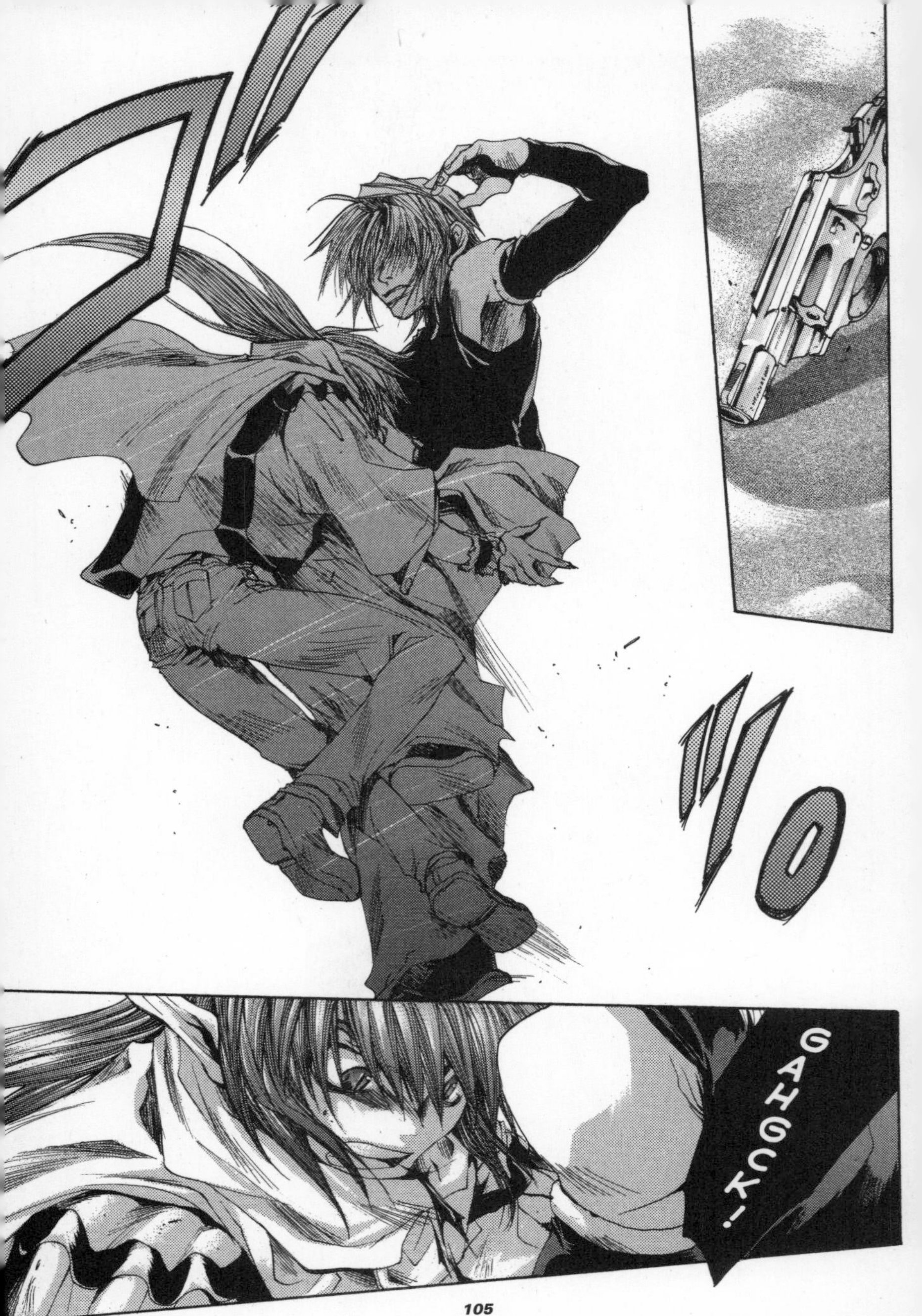
GAHGCK!

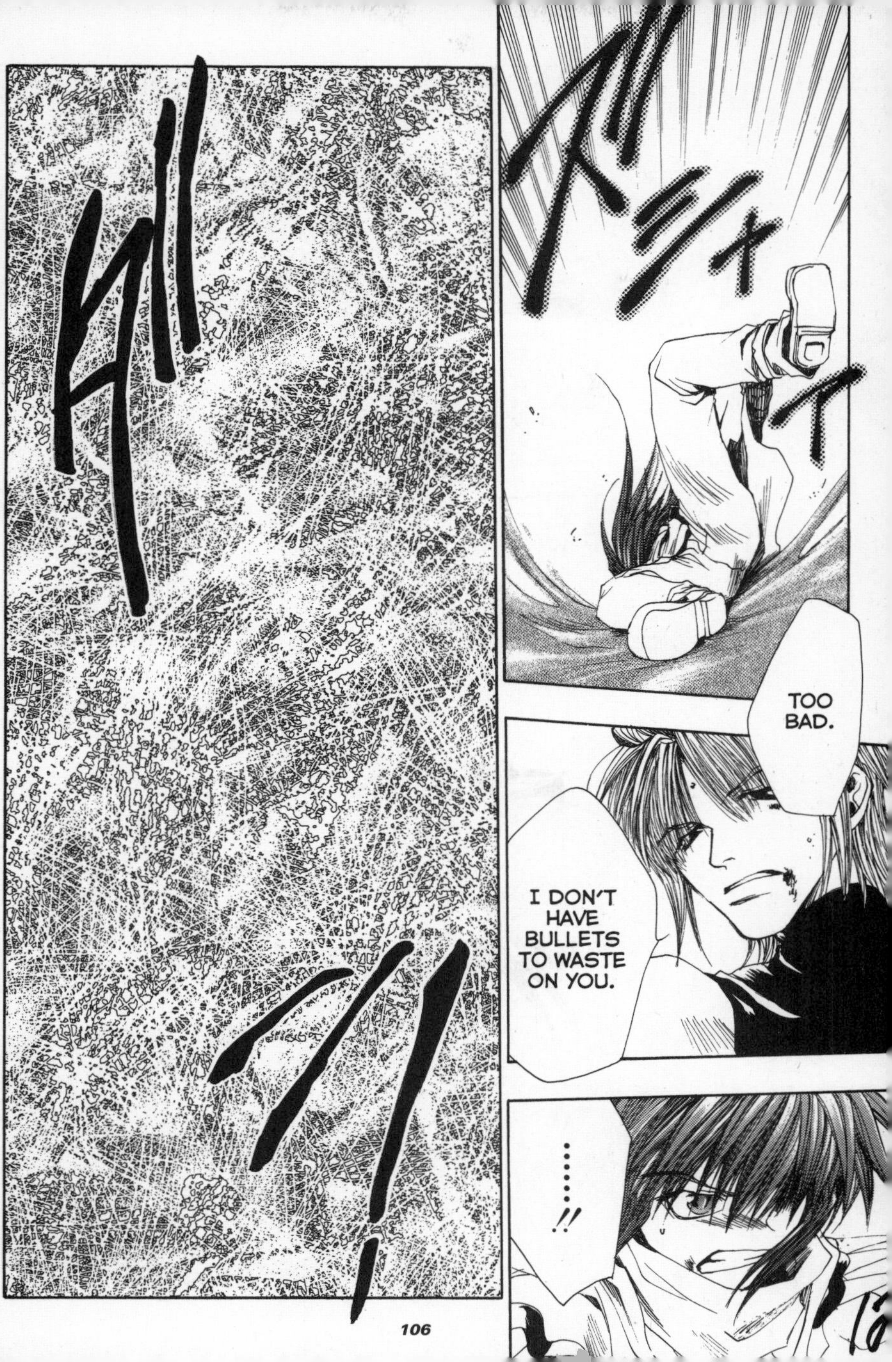
TOO BAD.
I DON'T HAVE BULLETS TO WASTE ON YOU.
......!!

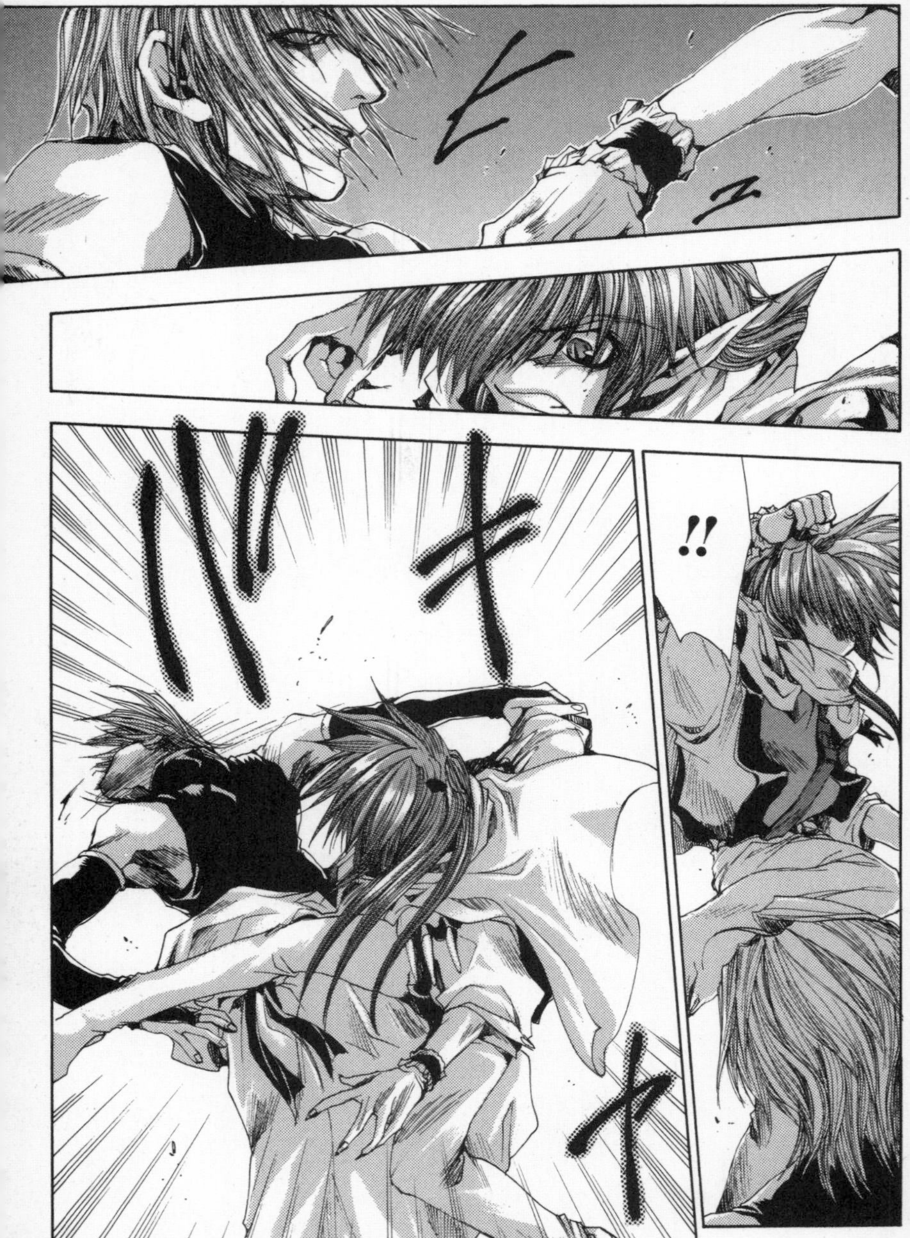

バキ
!!

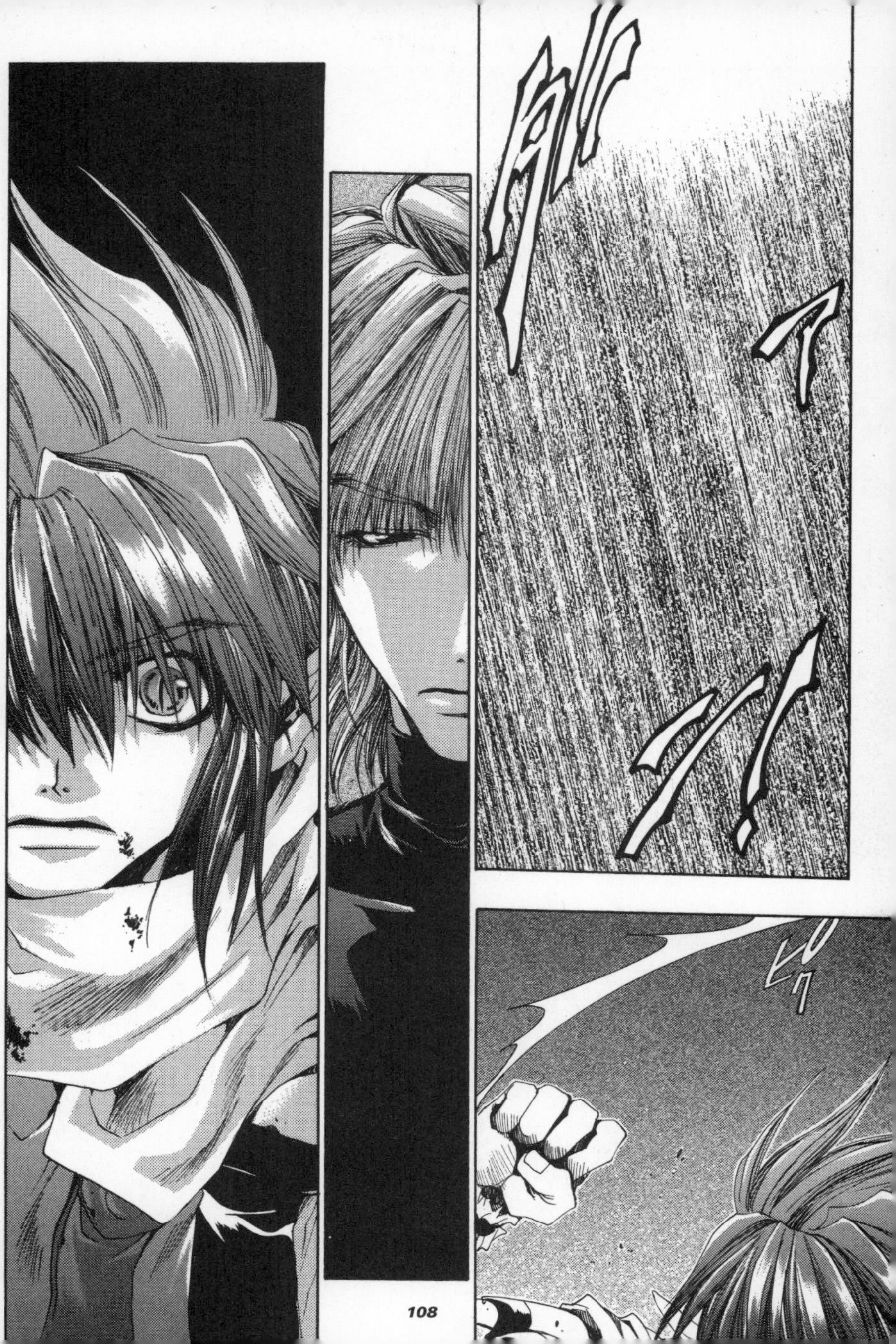

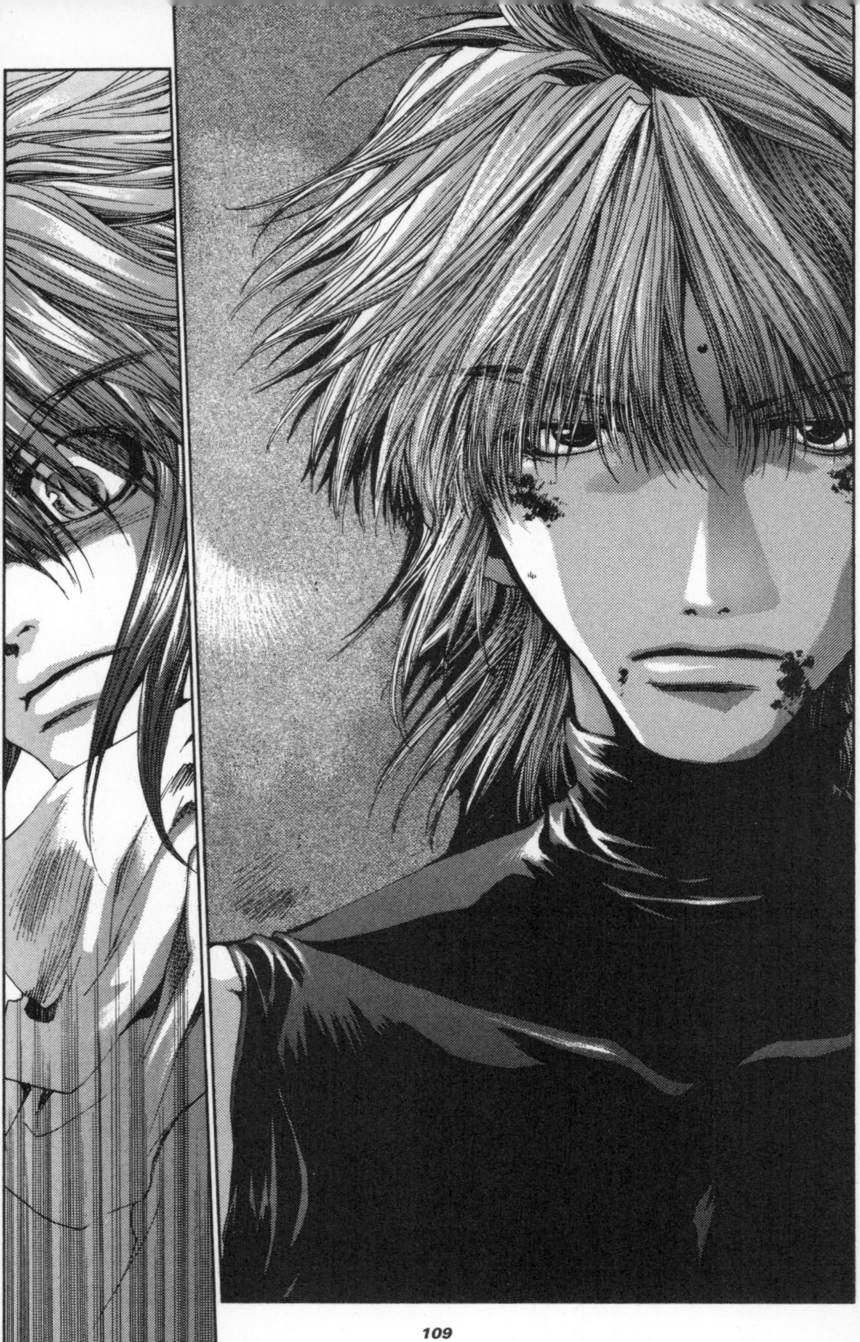

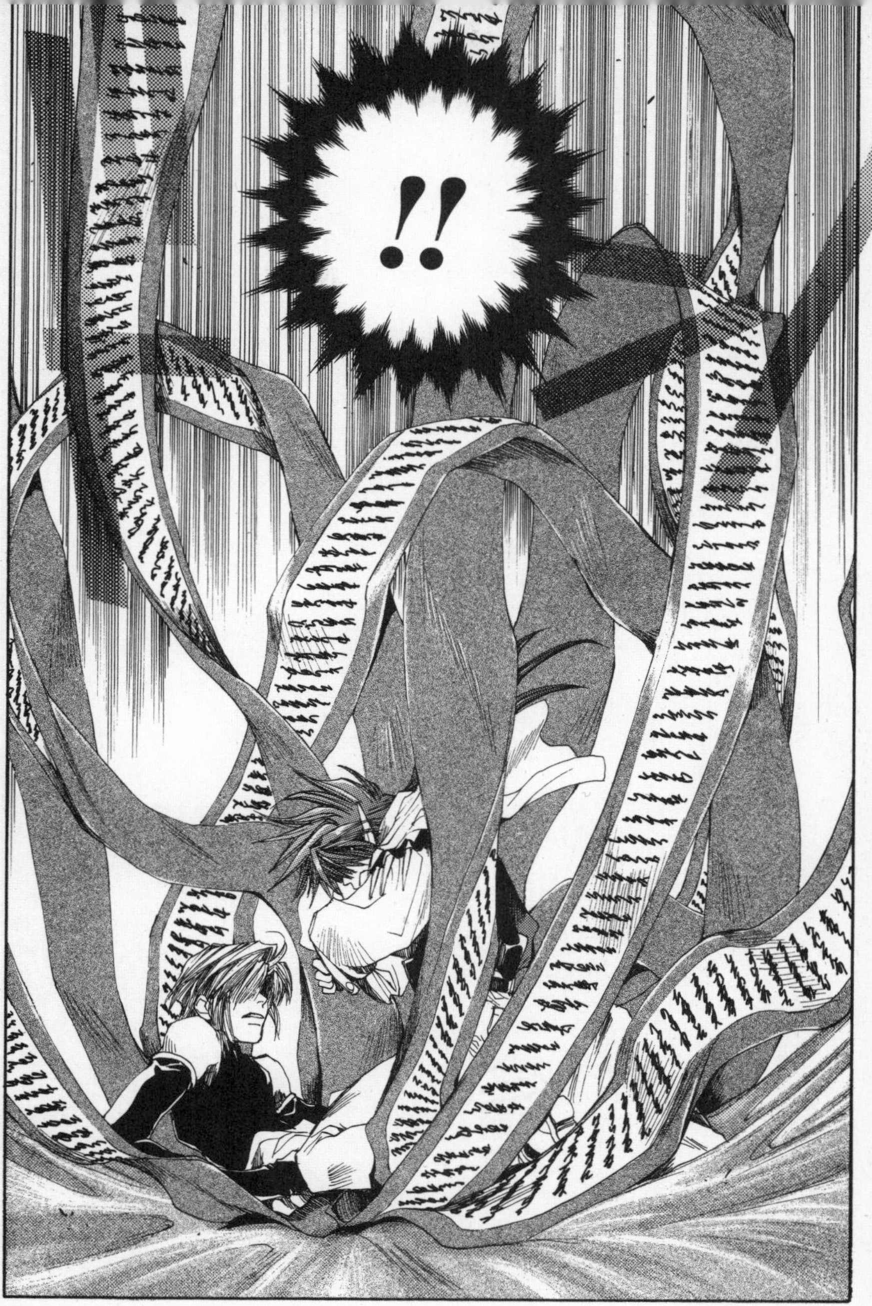
!!

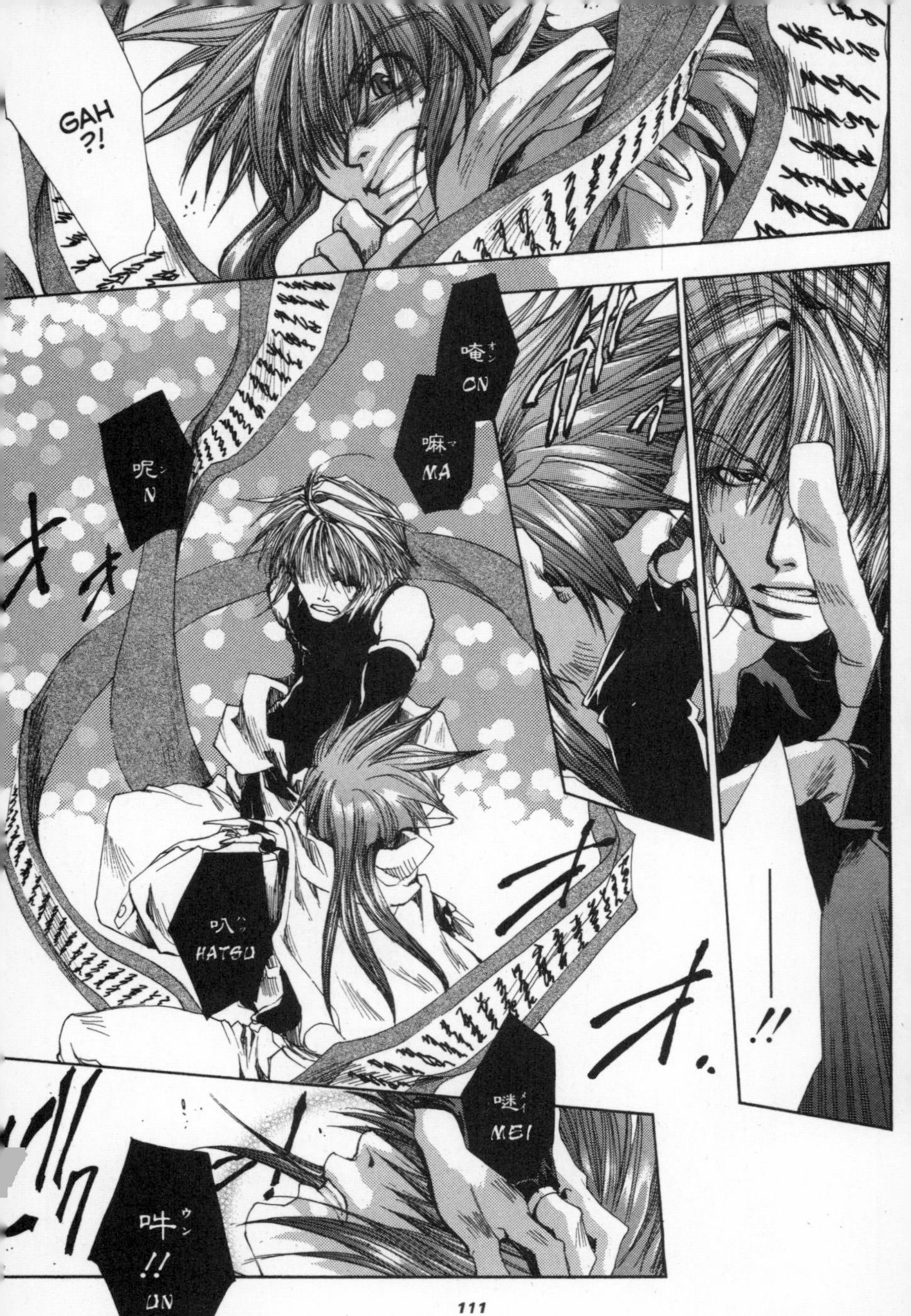
GAH ?!
—!!
唵 ON
嘛 MA
呢 N
叭 HATSU
咪 MEI
吽!! UN

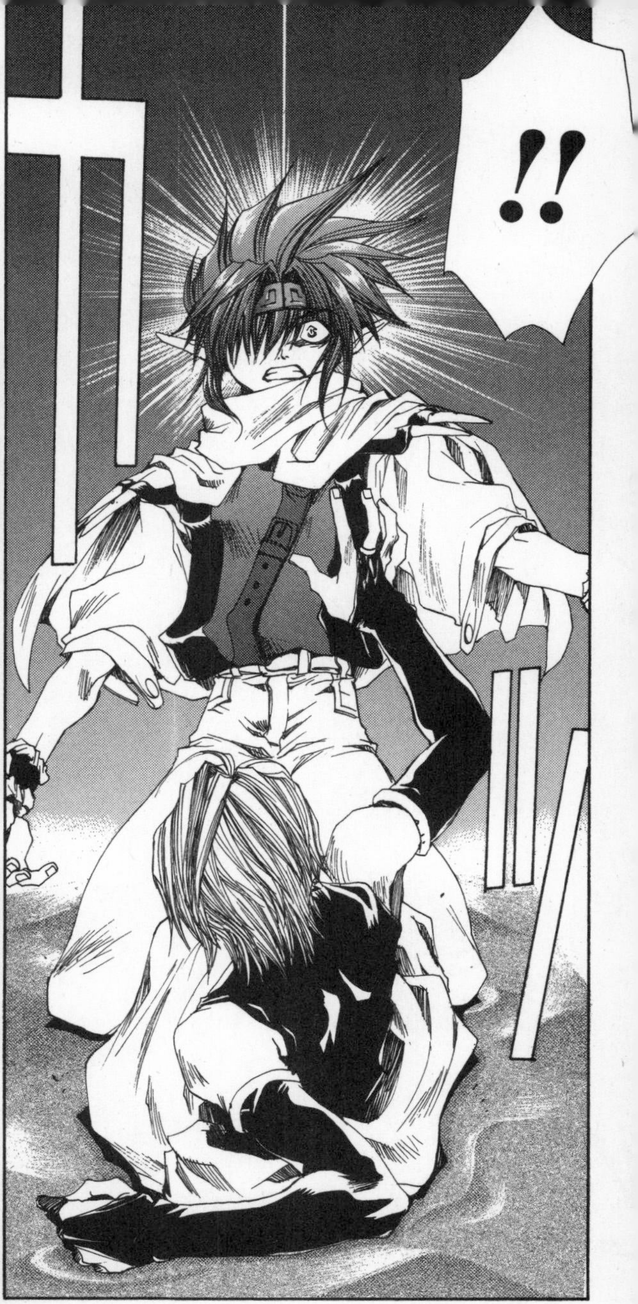
!!

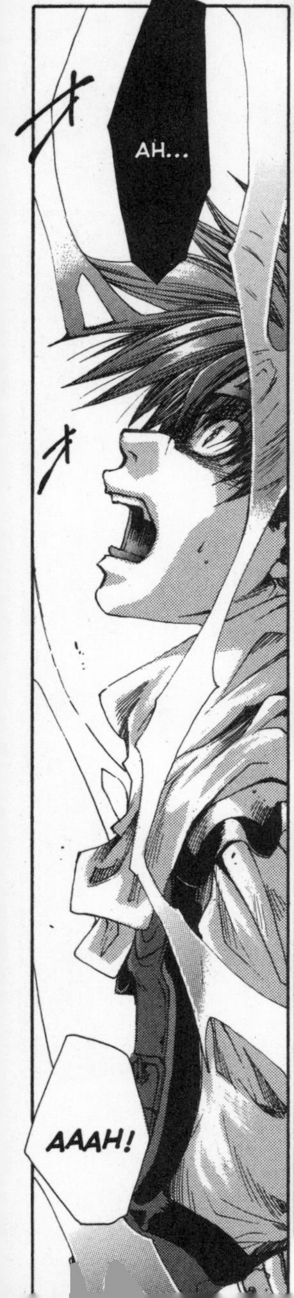
AH...
AAAH!

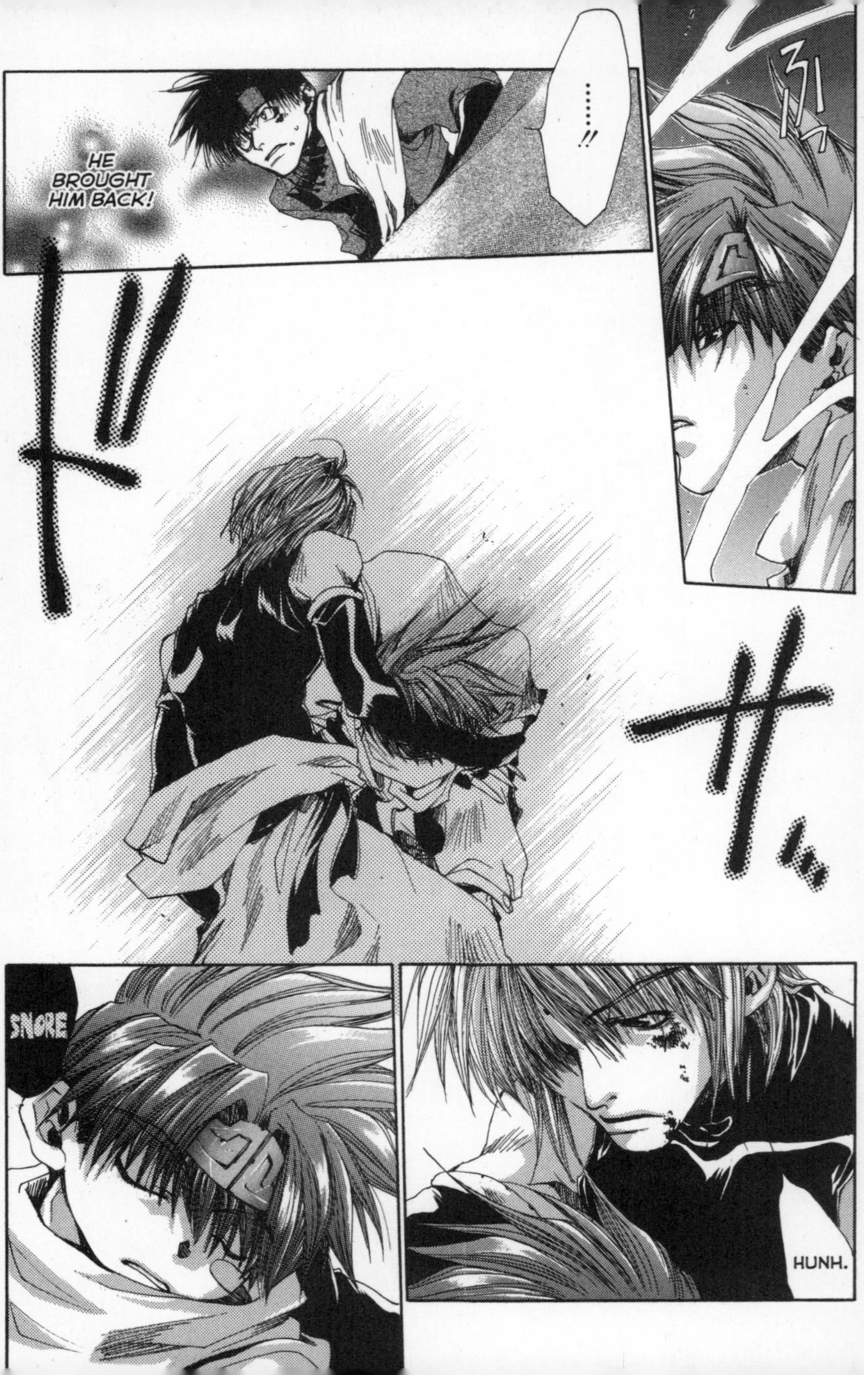
......!!
HE BROUGHT HIM BACK!
HUNH.
SNORE

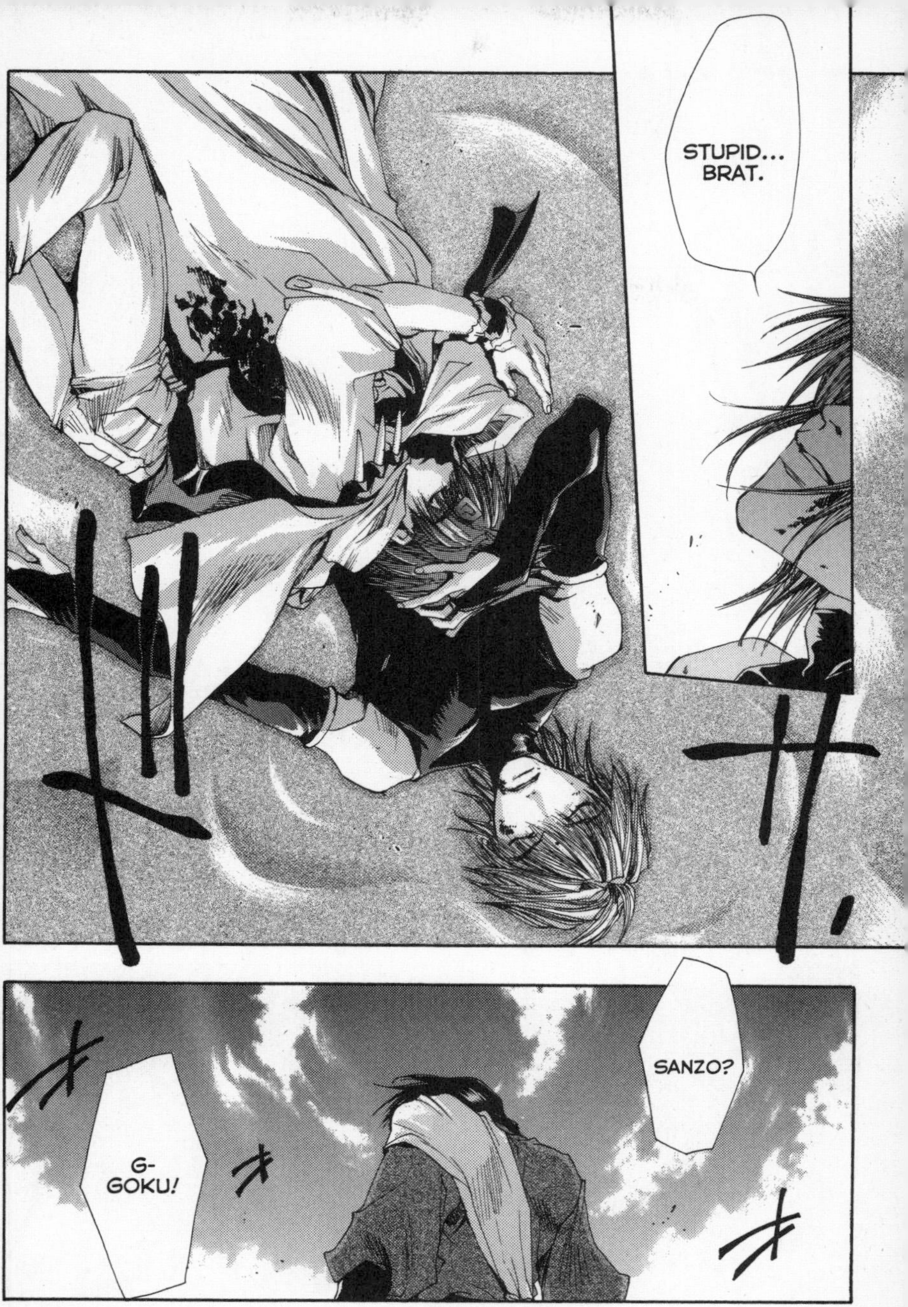
STUPID... BRAT.
SANZO?
G-GOKU!

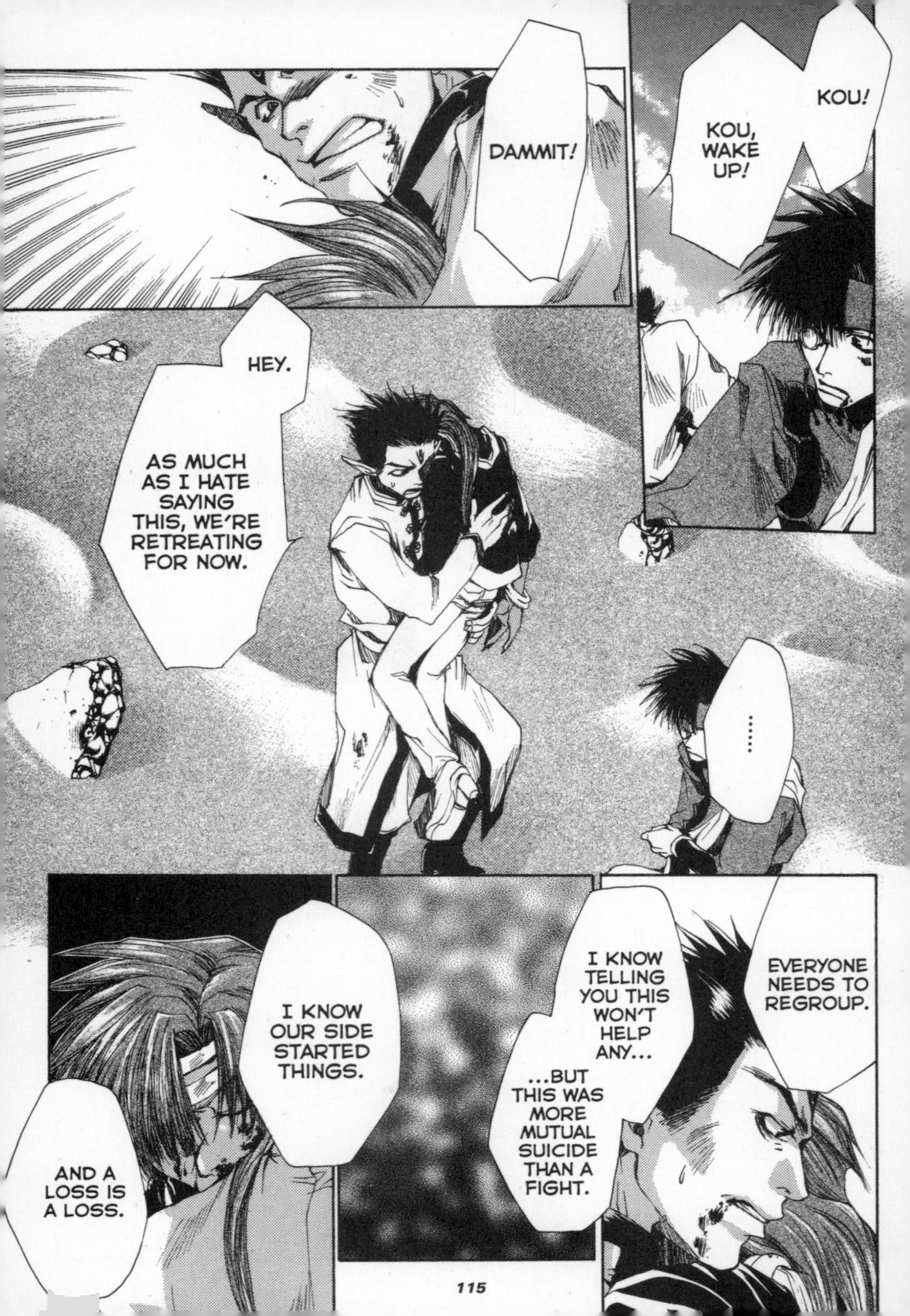
KOU!
KOU, WAKE UP!
DAMMIT!
HEY.
AS MUCH AS I HATE SAYING THIS, WE'RE RETREATING FOR NOW.
......
EVERYONE NEEDS TO REGROUP.
I KNOW TELLING YOU THIS WON'T HELP ANY...
...BUT THIS WAS MORE MUTUAL SUICIDE THAN A FIGHT.
I KNOW OUR SIDE STARTED THINGS.
AND A LOSS IS A LOSS.

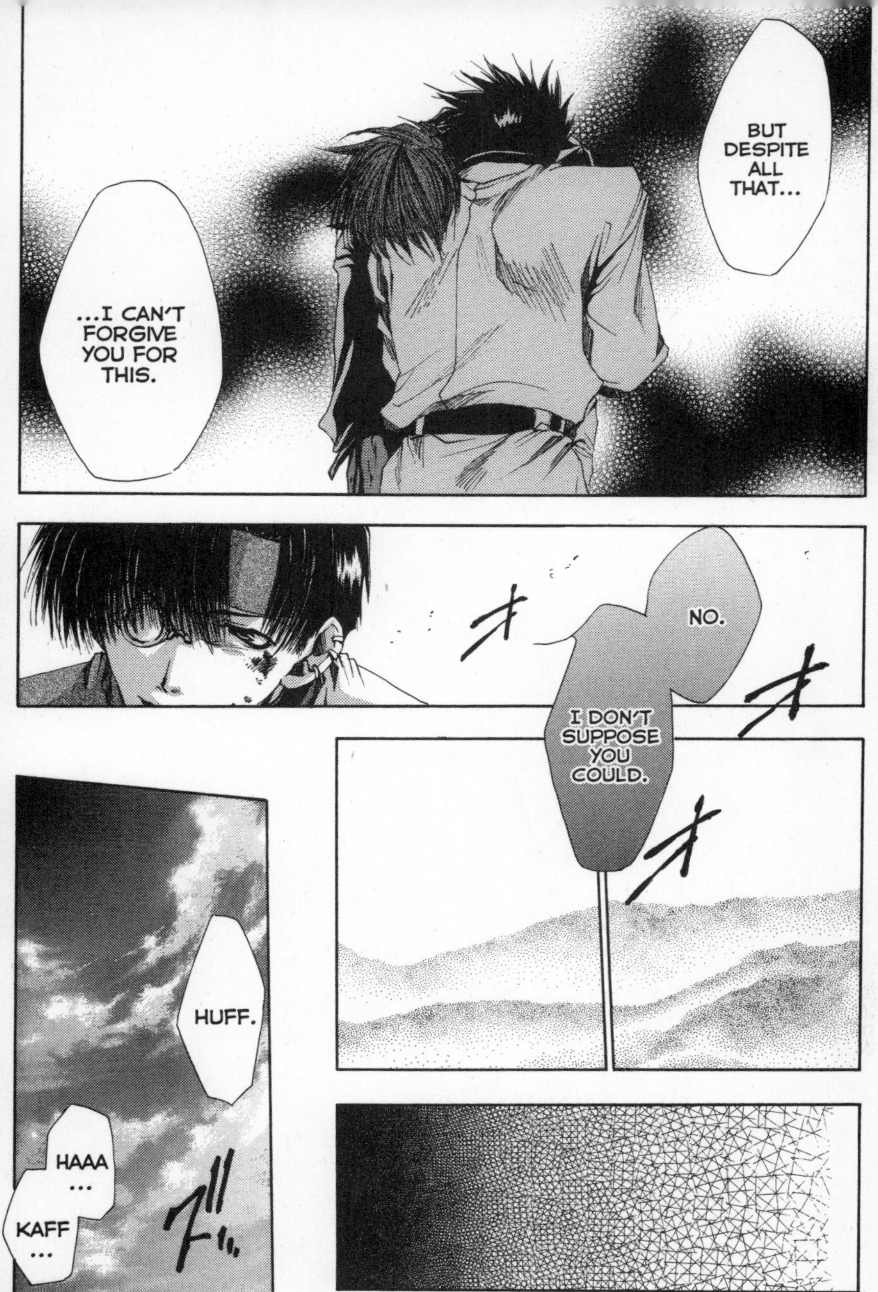
BUT DESPITE ALL THAT...
...I CAN'T FORGIVE YOU FOR THIS.
NO.
I DON'T SUPPOSE YOU COULD.
HUFF.
HAAA...
KAFF...

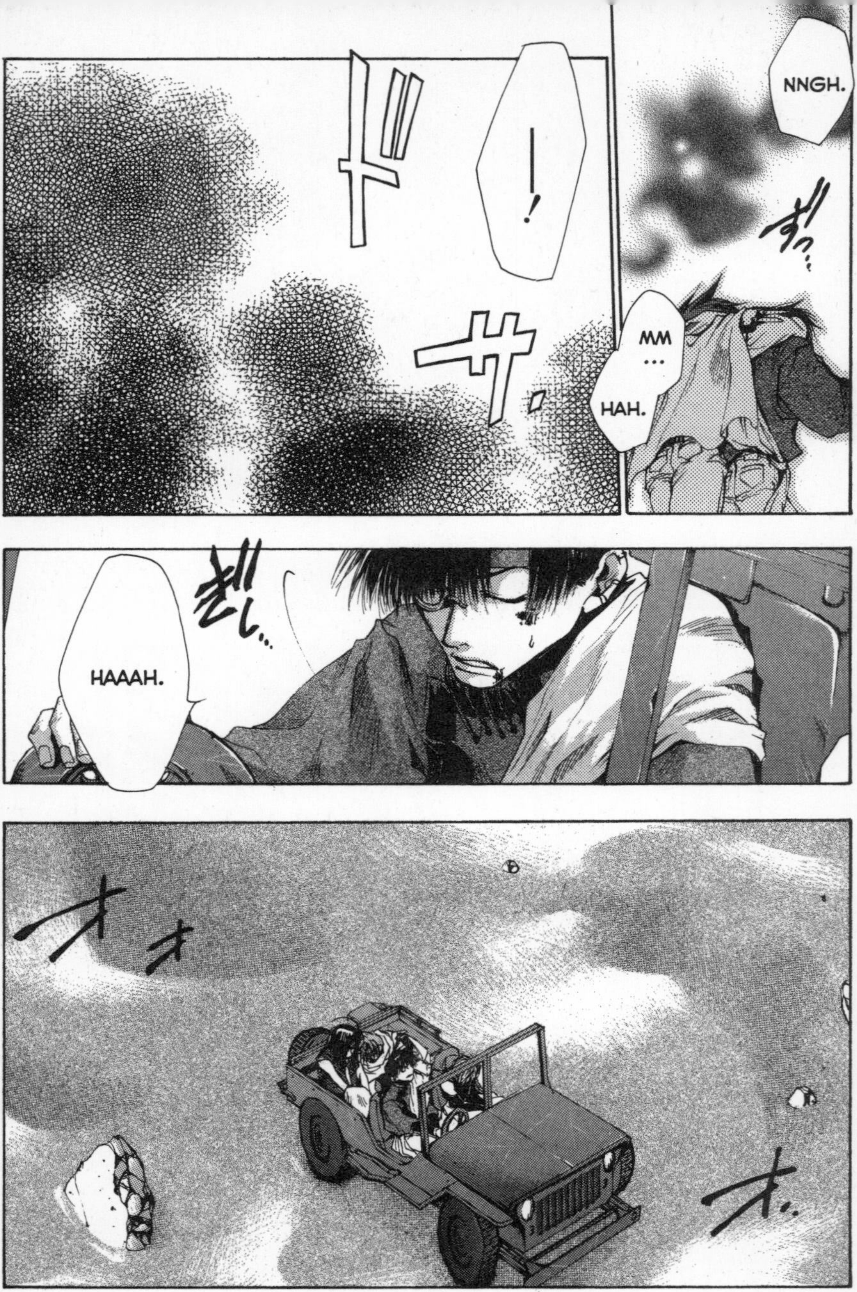
NNGH.
MM ...
HAH.
—!
HAAAH.

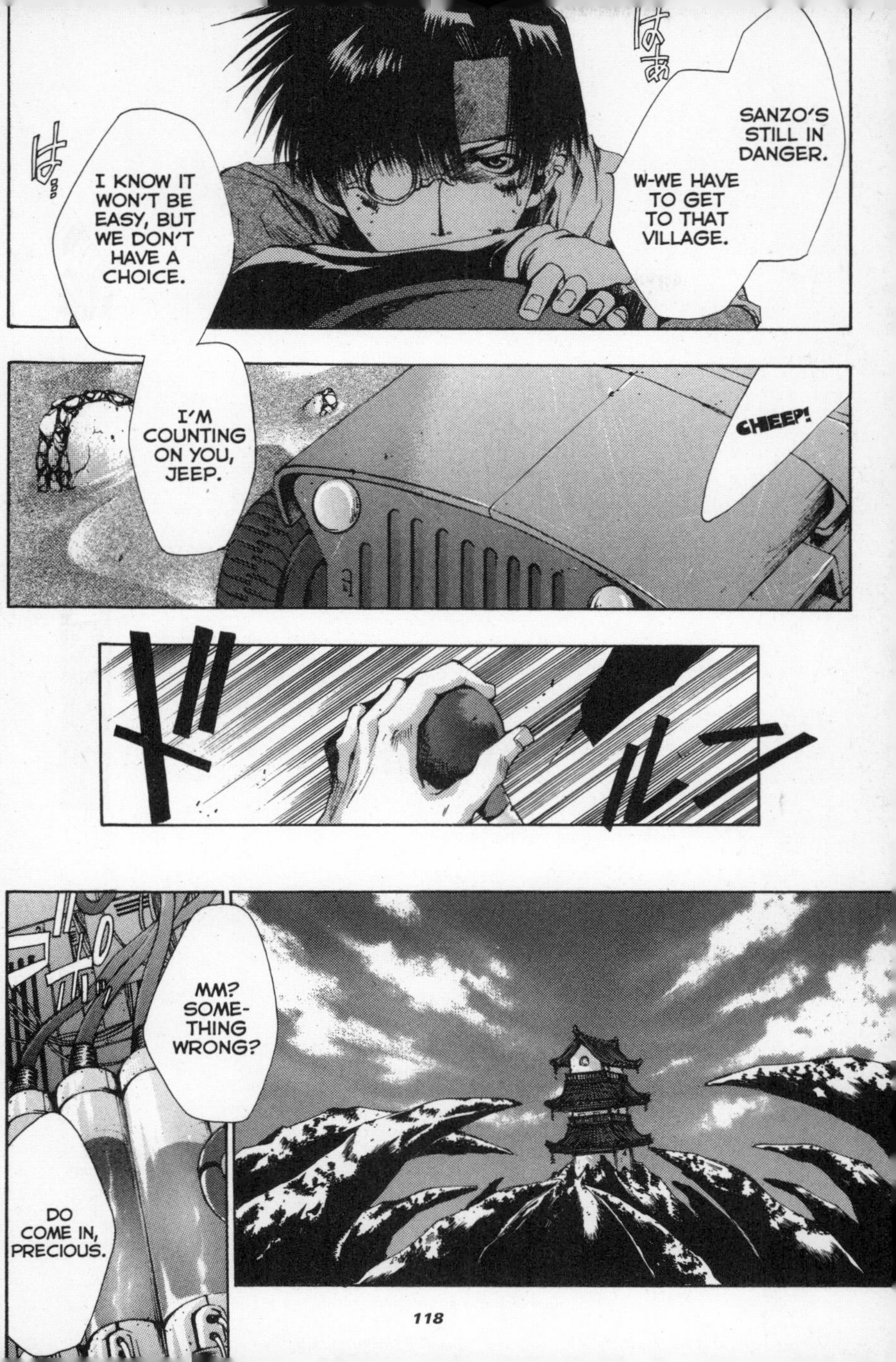
はあ
SANZO'S STILL IN DANGER.
W-WE HAVE TO GET TO THAT VILLAGE.
は…
I KNOW IT WON'T BE EASY, BUT WE DON'T HAVE A CHOICE.
I'M COUNTING ON YOU, JEEP.
CHEEP!
MM? SOME-THING WRONG?
DO COME IN, PRECIOUS.

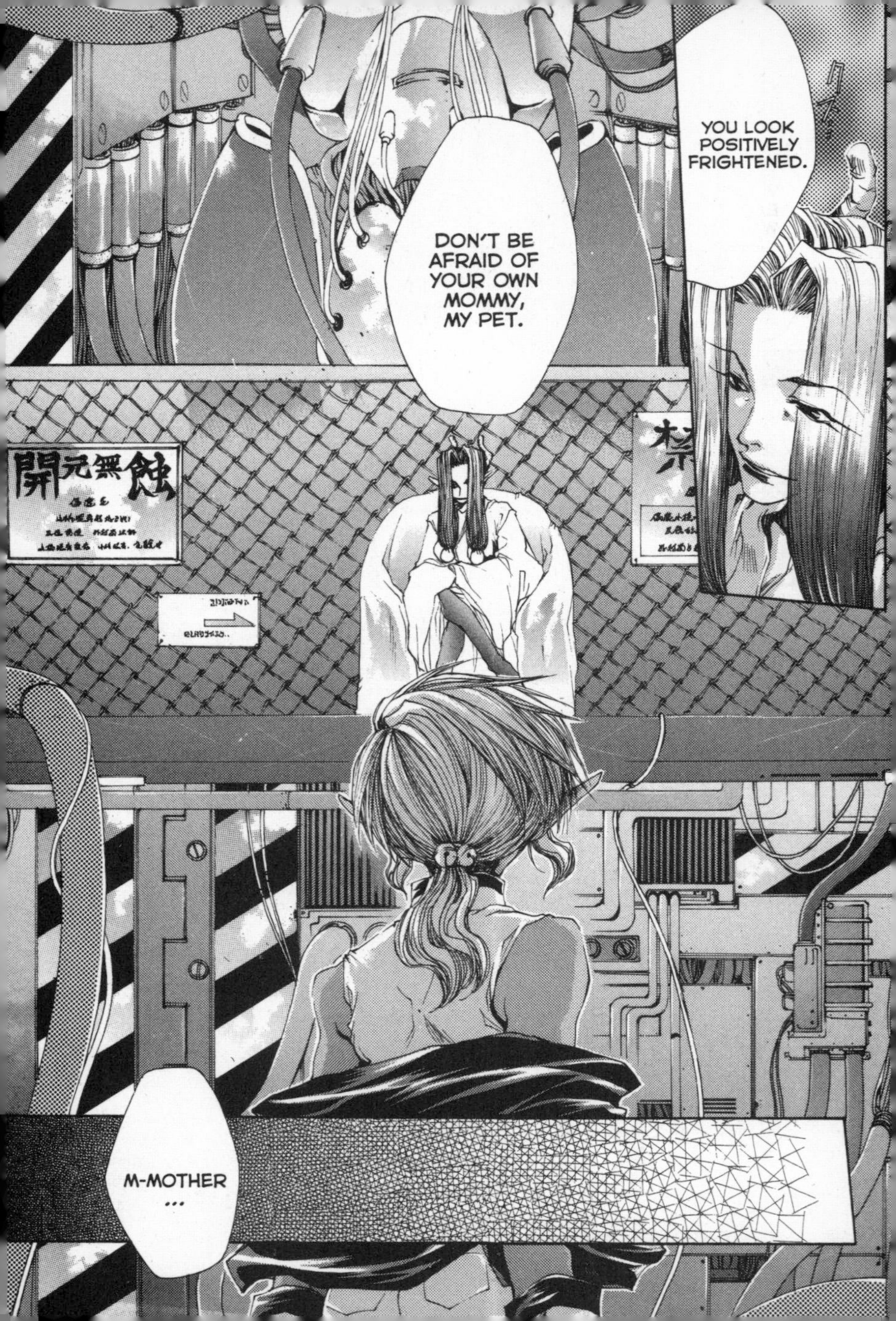
YOU LOOK POSITIVELY FRIGHTENED.
DON'T BE AFRAID OF YOUR OWN MOMMY, MY PET.
M-MOTHER ...

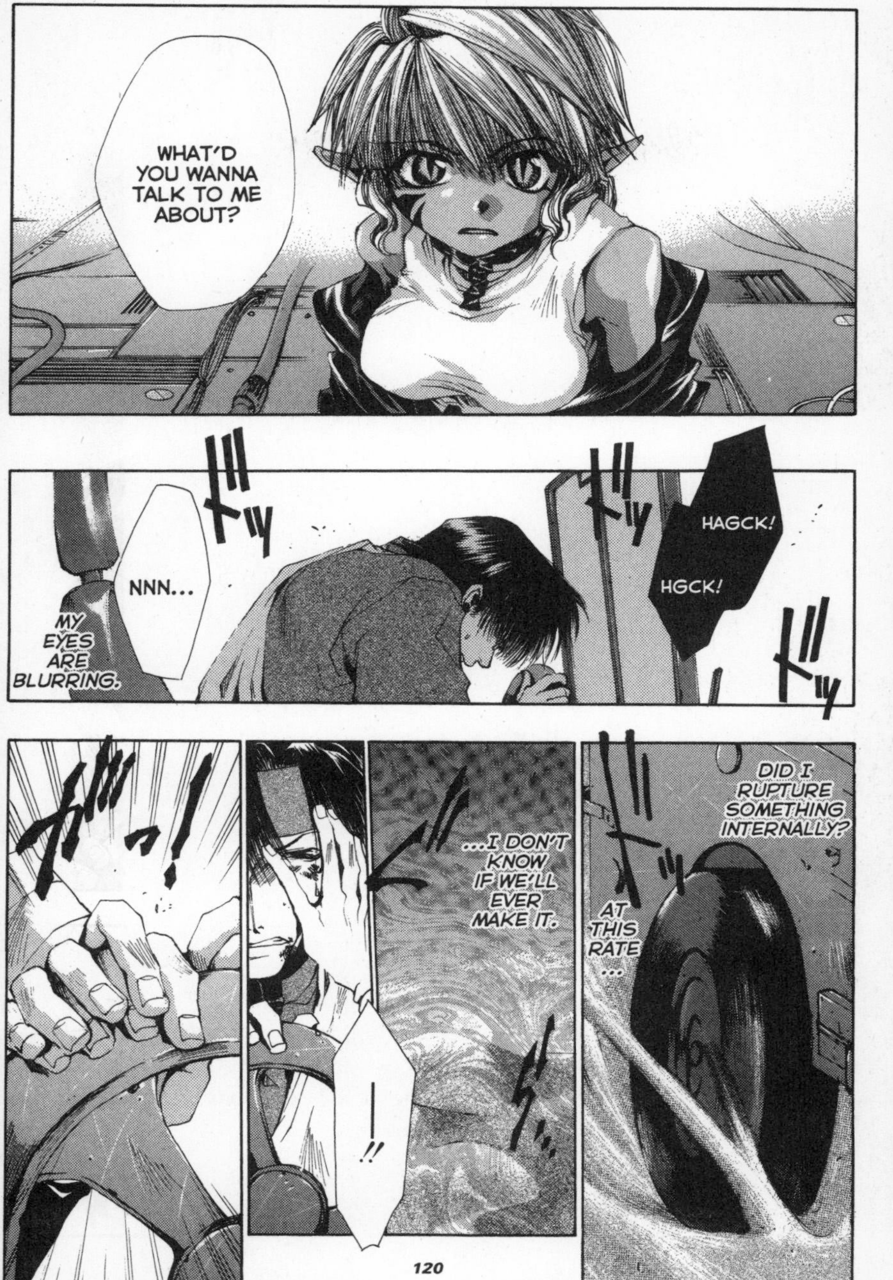
WHAT'D YOU WANNA TALK TO ME ABOUT?
HAGCK!
HGCK!
NNN...
MY EYES ARE BLURRING.
DID I RUPTURE SOMETHING INTERNALLY?
AT THIS RATE ...
...I DON'T KNOW IF WE'LL EVER MAKE IT.
—!!

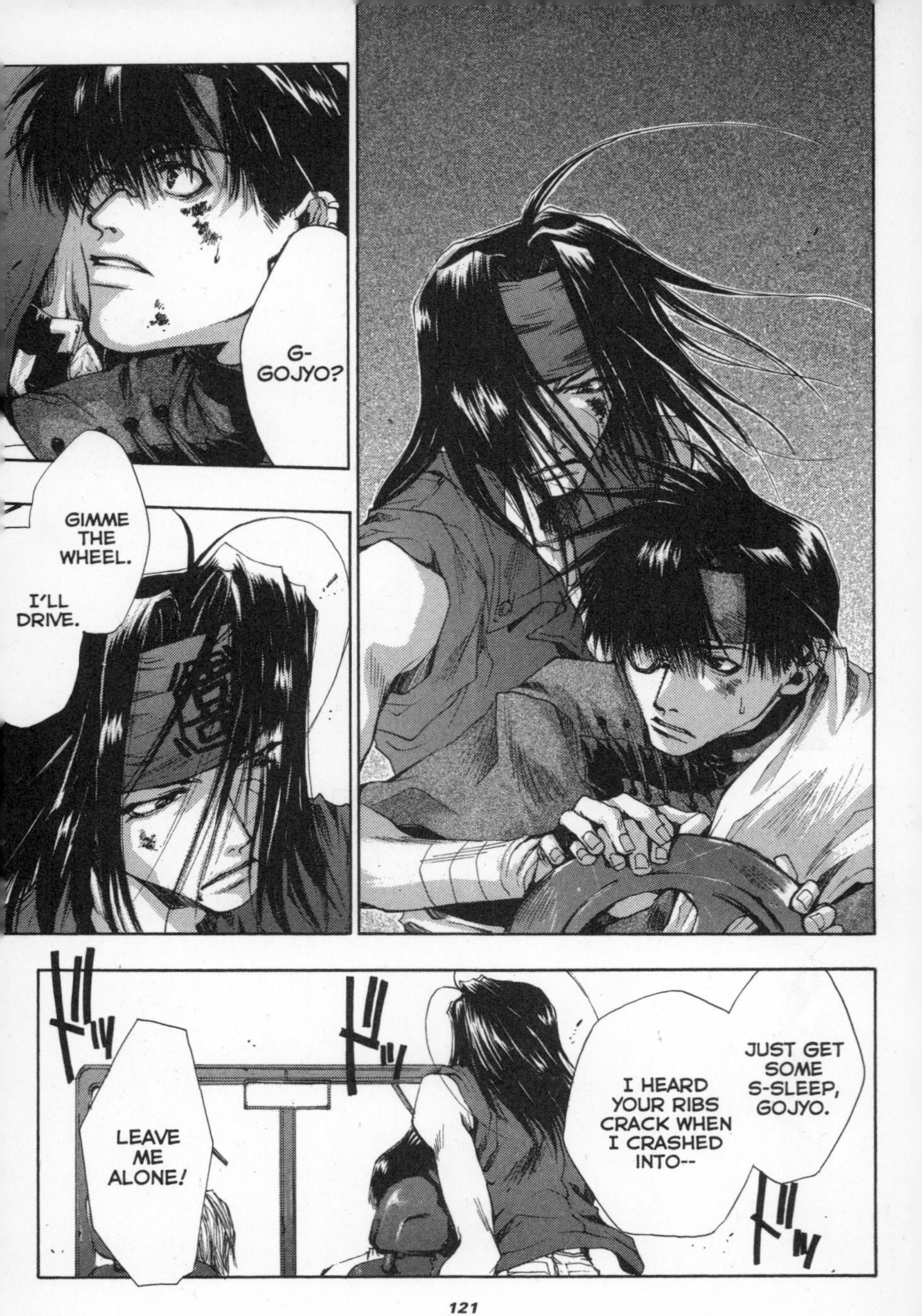
G-GOJYO?
GIMME THE WHEEL.
I'LL DRIVE.
JUST GET SOME S-SLEEP, GOJYO.
I HEARD YOUR RIBS CRACK WHEN I CRASHED INTO--
LEAVE ME ALONE!

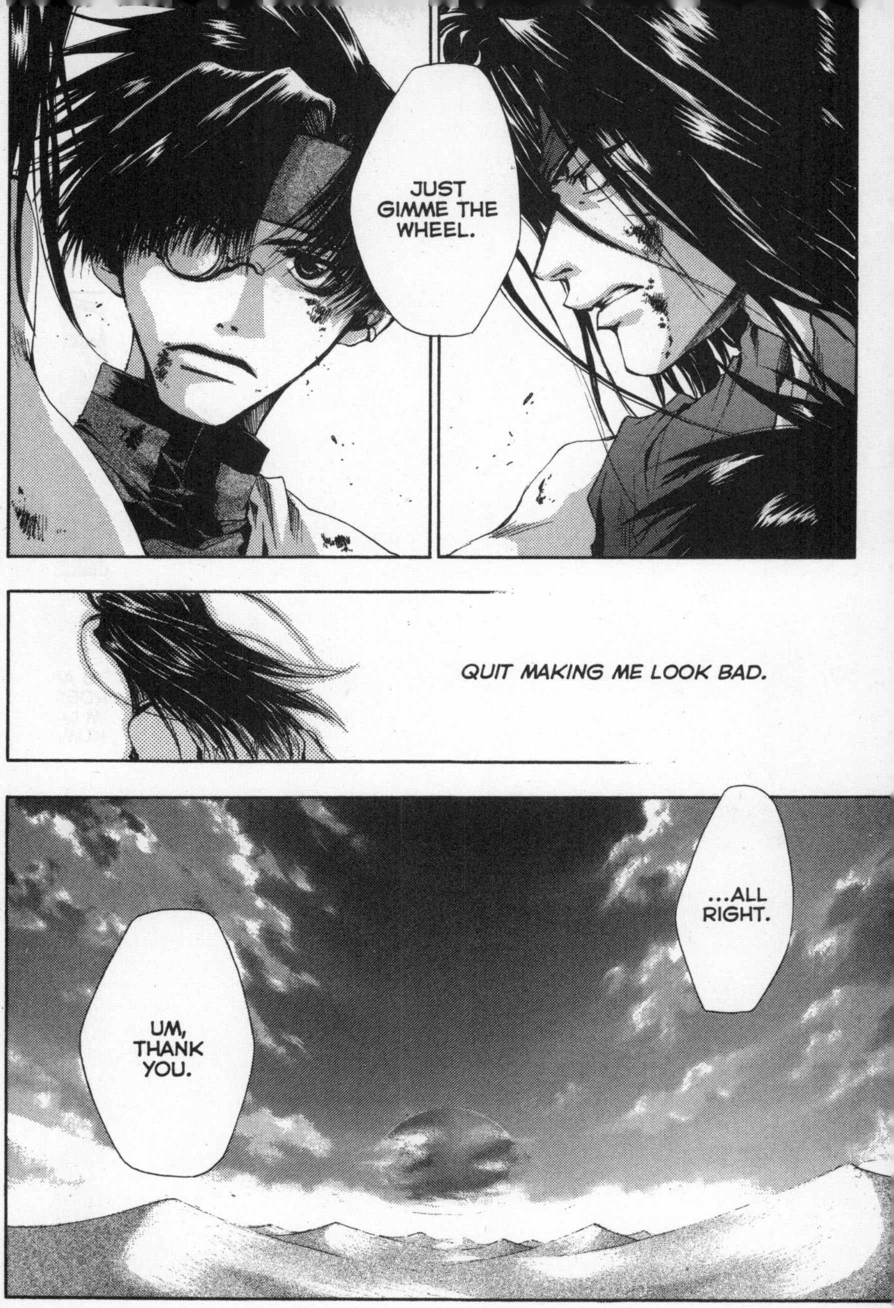
JUST GIMME THE WHEEL.
QUIT MAKING ME LOOK BAD.
...ALL RIGHT.
UM, THANK YOU.

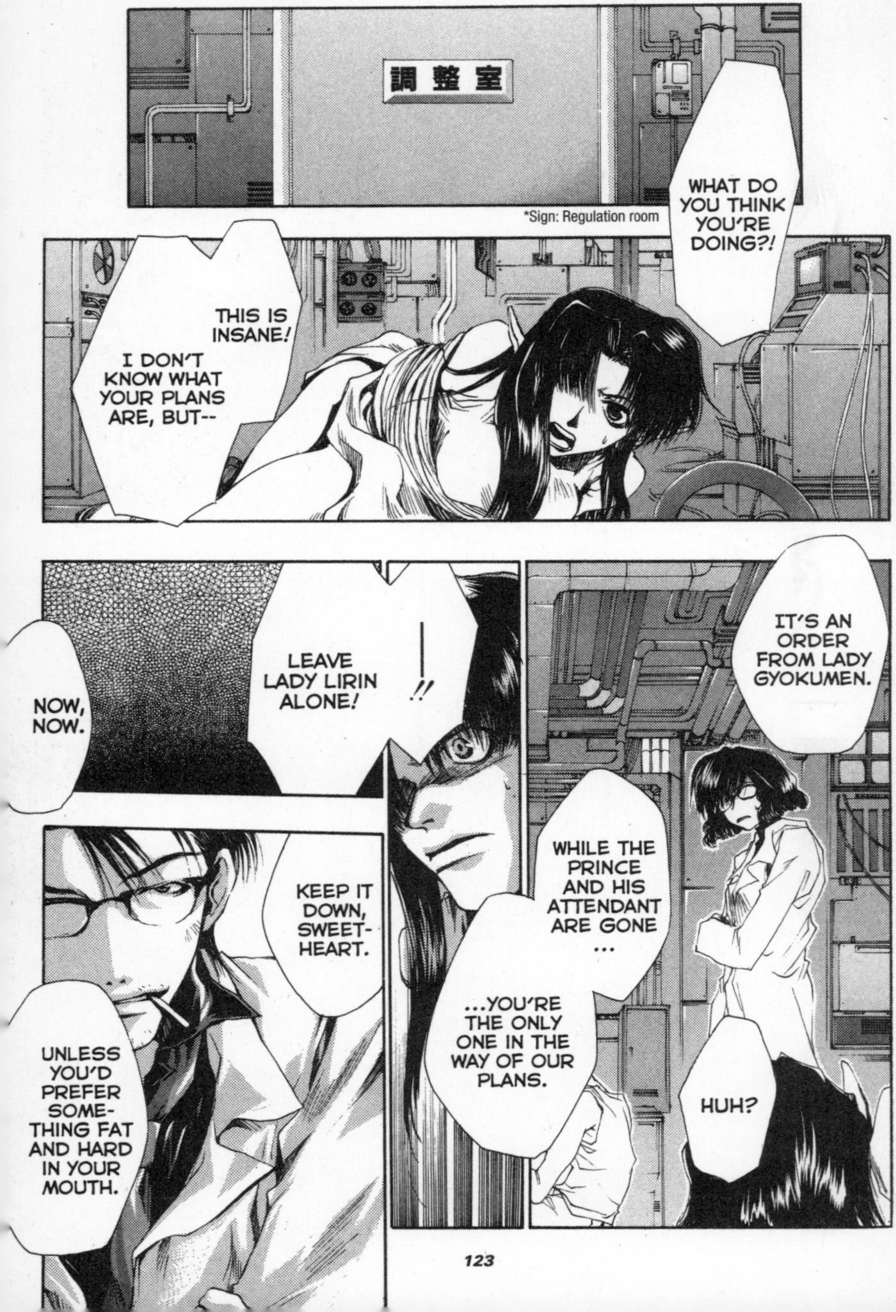
調整室
*Sign: Regulation room
WHAT DO YOU THINK YOU'RE DOING?!
THIS IS INSANE!
I DON'T KNOW WHAT YOUR PLANS ARE, BUT--
IT'S AN ORDER FROM LADY GYOKUMEN.
WHILE THE PRINCE AND HIS ATTENDANT ARE GONE...
...YOU'RE THE ONLY ONE IN THE WAY OF OUR PLANS.
HUH?
LEAVE LADY LIRIN ALONE!
—!!
NOW, NOW.
KEEP IT DOWN, SWEET-HEART.
UNLESS YOU'D PREFER SOME-THING FAT AND HARD IN YOUR MOUTH.

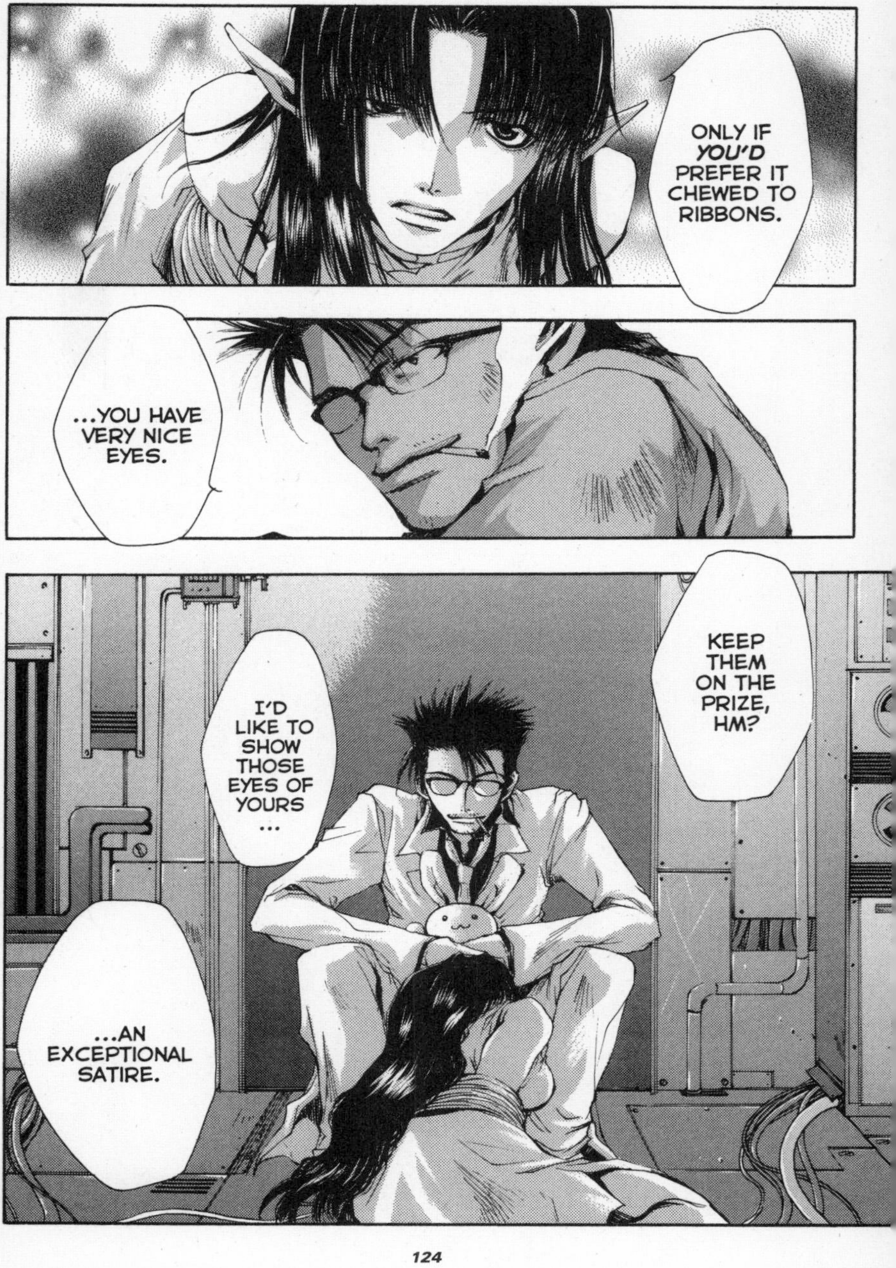
ONLY IF *YOU'D* PREFER IT CHEWED TO RIBBONS.
...YOU HAVE VERY NICE EYES.
KEEP THEM ON THE PRIZE, HM?
I'D LIKE TO SHOW THOSE EYES OF YOURS ...
...AN EXCEPTIONAL SATIRE.

IT'S ONLY FOR THEMSELVES THAT
PEOPLE LIVE AND DIE.

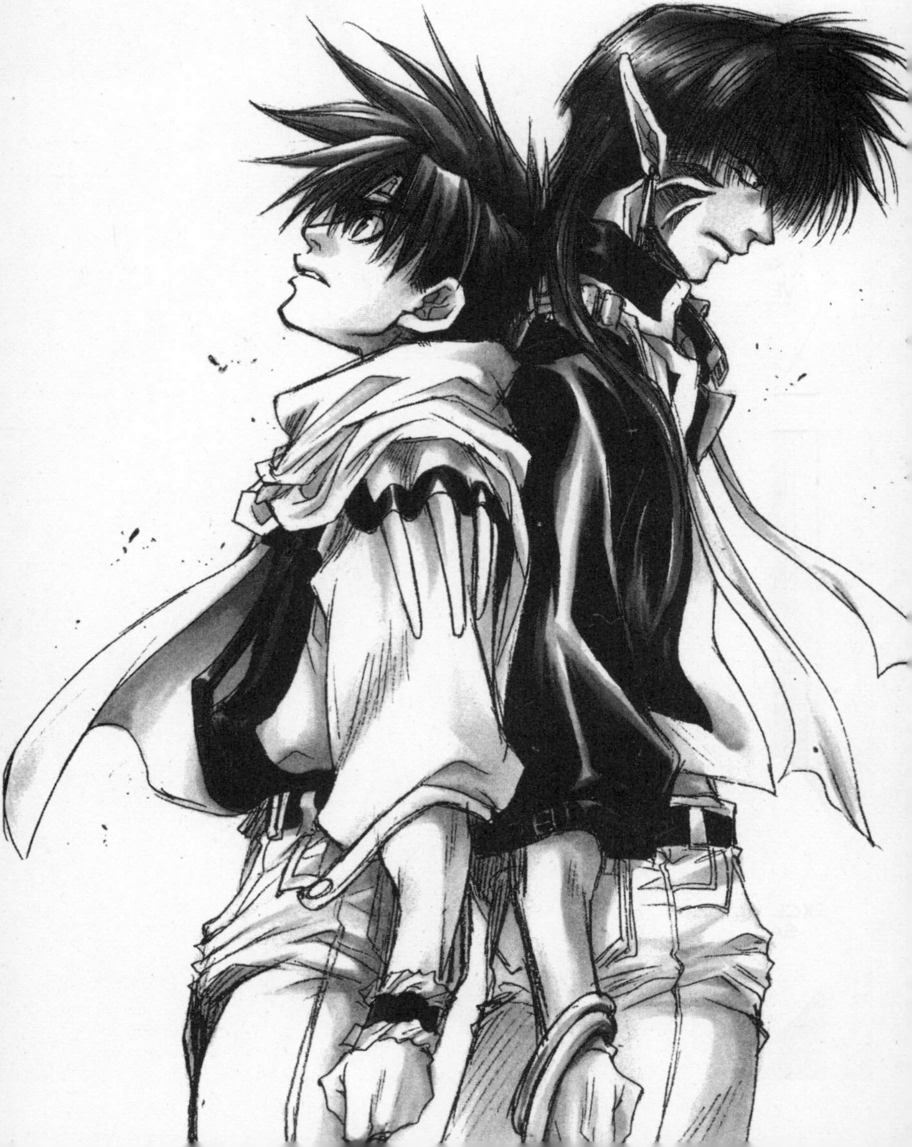

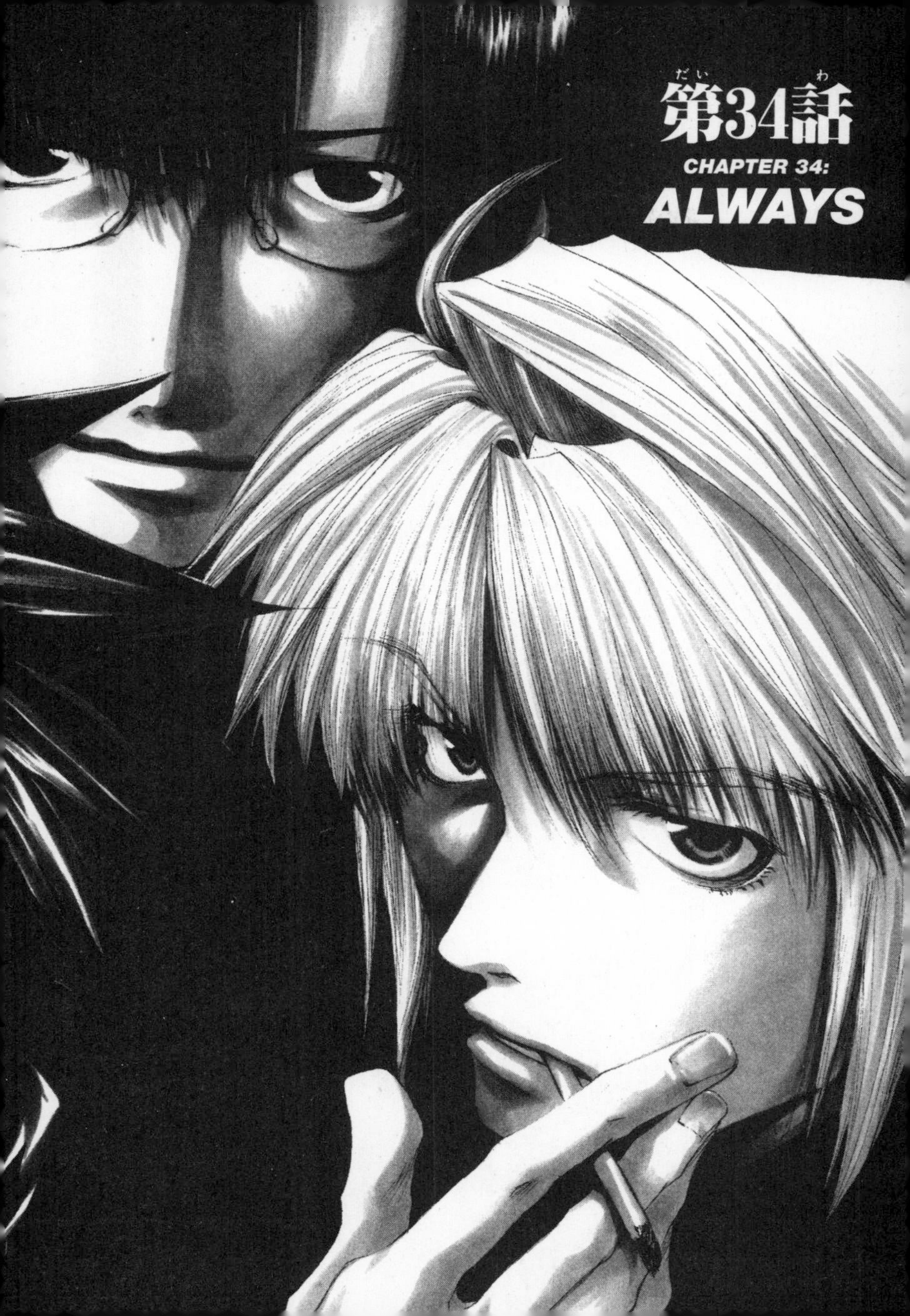
だい わ
第34話
CHAPTER 34:
ALWAYS

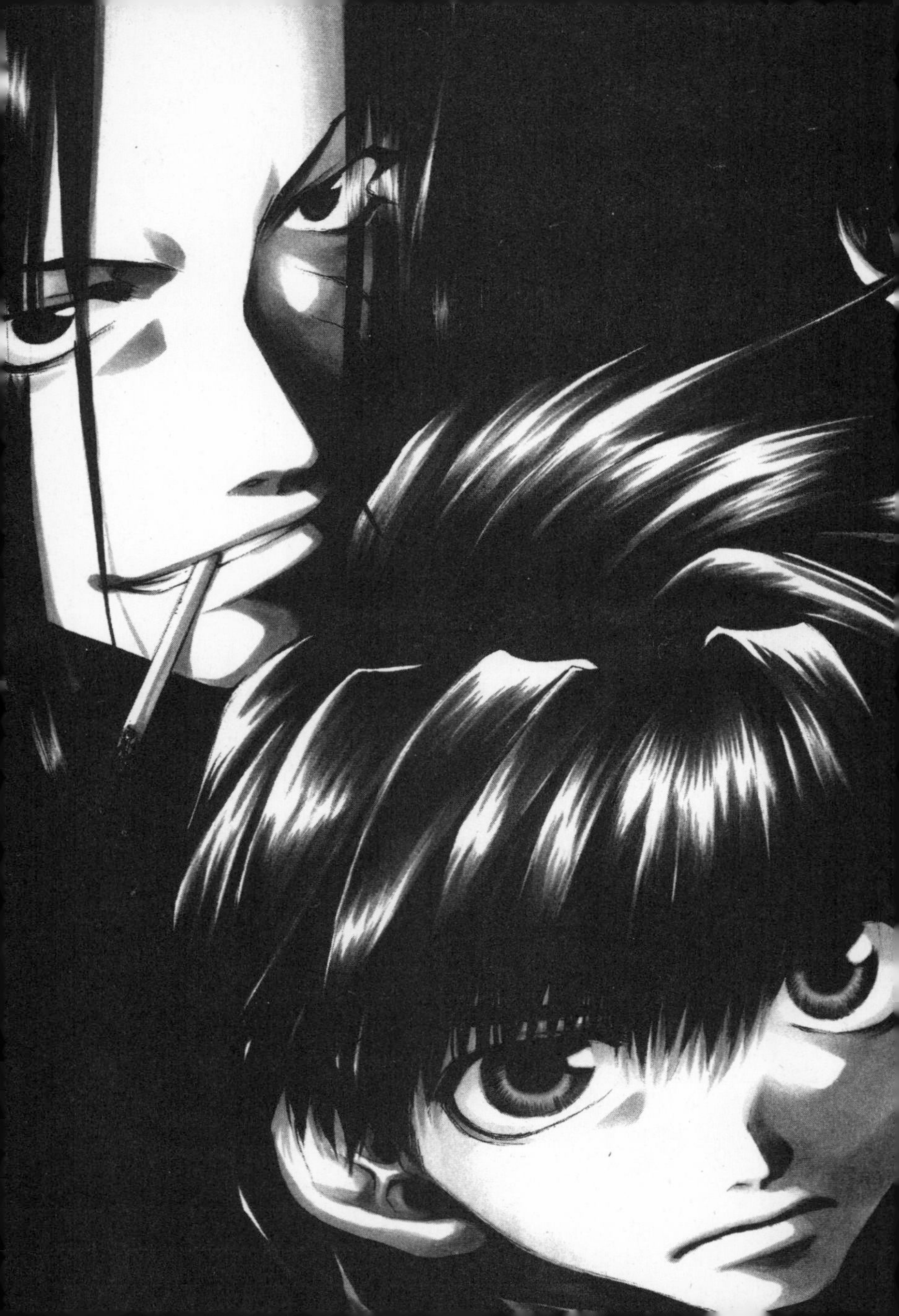

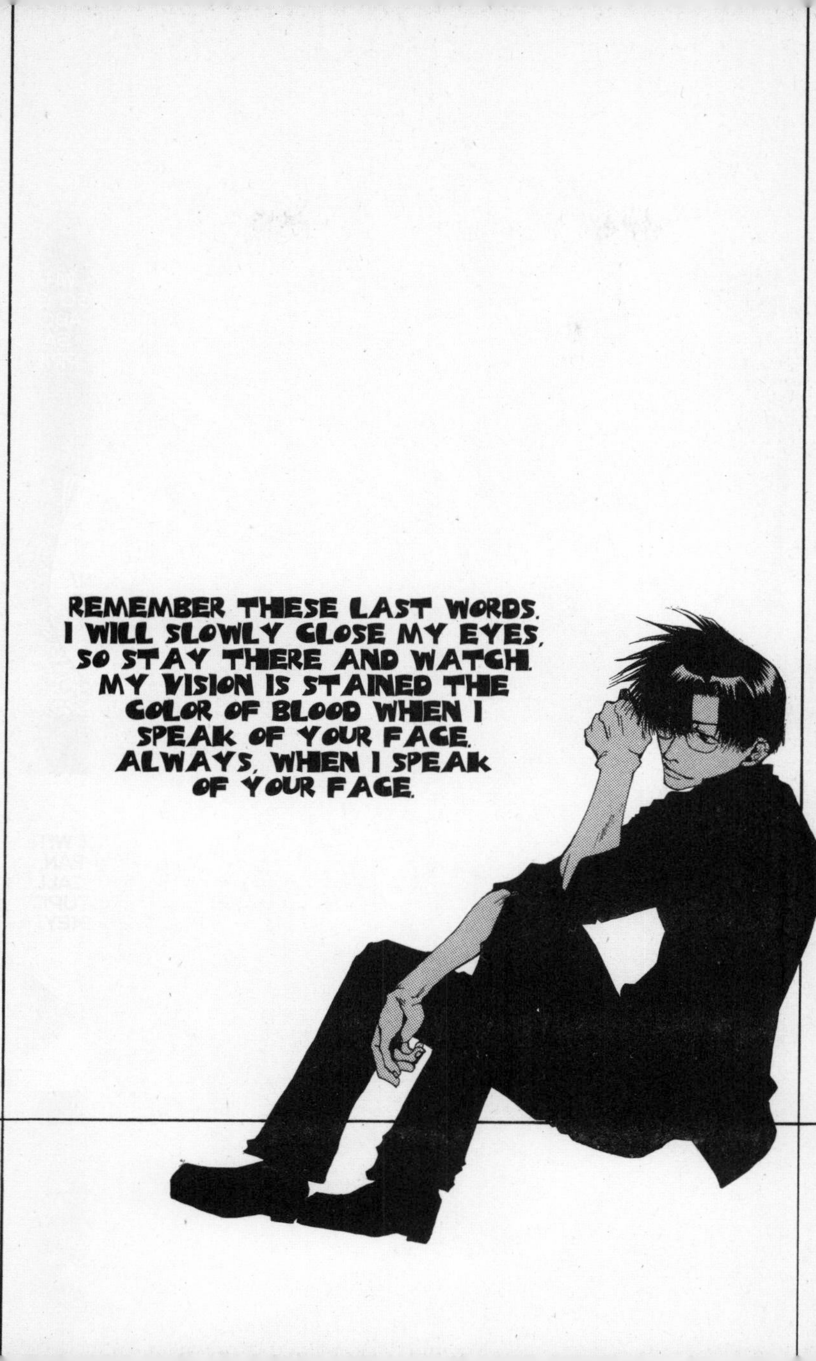
REMEMBER THESE LAST WORDS.
I WILL SLOWLY CLOSE MY EYES,
SO STAY THERE AND WATCH.
MY VISION IS STAINED THE
COLOR OF BLOOD WHEN I
SPEAK OF YOUR FACE.
ALWAYS, WHEN I SPEAK
OF YOUR FACE.

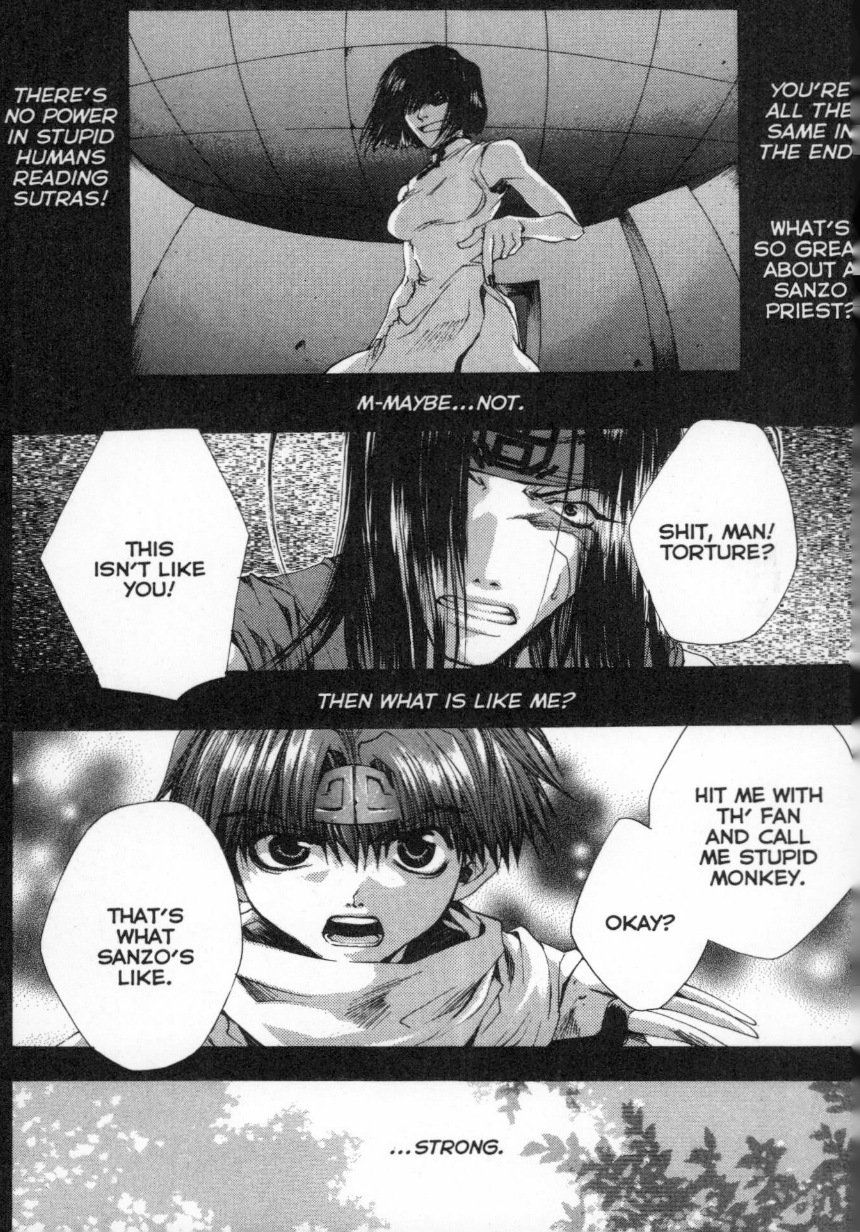
YOU'RE ALL THE SAME IN THE END
WHAT'S SO GREA ABOUT A SANZO PRIEST?
THERE'S NO POWER IN STUPID HUMANS READING SUTRAS!
M-MAYBE...NOT.
SHIT, MAN! TORTURE?
THIS ISN'T LIKE YOU!
THEN WHAT IS LIKE ME?
HIT ME WITH TH' FAN AND CALL ME STUPID MONKEY.
OKAY?
THAT'S WHAT SANZO'S LIKE.
...STRONG.

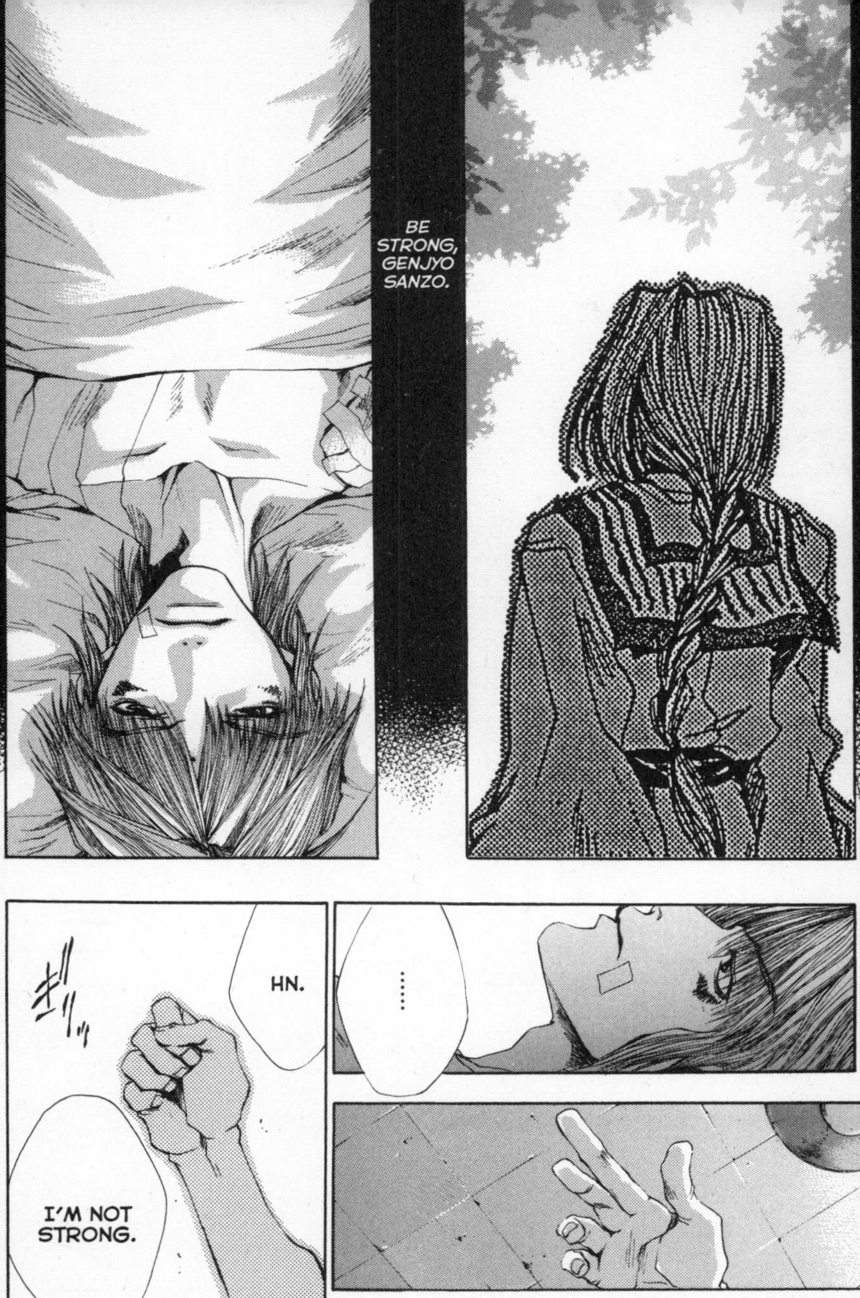

BE STRONG, GENJYO SANZO.
……
HN.
ギリッ
I'M NOT STRONG.

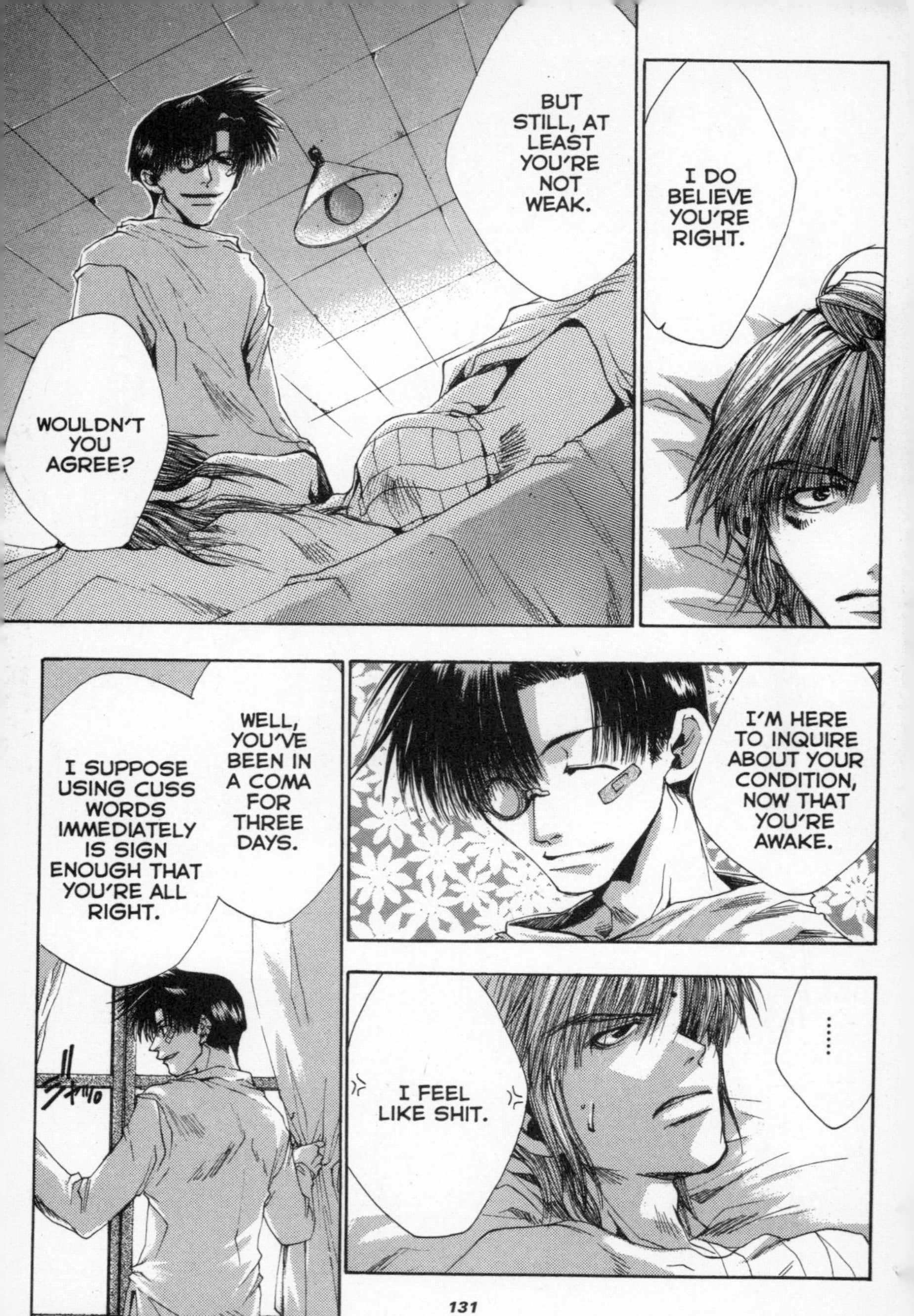
I DO BELIEVE YOU'RE RIGHT.
BUT STILL, AT LEAST YOU'RE NOT WEAK.
WOULDN'T YOU AGREE?
I'M HERE TO INQUIRE ABOUT YOUR CONDITION, NOW THAT YOU'RE AWAKE.
......
I FEEL LIKE SHIT.
WELL, YOU'VE BEEN IN A COMA FOR THREE DAYS.
I SUPPOSE USING CUSS WORDS IMMEDIATELY IS SIGN ENOUGH THAT YOU'RE ALL RIGHT.

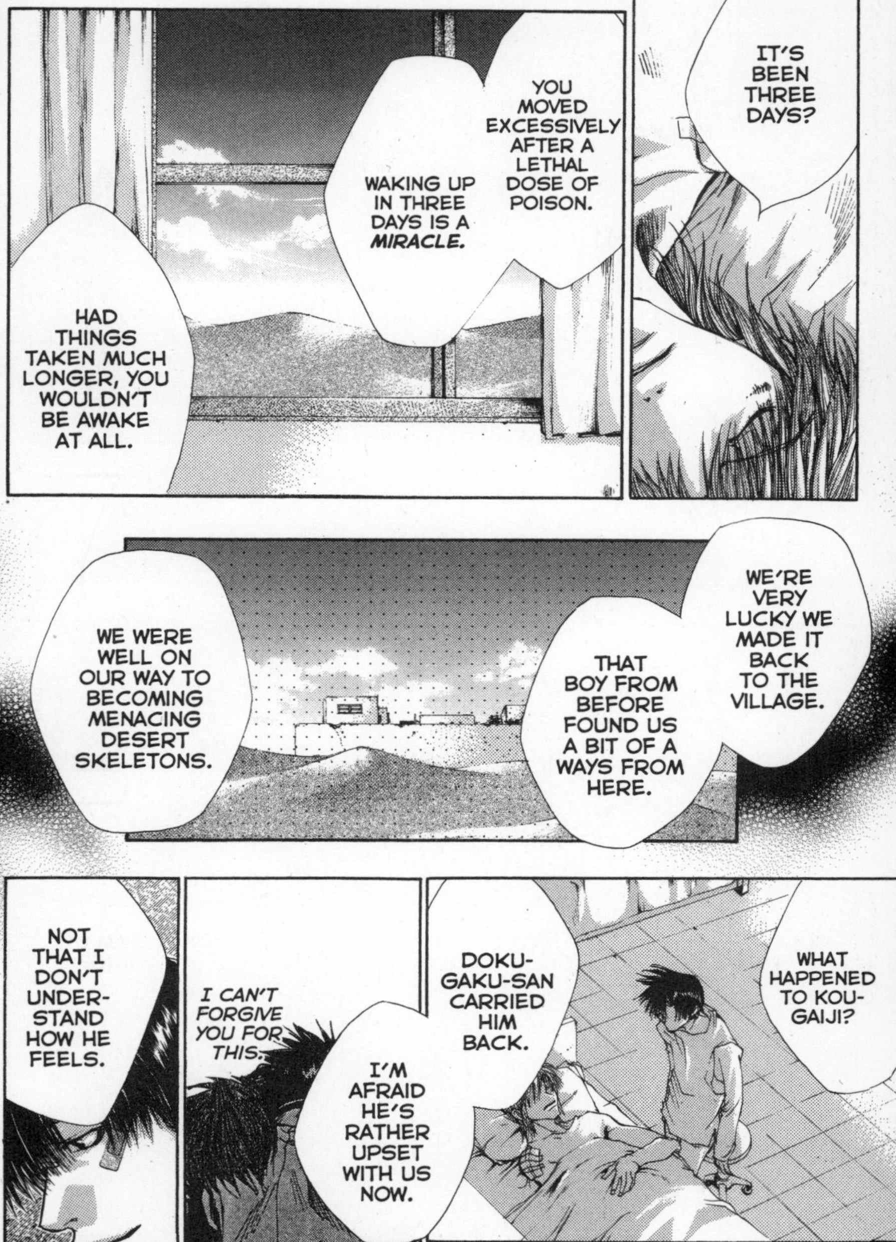
IT'S BEEN THREE DAYS?
YOU MOVED EXCESSIVELY AFTER A LETHAL DOSE OF POISON.
WAKING UP IN THREE DAYS IS A *MIRACLE.*
HAD THINGS TAKEN MUCH LONGER, YOU WOULDN'T BE AWAKE AT ALL.
WE'RE VERY LUCKY WE MADE IT BACK TO THE VILLAGE.
THAT BOY FROM BEFORE FOUND US A BIT OF A WAYS FROM HERE.
WE WERE WELL ON OUR WAY TO BECOMING MENACING DESERT SKELETONS.
WHAT HAPPENED TO KOU-GAIJI?
DOKU-GAKU-SAN CARRIED HIM BACK.
I'M AFRAID HE'S RATHER UPSET WITH US NOW.
I CAN'T FORGIVE YOU FOR THIS.
NOT THAT I DON'T UNDER-STAND HOW HE FEELS.

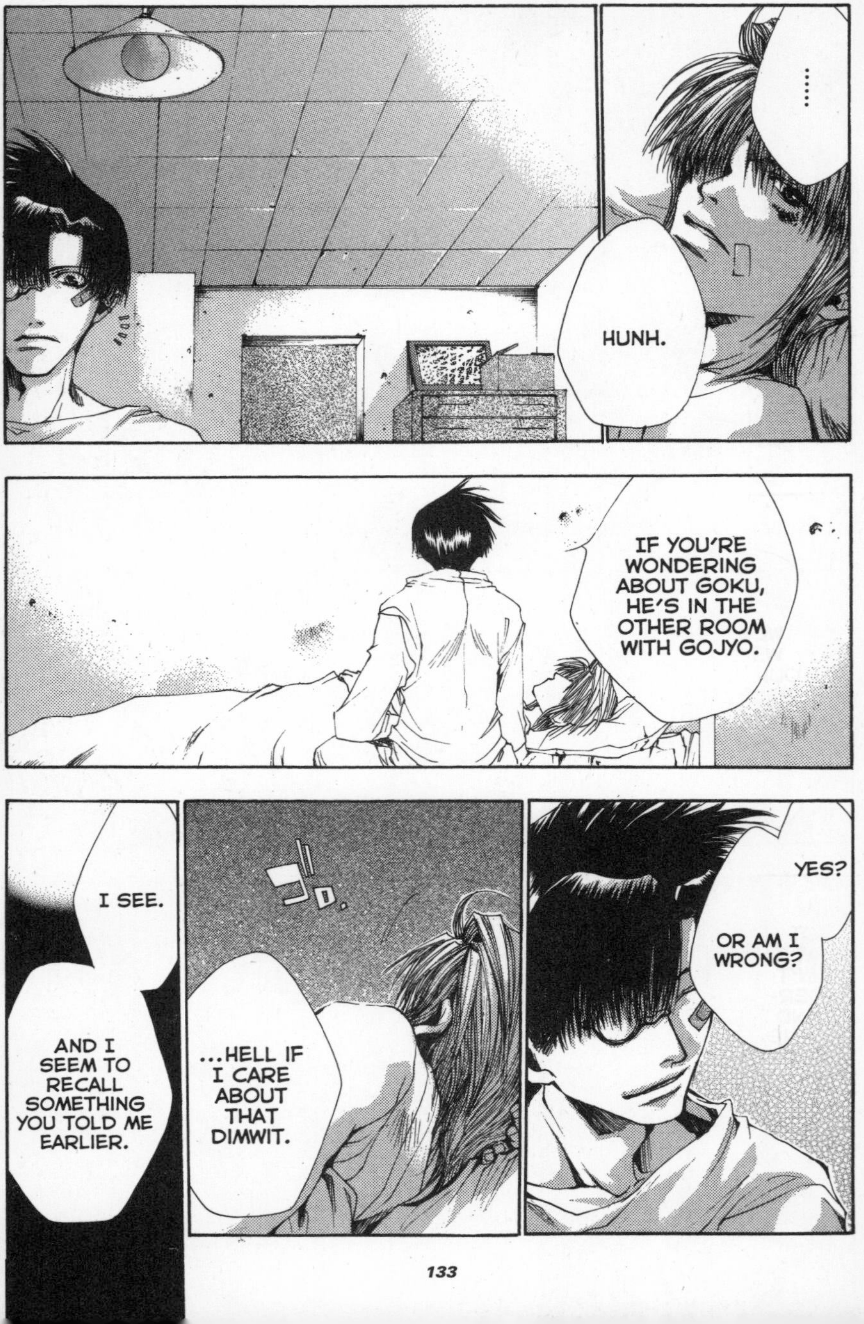
……
HUNH.
IF YOU'RE WONDERING ABOUT GOKU, HE'S IN THE OTHER ROOM WITH GOJYO.
YES?
OR AM I WRONG?
ゴロ。
...HELL IF I CARE ABOUT THAT DIMWIT.
I SEE.
AND I SEEM TO RECALL SOMETHING YOU TOLD ME EARLIER.

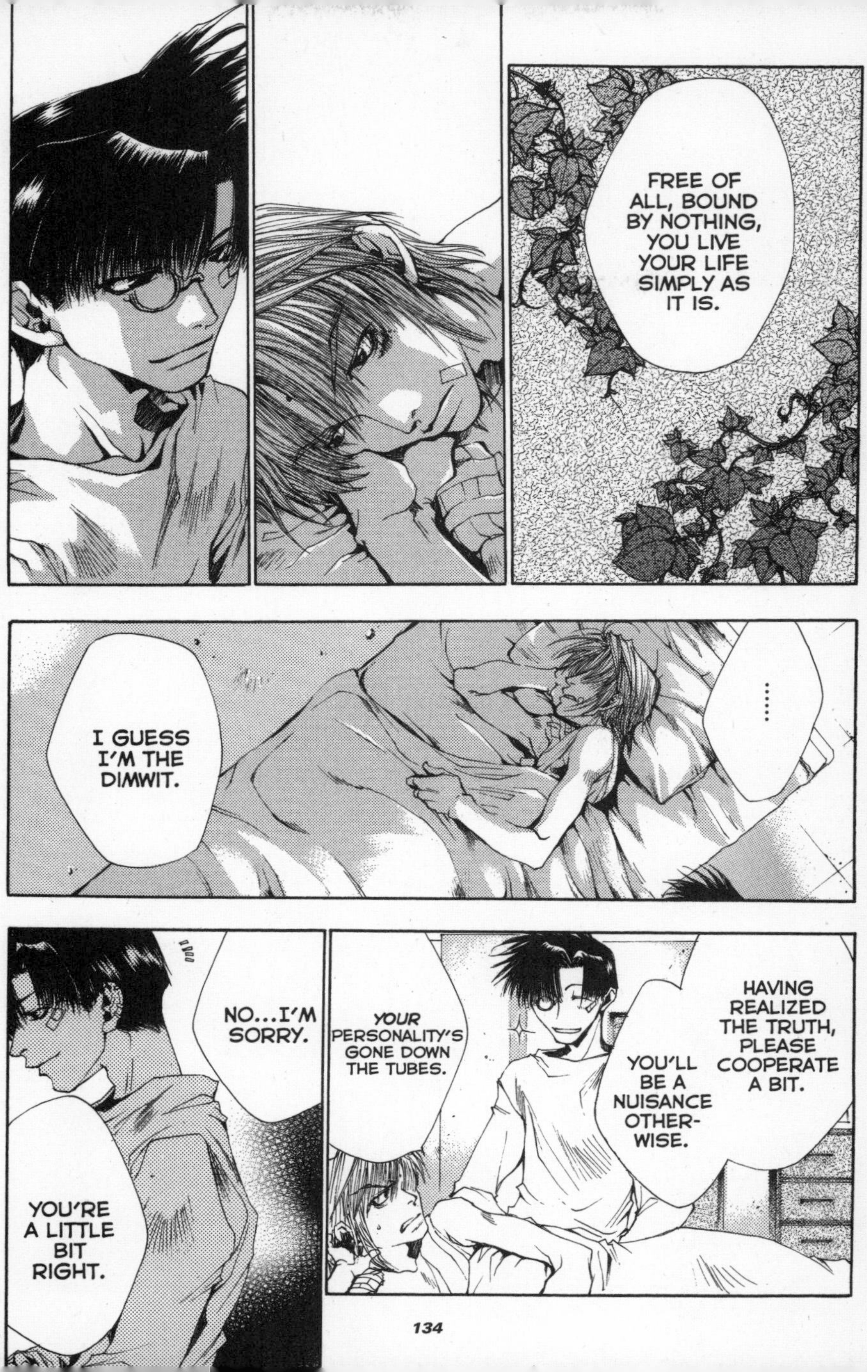
FREE OF ALL, BOUND BY NOTHING, YOU LIVE YOUR LIFE SIMPLY AS IT IS.
......
I GUESS I'M THE DIMWIT.
HAVING REALIZED THE TRUTH, PLEASE COOPERATE A BIT.
YOU'LL BE A NUISANCE OTHERWISE.
YOUR PERSONALITY'S GONE DOWN THE TUBES.
NO...I'M SORRY.
YOU'RE A LITTLE BIT RIGHT.

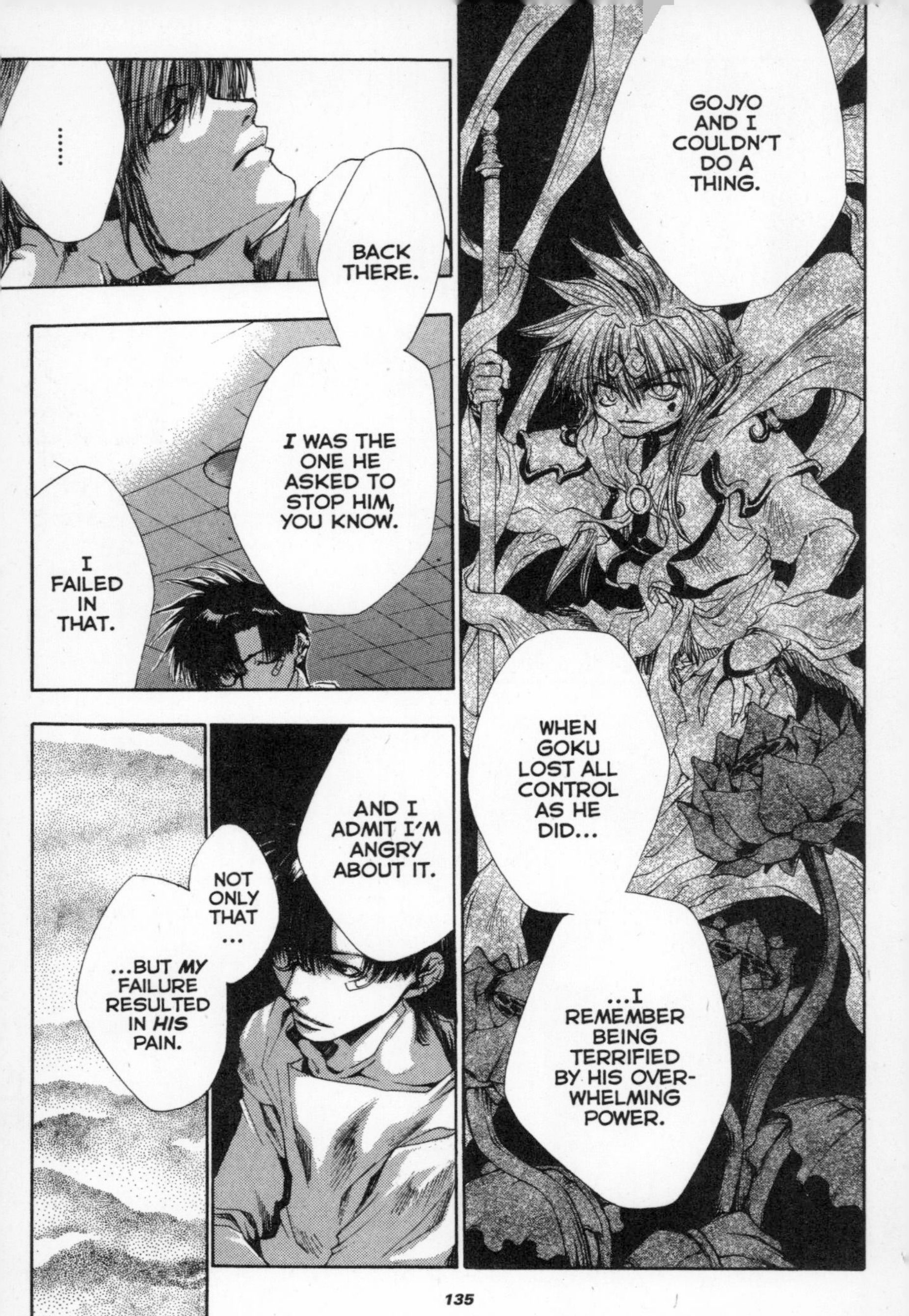
GOJYO AND I COULDN'T DO A THING.
WHEN GOKU LOST ALL CONTROL AS HE DID...
...I REMEMBER BEING TERRIFIED BY HIS OVER-WHELMING POWER.
......
BACK THERE.
I WAS THE ONE HE ASKED TO STOP HIM, YOU KNOW.
I FAILED IN THAT.
AND I ADMIT I'M ANGRY ABOUT IT.
NOT ONLY THAT...
...BUT *MY* FAILURE RESULTED IN *HIS* PAIN.

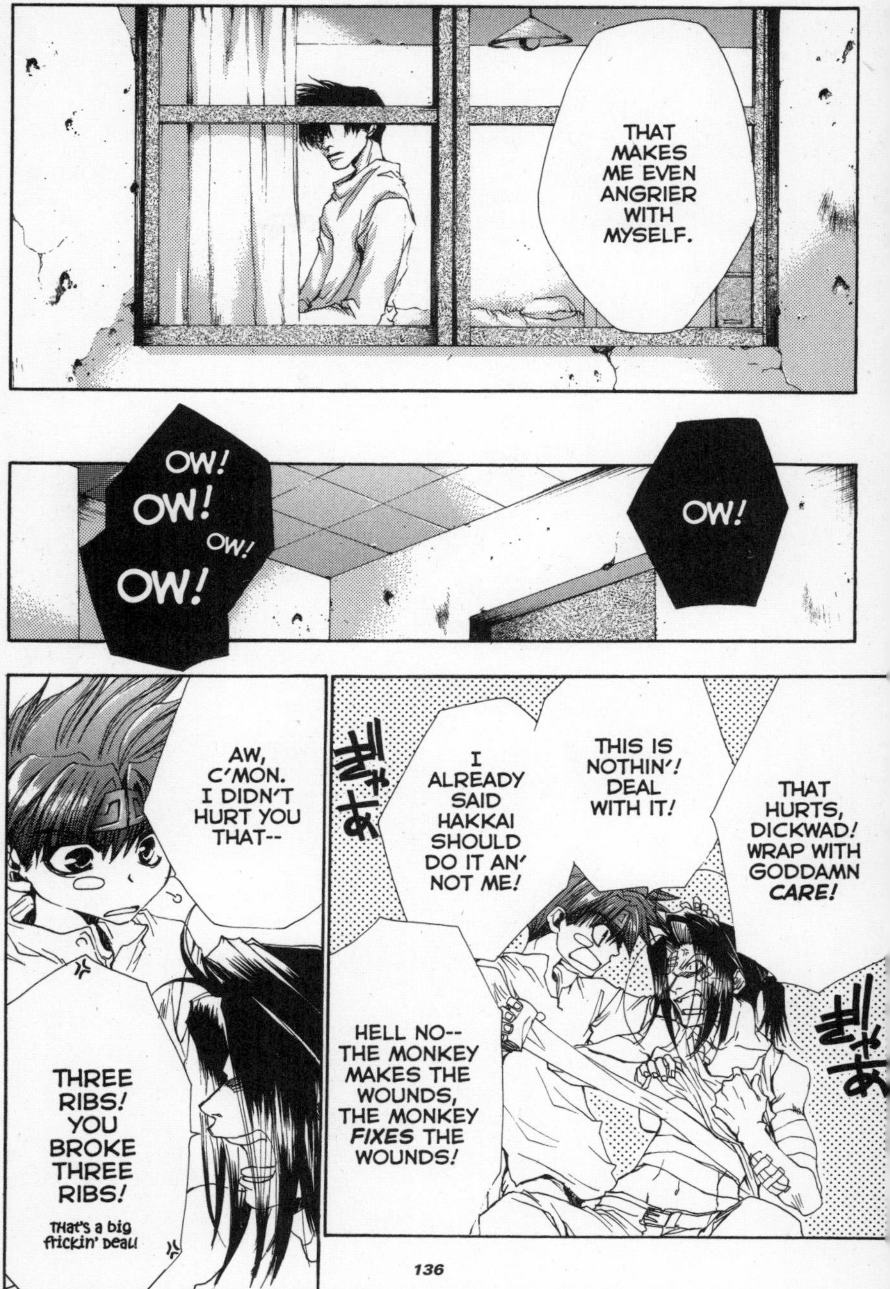

THAT MAKES ME EVEN ANGRIER WITH MYSELF.
OW!
OW! OW! OW! OW!
ぎゃあ
THAT HURTS, DICKWAD! WRAP WITH GODDAMN CARE!
THIS IS NOTHIN'! DEAL WITH IT!
I ALREADY SAID HAKKAI SHOULD DO IT AN' NOT ME!
ぎゃあ
HELL NO-- THE MONKEY MAKES THE WOUNDS, THE MONKEY FIXES THE WOUNDS!
AW, C'MON. I DIDN'T HURT YOU THAT--
THREE RIBS! YOU BROKE THREE RIBS!
THAT'S a big frickin' deal!

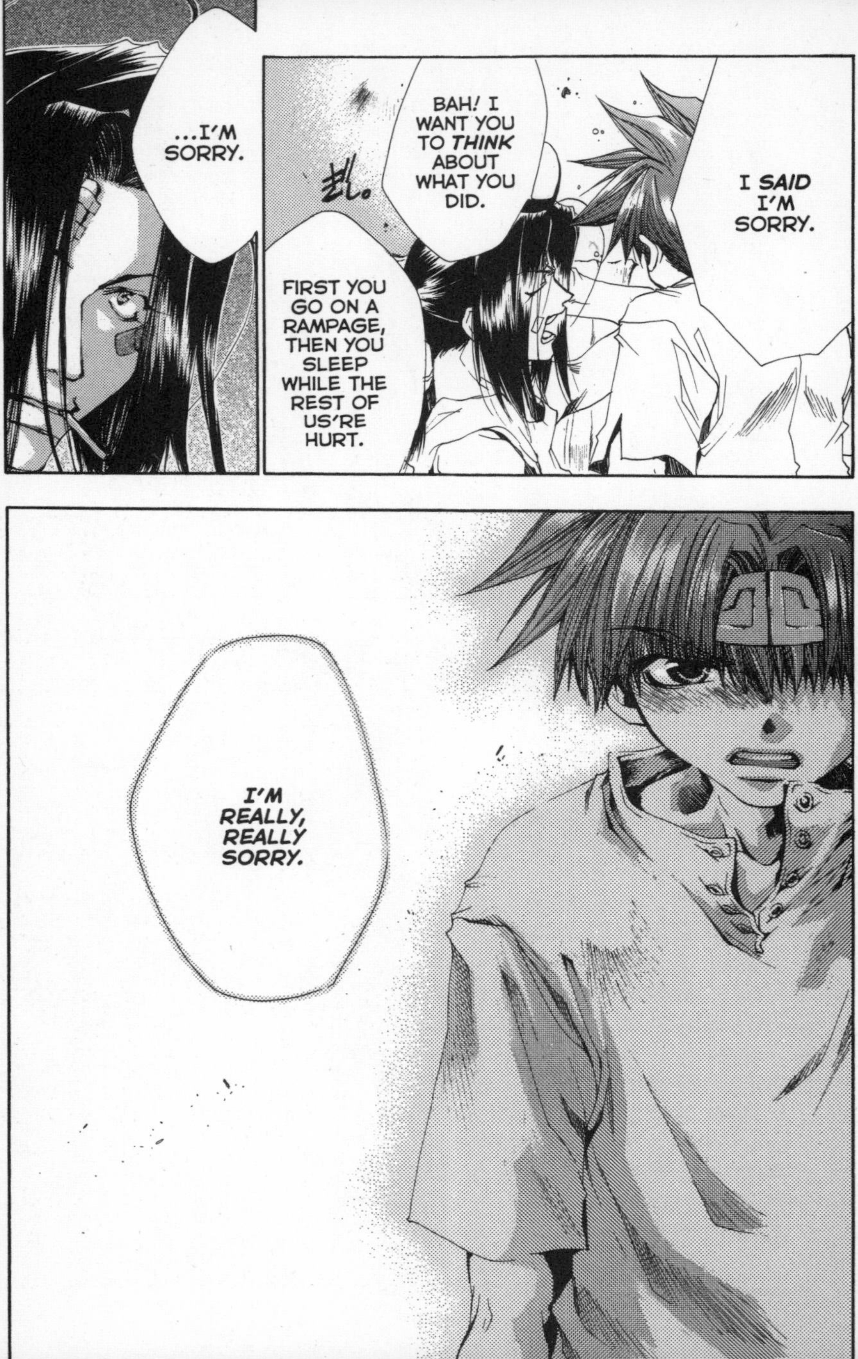
I SAID I'M SORRY.
BAH! I WANT YOU TO THINK ABOUT WHAT YOU DID.
FIRST YOU GO ON A RAMPAGE, THEN YOU SLEEP WHILE THE REST OF US'RE HURT.
...I'M SORRY.
I'M REALLY, REALLY SORRY.

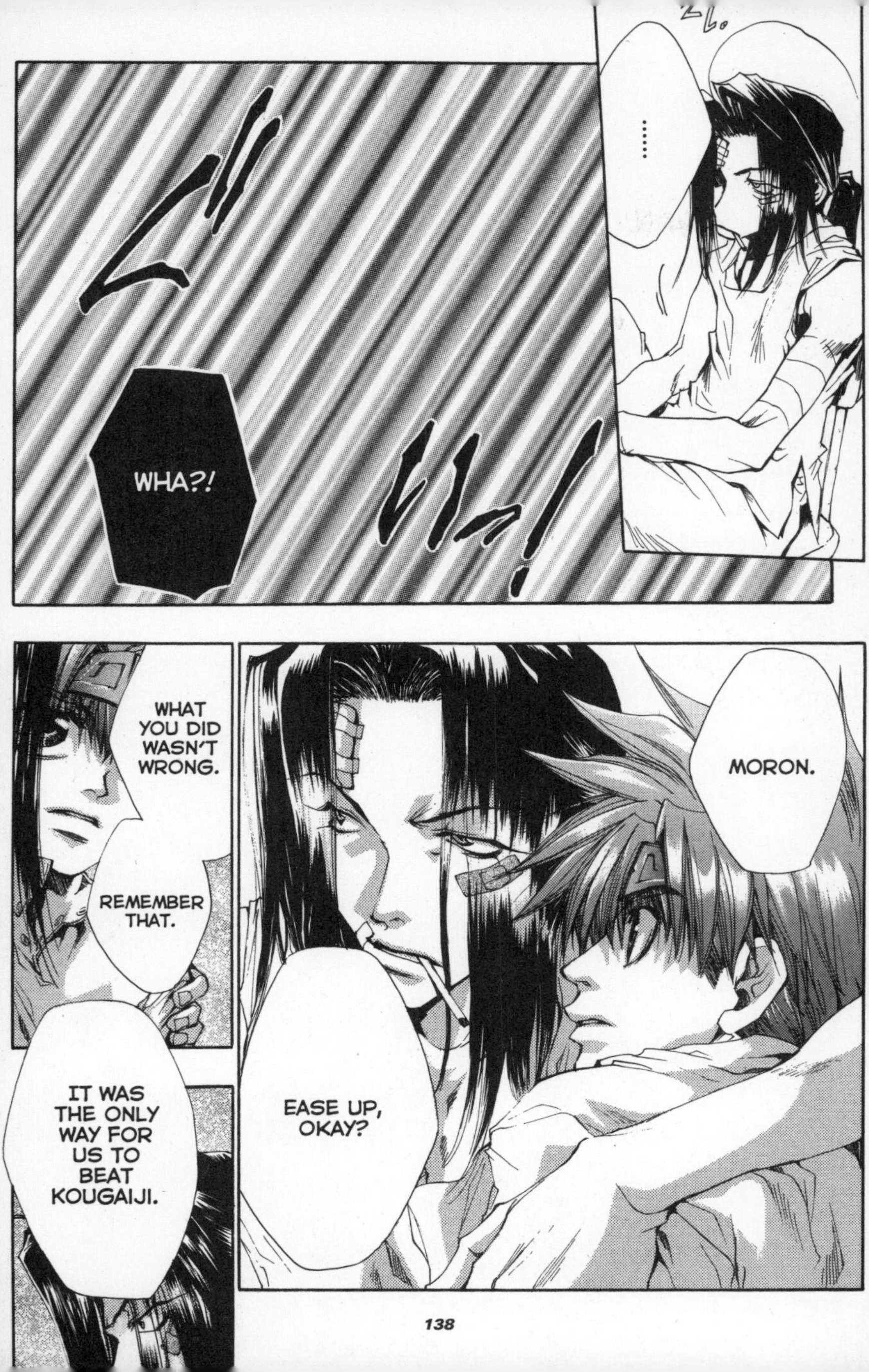
......
WHA?!
MORON.
EASE UP, OKAY?
WHAT YOU DID WASN'T WRONG.
REMEMBER THAT.
IT WAS THE ONLY WAY FOR US TO BEAT KOUGAIJI.

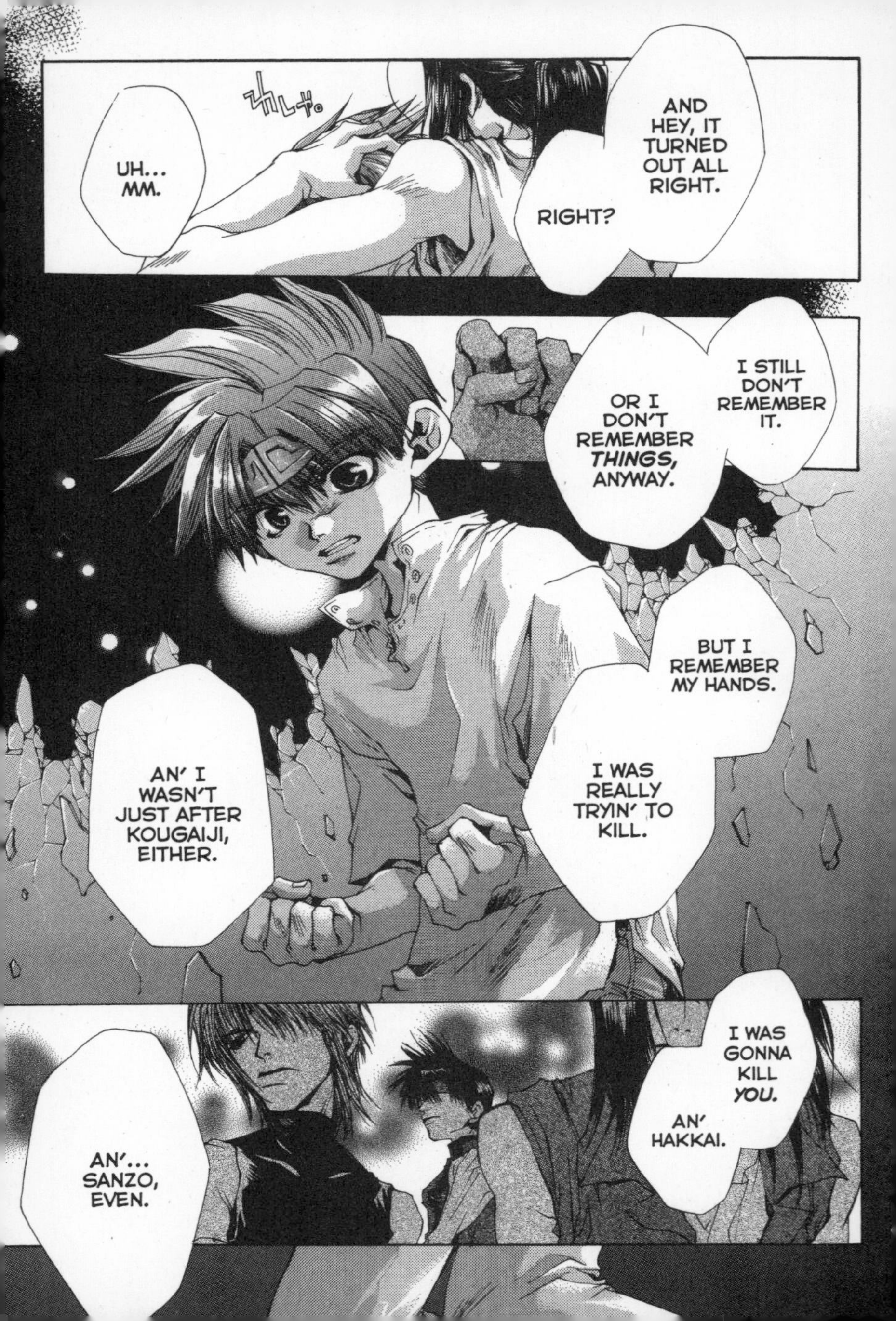
AND HEY, IT TURNED OUT ALL RIGHT.
RIGHT?
UH... MM.
I STILL DON'T REMEMBER IT.
OR I DON'T REMEMBER *THINGS*, ANYWAY.
BUT I REMEMBER MY HANDS.
I WAS REALLY TRYIN' TO KILL.
AN' I WASN'T JUST AFTER KOUGAIJI, EITHER.
I WAS GONNA KILL *YOU*.
AN' HAKKAI.
AN'... SANZO, EVEN.

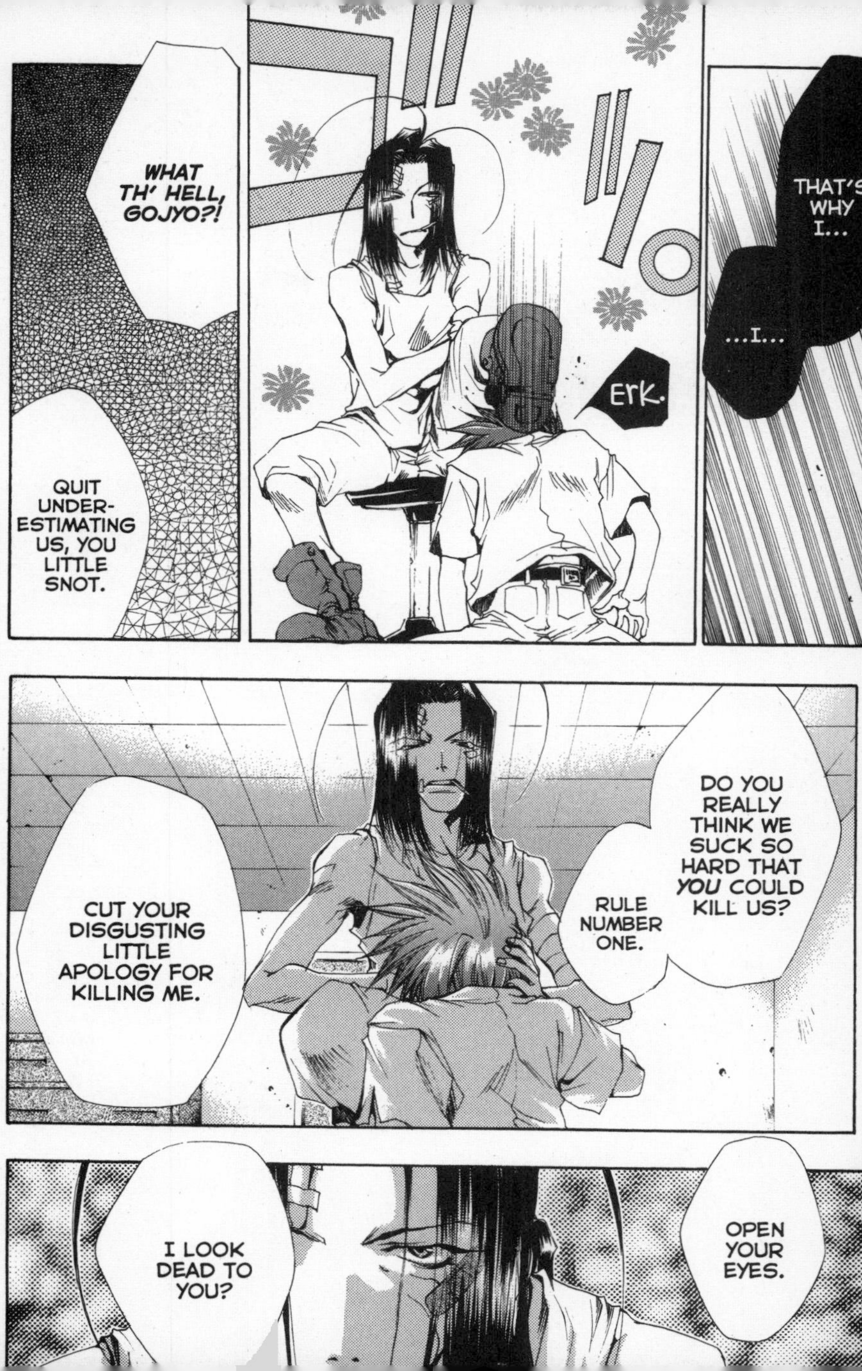
THAT'S WHY I...
...I...
Erk.
WHAT TH' HELL, GOJYO?!
QUIT UNDER-ESTIMATING US, YOU LITTLE SNOT.
DO YOU REALLY THINK WE SUCK SO HARD THAT *YOU* COULD KILL US?
RULE NUMBER ONE.
CUT YOUR DISGUSTING LITTLE APOLOGY FOR KILLING ME.
OPEN YOUR EYES.
I LOOK DEAD TO YOU?

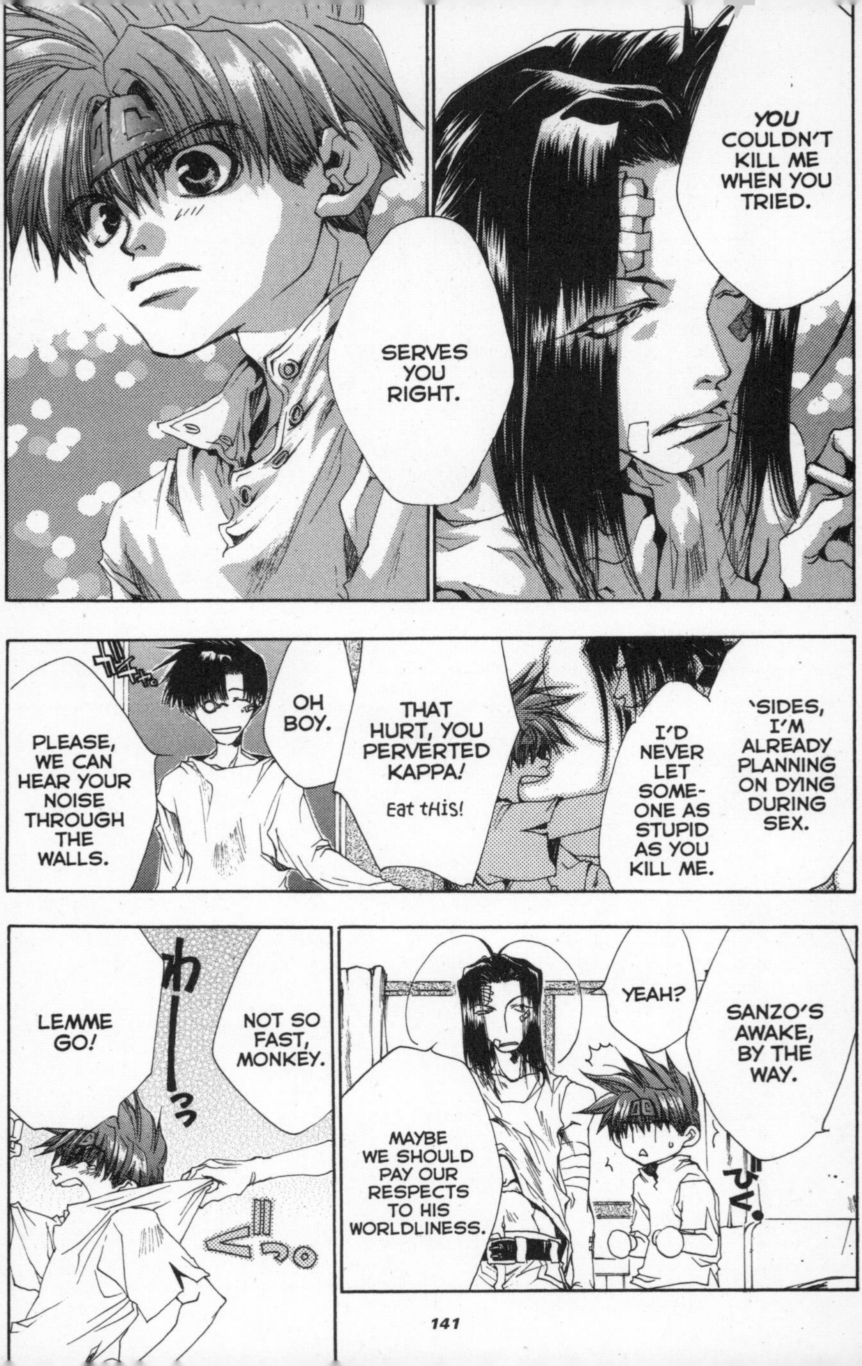
YOU COULDN'T KILL ME WHEN YOU TRIED.
SERVES YOU RIGHT.
'SIDES, I'M ALREADY PLANNING ON DYING DURING SEX.
I'D NEVER LET SOME-ONE AS STUPID AS YOU KILL ME.
THAT HURT, YOU PERVERTED KAPPA!
Eat tHIS!
OH BOY.
PLEASE, WE CAN HEAR YOUR NOISE THROUGH THE WALLS.
SANZO'S AWAKE, BY THE WAY.
YEAH?
MAYBE WE SHOULD PAY OUR RESPECTS TO HIS WORLDLINESS.
NOT SO FAST, MONKEY.
LEMME GO!

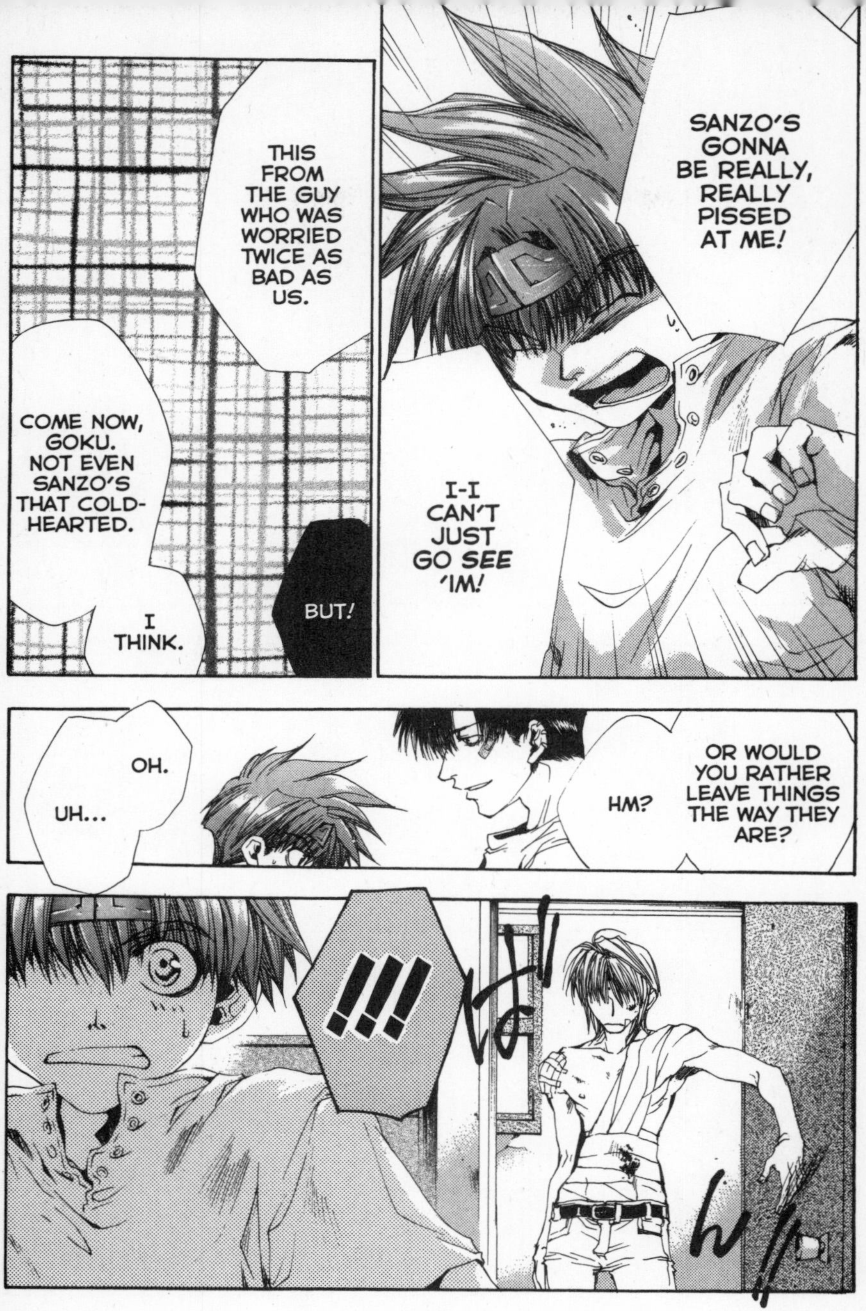
SANZO'S GONNA BE REALLY, REALLY PISSED AT ME!
I-I CAN'T JUST GO SEE 'IM!
THIS FROM THE GUY WHO WAS WORRIED TWICE AS BAD AS US.
BUT!
COME NOW, GOKU. NOT EVEN SANZO'S THAT COLD-HEARTED.
I THINK.
OR WOULD YOU RATHER LEAVE THINGS THE WAY THEY ARE?
HM?
OH.
UH...
!!!

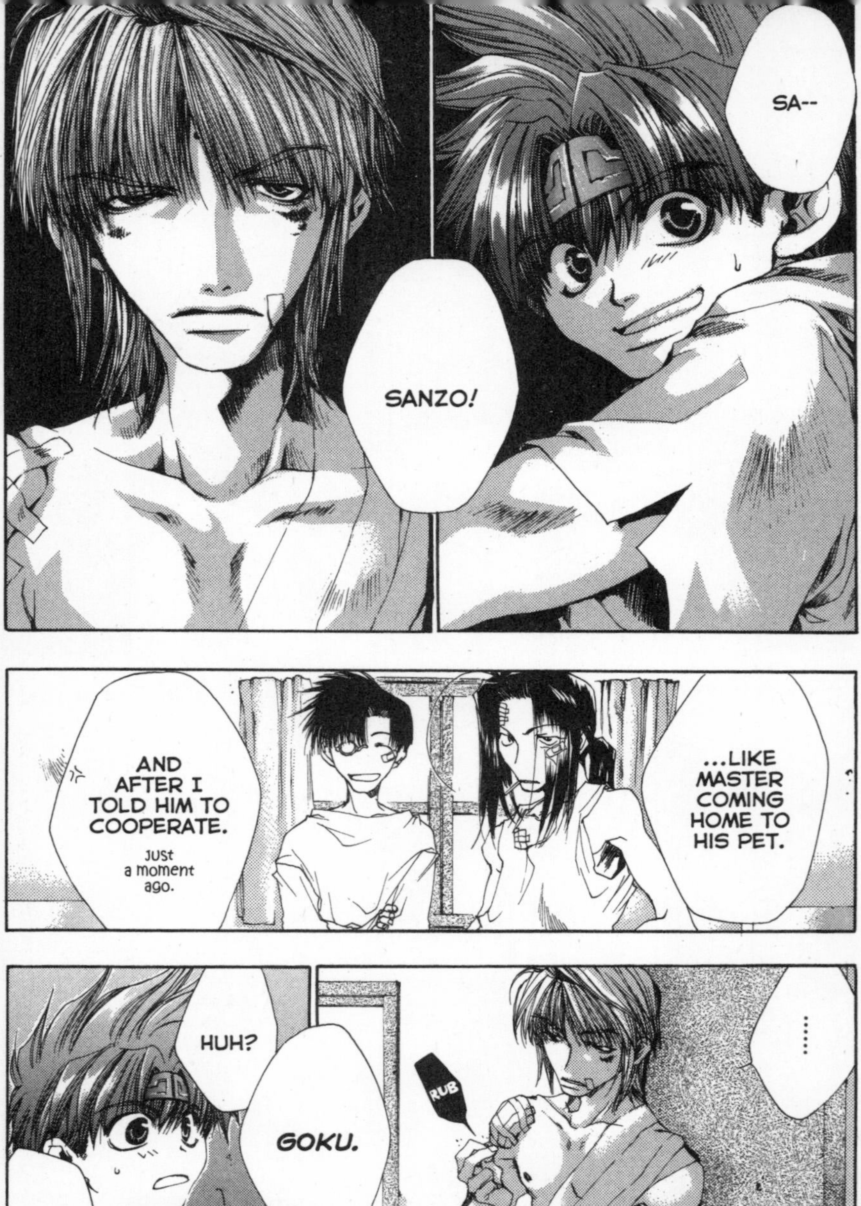
SA--
SANZO!
...LIKE MASTER COMING HOME TO HIS PET.
AND AFTER I TOLD HIM TO COOPERATE.
JUST a moment ago.
......
RUB
GOKU.
HUH?
UH, WHAT?
はっ

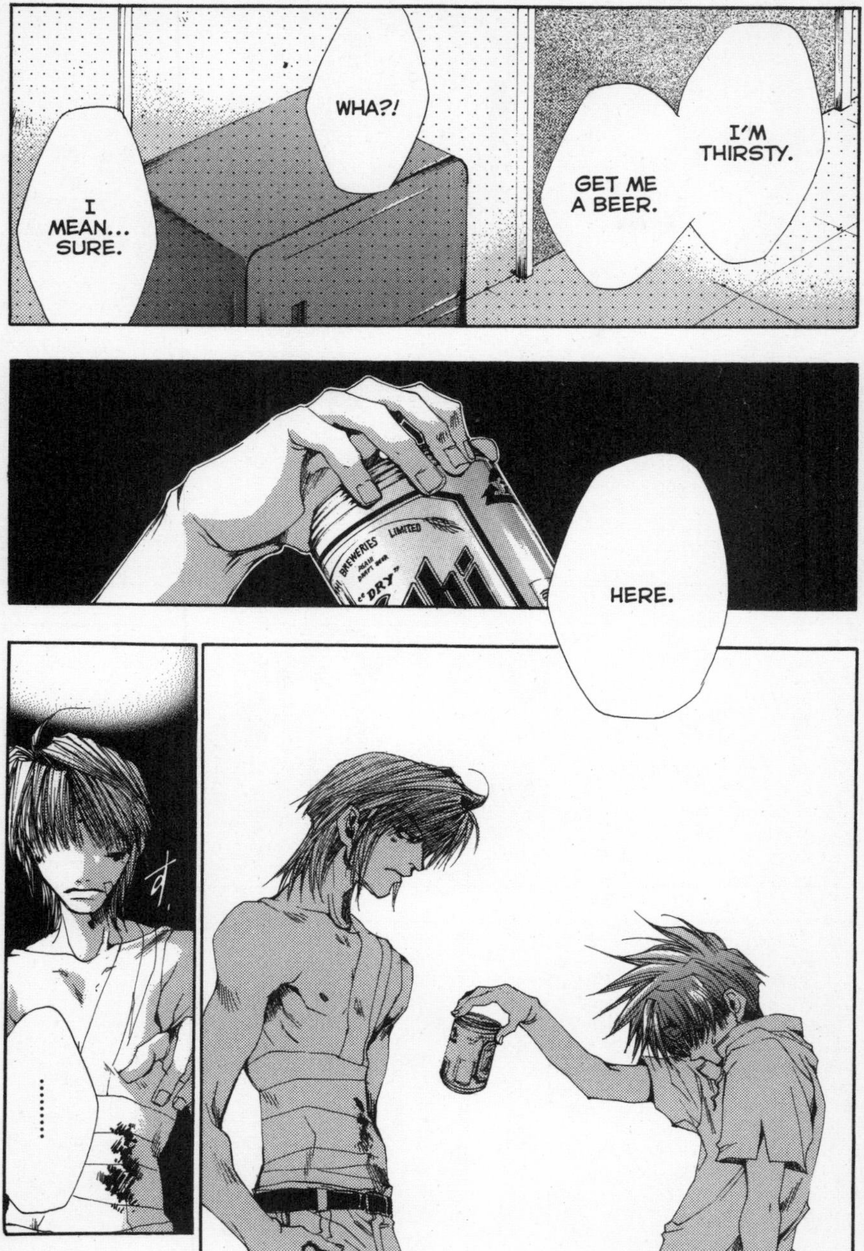
I'M THIRSTY.
GET ME A BEER.
WHA?!
I MEAN... SURE.
BREWERIES LIMITED
"DRY"
HERE.
す
....

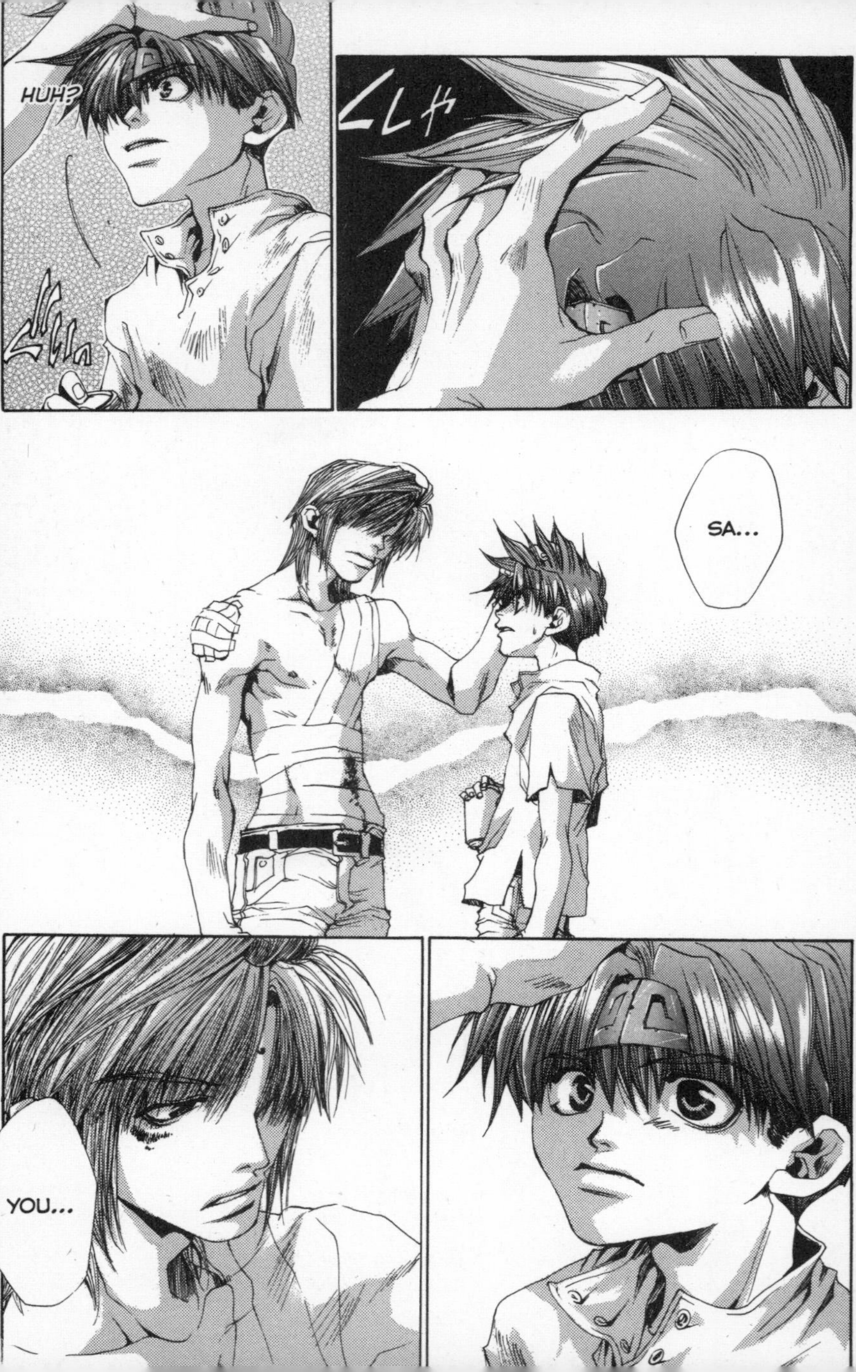
HUH?
SA...
YOU...

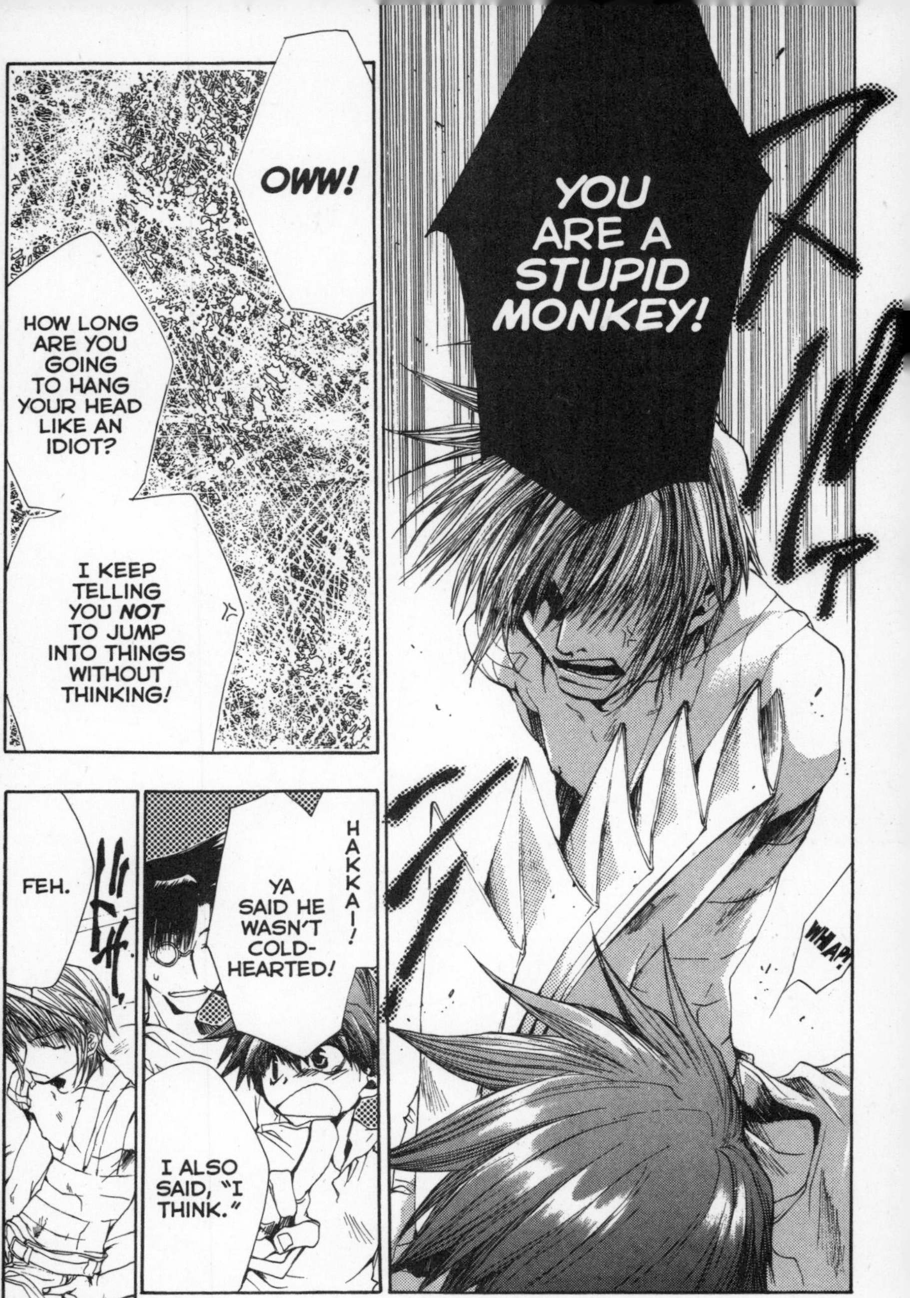
YOU ARE A STUPID MONKEY!
WHAP!
OWW!
HOW LONG ARE YOU GOING TO HANG YOUR HEAD LIKE AN IDIOT?
I KEEP TELLING YOU *NOT* TO JUMP INTO THINGS WITHOUT THINKING!
HAKKAI!
YA SAID HE WASN'T COLD-HEARTED!
I ALSO SAID, "I THINK."
FEH.

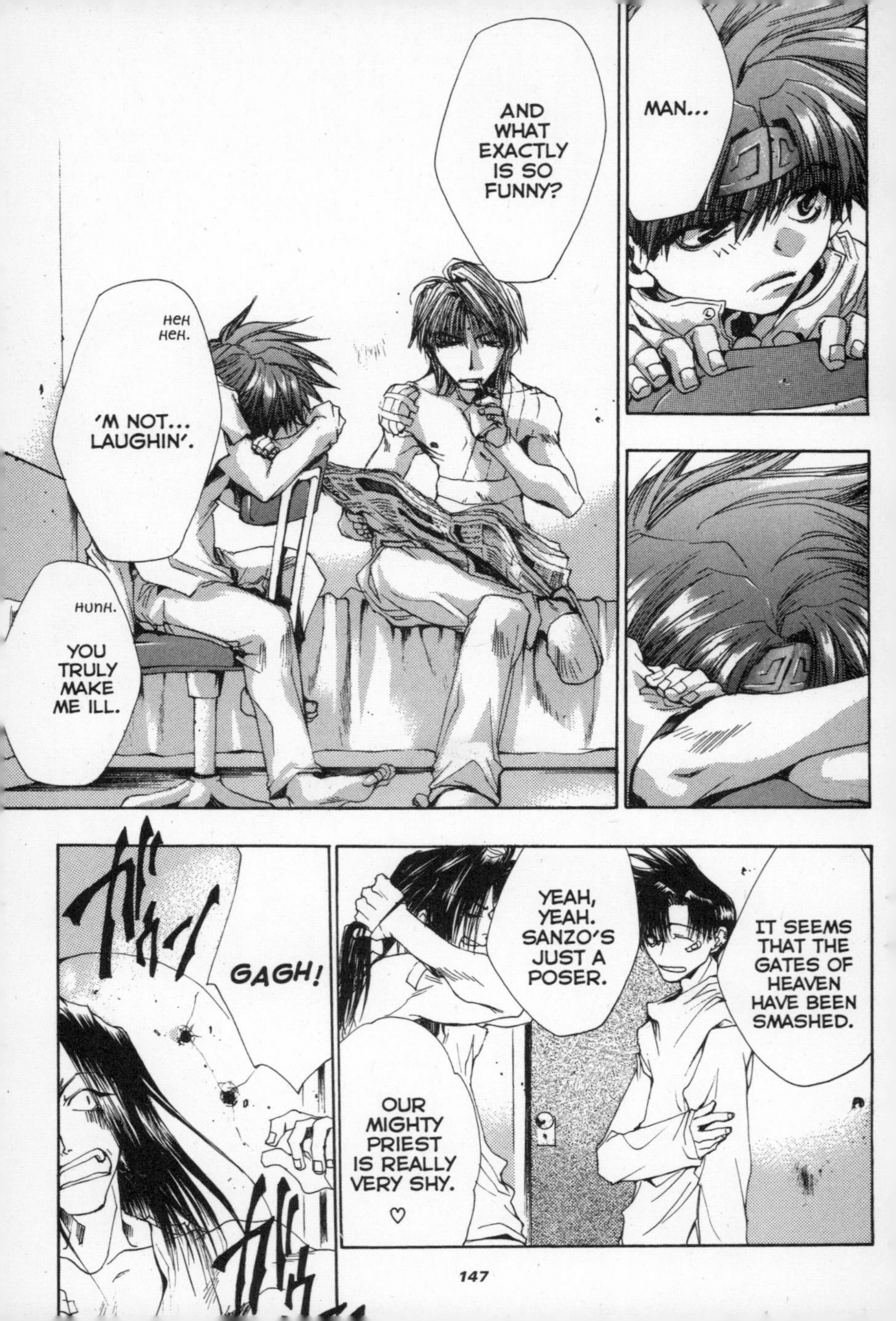
MAN...
AND WHAT EXACTLY IS SO FUNNY?
HEH HEH.
'M NOT... LAUGHIN'.
HUNH.
YOU TRULY MAKE ME ILL.
IT SEEMS THAT THE GATES OF HEAVEN HAVE BEEN SMASHED.
YEAH, YEAH. SANZO'S JUST A POSER.
OUR MIGHTY PRIEST IS REALLY VERY SHY. ♡
GAGH!

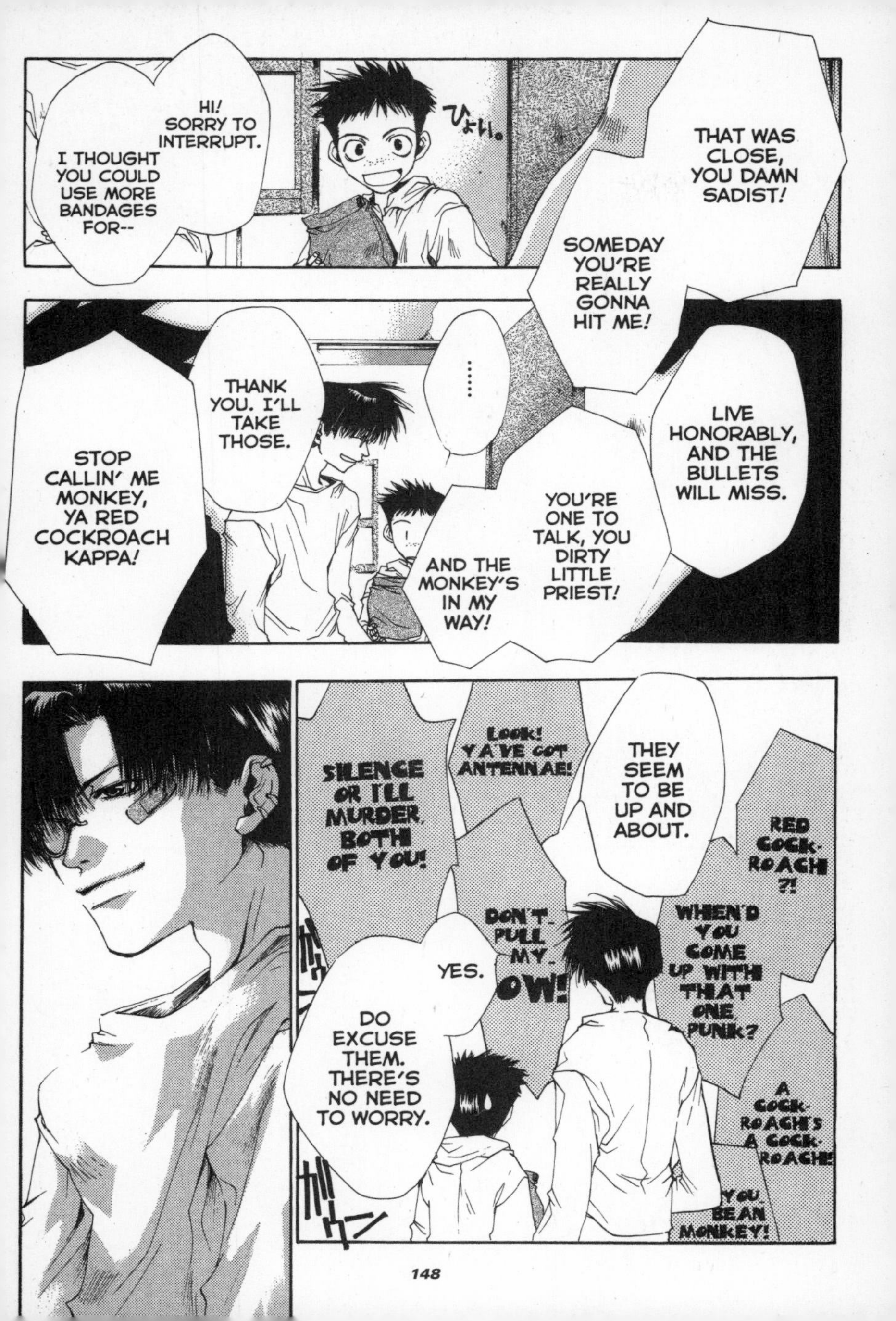
THAT WAS CLOSE, YOU DAMN SADIST!
SOMEDAY YOU'RE REALLY GONNA HIT ME!
ひょい。
HI! SORRY TO INTERRUPT.
I THOUGHT YOU COULD USE MORE BANDAGES FOR--
LIVE HONORABLY, AND THE BULLETS WILL MISS.
YOU'RE ONE TO TALK, YOU DIRTY LITTLE PRIEST!
AND THE MONKEY'S IN MY WAY!
......
THANK YOU. I'LL TAKE THOSE.
STOP CALLIN' ME MONKEY, YA RED COCKROACH KAPPA!
RED COCKROACH?!
A COCKROACH'S A COCKROACH!
YOU BEAN MONKEY!
WHEN'D YOU COME UP WITH THAT ONE, PUNK?
THEY SEEM TO BE UP AND ABOUT.
LOOK! YA'VE GOT ANTENNAE!
DON'T PULL MY- OW!
SILENCE OR I'LL MURDER BOTH OF YOU!
YES.
DO EXCUSE THEM. THERE'S NO NEED TO WORRY.

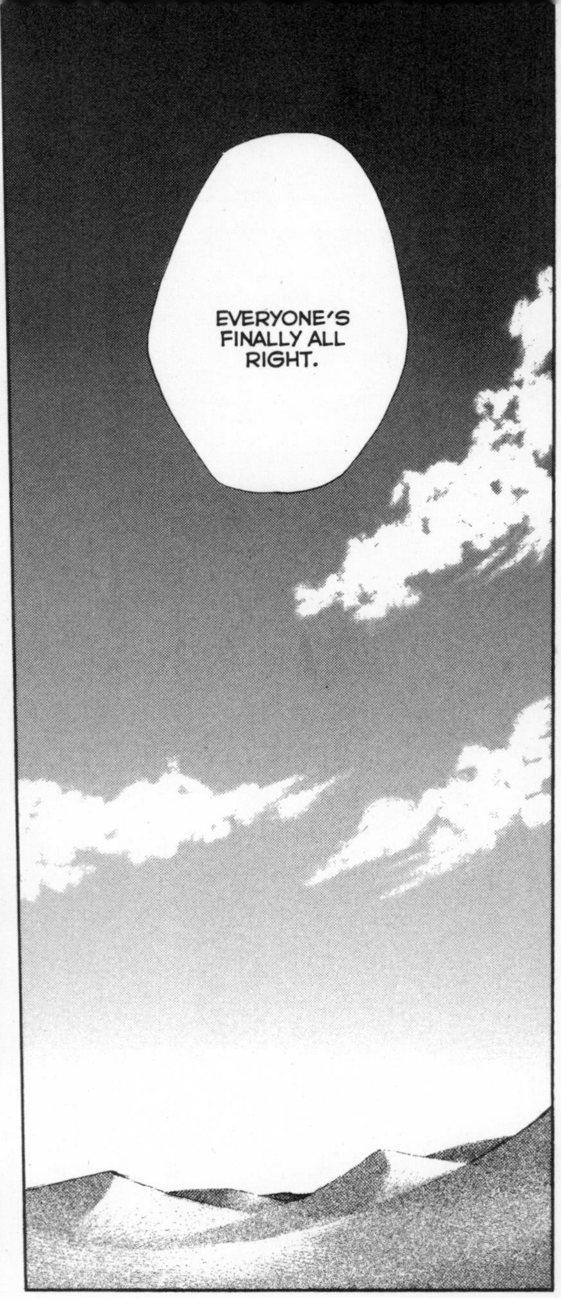
EVERYONE'S FINALLY ALL RIGHT.
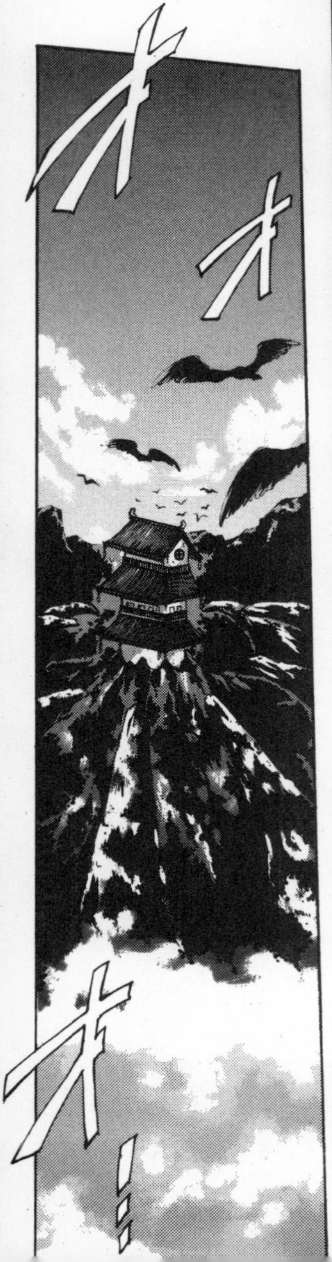
オオオ!!

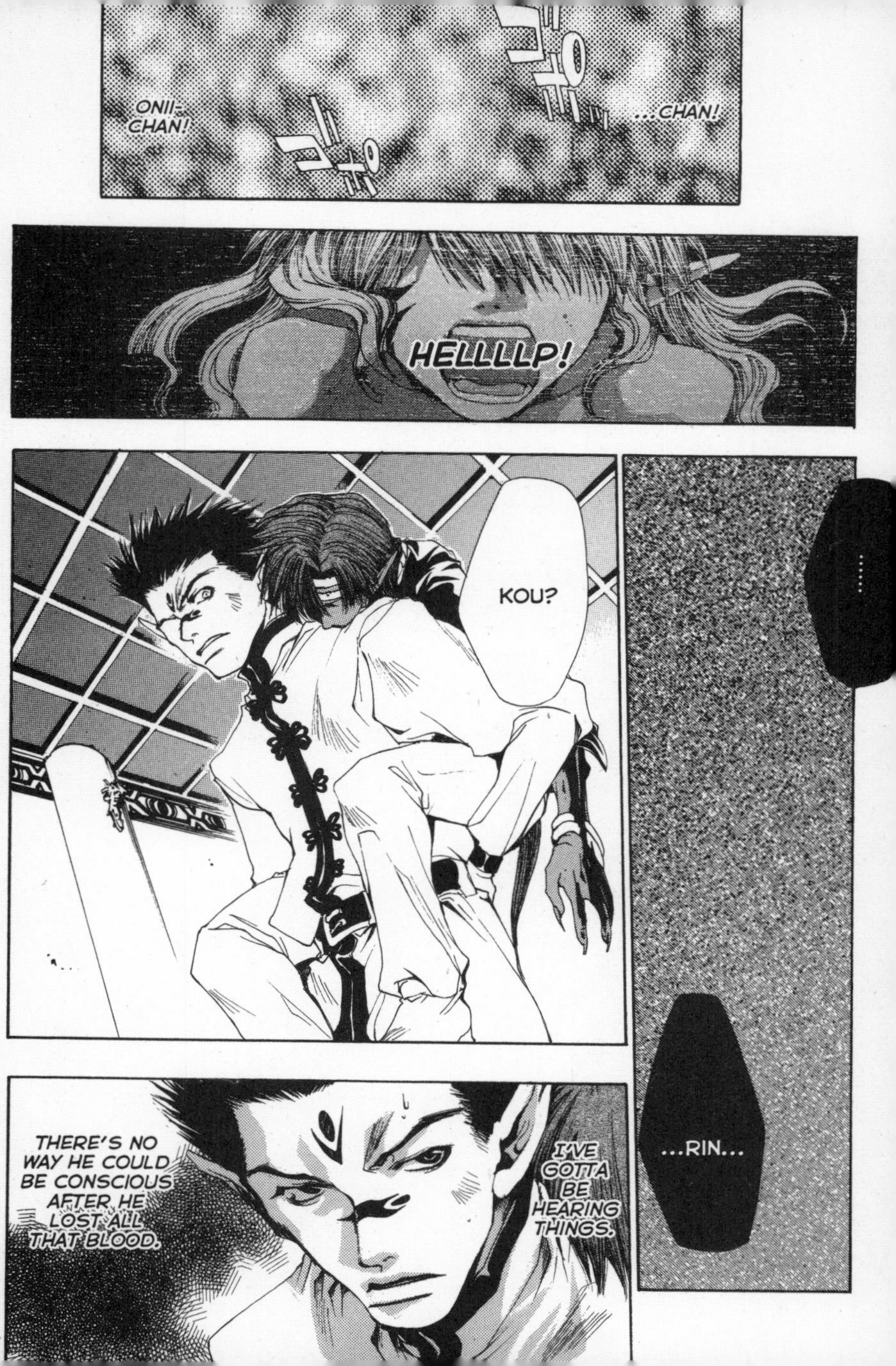
...CHAN!
ONII-CHAN!
HELLLLP!
......
...RIN...
KOU?
I'VE GOTTA BE HEARING THINGS.
THERE'S NO WAY HE COULD BE CONSCIOUS AFTER HE LOST ALL THAT BLOOD.

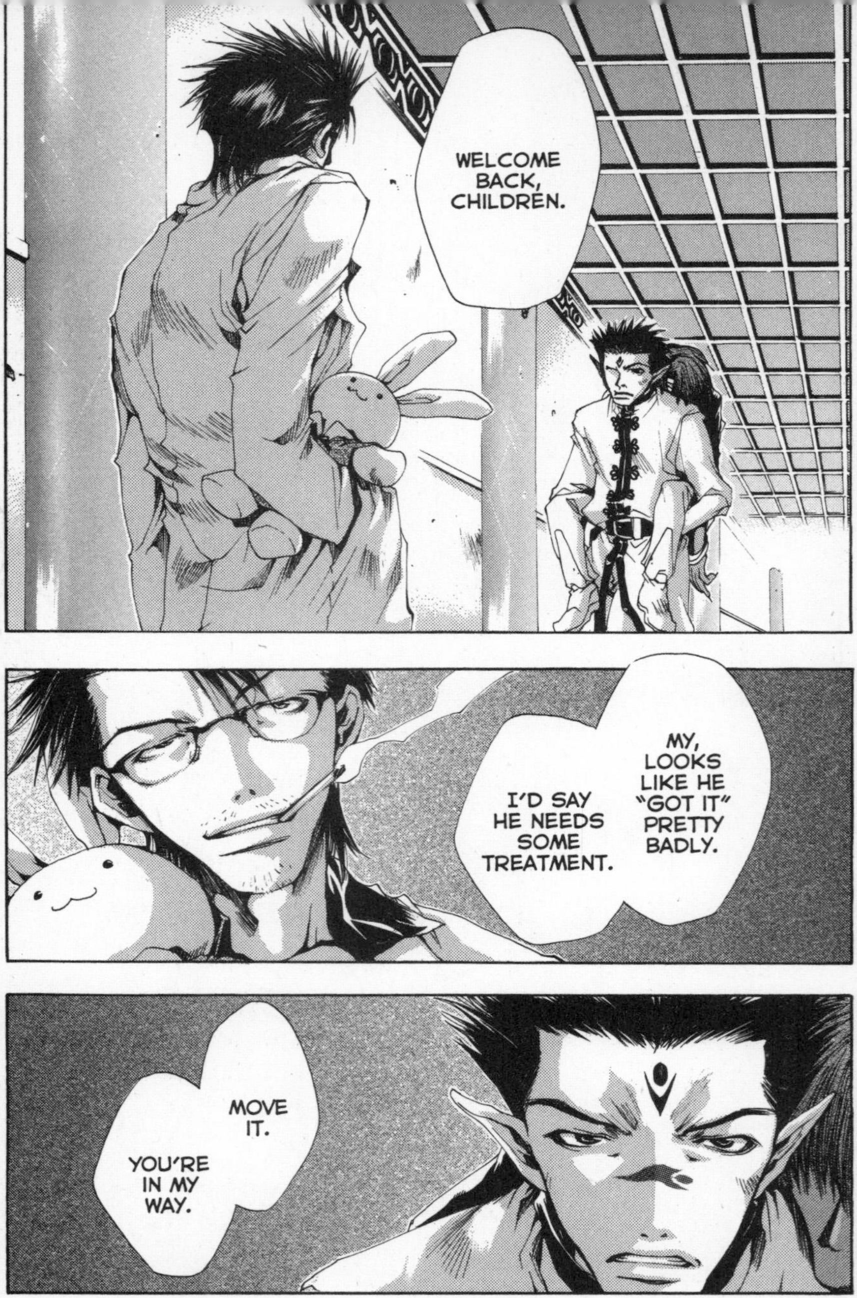
WELCOME BACK, CHILDREN.
MY, LOOKS LIKE HE "GOT IT" PRETTY BADLY.
I'D SAY HE NEEDS SOME TREATMENT.
MOVE IT.
YOU'RE IN MY WAY.

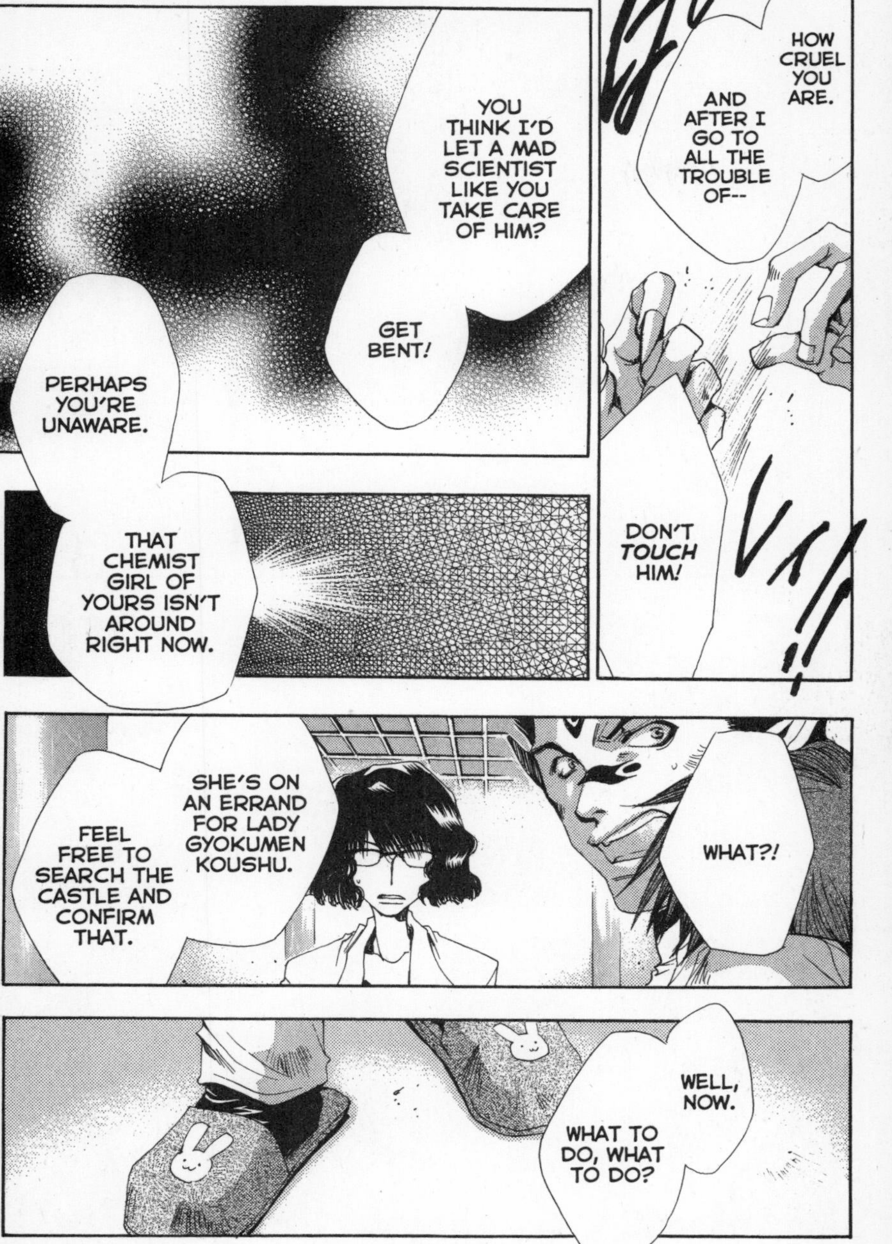
HOW CRUEL YOU ARE.
AND AFTER I GO TO ALL THE TROUBLE OF--
DON'T *TOUCH* HIM!
YOU THINK I'D LET A MAD SCIENTIST LIKE YOU TAKE CARE OF HIM?
GET BENT!
PERHAPS YOU'RE UNAWARE.
THAT CHEMIST GIRL OF YOURS ISN'T AROUND RIGHT NOW.
WHAT?!
SHE'S ON AN ERRAND FOR LADY GYOKUMEN KOUSHU.
FEEL FREE TO SEARCH THE CASTLE AND CONFIRM THAT.
WELL, NOW.
WHAT TO DO, WHAT TO DO?

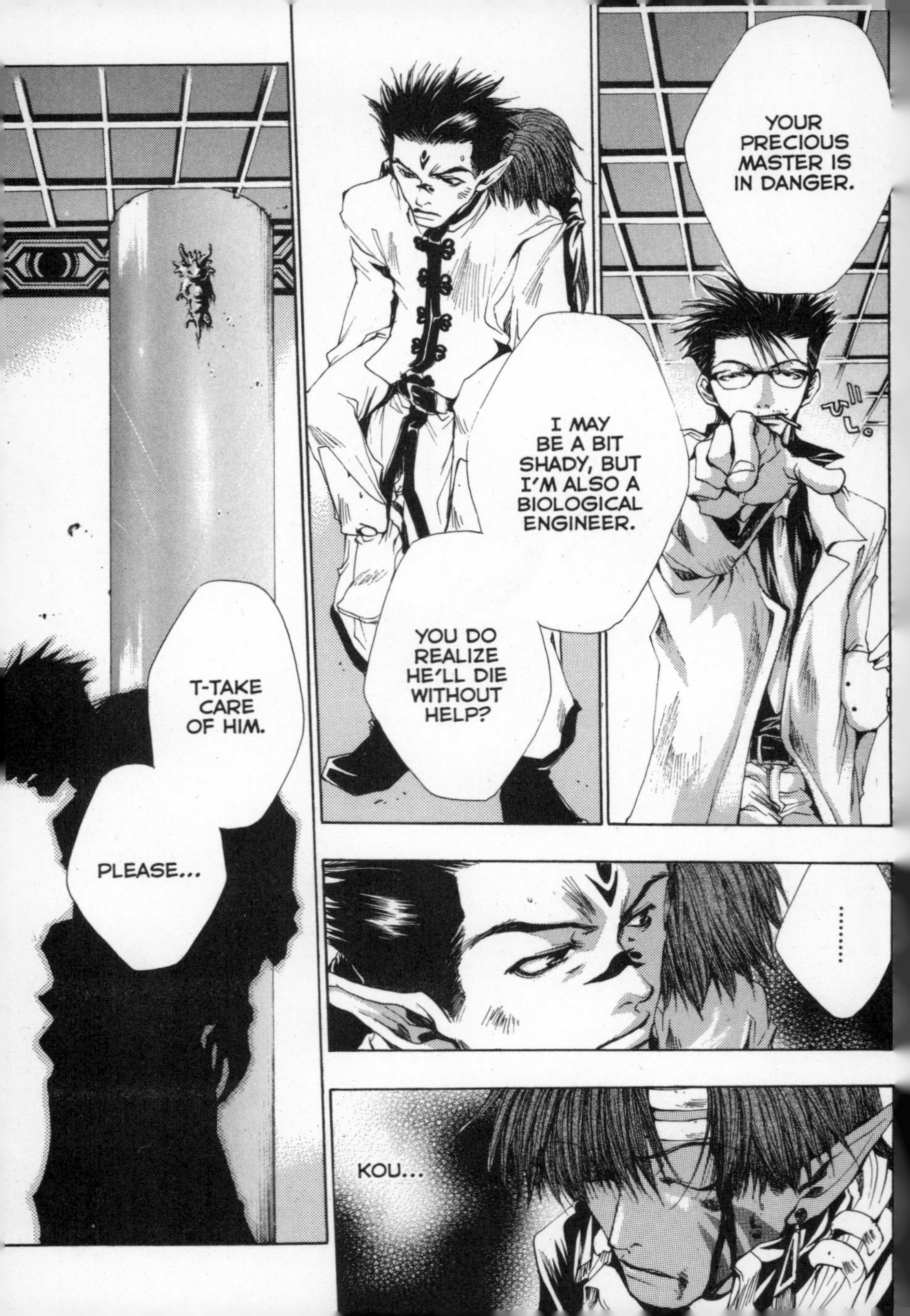
YOUR PRECIOUS MASTER IS IN DANGER.
I MAY BE A BIT SHADY, BUT I'M ALSO A BIOLOGICAL ENGINEER.
YOU DO REALIZE HE'LL DIE WITHOUT HELP?
......
KOU...
T-TAKE CARE OF HIM.
PLEASE...

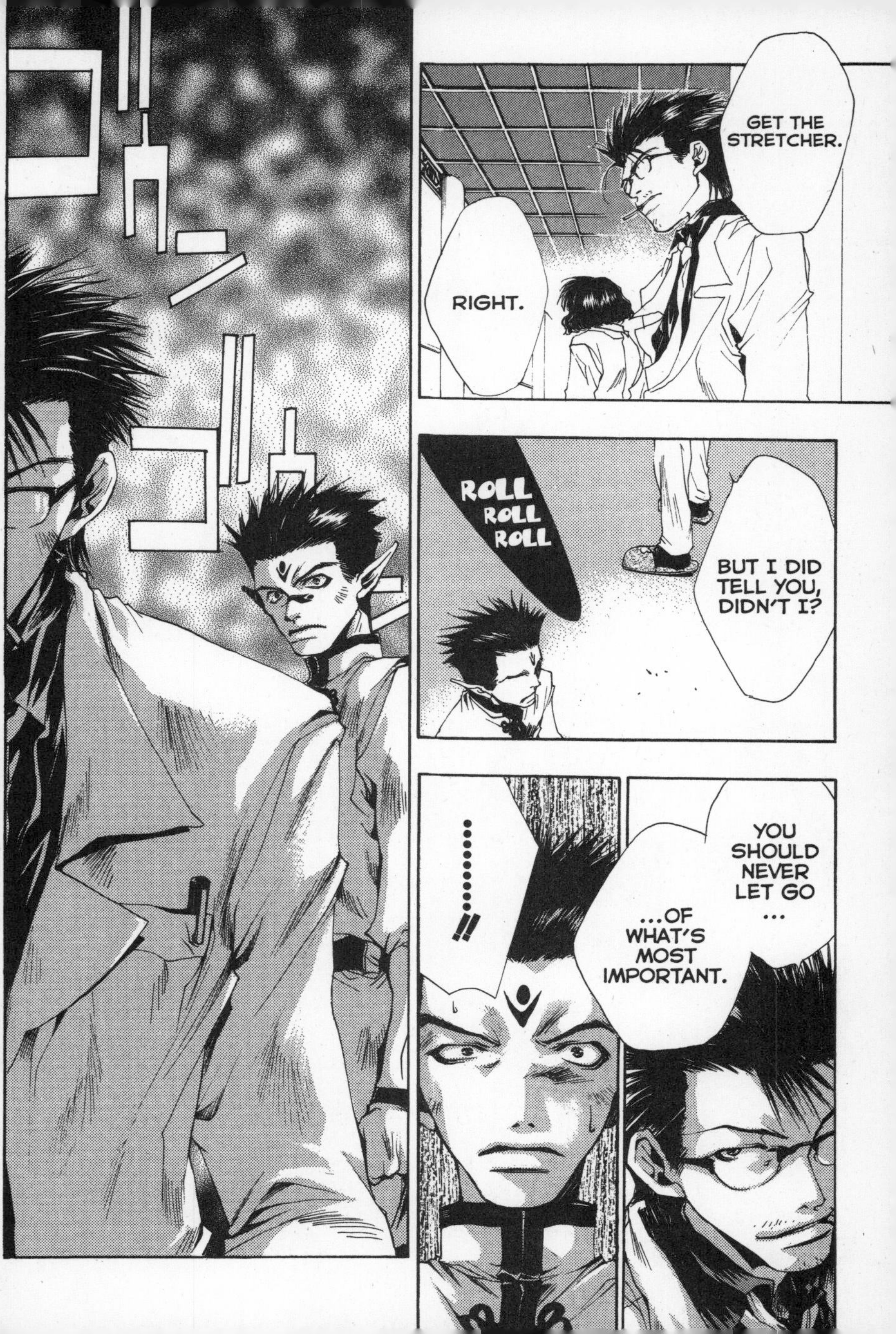
GET THE STRETCHER.
RIGHT.
BUT I DID TELL YOU, DIDN'T I?
ROLL ROLL ROLL
YOU SHOULD NEVER LET GO ...
...OF WHAT'S MOST IMPORTANT.
........!!

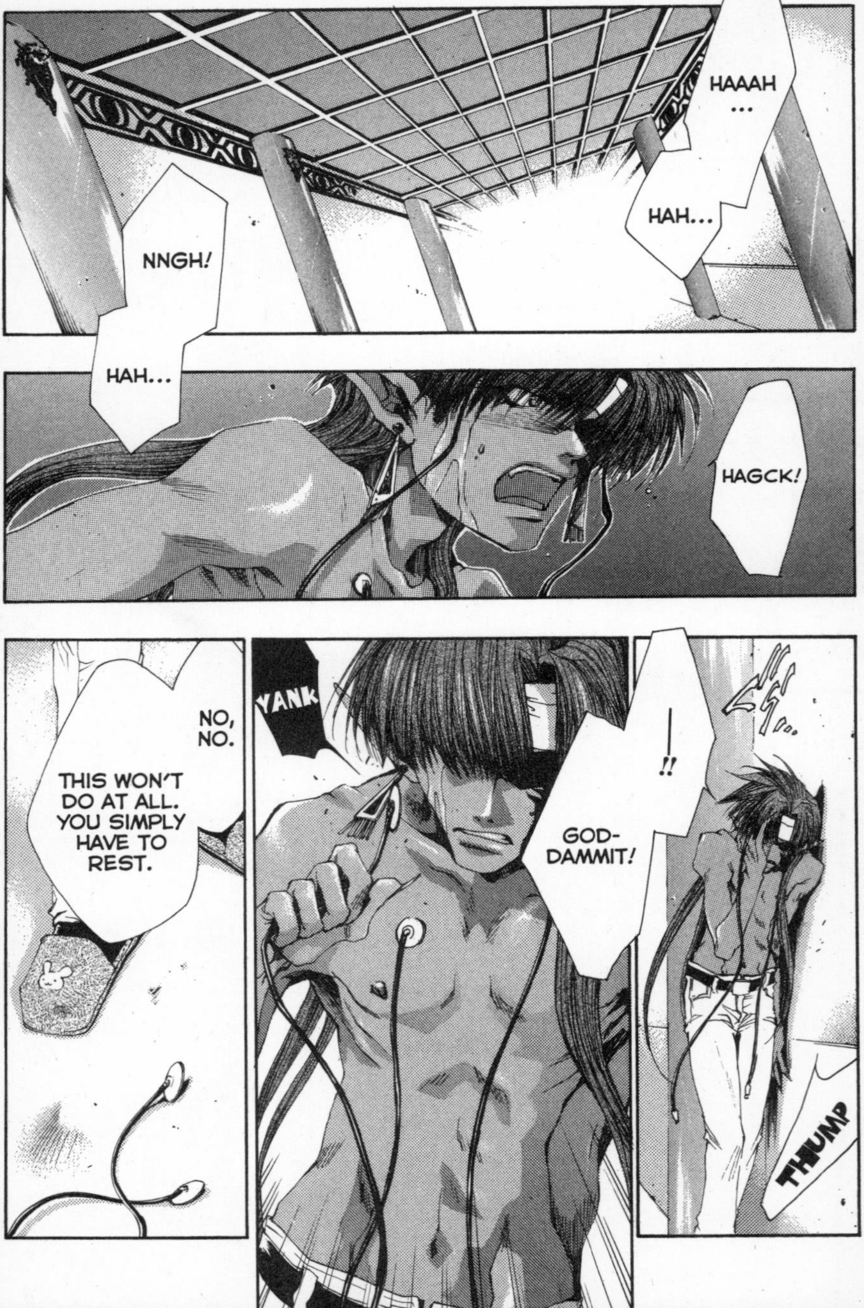
HAAAH ...
HAH...
NNGH!
HAH...
HAGCK!
THUMP
—!!
GOD-DAMMIT!
YANK
NO, NO.
THIS WON'T DO AT ALL. YOU SIMPLY HAVE TO REST.

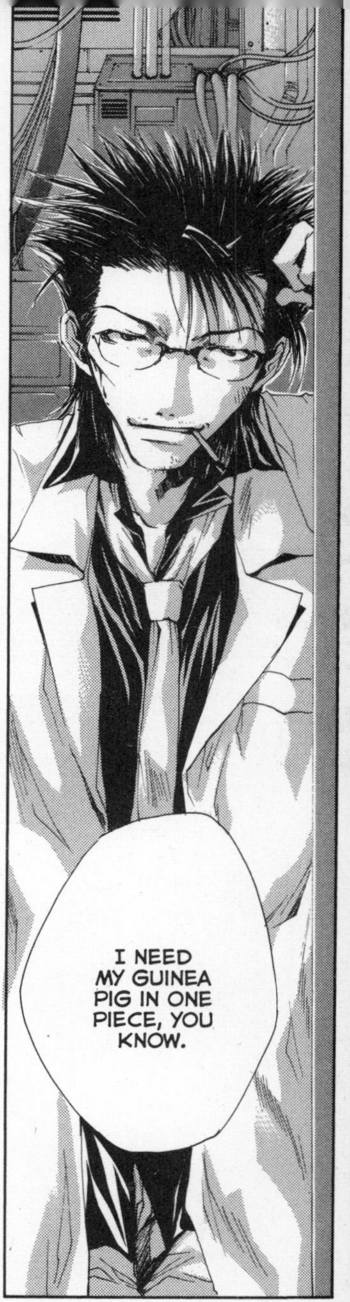
I NEED MY GUINEA PIG IN ONE PIECE, YOU KNOW.

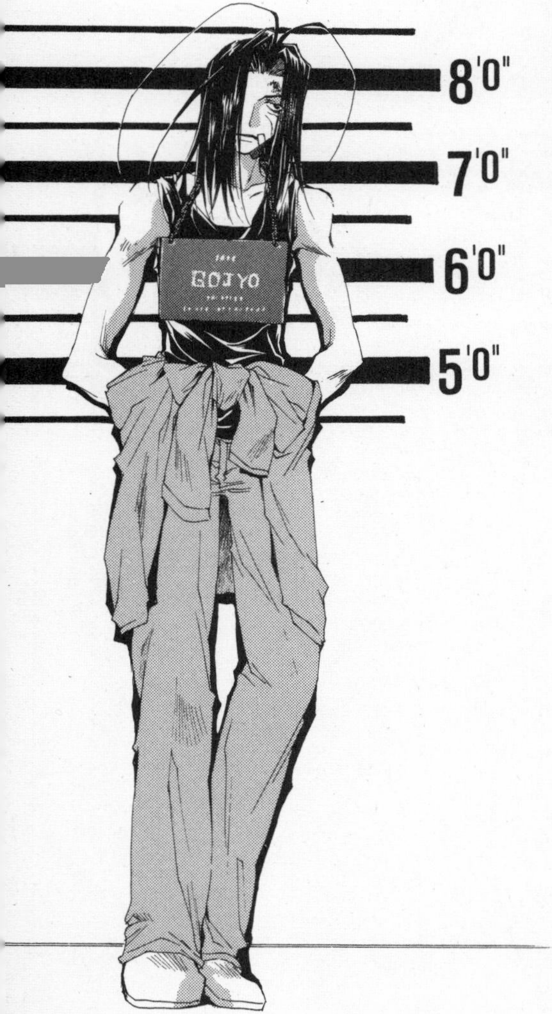
8'0"
7'0"
6'0"
5'0"
GOJYO

第35話 (だいわ)

CHAPTER 35: OPPOSITE

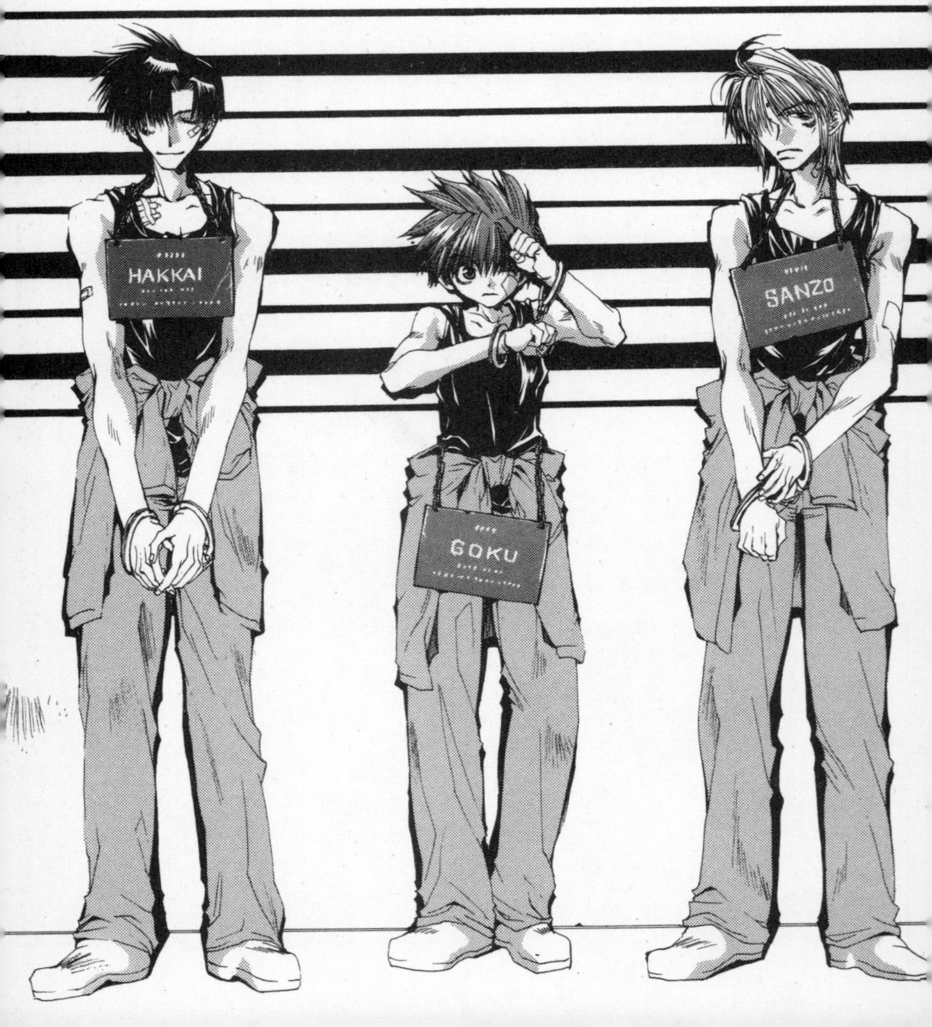

HAKKAI
GOKU
SANZO

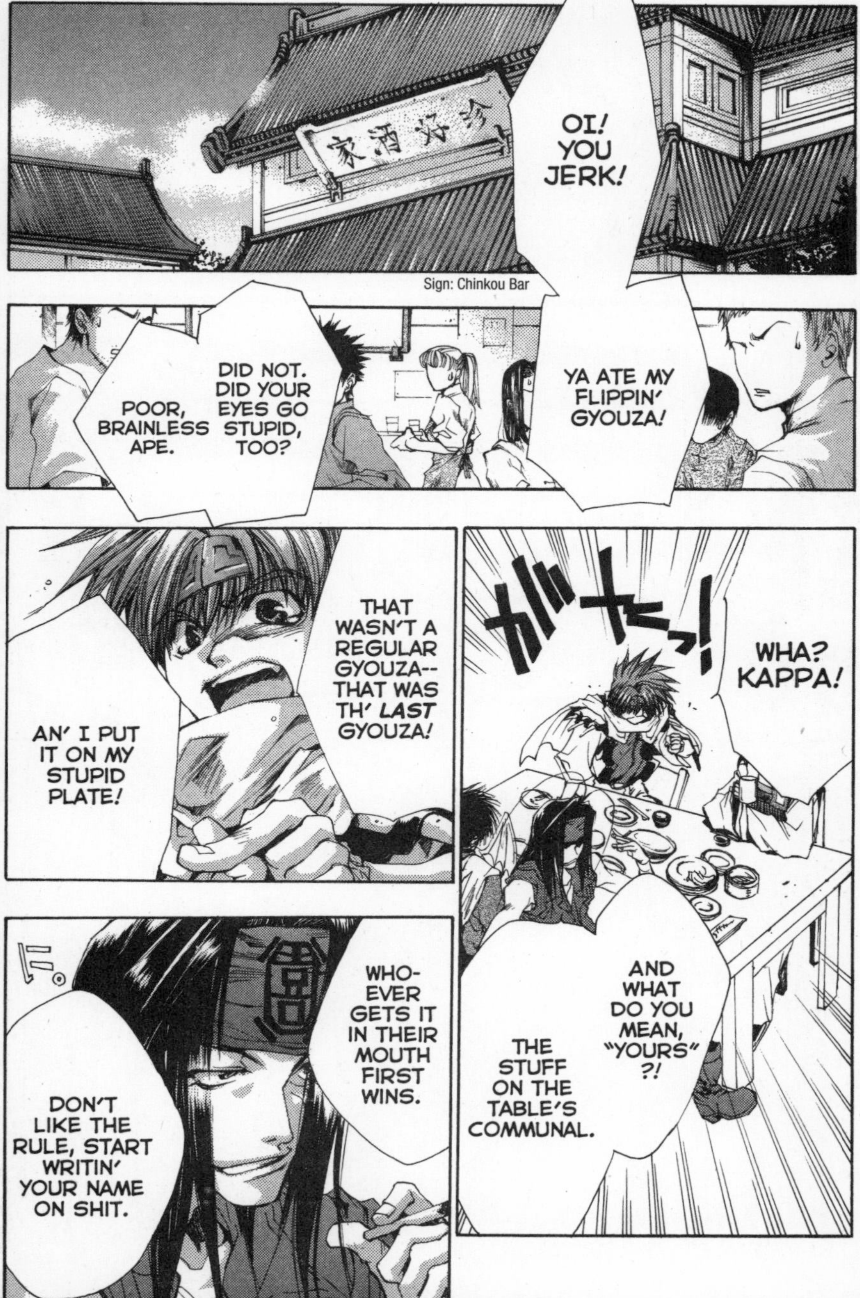
OI! YOU JERK!
Sign: Chinkou Bar
YA ATE MY FLIPPIN' GYOUZA!
DID NOT. DID YOUR EYES GO STUPID, TOO?
POOR, BRAINLESS APE.
WHA? KAPPA!
AND WHAT DO YOU MEAN, "YOURS"?!
THE STUFF ON THE TABLE'S COMMUNAL.
THAT WASN'T A REGULAR GYOUZA-- THAT WAS TH' *LAST* GYOUZA!
AN' I PUT IT ON MY STUPID PLATE!
WHO-EVER GETS IT IN THEIR MOUTH FIRST WINS.
DON'T LIKE THE RULE, START WRITIN' YOUR NAME ON SHIT.

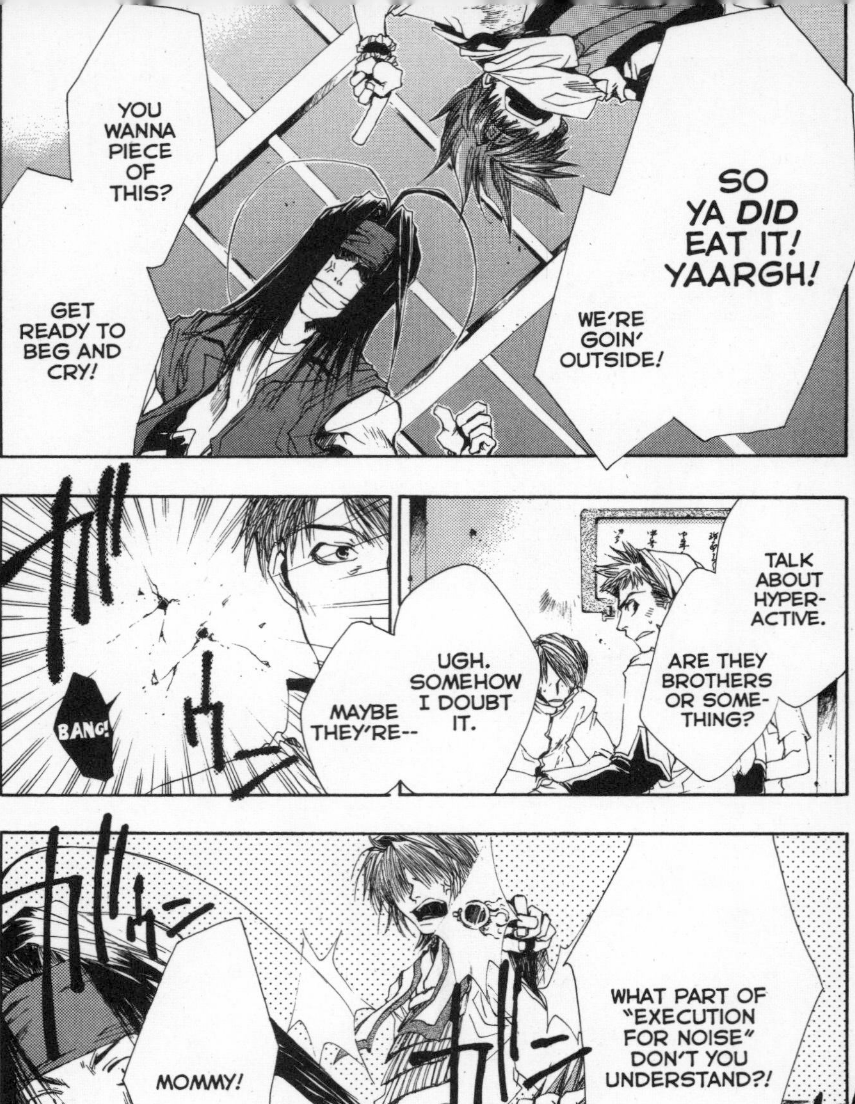
SO YA *DID* EAT IT! YAARGH!
WE'RE GOIN' OUTSIDE!
YOU WANNA PIECE OF THIS?
GET READY TO BEG AND CRY!
TALK ABOUT HYPER-ACTIVE.
ARE THEY BROTHERS OR SOME-THING?
UGH. SOMEHOW I DOUBT IT.
MAYBE THEY'RE--
BANG!
WHAT PART OF "EXECUTION FOR NOISE" DON'T YOU UNDERSTAND?!
MOMMY!

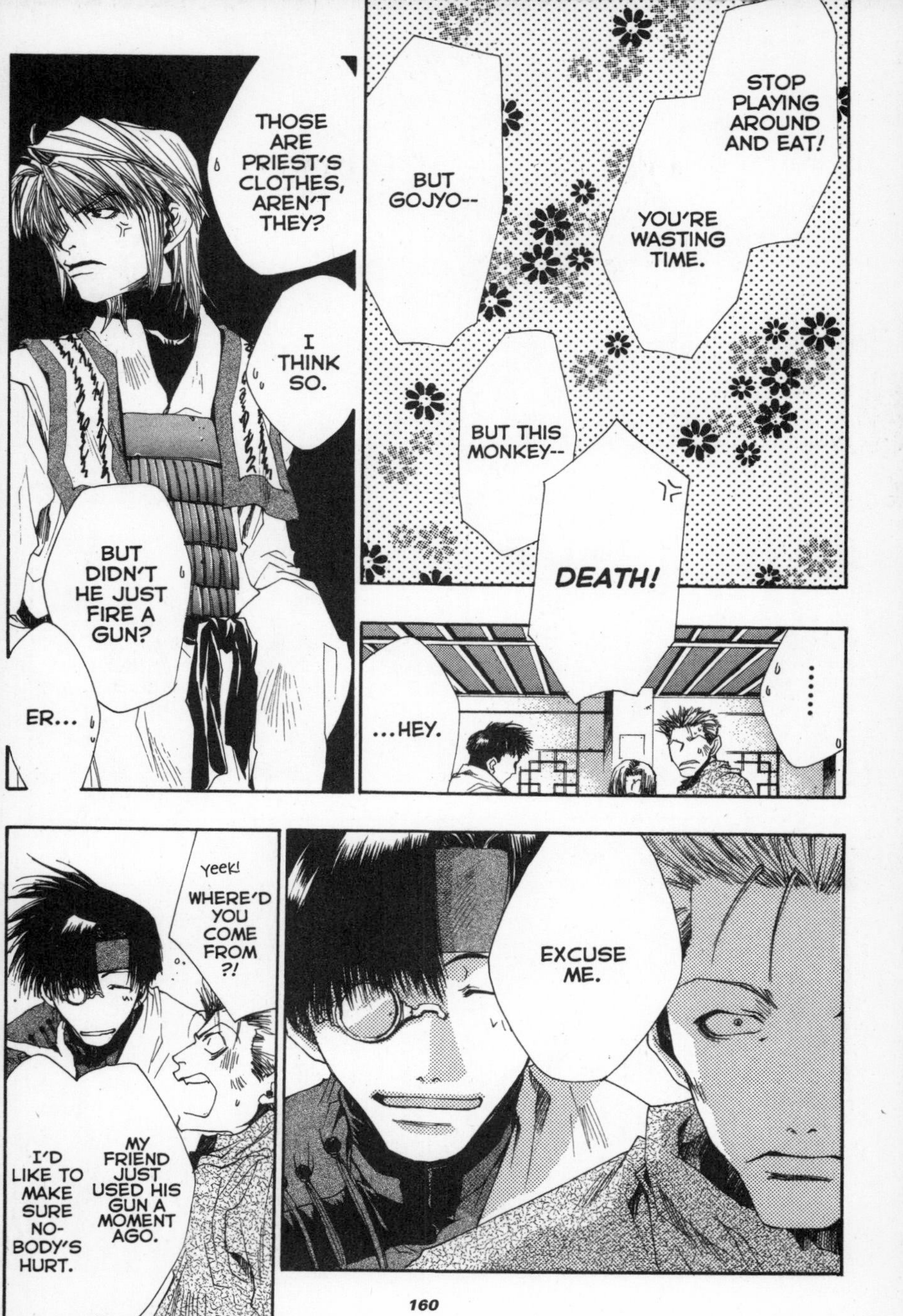
STOP PLAYING AROUND AND EAT!
YOU'RE WASTING TIME.
BUT GOJYO--
BUT THIS MONKEY--
DEATH!
......
...HEY.
THOSE ARE PRIEST'S CLOTHES, AREN'T THEY?
I THINK SO.
BUT DIDN'T HE JUST FIRE A GUN?
ER...
EXCUSE ME.
Yeek! WHERE'D YOU COME FROM ?!
MY FRIEND JUST USED HIS GUN A MOMENT AGO.
I'D LIKE TO MAKE SURE NO-BODY'S HURT.

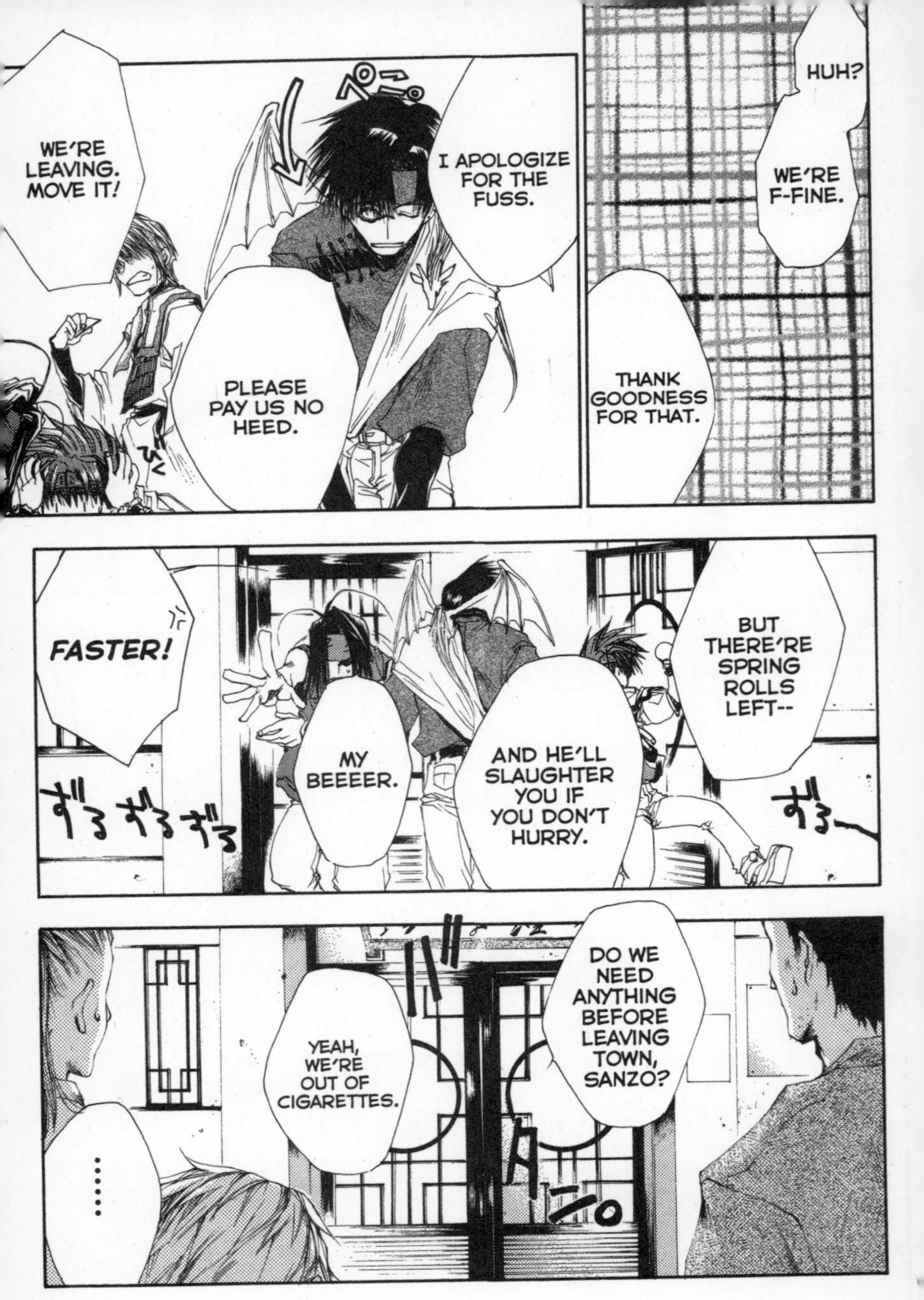
HUH?
WE'RE F-FINE.
THANK GOODNESS FOR THAT.
I APOLOGIZE FOR THE FUSS.
WE'RE LEAVING. MOVE IT!
PLEASE PAY US NO HEED.
BUT THERE'RE SPRING ROLLS LEFT--
ずるー
AND HE'LL SLAUGHTER YOU IF YOU DON'T HURRY.
MY BEEEER.
FASTER!
ずるずるずる
DO WE NEED ANYTHING BEFORE LEAVING TOWN, SANZO?
YEAH, WE'RE OUT OF CIGARETTES.
......

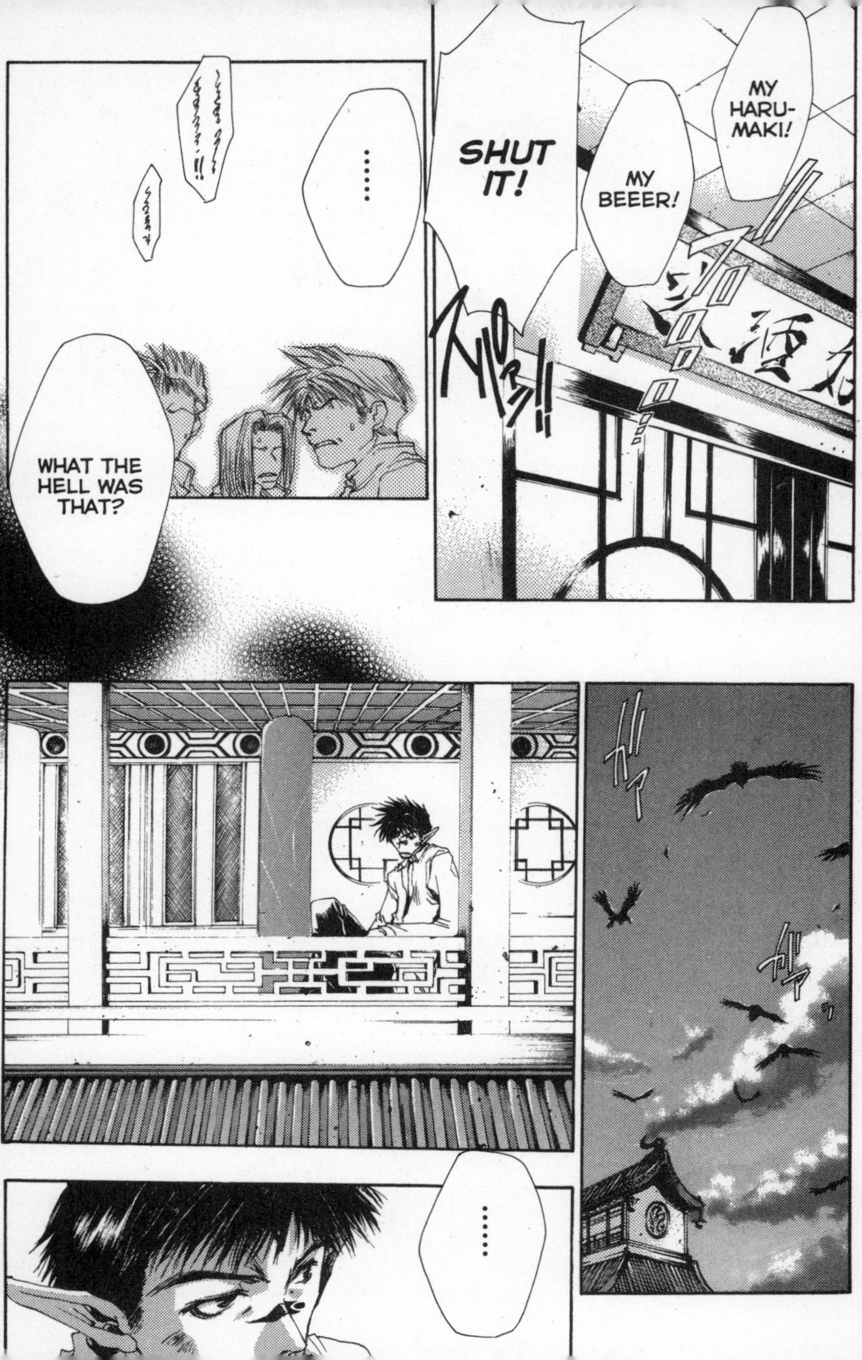
MY HARU-MAKI!
MY BEEER!
SHUT IT!
......
WHAT THE HELL WAS THAT?
......

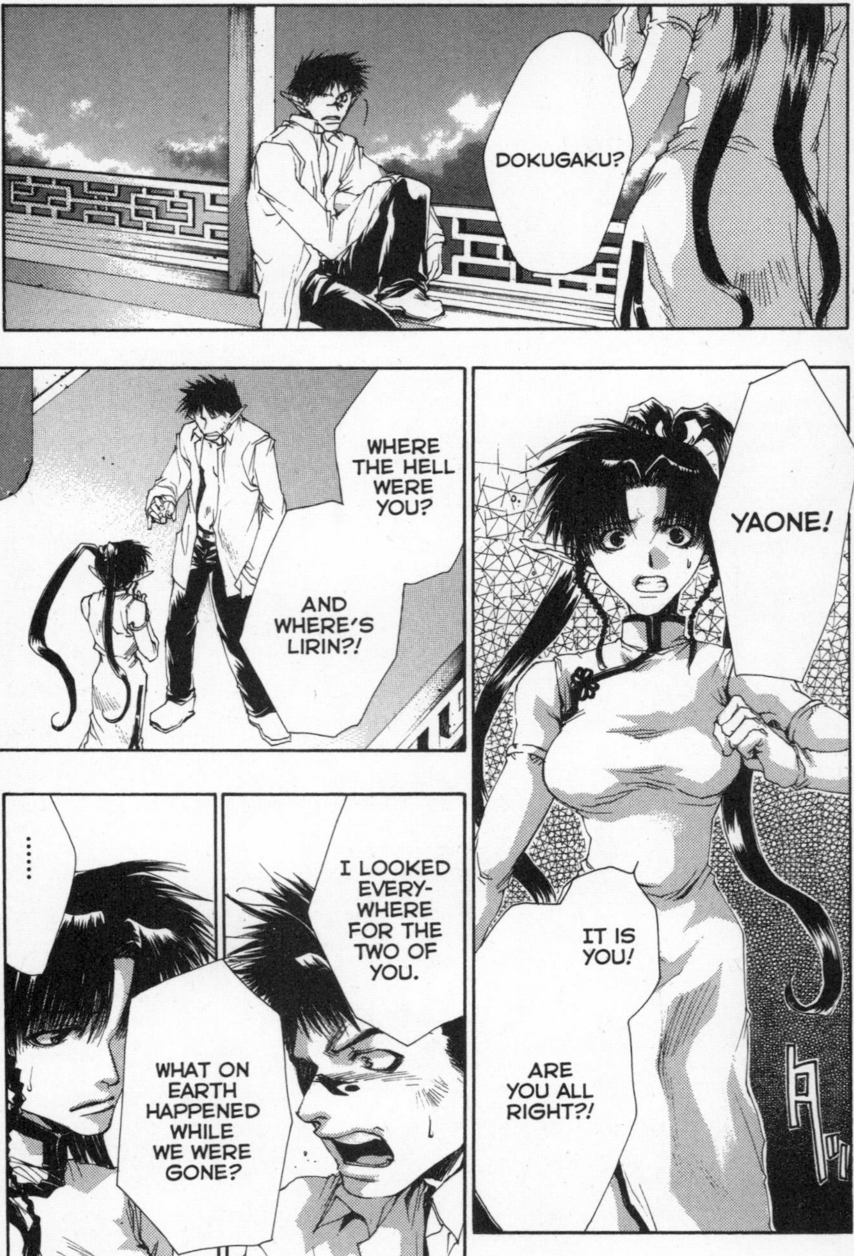
DOKUGAKU?
YAONE!
IT IS YOU!
ARE YOU ALL RIGHT?!
WHERE THE HELL WERE YOU?
AND WHERE'S LIRIN?!
I LOOKED EVERY-WHERE FOR THE TWO OF YOU.
WHAT ON EARTH HAPPENED WHILE WE WERE GONE?
......

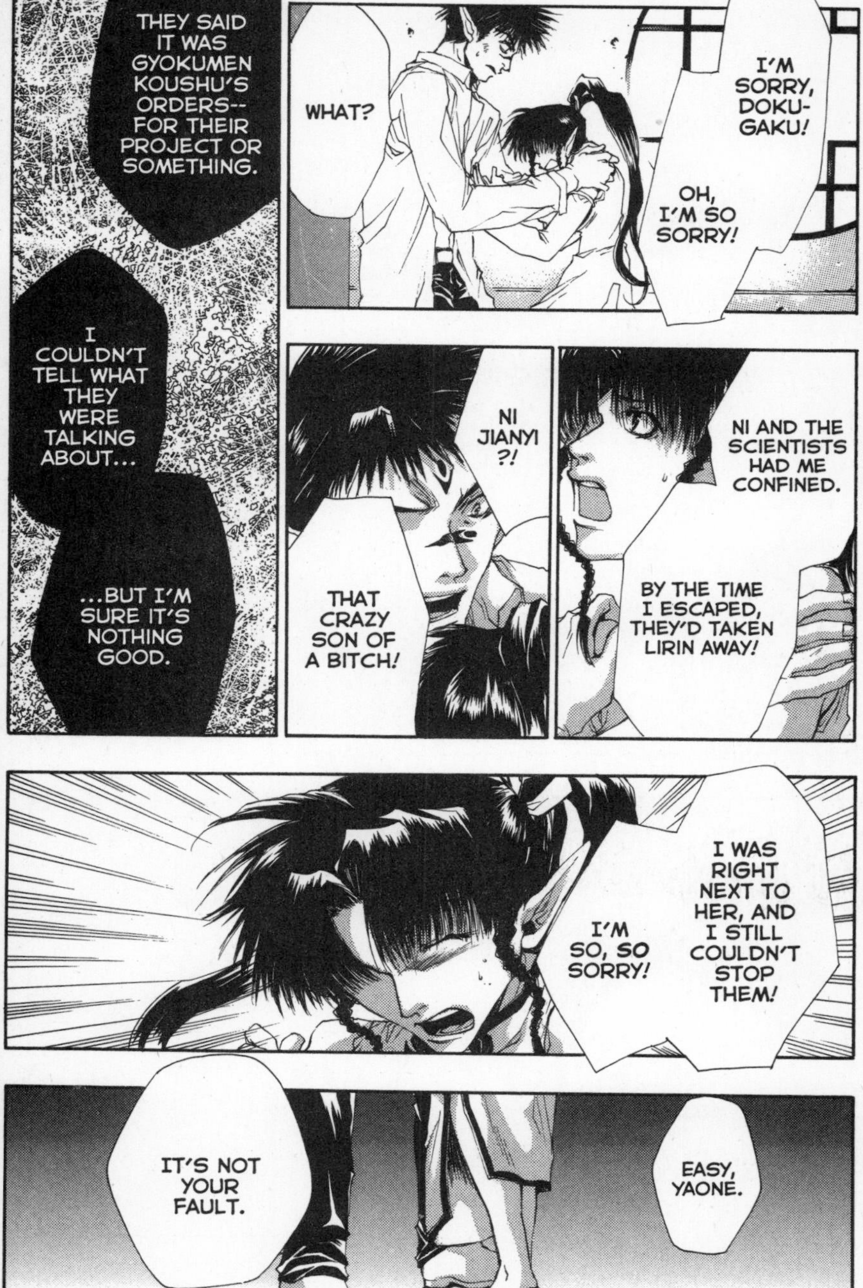
I'M SORRY, DOKU-GAKU!
OH, I'M SO SORRY!
WHAT?
NI AND THE SCIENTISTS HAD ME CONFINED.
BY THE TIME I ESCAPED, THEY'D TAKEN LIRIN AWAY!
NI JIANYI?!
THAT CRAZY SON OF A BITCH!
THEY SAID IT WAS GYOKUMEN KOUSHU'S ORDERS--FOR THEIR PROJECT OR SOMETHING.
I COULDN'T TELL WHAT THEY WERE TALKING ABOUT...
...BUT I'M SURE IT'S NOTHING GOOD.
I WAS RIGHT NEXT TO HER, AND I STILL COULDN'T STOP THEM!
I'M SO, SO SORRY!
EASY, YAONE.
IT'S NOT YOUR FAULT.

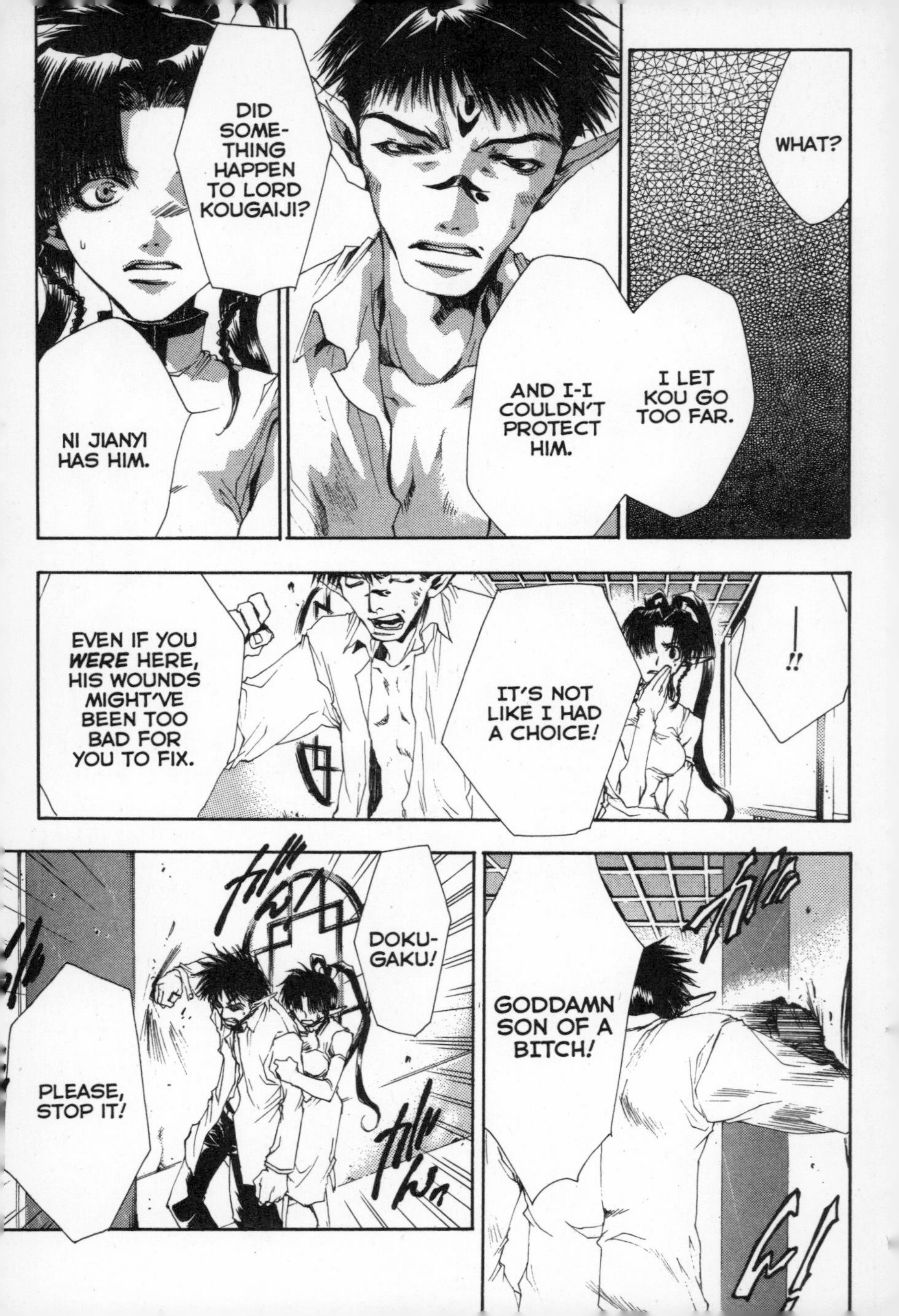
WHAT?
I LET KOU GO TOO FAR.
AND I-I COULDN'T PROTECT HIM.
DID SOMETHING HAPPEN TO LORD KOUGAIJI?
NI JIANYI HAS HIM.
!!
IT'S NOT LIKE I HAD A CHOICE!
EVEN IF YOU *WERE* HERE, HIS WOUNDS MIGHT'VE BEEN TOO BAD FOR YOU TO FIX.
GODDAMN SON OF A BITCH!
DOKU-GAKU!
PLEASE, STOP IT!

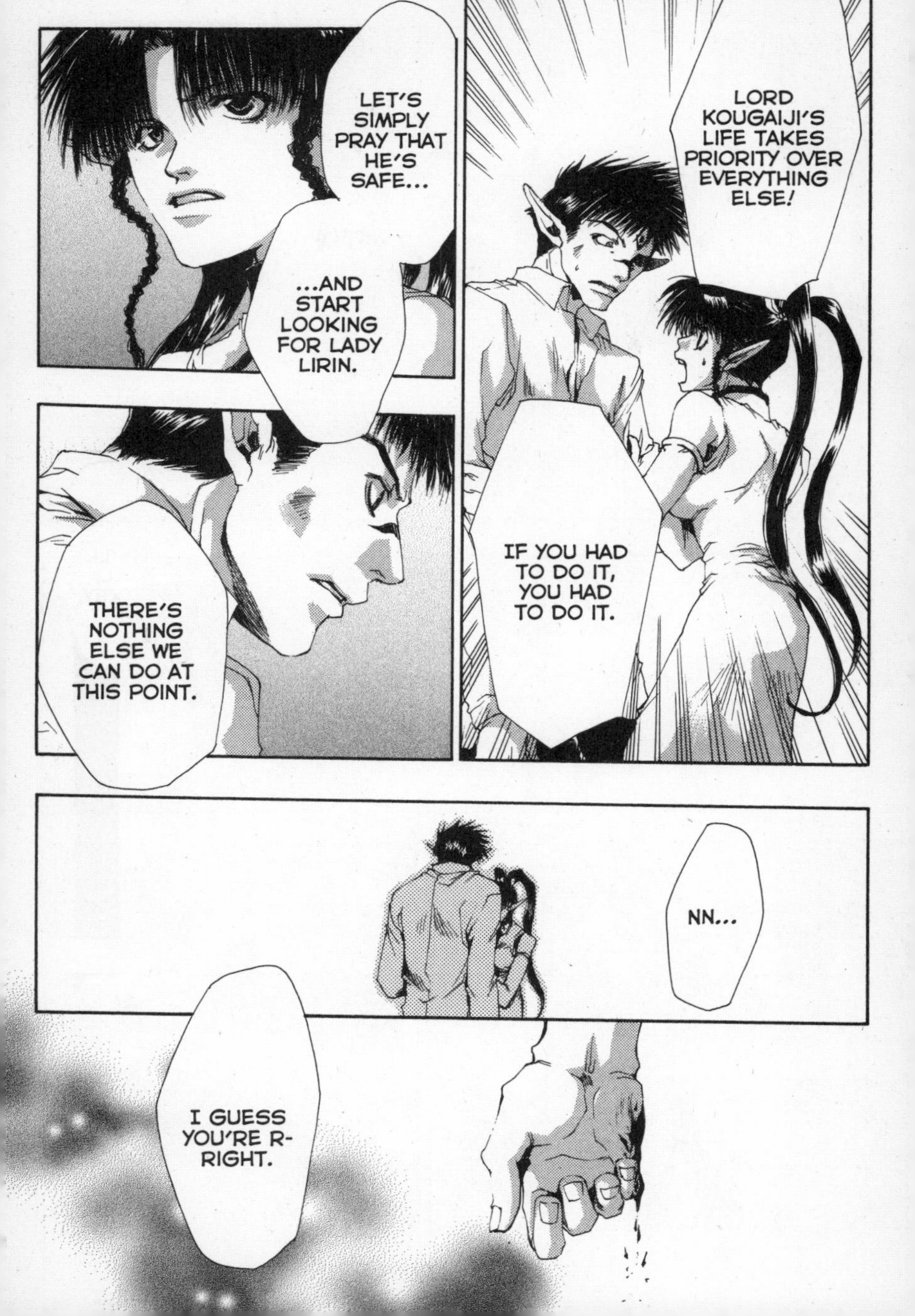
LORD KOUGAIJI'S LIFE TAKES PRIORITY OVER EVERYTHING ELSE!
IF YOU HAD TO DO IT, YOU HAD TO DO IT.
LET'S SIMPLY PRAY THAT HE'S SAFE...
...AND START LOOKING FOR LADY LIRIN.
THERE'S NOTHING ELSE WE CAN DO AT THIS POINT.
NN...
I GUESS YOU'RE R-RIGHT.

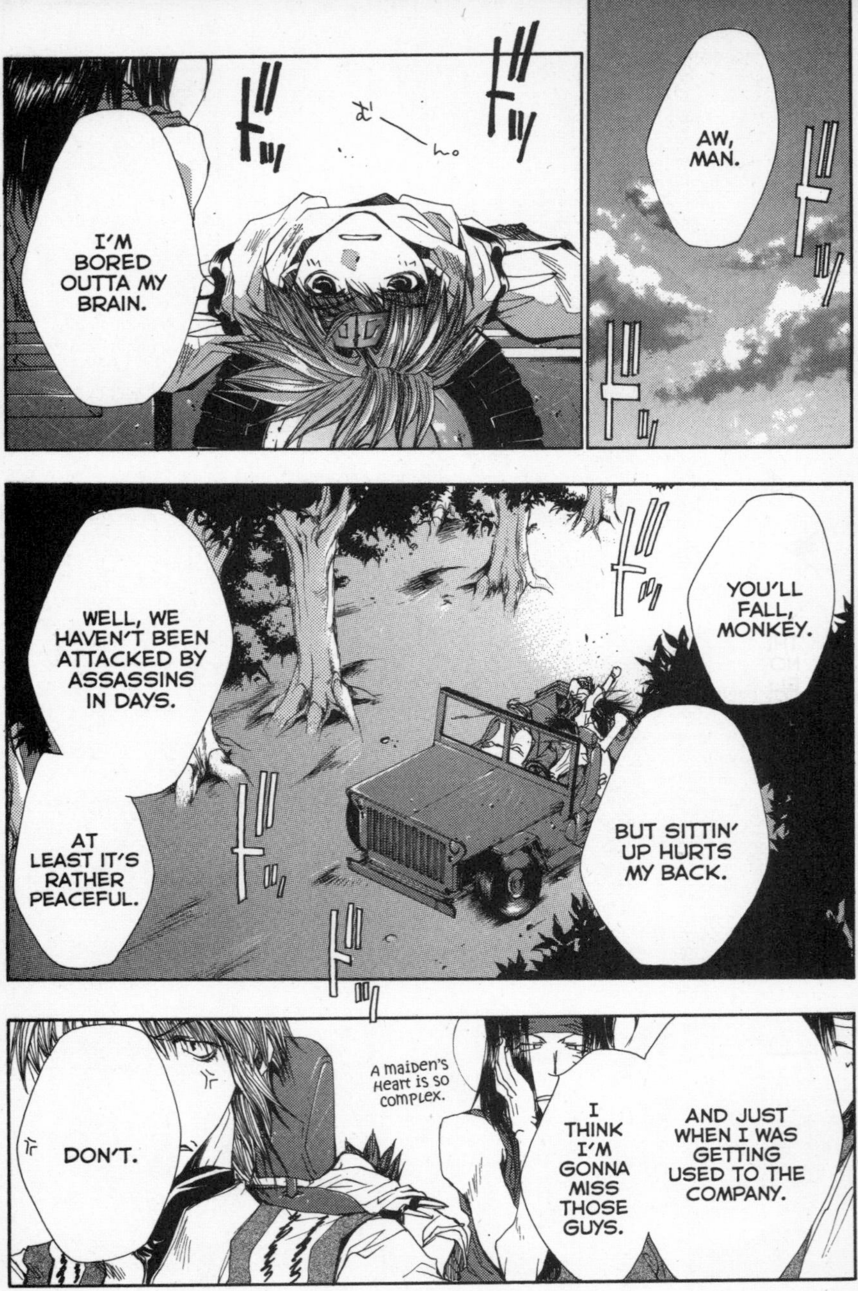
AW, MAN.
I'M BORED OUTTA MY BRAIN.
YOU'LL FALL, MONKEY.
BUT SITTIN' UP HURTS MY BACK.
WELL, WE HAVEN'T BEEN ATTACKED BY ASSASSINS IN DAYS.
AT LEAST IT'S RATHER PEACEFUL.
AND JUST WHEN I WAS GETTING USED TO THE COMPANY.
I THINK I'M GONNA MISS THOSE GUYS.
A MAIDEN'S HEART IS SO COMPLEX.
DON'T.

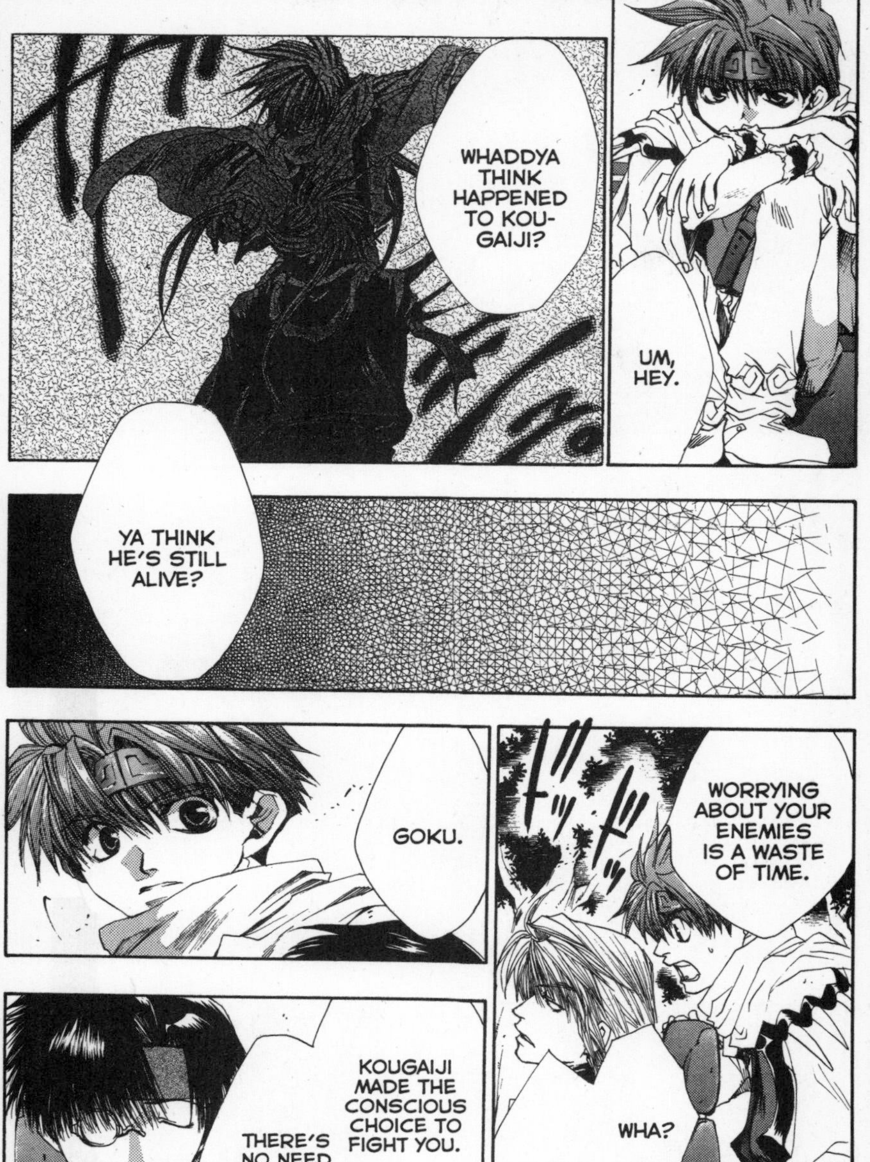
UM, HEY.
WHADDYA THINK HAPPENED TO KOU-GAIJI?
YA THINK HE'S STILL ALIVE?
WORRYING ABOUT YOUR ENEMIES IS A WASTE OF TIME.
WHA?
BUT I--
GOKU.
KOUGAIJI MADE THE CONSCIOUS CHOICE TO FIGHT YOU.
THERE'S NO NEED FOR YOU TO WORRY.

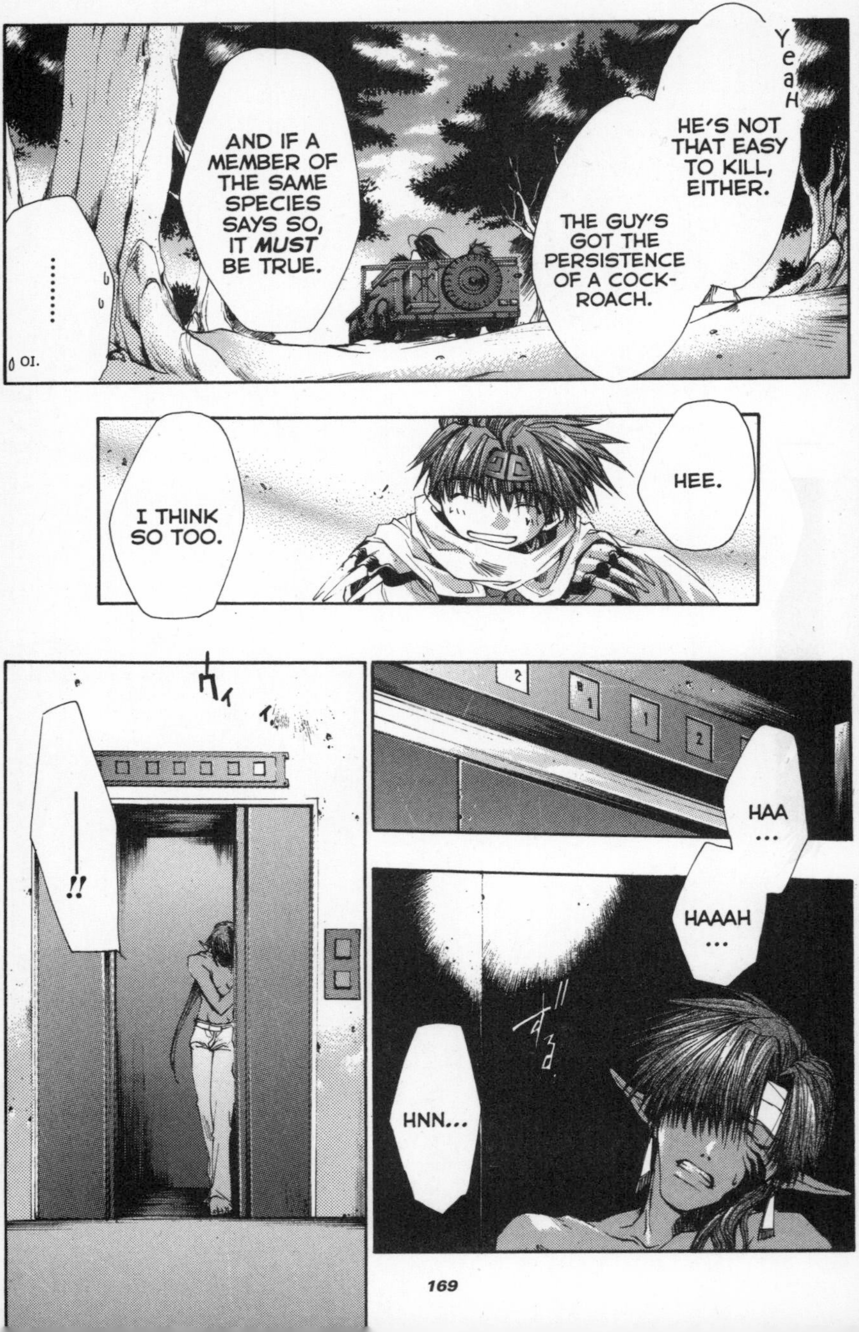
Yeah
HE'S NOT THAT EASY TO KILL, EITHER.
THE GUY'S GOT THE PERSISTENCE OF A COCK-ROACH.
AND IF A MEMBER OF THE SAME SPECIES SAYS SO, IT MUST BE TRUE.
....
OI.
HEE.
I THINK SO TOO.
HAA...
HAAAH...
HNN...
—!!

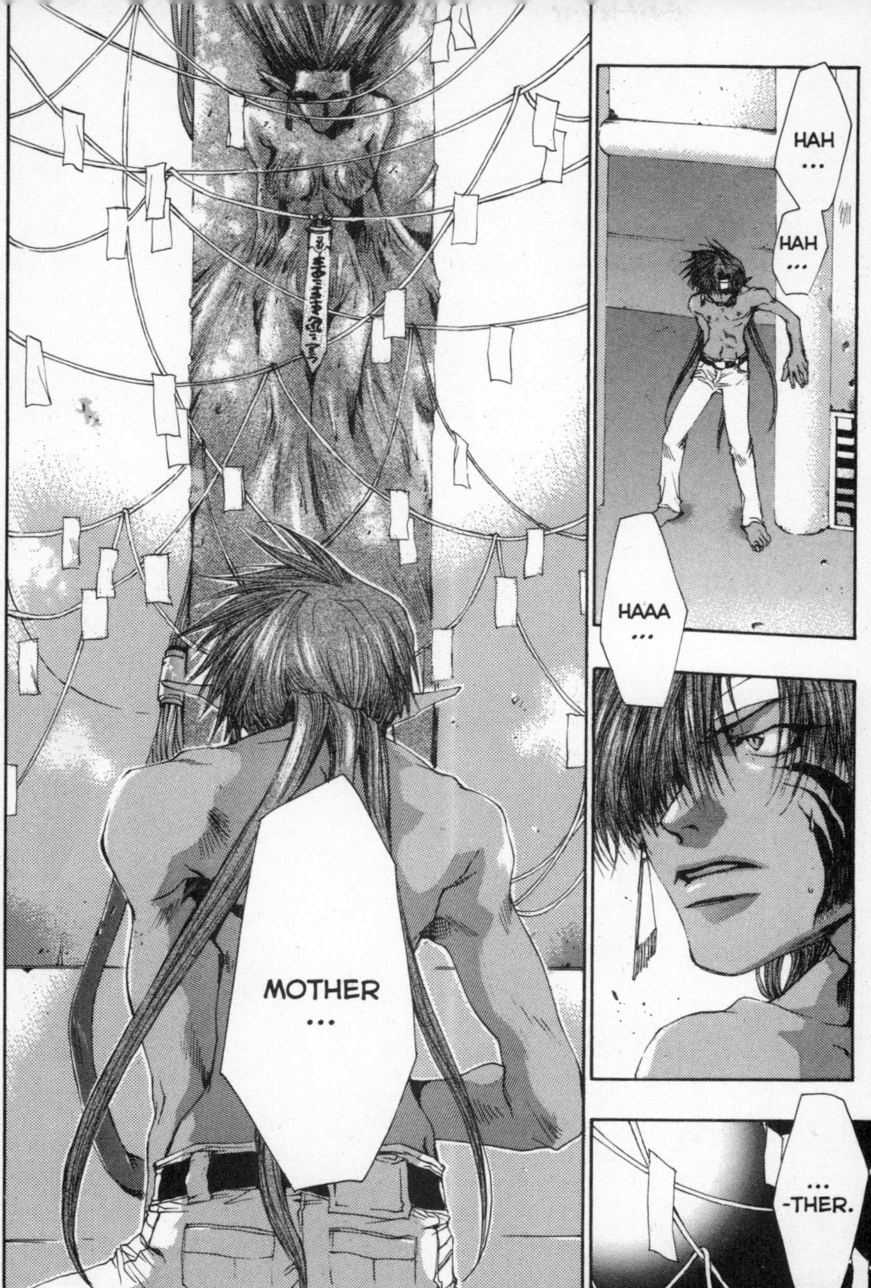
HAH ...
HAH ...
HAAA ...
... -THER.
MOTHER ...

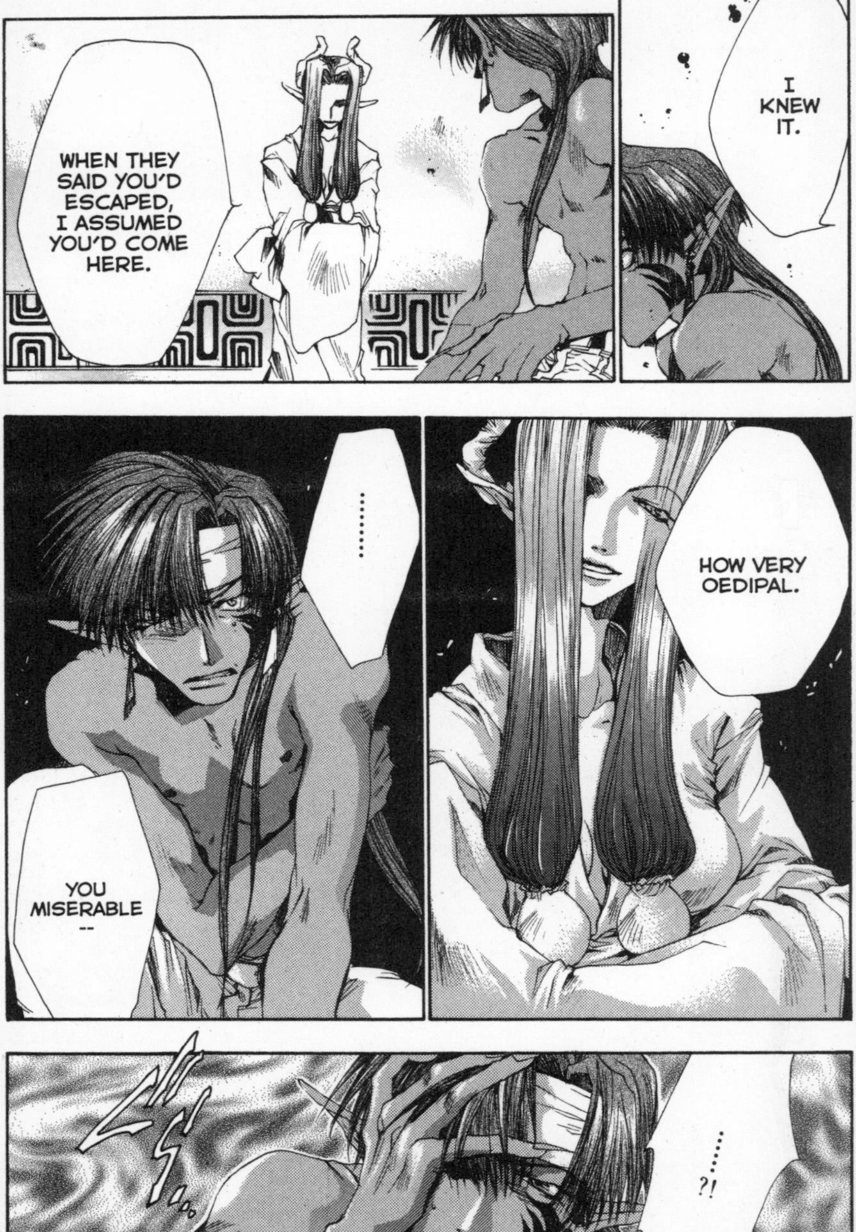

I KNEW IT.
WHEN THEY SAID YOU'D ESCAPED, I ASSUMED YOU'D COME HERE.
HOW VERY OEDIPAL.
....
YOU MISERABLE --
......?!

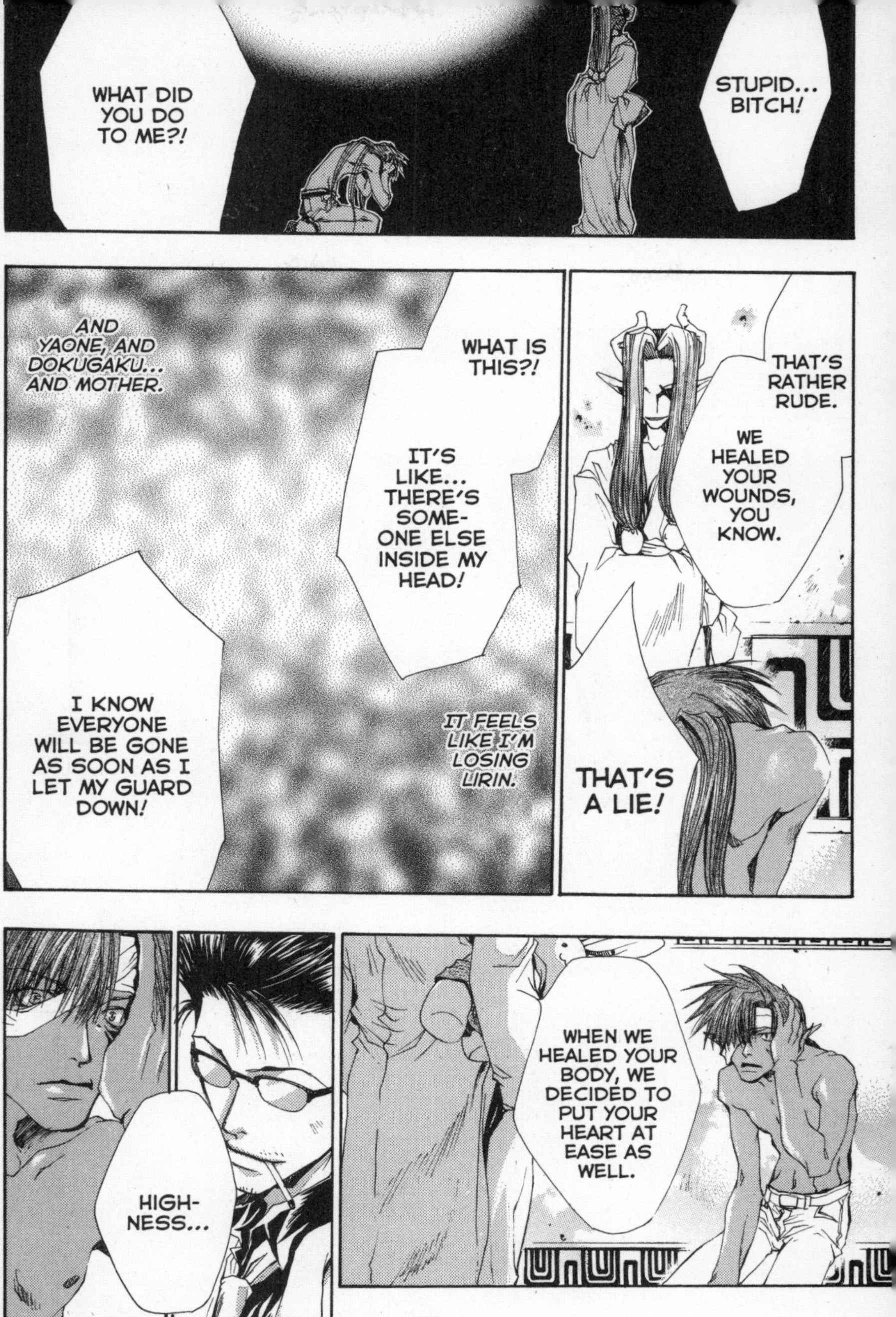
STUPID... BITCH!
WHAT DID YOU DO TO ME?!
THAT'S RATHER RUDE.
WE HEALED YOUR WOUNDS, YOU KNOW.
THAT'S A LIE!
WHAT IS THIS?!
IT'S LIKE... THERE'S SOME-ONE ELSE INSIDE MY HEAD!
AND YAONE, AND DOKUGAKU... AND MOTHER.
IT FEELS LIKE I'M LOSING LIRIN.
I KNOW EVERYONE WILL BE GONE AS SOON AS I LET MY GUARD DOWN!
WHEN WE HEALED YOUR BODY, WE DECIDED TO PUT YOUR HEART AT EASE AS WELL.
HIGH-NESS...

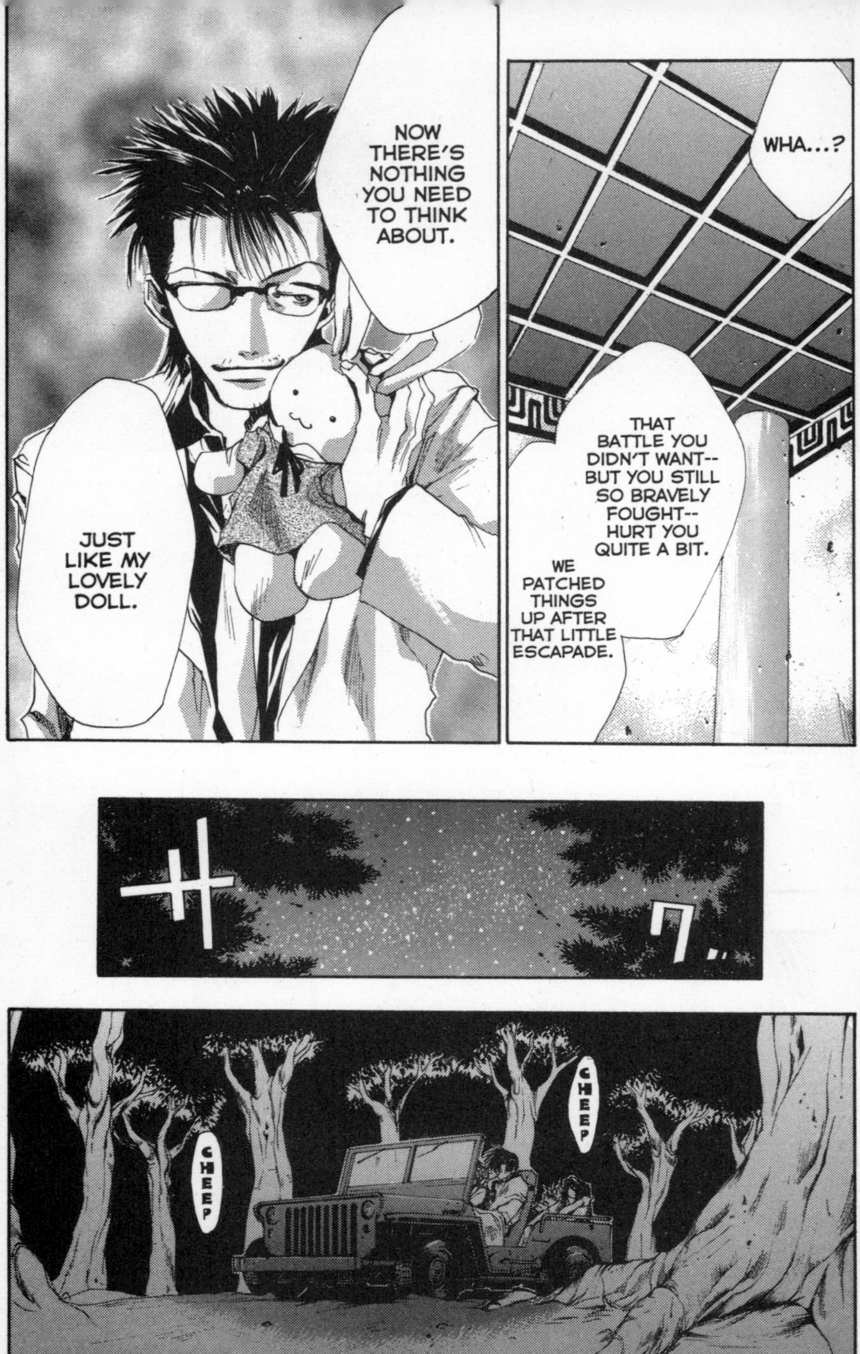
WHA...?
THAT BATTLE YOU DIDN'T WANT-- BUT YOU STILL SO BRAVELY FOUGHT-- HURT YOU QUITE A BIT.
WE PATCHED THINGS UP AFTER THAT LITTLE ESCAPADE.
NOW THERE'S NOTHING YOU NEED TO THINK ABOUT.
JUST LIKE MY LOVELY DOLL.
CHEEP
CHEEP

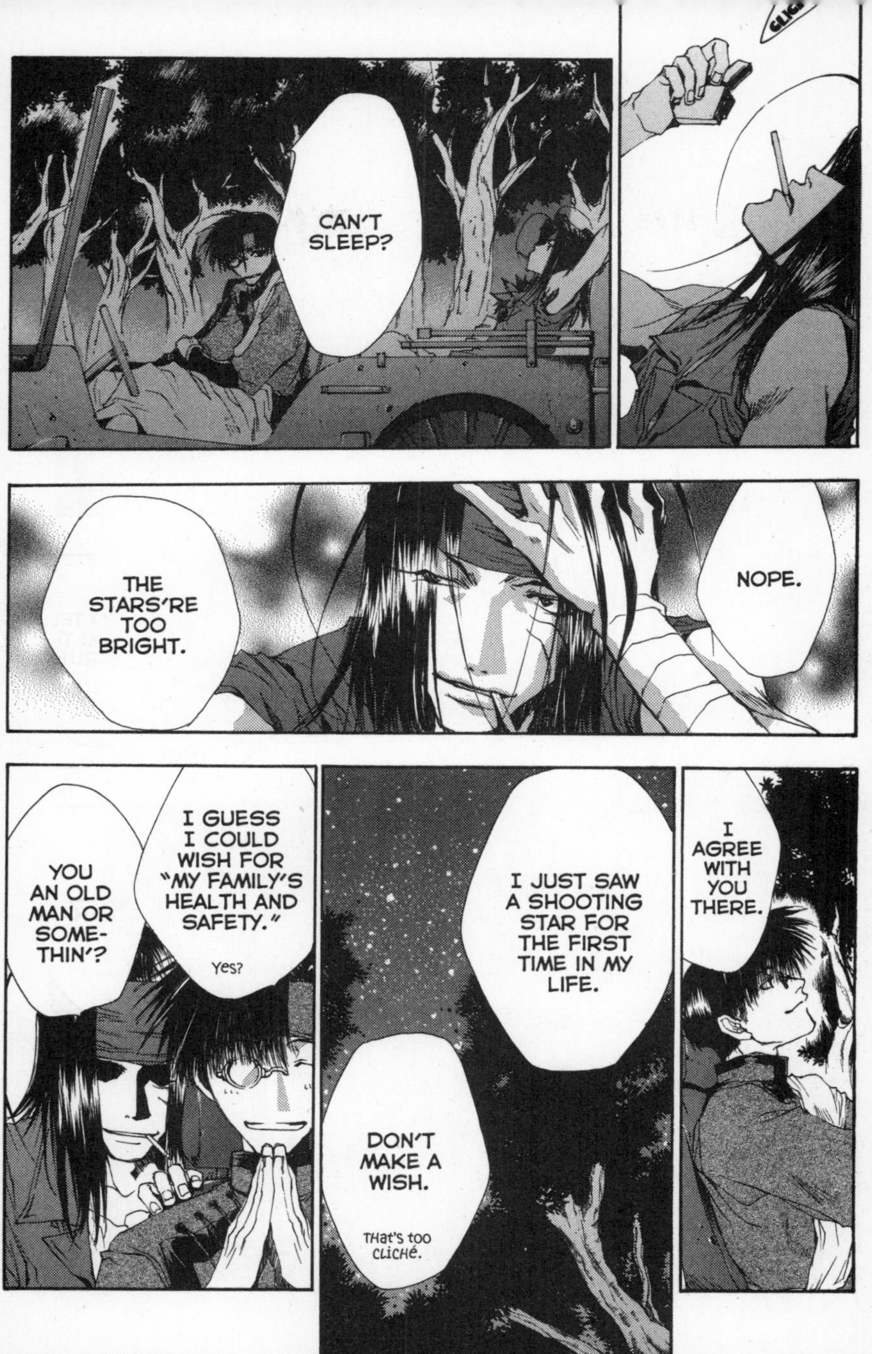
CLIC
CAN'T SLEEP?
NOPE.
THE STARS'RE TOO BRIGHT.
I AGREE WITH YOU THERE.
I JUST SAW A SHOOTING STAR FOR THE FIRST TIME IN MY LIFE.
DON'T MAKE A WISH.
That's too cliché.
I GUESS I COULD WISH FOR "MY FAMILY'S HEALTH AND SAFETY."
Yes?
YOU AN OLD MAN OR SOME-THIN'?

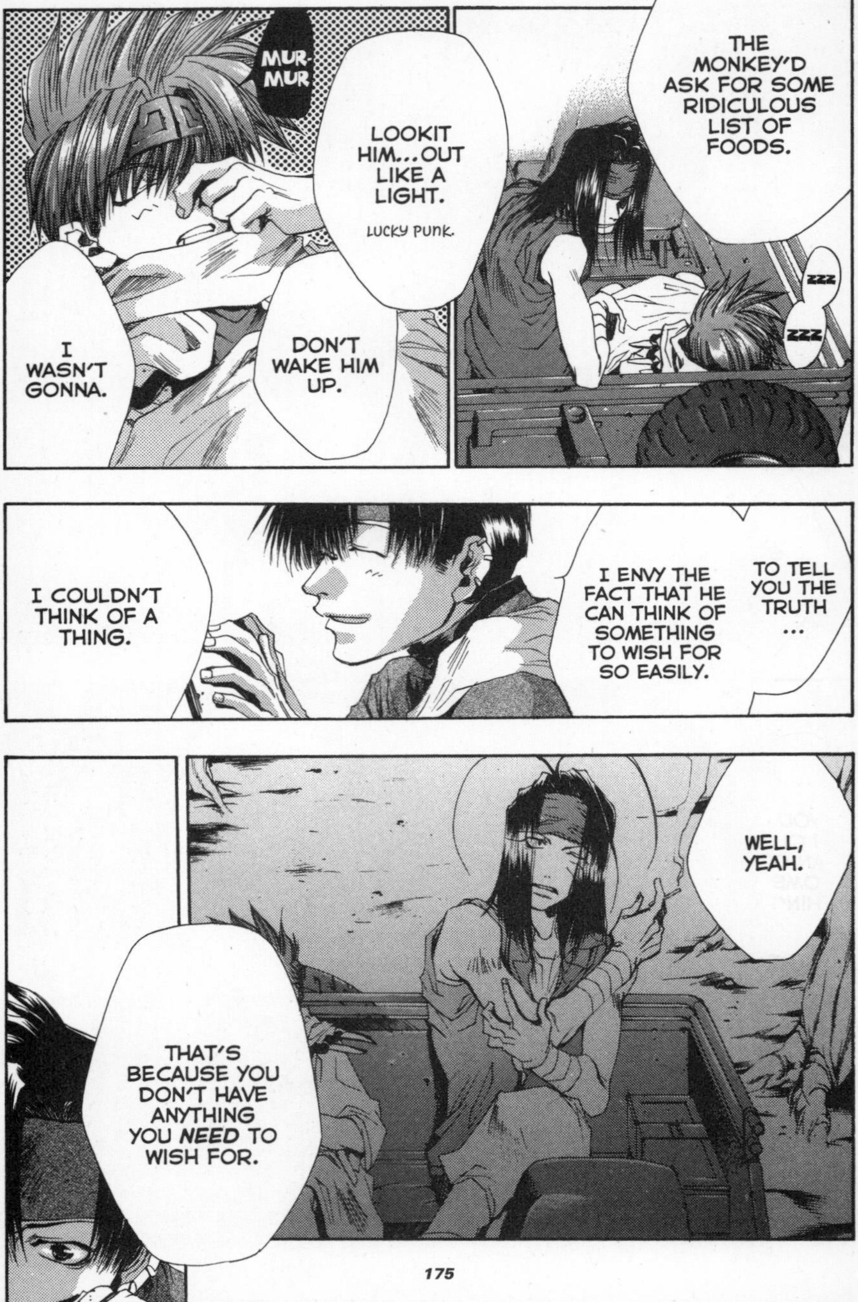
THE MONKEY'D ASK FOR SOME RIDICULOUS LIST OF FOODS.
ZZZ
ZZZ
MUR-MUR
LOOKIT HIM...OUT LIKE A LIGHT.
LUCKY PUNK.
DON'T WAKE HIM UP.
I WASN'T GONNA.
TO TELL YOU THE TRUTH ...
I ENVY THE FACT THAT HE CAN THINK OF SOMETHING TO WISH FOR SO EASILY.
I COULDN'T THINK OF A THING.
WELL, YEAH.
THAT'S BECAUSE YOU DON'T HAVE ANYTHING YOU NEED TO WISH FOR.

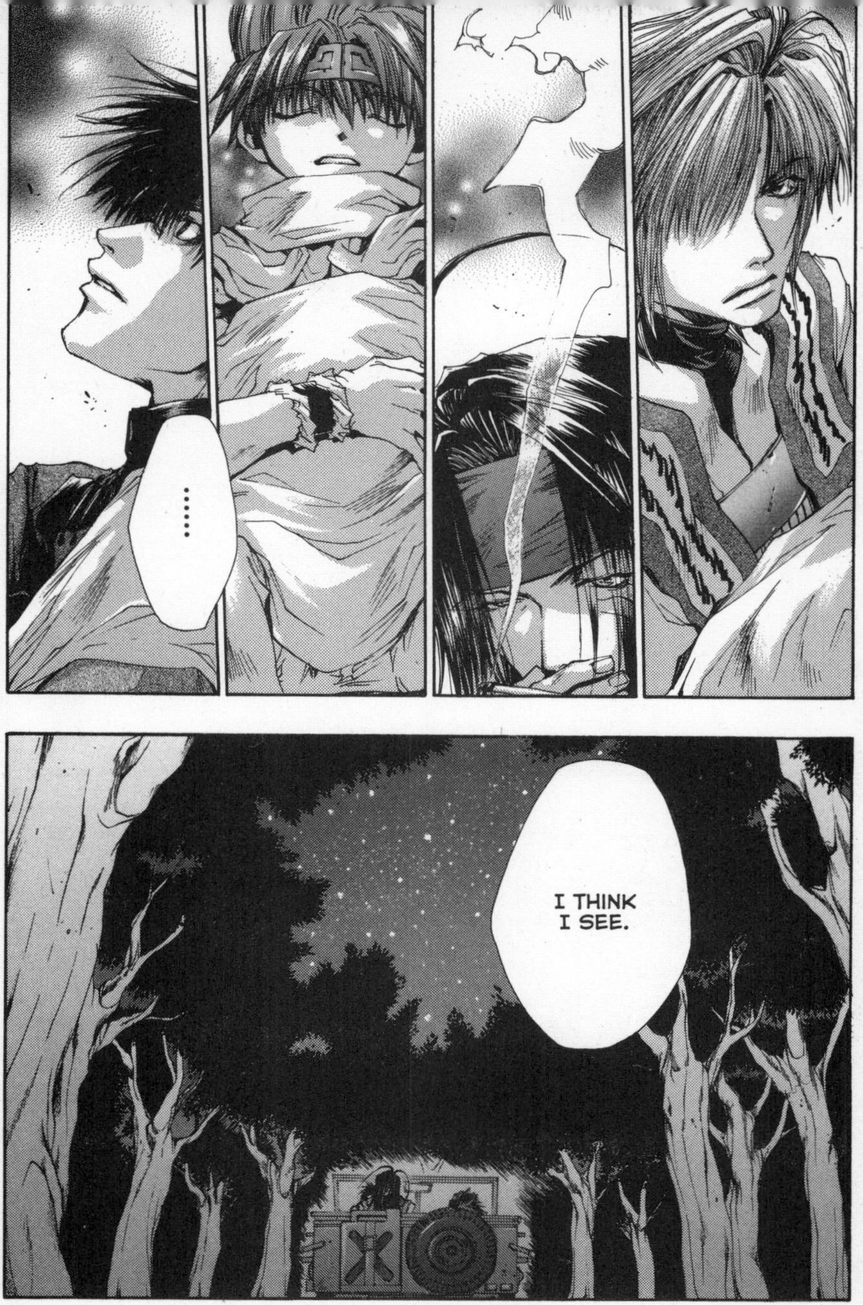
......
I THINK I SEE.

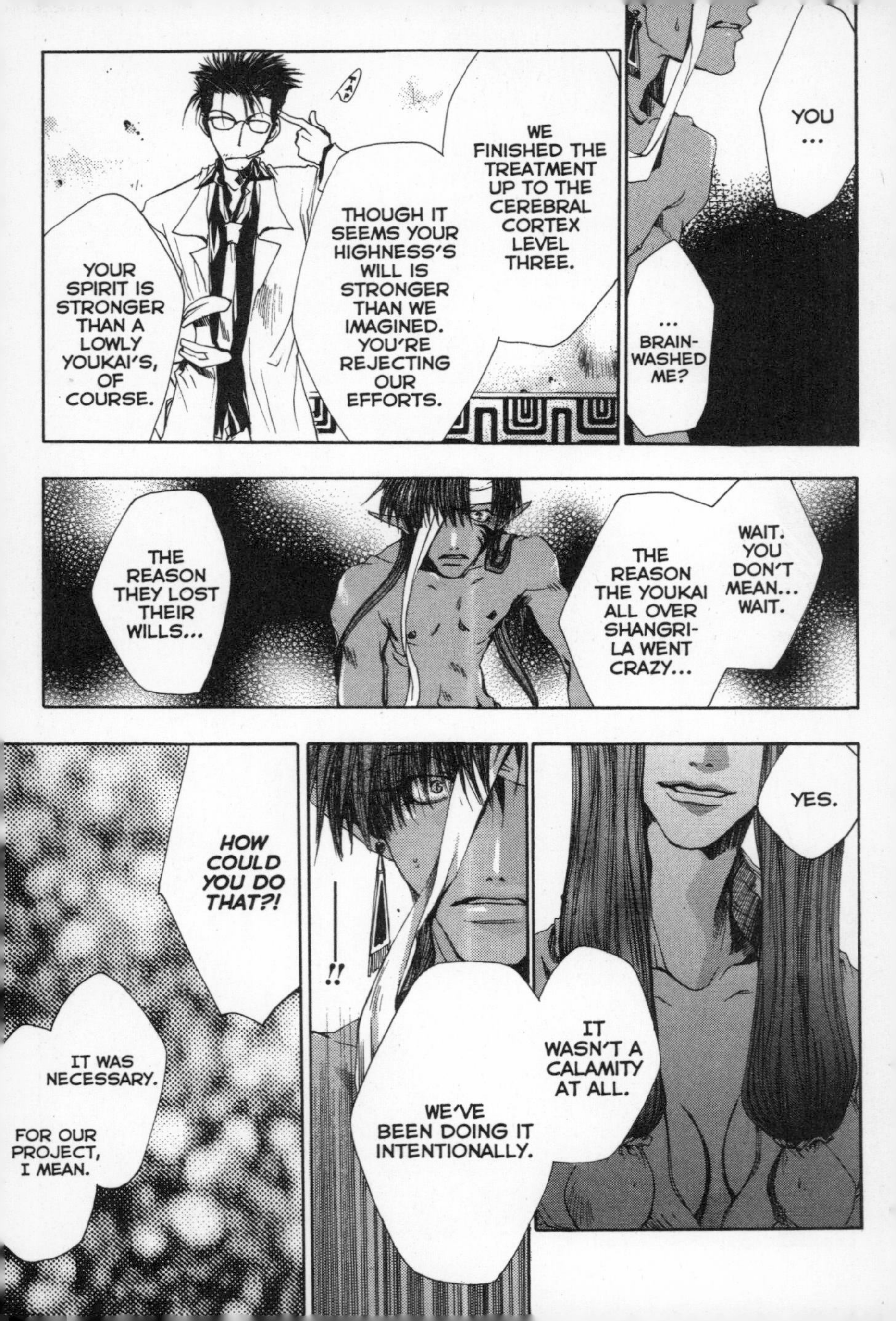
YOU ...
... BRAIN-WASHED ME?
WE FINISHED THE TREATMENT UP TO THE CEREBRAL CORTEX LEVEL THREE.
TAP
THOUGH IT SEEMS YOUR HIGHNESS'S WILL IS STRONGER THAN WE IMAGINED. YOU'RE REJECTING OUR EFFORTS.
YOUR SPIRIT IS STRONGER THAN A LOWLY YOUKAI'S, OF COURSE.
WAIT. YOU DON'T MEAN... WAIT.
THE REASON THE YOUKAI ALL OVER SHANGRI-LA WENT CRAZY...
THE REASON THEY LOST THEIR WILLS...
YES.
IT WASN'T A CALAMITY AT ALL.
WE'VE BEEN DOING IT INTENTIONALLY.
!!
HOW COULD YOU DO THAT?!
IT WAS NECESSARY.
FOR OUR PROJECT, I MEAN.

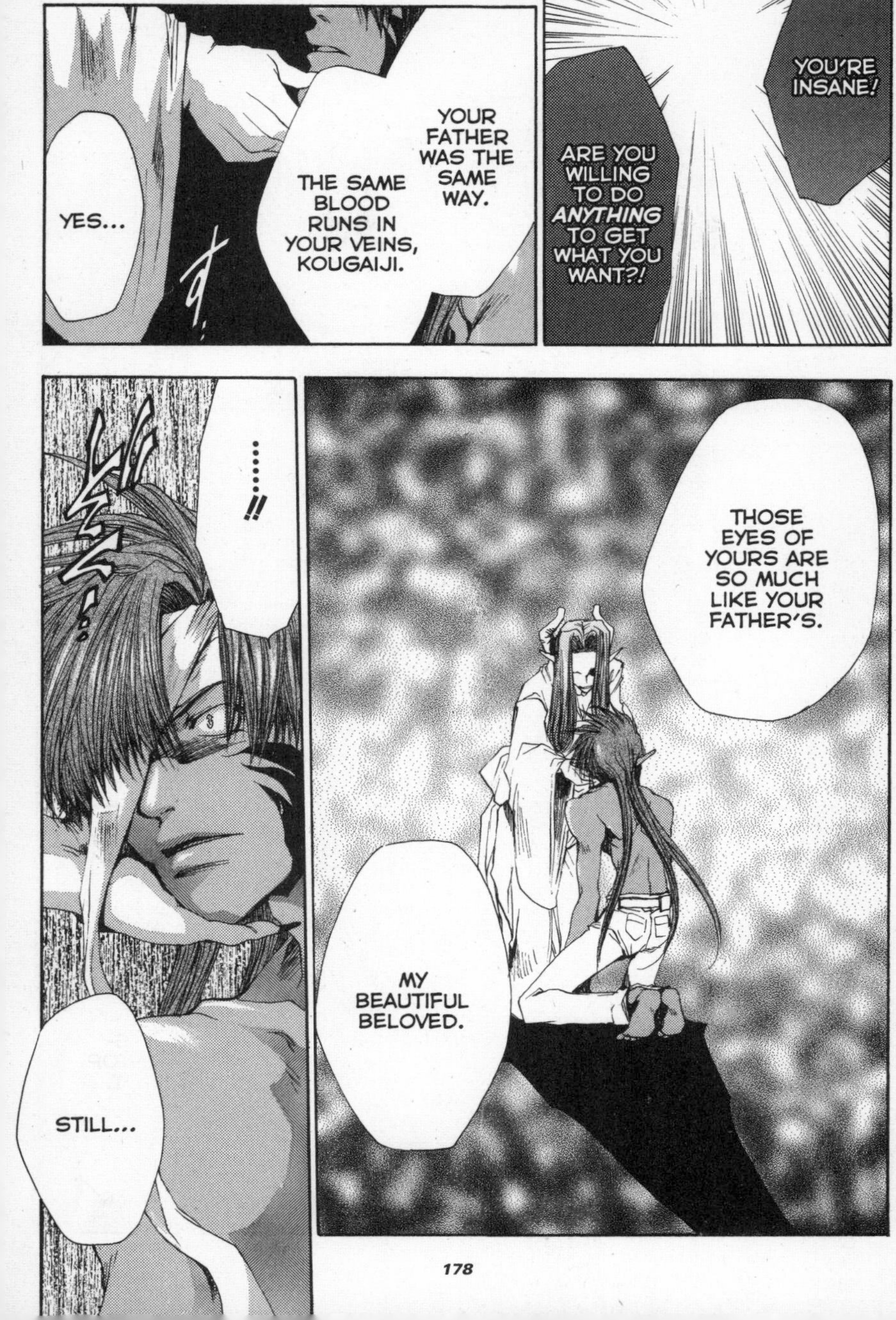
YOU'RE INSANE!
ARE YOU WILLING TO DO *ANYTHING* TO GET WHAT YOU WANT?!
YOUR FATHER WAS THE SAME WAY.
THE SAME BLOOD RUNS IN YOUR VEINS, KOUGAIJI.
YES...
THOSE EYES OF YOURS ARE SO MUCH LIKE YOUR FATHER'S.
MY BEAUTIFUL BELOVED.
......!!
STILL...

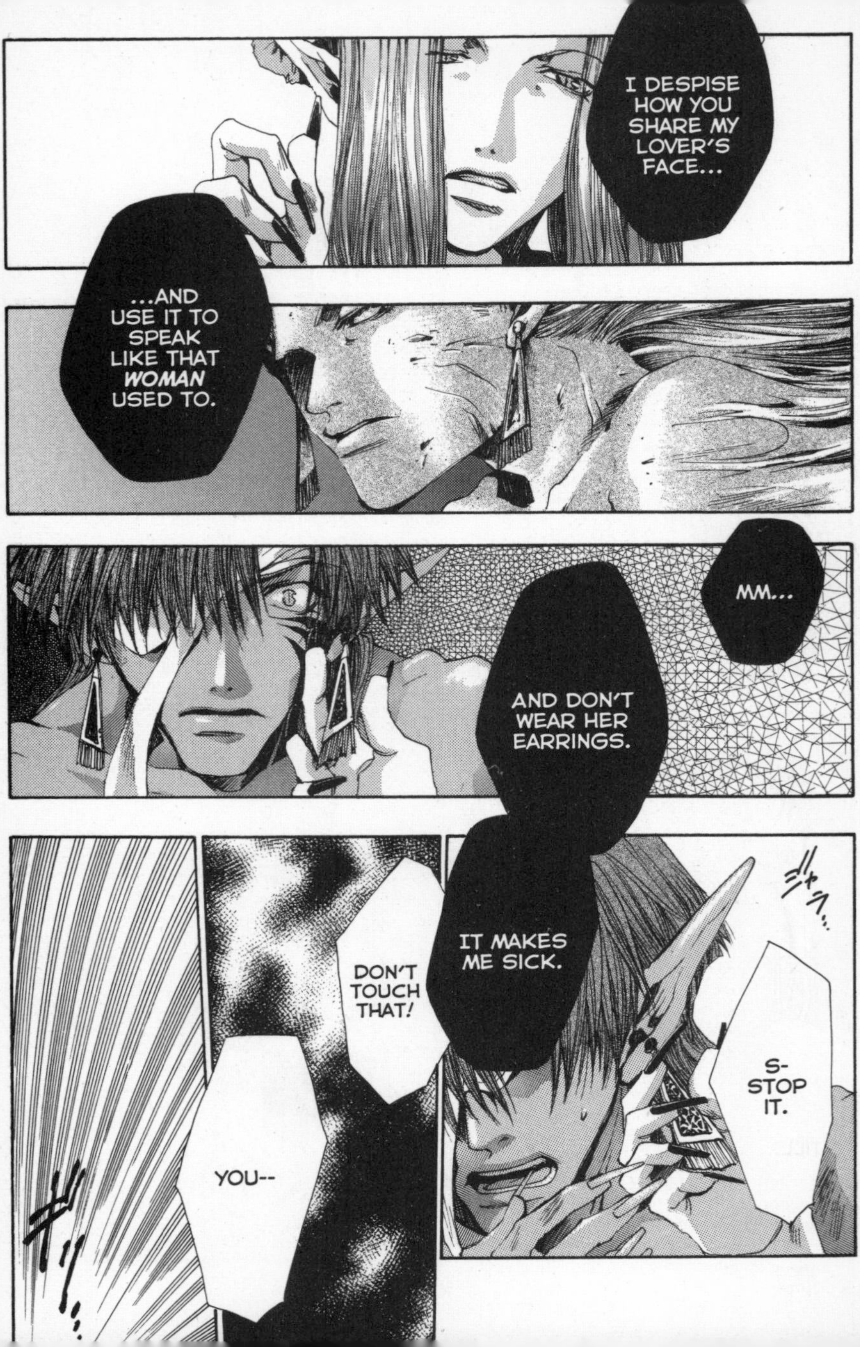
I DESPISE HOW YOU SHARE MY LOVER'S FACE...
...AND USE IT TO SPEAK LIKE THAT *WOMAN* USED TO.
MM...
AND DON'T WEAR HER EARRINGS.
IT MAKES ME SICK.
S-STOP IT.
DON'T TOUCH THAT!
YOU--

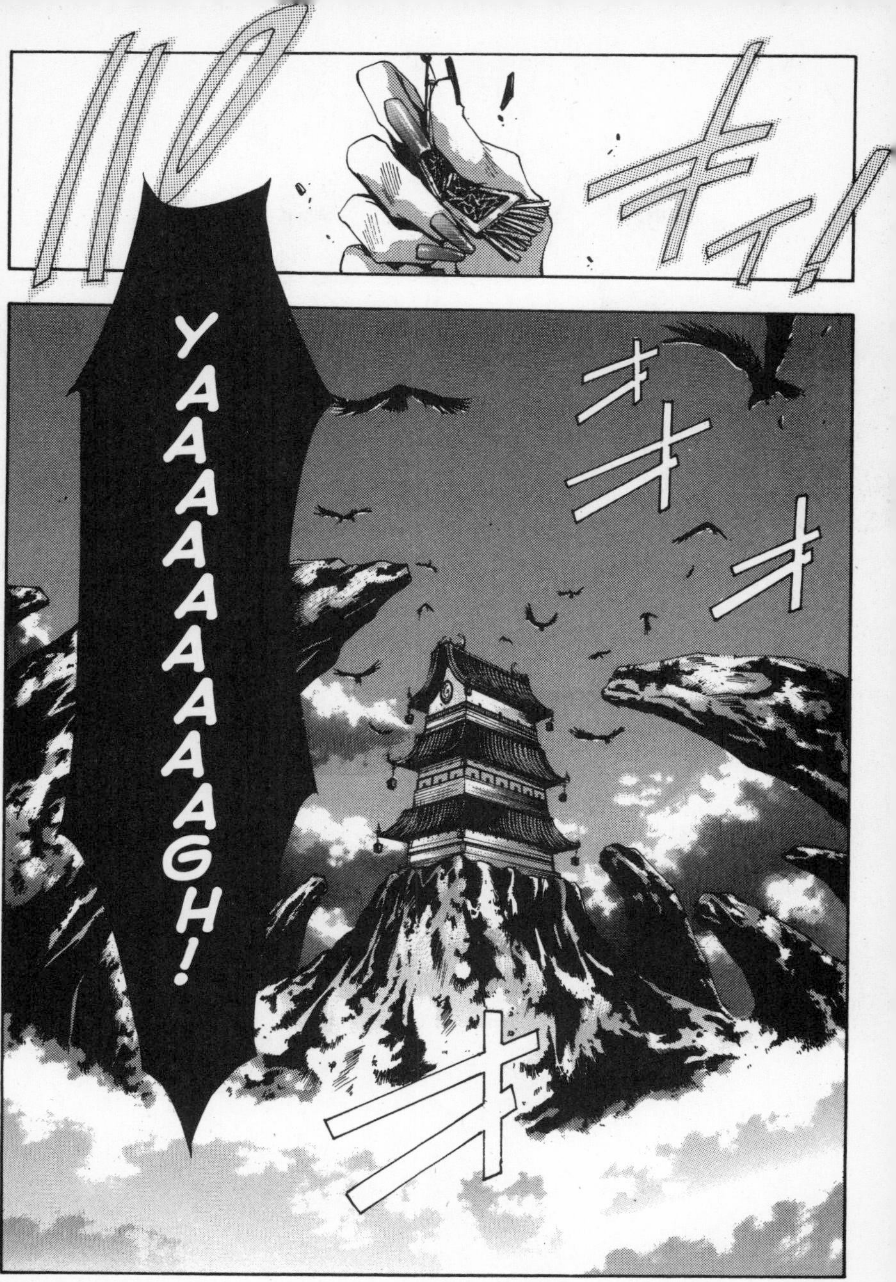
YAAAAAAAAAGH!

第36話 CHAPTER 36: WISH

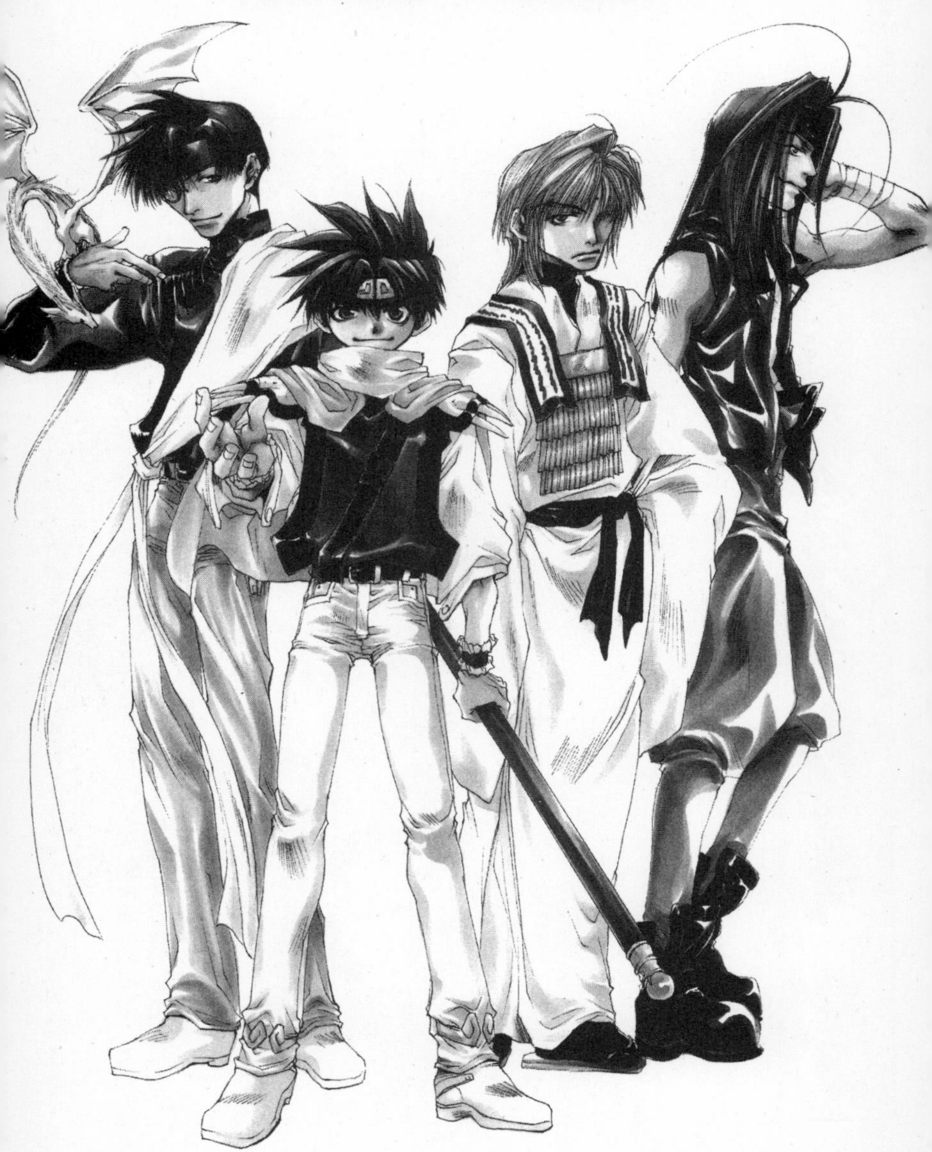

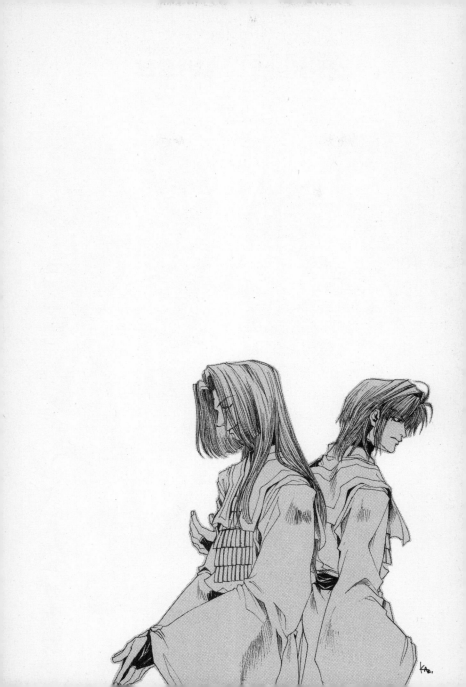

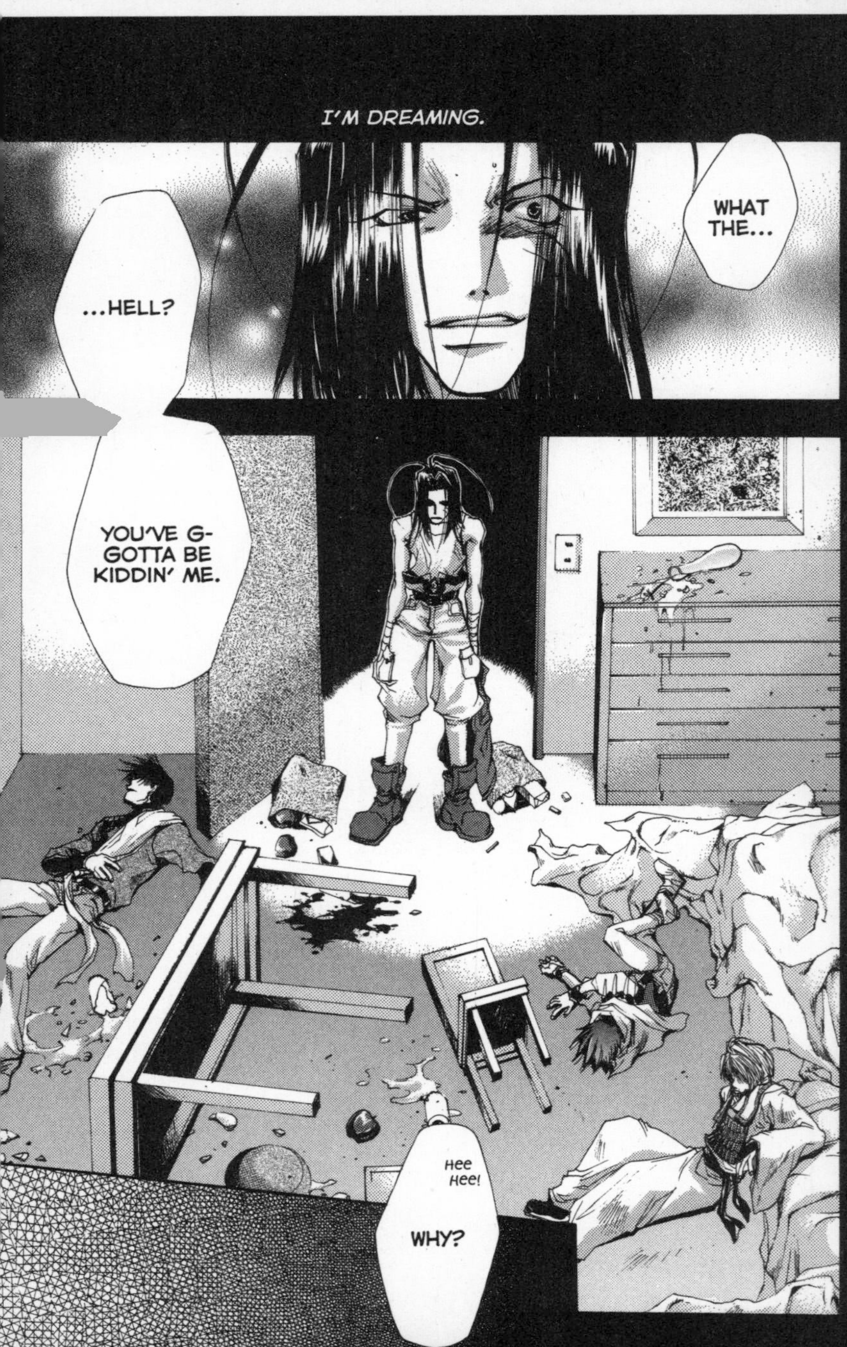
I'M DREAMING.
WHAT THE...
...HELL?
YOU'VE G-GOTTA BE KIDDIN' ME.
Hee Hee!
WHY?

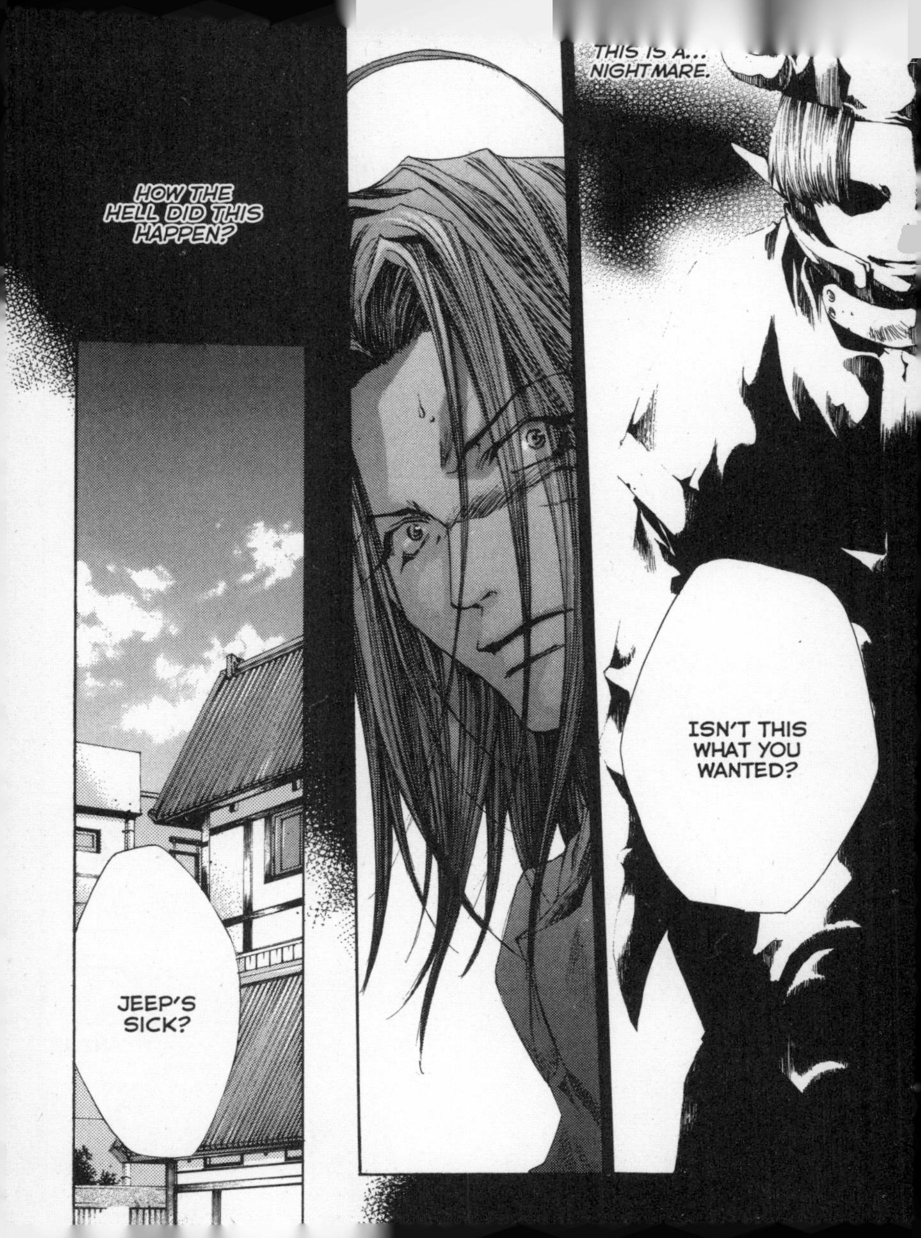
THIS IS A... NIGHTMARE.
ISN'T THIS WHAT YOU WANTED?
HOW THE HELL DID THIS HAPPEN?
JEEP'S SICK?

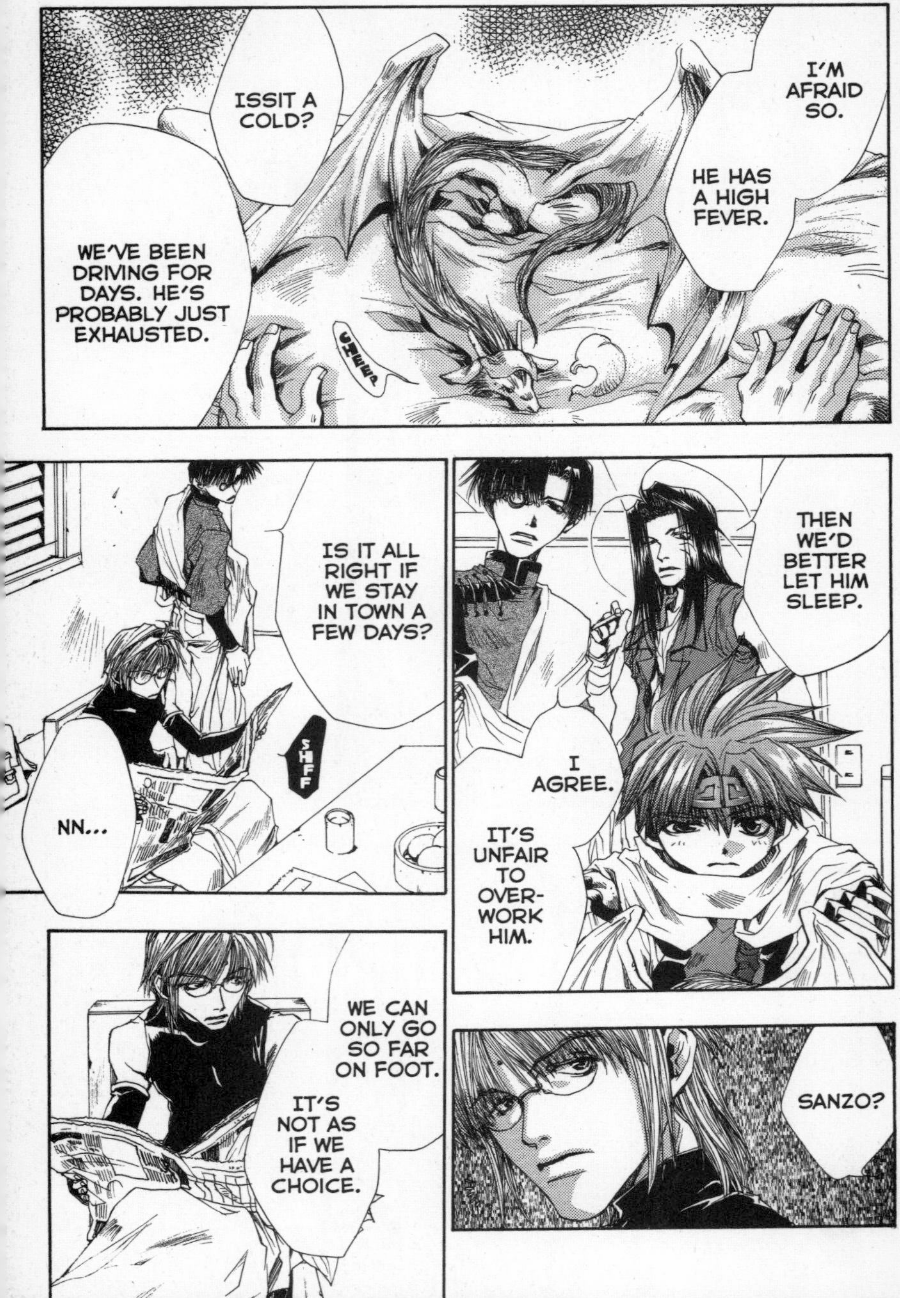
I'M AFRAID SO.
HE HAS A HIGH FEVER.
ISSIT A COLD?
WE'VE BEEN DRIVING FOR DAYS. HE'S PROBABLY JUST EXHAUSTED.
THEN WE'D BETTER LET HIM SLEEP.
I AGREE.
IT'S UNFAIR TO OVER-WORK HIM.
IS IT ALL RIGHT IF WE STAY IN TOWN A FEW DAYS?
SHFF
NN...
SANZO?
WE CAN ONLY GO SO FAR ON FOOT.
IT'S NOT AS IF WE HAVE A CHOICE.

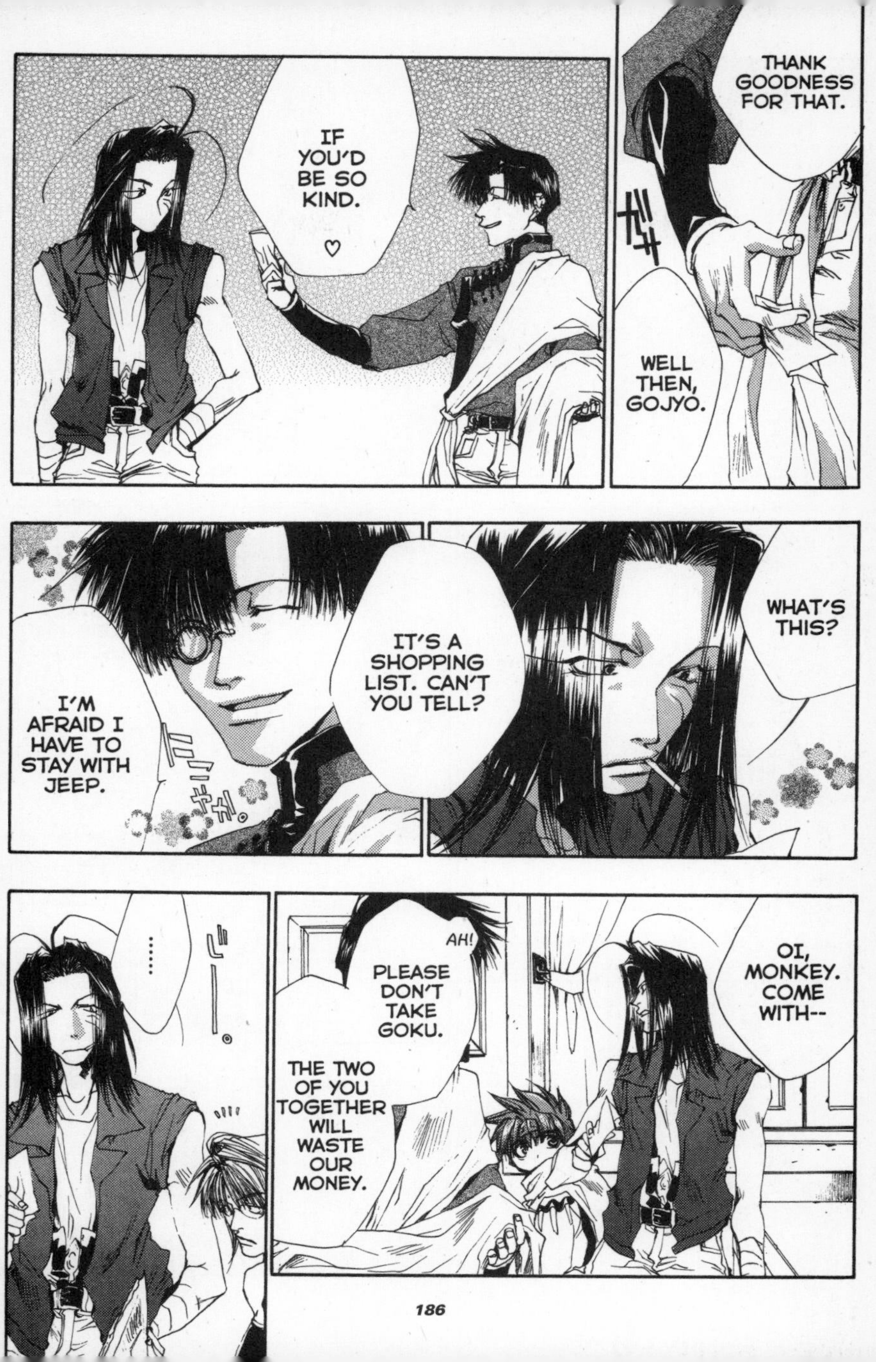
THANK GOODNESS FOR THAT.
WELL THEN, GOJYO.
IF YOU'D BE SO KIND. ♡
WHAT'S THIS?
IT'S A SHOPPING LIST. CAN'T YOU TELL?
I'M AFRAID I HAVE TO STAY WITH JEEP.
OI, MONKEY. COME WITH--
AH!
PLEASE DON'T TAKE GOKU.
THE TWO OF YOU TOGETHER WILL WASTE OUR MONEY.
......

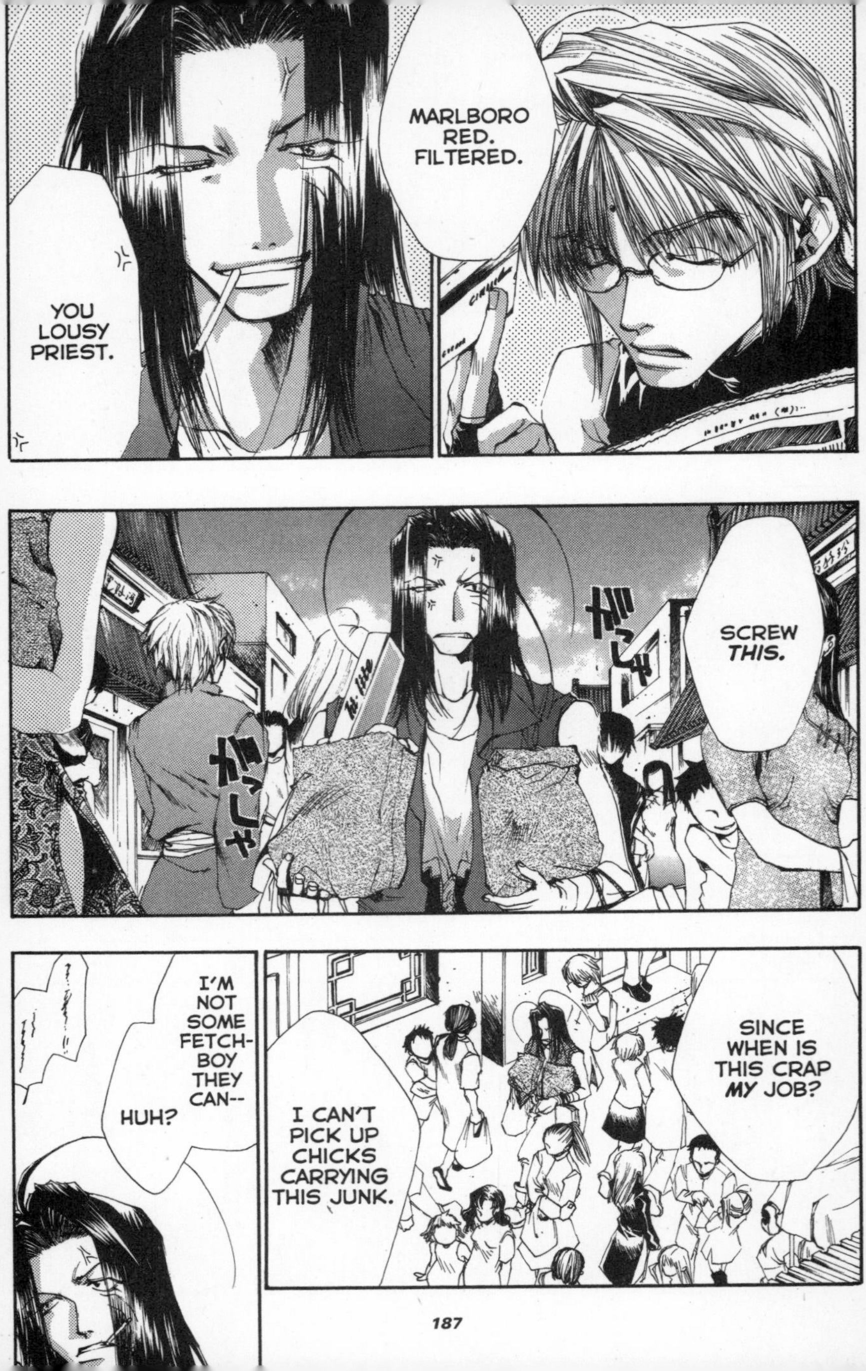
MARLBORO RED. FILTERED.
YOU LOUSY PRIEST.
SCREW *THIS.*
SINCE WHEN IS THIS CRAP *MY* JOB?
I CAN'T PICK UP CHICKS CARRYING THIS JUNK.
I'M NOT SOME FETCH-BOY THEY CAN--
HUH?

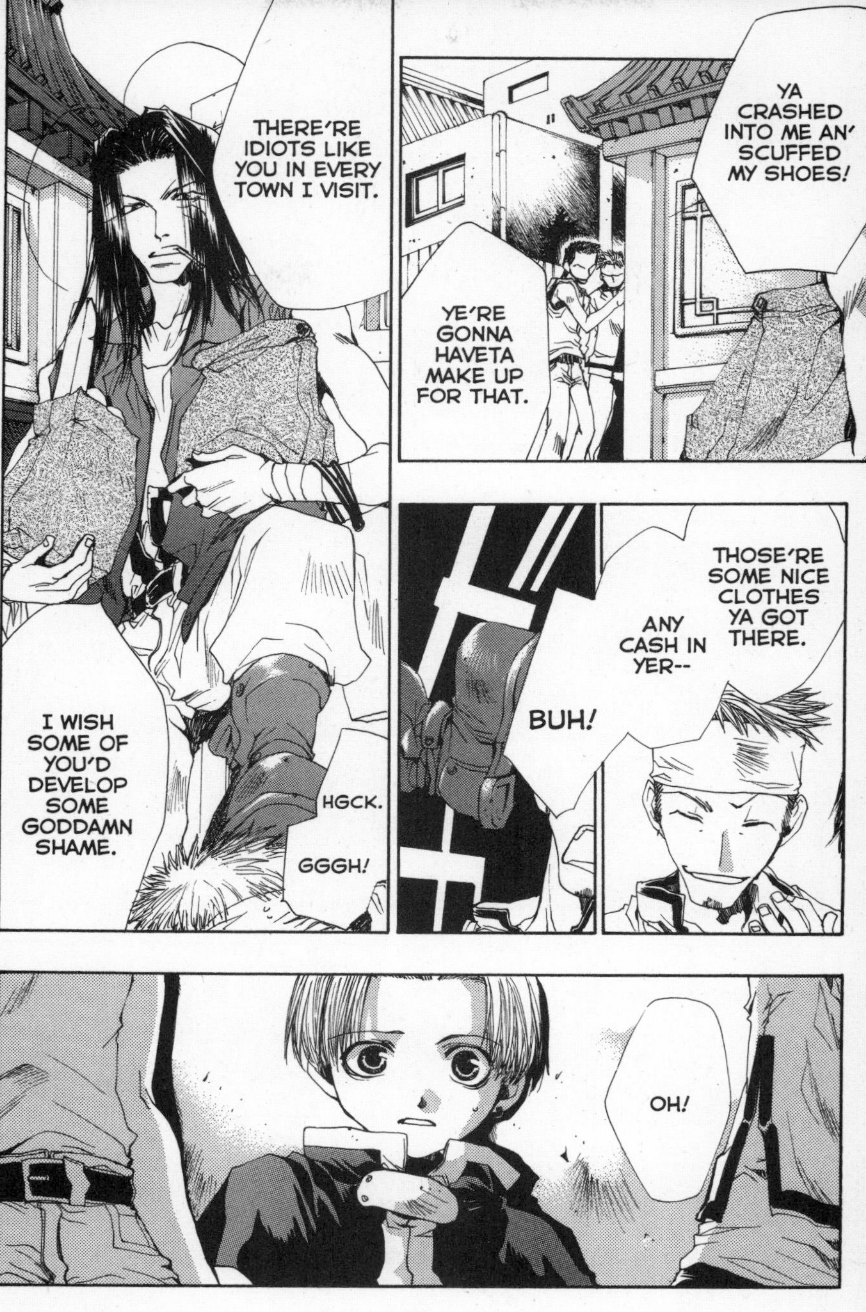
YA CRASHED INTO ME AN' SCUFFED MY SHOES!
YE'RE GONNA HAVETA MAKE UP FOR THAT.
THOSE'RE SOME NICE CLOTHES YA GOT THERE.
ANY CASH IN YER--
BUH!
THERE'RE IDIOTS LIKE YOU IN EVERY TOWN I VISIT.
I WISH SOME OF YOU'D DEVELOP SOME GODDAMN SHAME.
HGCK.
GGGH!
OH!

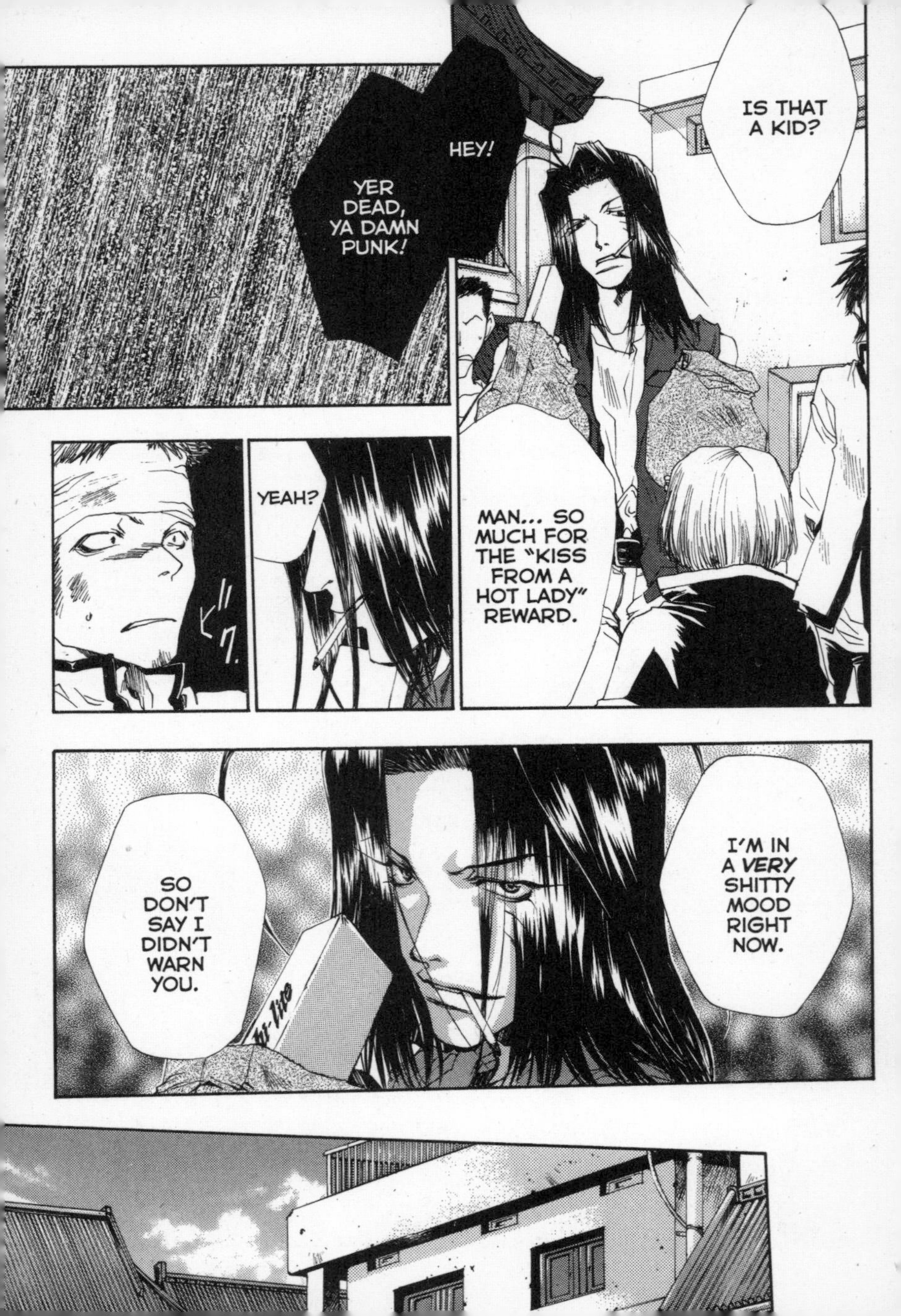
IS THAT A KID?
MAN... SO MUCH FOR THE "KISS FROM A HOT LADY" REWARD.
HEY!
YER DEAD, YA DAMN PUNK!
YEAH?
I'M IN A *VERY* SHITTY MOOD RIGHT NOW.
SO DON'T SAY I DIDN'T WARN YOU.

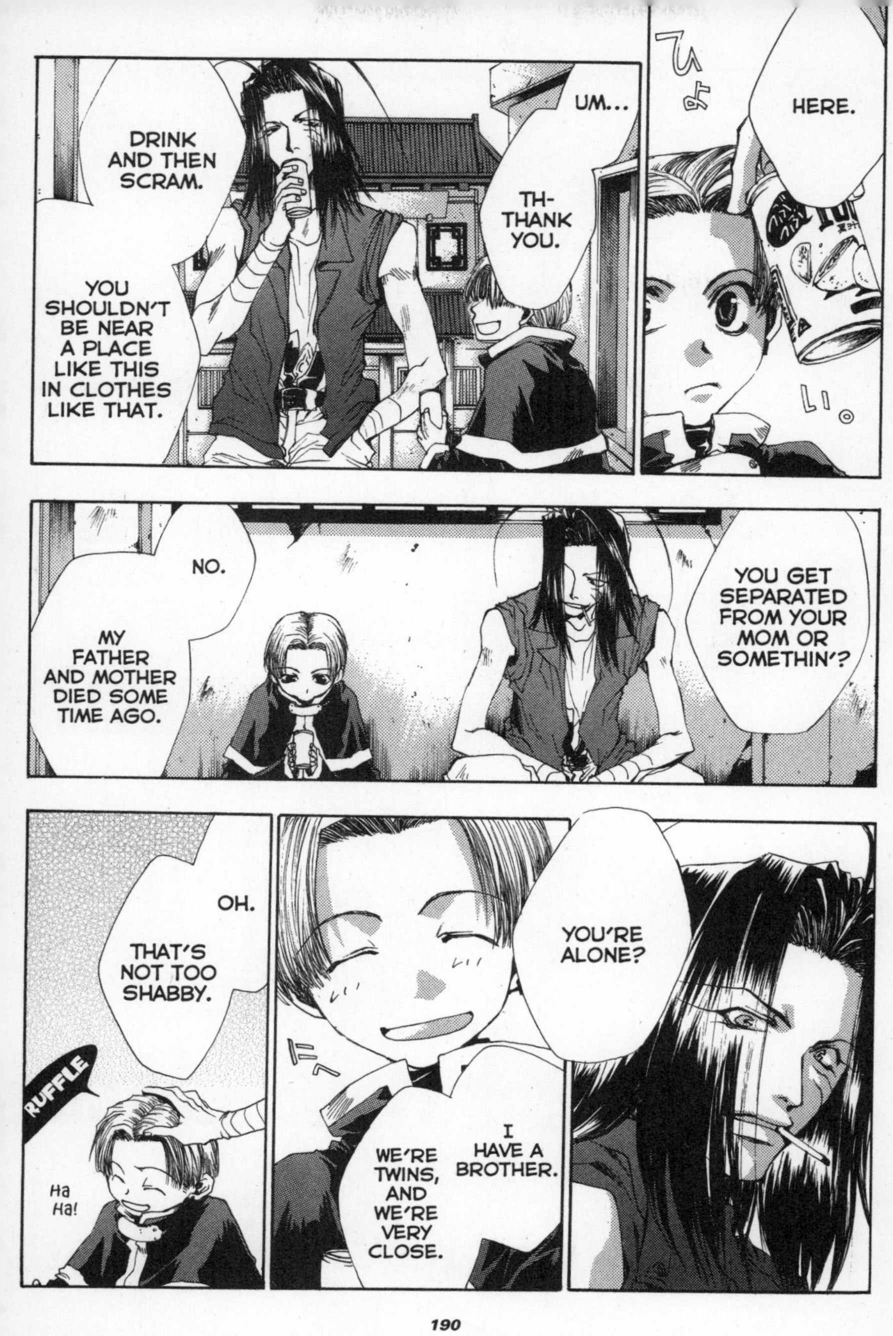
ひょ
HERE.
い。
UM...
TH-THANK YOU.
DRINK AND THEN SCRAM.
YOU SHOULDN'T BE NEAR A PLACE LIKE THIS IN CLOTHES LIKE THAT.
YOU GET SEPARATED FROM YOUR MOM OR SOMETHIN'?
NO.
MY FATHER AND MOTHER DIED SOME TIME AGO.
YOU'RE ALONE?
I HAVE A BROTHER.
WE'RE TWINS, AND WE'RE VERY CLOSE.
OH.
THAT'S NOT TOO SHABBY.
RUFFLE
Ha Ha!

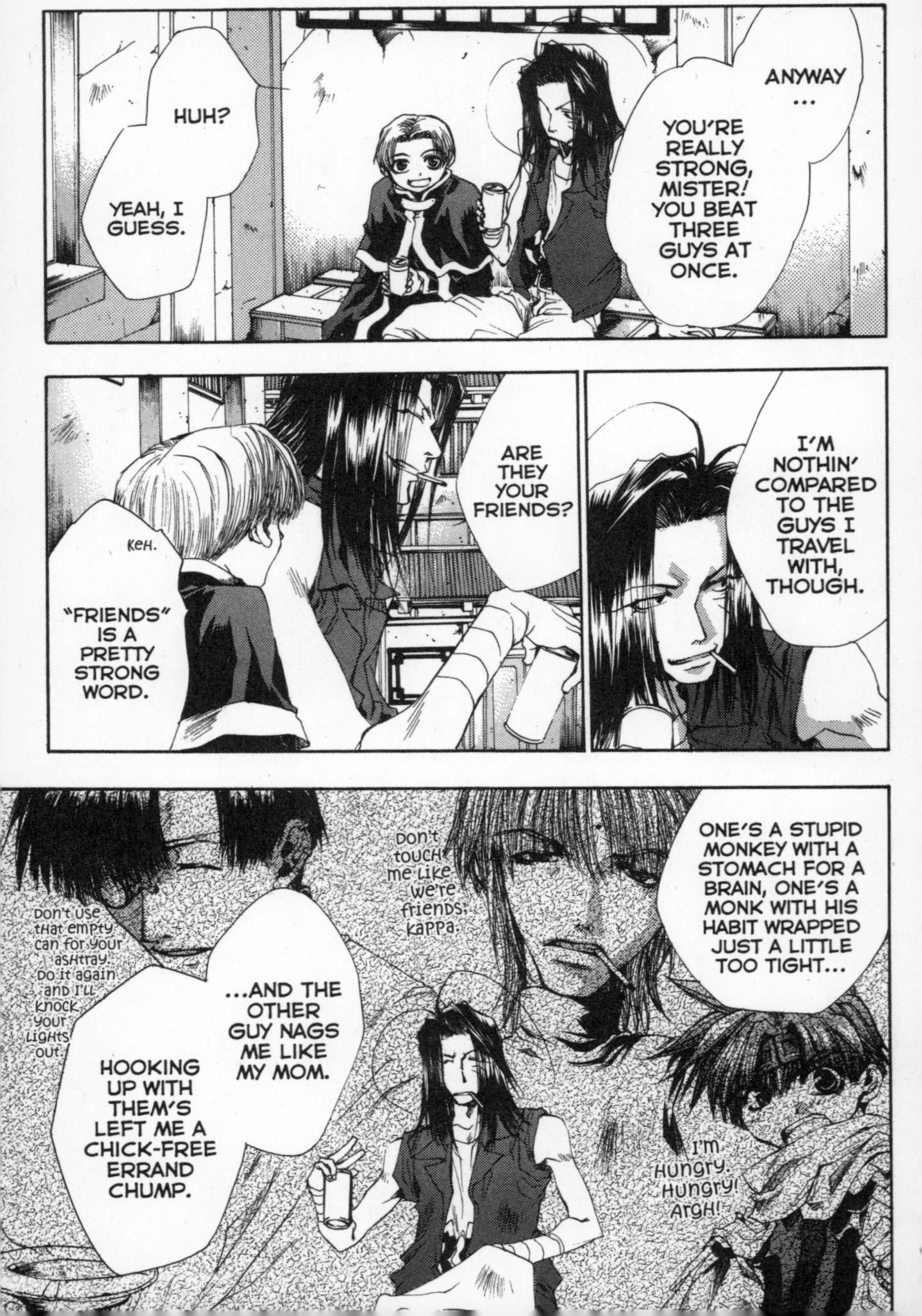
ANYWAY ...
YOU'RE REALLY STRONG, MISTER! YOU BEAT THREE GUYS AT ONCE.
HUH?
YEAH, I GUESS.
I'M NOTHIN' COMPARED TO THE GUYS I TRAVEL WITH, THOUGH.
ARE THEY YOUR FRIENDS?
KEH.
"FRIENDS" IS A PRETTY STRONG WORD.
ONE'S A STUPID MONKEY WITH A STOMACH FOR A BRAIN, ONE'S A MONK WITH HIS HABIT WRAPPED JUST A LITTLE TOO TIGHT...
Don't touch me like we're friends, kappa.
...AND THE OTHER GUY NAGS ME LIKE MY MOM.
Don't use that empty can for your ashtray. Do it again and I'll knock your lights out.
I'm Hungry. Hungry! Argh!
HOOKING UP WITH THEM'S LEFT ME A CHICK-FREE ERRAND CHUMP.

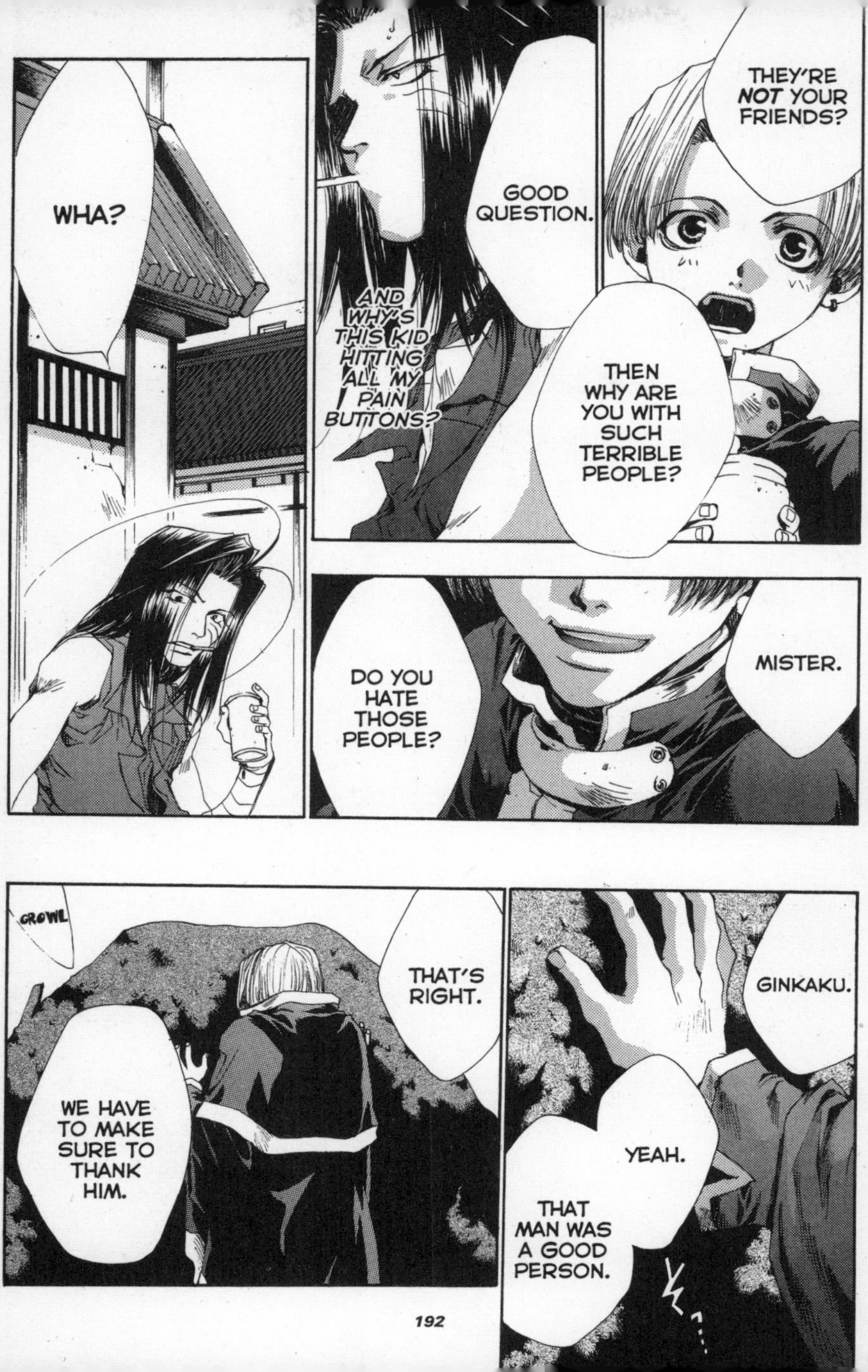
THEY'RE *NOT* YOUR FRIENDS?
THEN WHY ARE YOU WITH SUCH TERRIBLE PEOPLE?
GOOD QUESTION.
AND WHY'S THIS KID HITTING ALL MY PAIN BUTTONS?
MISTER.
DO YOU HATE THOSE PEOPLE?
WHA?
GINKAKU.
YEAH.
THAT MAN WAS A GOOD PERSON.
THAT'S RIGHT.
WE HAVE TO MAKE SURE TO THANK HIM.
GROWL

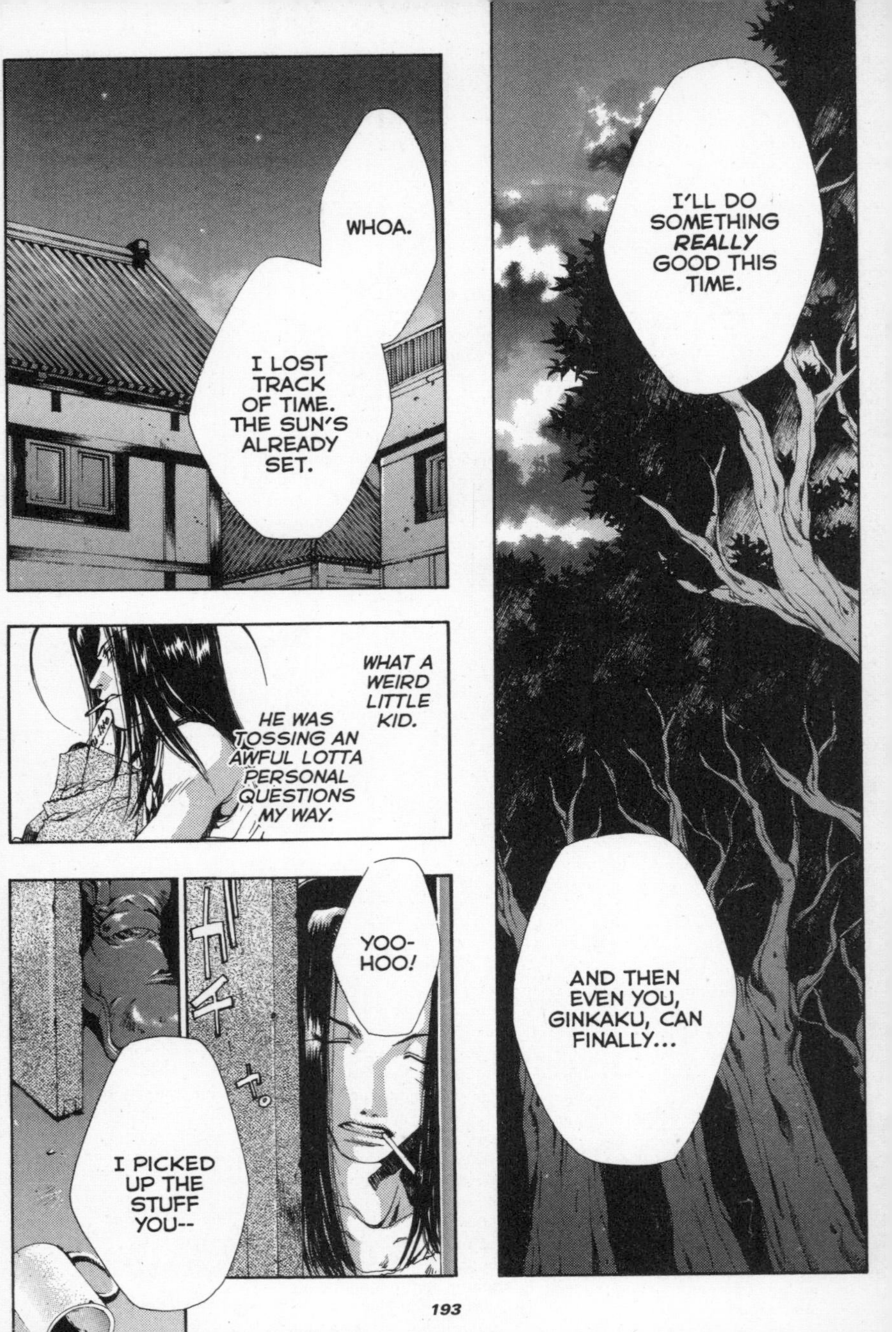
I'LL DO SOMETHING *REALLY* GOOD THIS TIME.
AND THEN EVEN YOU, GINKAKU, CAN FINALLY...
WHOA.
I LOST TRACK OF TIME. THE SUN'S ALREADY SET.
WHAT A WEIRD LITTLE KID.
HE WAS TOSSING AN AWFUL LOTTA PERSONAL QUESTIONS MY WAY.
YOO-HOO!
I PICKED UP THE STUFF YOU--

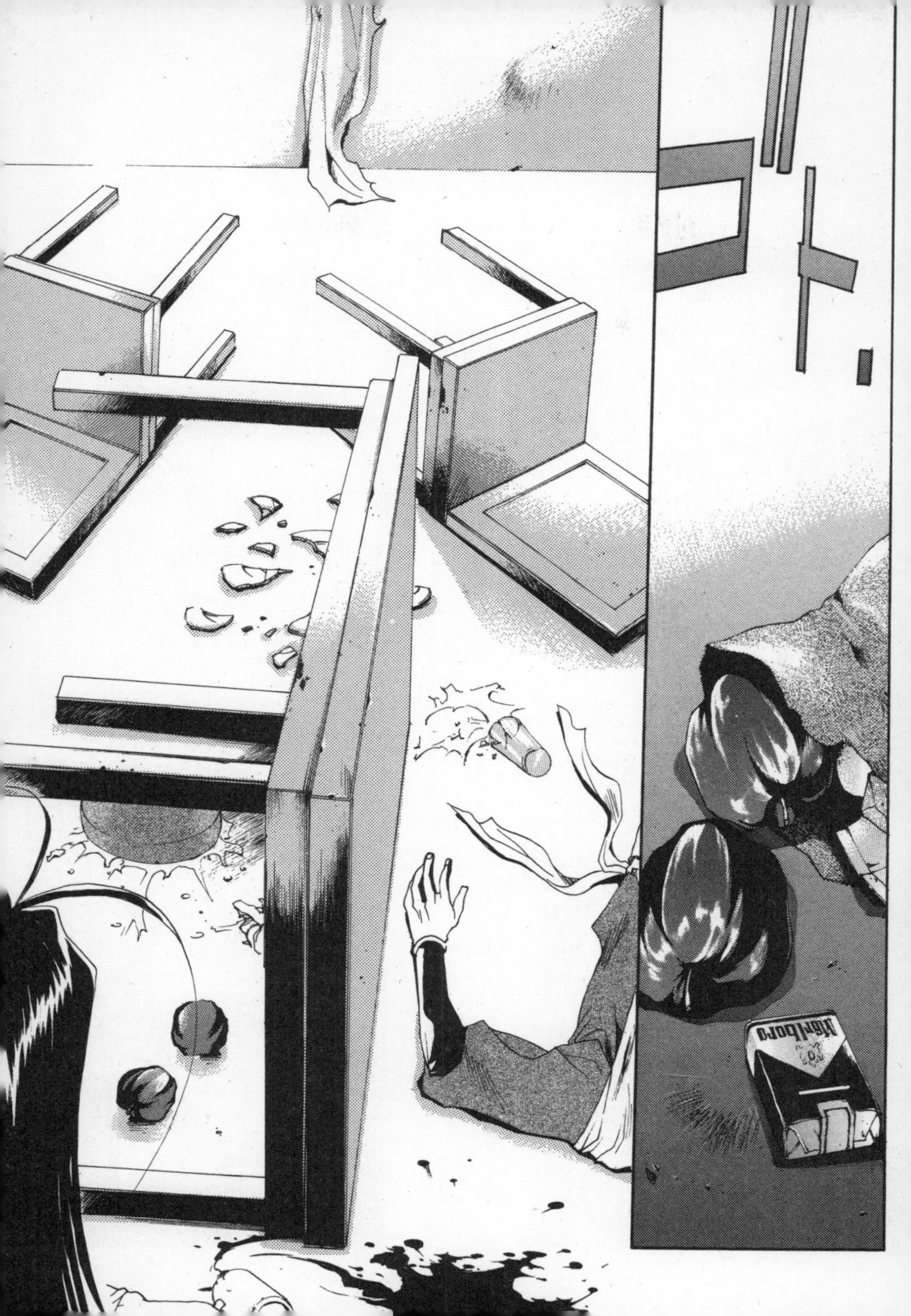
Marlboro

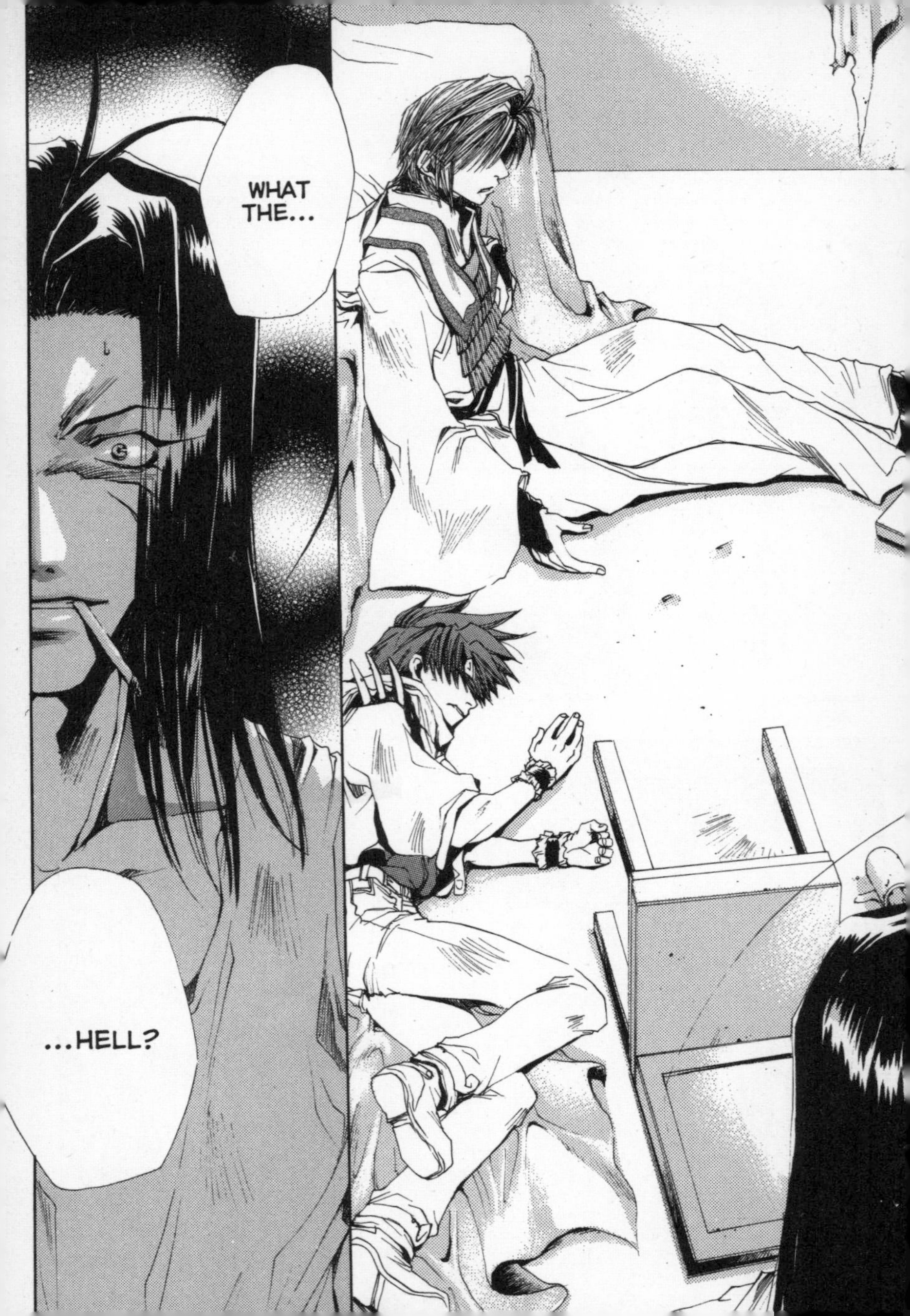
WHAT THE...
...HELL?

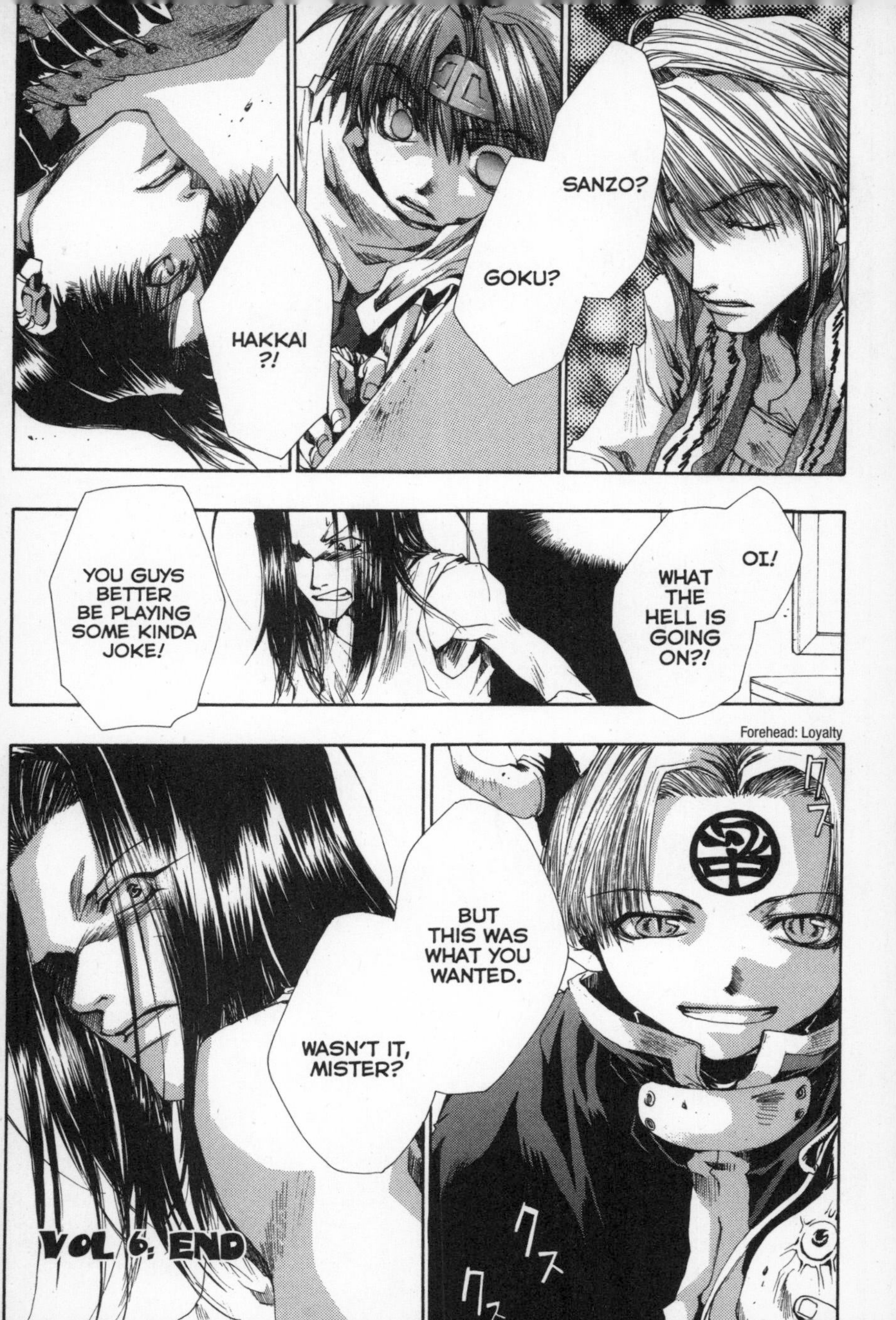
SANZO?
GOKU?
HAKKAI ?!
OI!
WHAT THE HELL IS GOING ON?!
YOU GUYS BETTER BE PLAYING SOME KINDA JOKE!
Forehead: Loyalty
クス
BUT THIS WAS WHAT YOU WANTED.
WASN'T IT, MISTER?
クス
クス
VOL 6: END

STAFF

ORIGINAL WORKS

Kazuya Minekura

ASSISTANTS

Azuma Asu

Jiro suzuki

EDITOR

Yousuke Sugino

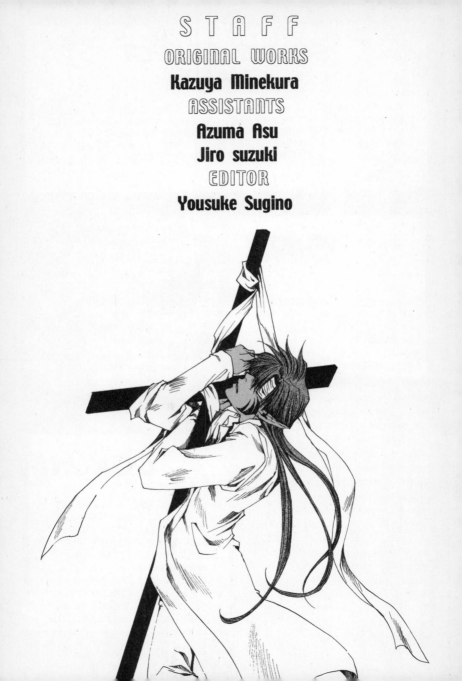

SOUND EFFECT CHART

THE FOLLOWING IS A LIST OF THE SOUND EFFECTS USED IN SAIYUKI. EACH SOUND IS LABELED BY PAGE AND PANEL NUMBER, SEPARATED BY A PERIOD. THE FIRST DESCRIPTION (IN BOLD) IS THE PHONETIC READING OF THE JAPANESE, AND IS FOLLOWED BY THE EQUIVALENT ENGLISH SOUND OR A DESCRIPTION.

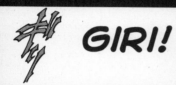 GIRI!

THIS USEFUL SOUND EFFECT HAS A COUPLE OF FUNCTIONS: IT CAN BE EITHER THE SOUND OF GRINDING TEETH OR TWO COMBATANTS STRUGGLING AGAINST EACH OTHER.

25.2 **ZA:** RUSH
25.3 **ZAZA:** RUSH
25.4 **ZAZA:** RUSH
26.1 **DO!:** WHAM
26.5 **GO!...:** ROAR
27.1 **BUWA!:** KABOOM!
28.2 **GEHO!:** COUGH!
29.3 **FURA:** WOBBLE
29.5 **DO!:** FWUMP
31.3 **OOO...:** HOWLING WIND
32.3 **ZA!...:** GRAB
32.4 **OOO:** HOWLING WIND
39.5 **OOO:** HOWLING WIND
40.2 **OOO...:** HOWLING WIND
40.5 **OO:** HOWLING WIND
41.2 **O:** HOWLING WIND
42.1 **ZA!!:** RUSH

13.4 **GIKU.:** TWITCH
14.1 **PAN!:** WHAP!
16.1 **GURI!:** SHAKE
17.1 **OO:** GROAN
18.6 **PARA...:** CRUMBLE
18.7 **GOGO:** OMINOUS
19.1 **ZUUN!:** RUMBLE
20.4 **ZU:** CRACK
21.1 **BAAN!:** KSSHH!
21.2 **ZAZAZA:** RUSH
21.3 **ZA:** RUSH
22.3 **ZUZUZU:** CRACK
23.1 **DOOON!:** BOOM
24.2 **OOO:** ROAR
25.1 **ZA:** RUSH

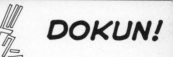 DOKUN!

IN MOST MANGA, A PLEASANT LITTLE "DOKI DOKI" IS THE PREFERRED SOUND FOR HEARTBEATS, BUT IN SAIYUKI, THEY NEEDED TO KICK IT UP A NOTCH. "DOKUN" IS THE SOUND OF A PARTICULARLY STRONG HEARTBEAT, USUALLY RESERVED FOR MOMENTS OF EXTREME SHOCK OR DEMONIC TRANSFORMATION.

67.1	ZA!: RUSH
67.2	OOOO: HOWLING WIND
67.3	ZOZO...: WHUSH
68.4	DOON: BOOM

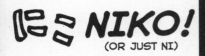

NIKO!

(OR JUST NI)

IT TAKES 26 MUS-CLES TO SMILE, OR JUST TWO KATAKANA! "NIKO," REPEATED AS MUCH AS YOU WANT FOR EMPHASIS, GIVES THE READER AN INDICATION OF JUST HOW BIG A SMILE IS.

68.1	ZAA!!: WHOOSH
68.3	BOKII: KAWHAM
70.1	BUSHUU: CRASPLURT
71.1	GUI!: YANK
71.3	ZASHU.: SLASH
72.1	BUSHU.: SPLURT
74.1	ZASHUZASHU: SLASH-SLASH
74.5	GIRI...: GRIND
75.1	BA!!: SPRING
75.2	DA!.: DASH
75.3	ZAN.: SWISH
77.1	TO!.: TAP
78.1	GOKYA!: KAWHAM
78.2	DOSAA: KATHUD
80.1	ZAA!: POSE
80.3	PIKU: TWITCH
80.4	CHAKI.: SHKK
81.2	HYUN!!: SWSH
81.3	BA!..: KA-
81.4	GAKII!!: WHANG
82.2	KUWA!: GWAH
82.4	GAKII: CRUNCH
83.3	BA!: DASH
84.3	PASHII!!: WHACK
84.1	BOKII: THWOCK
85.2	ZURU...: STAGGER

42.3	FOOO: WHOOSH
42.6	GO...: KA-
43.1	DONDOON!: BOOOOM!
45.1	DOKAA: WHACK
45.2	ZUSAA: CRASH
46.1	GABA!: SHOCK
47.1	BA!: BAM
47.2	ZA!.: RUSH
47.5	GO...: KA-
48.1	GO!: WHAM!
48.2	ZA!...: RUSH
49.2	ZAA!: WHOOSH
51.1	HA!: GASP
51.2	ZA!: RUSH
51.3	JA!...: CLANK
51.4	CHIN!: CHING
52.4	JA!.: SKSH
53.2	GAKII!!: CLANG
53.3	GIRIGIRI: GRIND
54.1	OOO..: HOWLING WIND
54.4	GIRI: GRIND
54.5	ZAKU...: SKSH
55.2	OO: HOWLING WIND
55.3	OOO: HOWLING WIND
56.1	TO!: THUNK
56.2	DOKUN.: HEART POUNDING
57.3	DOKUN: HEART POUNDING
57.4	OOO: HOWLING WIND
58.1	OOO...: HOWLING WIND
63.1	OOO...: HOWLING WIND
64.1	TO!: TAP
65.1	BAKII: KAWHAM

SHIN!

THE SOUND OF SILENCE. THE PERFECT "SOUND" EFFECT TO PUNCTUATE THOSE UNCOMFORTABLE MOMENTS WHERE THE LACK OF ANY ACTUAL SOUNDS JUST ISN'T SUFFICIENT. FOR EMPHASIS, YOU'LL USUALLY SEE A LONG LINE IN BETWEEN THE "SHI" AND THE "N," INDICATING PROLONGED SILENCE.

111.5 BIKUN!: SHOCK
112.1 KA!: SHINE
112.2 OO: HOWLING WIND
113.1 FU!: SIGH
113.3 DOSA...: THUD
114.2 DOSA.: THUD
114.3 OOO: HOWLING WIND

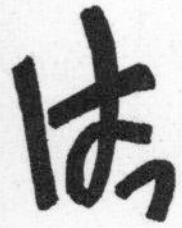
はっ

HAH!

THIS IS ONE OF THE MOST COMMON SOUNDS YOU'LL SEE IN MANGA. IT'S USED TO INDICATE SURPRISE AND IS USUALLY EQUIVALENT TO "GASP!" "H" ISN'T NECESSARILY VOCALIZED, THOUGH.

116.2 OOO: HOWLING WIND
116.6 ZU...: SLUMP
117.1 ZU!...: SLUMP
117.2 DOSA.: THUD
117.3 GISHI...: CREAK
117.4 OOO..: HOWLING WIND
118.1 HAAHA...: HUFF HUFF
118.3 DORUN: BRUUN
120.2 DO! DO! DO!: ENGINE RUMBLE
120.3 DO!: ENGINE RUMBLE
120.4 GURA...: WOBBLE
120.6 GA!!: GRAB
121.4 DO! DO! DO!: ENGINE RUMBLE
130.6 GIRI!: GRIND
131.5 JA!.: FLAP
133.5 GORO.: ROLL
136.3 GYAA GYAA: WAUGH WAUGH
137.1 GIKU.: TWITCH
138.1 GIKU.: TWITCH
138.2 GUI!!: GRAB
139.1 WASHA.: TOUSLE
140.2 GO!.: THWOCK
141.3 GACHA.: CLATCH
141.4 BIKU.: SHOCK

86.3 DOSA...: THUD
87.2 GO...!: KA-
87.3 DOON!: BOOM
87.4 ZAZA!.: SKSHH
88.1 OOO: HOWLING WIND
89.2 FU!.: SIGH
89.4 GO...: KA-
90.1 BA!..: SPRING
91.1 DAAN!: WHAM
91.2 MIKU!.: GRAB
92.1 BA!...: SPRING
93.1 DOGO!: WHACK
93.2 DOKAA!: KAWHAM
95.1 ZAA: POSE
96.2 BA!: SPRING
96.3 BAKYA!!: WHAM
96.3 DOKA!: WHACK
96.4 BAKI: THUD
97.4 GAUN!: BANG
102.3 OOOO: HOWLING WIND
102.5 ZAA..: POSE
103.5 DA!: DASH
105.2 GO!.: WHOCK
106.1 ZUSHAA: SKSHH

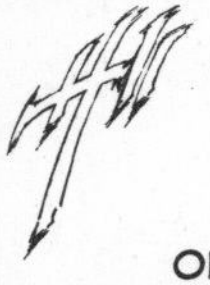

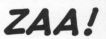

ZAA!

YOU'LL SEE THIS ONE A LOT IN *SAIYUKI*. "ZAA" INDICATES A DRAMATIC APPEARANCE. IF YOU WANT TO MAKE A LASTING IMPRESSION, ALWAYS COME IN WITH A COOL POSE AND A BIG "ZAA!"

106.3 BA!: KA-
106.4 DAN!: WHAM
107.1 HYU: SWSH
107.4 BAKYA: WHANG
108.1 DAAN!: WHAM
108.2 PIKU: TWITCH
111.3 GA!: GRAB
111.4 OOOO..: HOWLING WIND

161.3   ZURUX4: DRAG
161.4   BATAN.: SLAM
162.1   BURORORORO...:
VRURURURU
162.1   SUPAAN!!: VROOM!
162.3   GAA GAA: KAW KAW
163.2   TA!: DASH
165.5   GAN!: WHAM
165.6   GAN!X3: WHAM
167.1   DO! DO!: ENGINE RUMBLING
167.2   DO! DO!: ENGINE RUMBLING
167.2   OON.: ARGH
167.3   DO! DO! DO!: ENGINE RUMBLING
168.2   ZASHU.: SLASH
168.4   DO! DO!: ENGINE RUMBLING
169.4   ZURU..: DRAG
169.5   UII..: VMM
171.5   GURA...: STAGGER
173.3   SAWA..: WHOOSH
178.2   SU..: SHF
178.4   ZOKU!.: SHIVER
179.4   JARA...: CHINK
179.6   GIRI...: GRIND
180.1   PAKII!: SNAP
180.2   OOOO: HOWLING WIND
186.1   GASA: RUSTLE
186.4   NIKOYAKA.: SMILING
186.6   JII.: STARE
187.3   GASSHA GASSHA:
GROWL GROWL
188.3   DOKA: CLOMP
189.4   BIKU.: TWINGE
190.1   HYOI.: REACH
190.5   NIHE: HEH HEH
192.5   SO!...: SLIDE
193.4   GACHA.: CLATCH
194.1   GOTO.: KATHUNK
196.5   KUSU x3: HEH

141.5   WA!!: WAH!
141.5   GU!.: GRAB
142.4   BAN!!: BANG
143.5   HA!: GASP
144.4   SU.: SHF
145.1   KUSHA: TOUSLE
145.2   GUI!: GRAB
146.1   SUPAAN!: THWACK
146.4   DOSA.: WHUMP
147.5   GAUN GAUN: BANG BANG
148.1   HYOI: POP UP
148.3   GAUN GAUN: BANG BANG
149.2   OOO!.: HOWLING WIND

 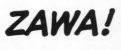

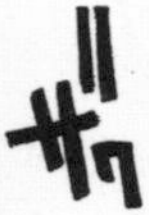

ZAWA!

NO ONE REALLY CARES WHAT ALL THOSE EXTRAS IN THE BACKGROUND ARE SAYING, RIGHT? THAT'S WHY MANGA-KA USE THIS HANDY SOUND EFFECT TO INDICATE BACKGROUND CHATTER. YOU'LL SEE IT HOVERING OVER CROWDED CITY STREETS OR CLASSROOMS THROUGHOUT MANGA. IT CAN ALSO BE USED TO INDICATE THE SOUND OF WIND BLOWING THROUGH THE LEAVES OF A TREE. AIN'T THAT SWEET?

150.1   GOBO GOBO: GLUB GLUB
152.1   BASHII!!: BASH
153.1   BIKU.: TWITCH
154.5   GOUN GOUN: KACHUG
KACHUG
155.3   GURA...: STAGGER
158.3   GATA!!: SHOCK
158.5   NI.: GRIN
159.3   GAUN: BANG
159.4   GAUN GAN GAUN: BANG
BANG BANG
161.2   PEKO.: BOW
161.2   BIKU BIKU: TWITCH TWITCH

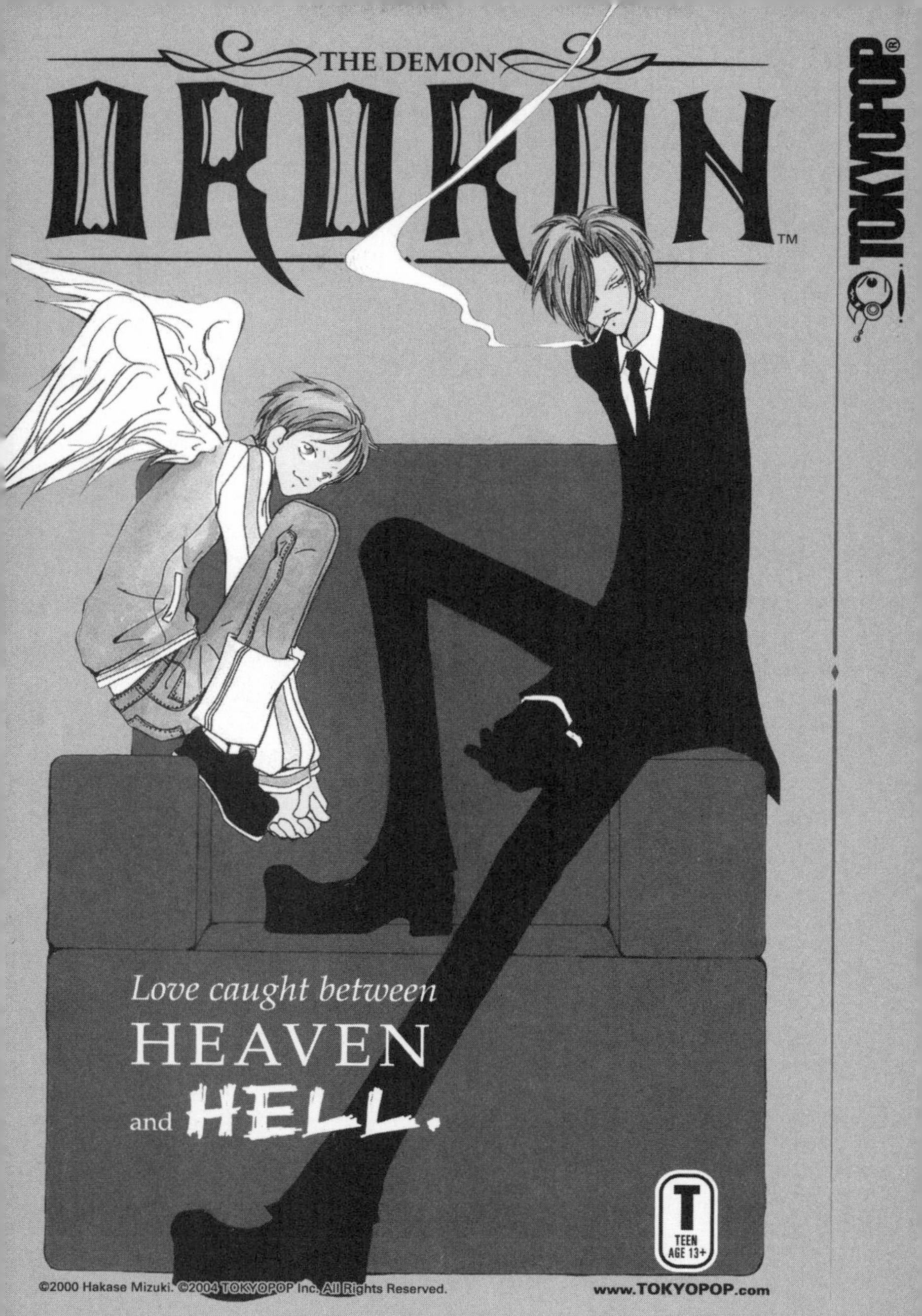
THE DEMON
ORORON™
TOKYOPOP®
Love caught between
HEAVEN
and HELL.
T
TEEN
AGE 13+

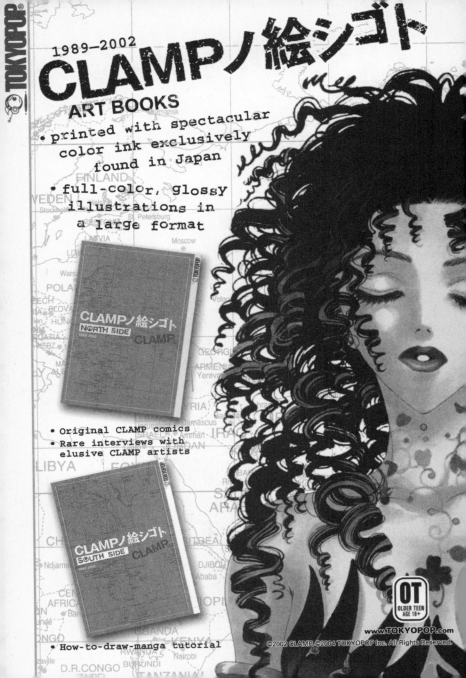

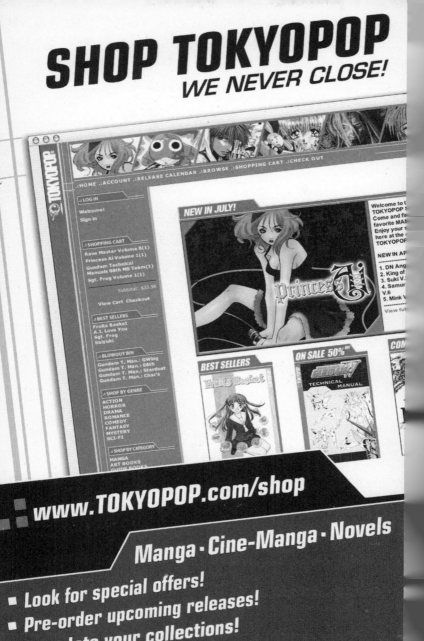

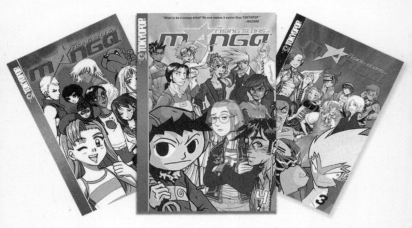
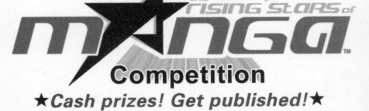

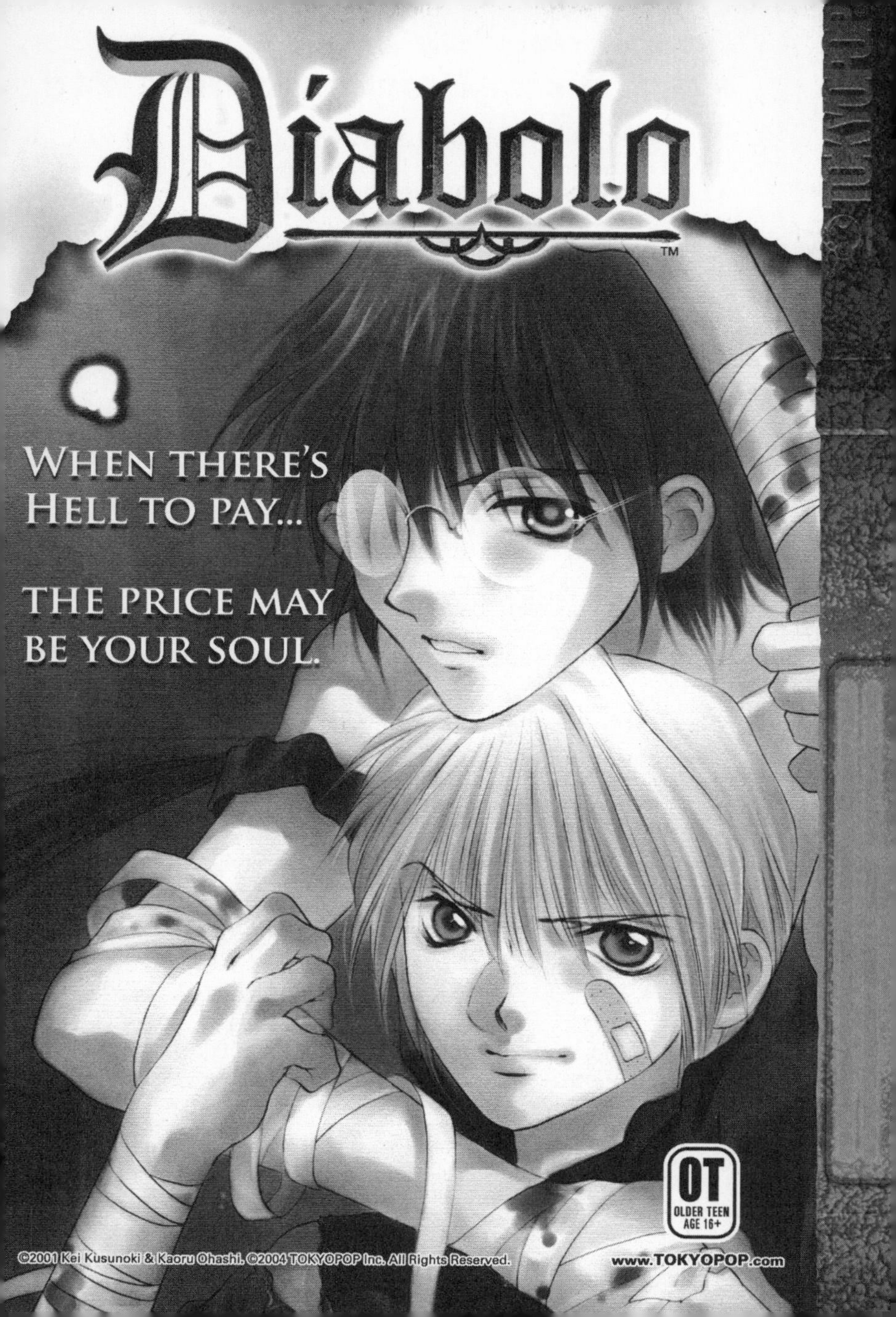

Diablo™
WHEN THERE'S HELL TO PAY...
THE PRICE MAY BE YOUR SOUL.
OT OLDER TEEN AGE 16+
©2001 Kei Kusunoki & Kaoru Ohashi. ©2004 TOKYOPOP Inc. All Rights Reserved.
www.TOKYOPOP.com
TOKYOPOP

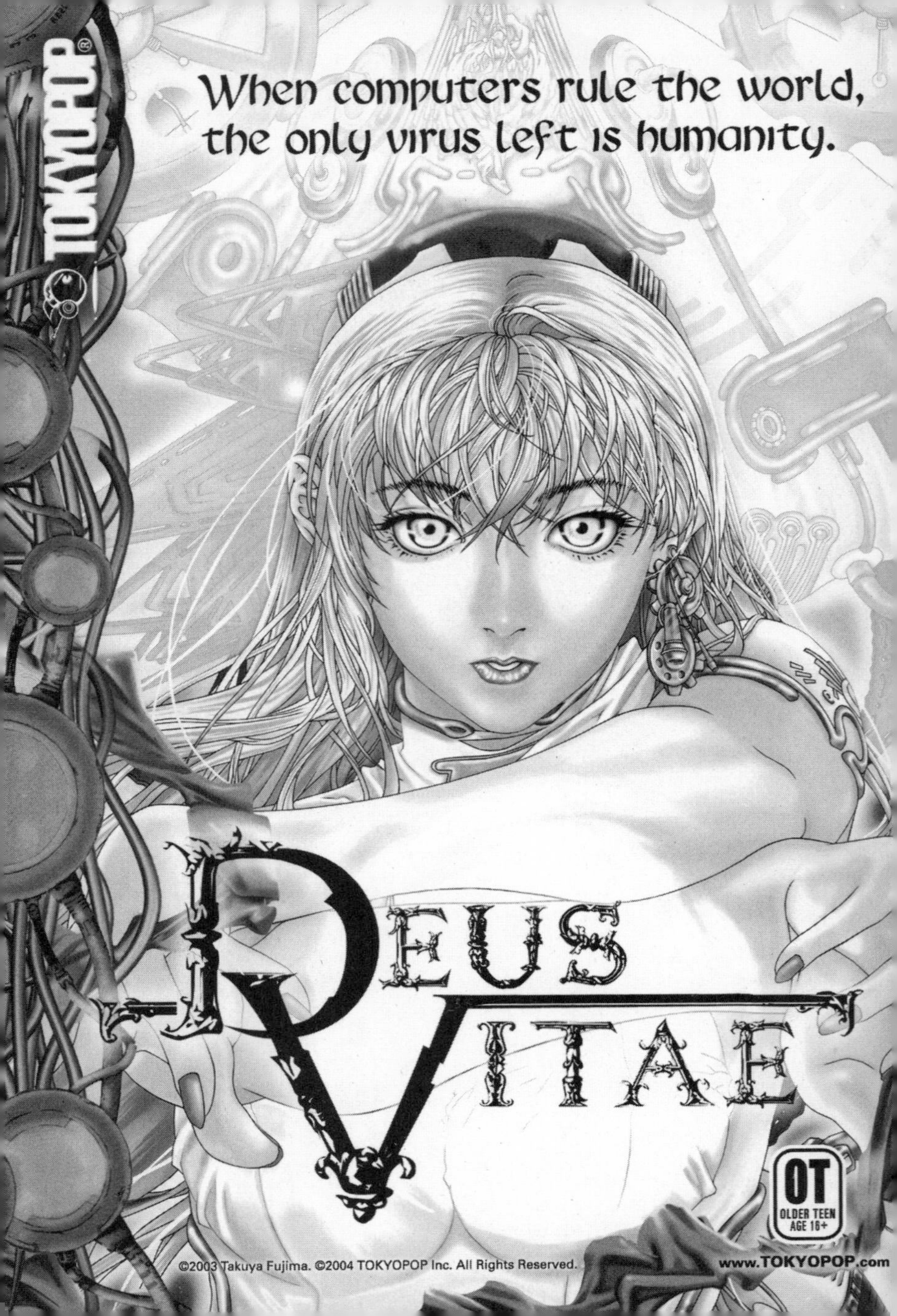

TOKYOPOP®
When computers rule the world,
the only virus left is humanity.
DEUS VITAE
OT
OLDER TEEN
AGE 16+
©2003 Takuya Fujima. ©2004 TOKYOPOP Inc. All Rights Reserved.
www.TOKYOPOP.com

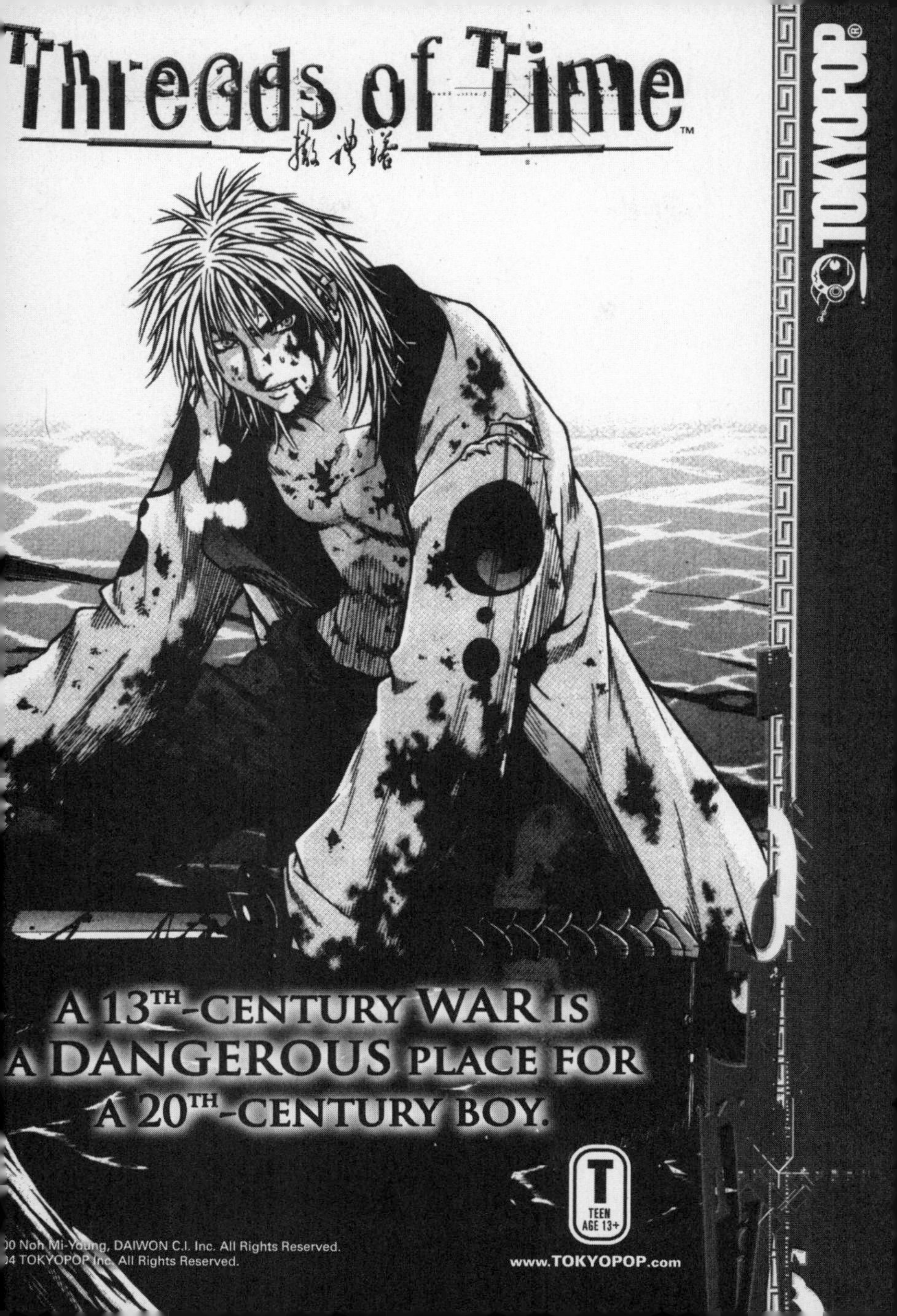
Threads of Time™
TOKYOPOP®
A 13TH-CENTURY WAR IS
A DANGEROUS PLACE FOR
A 20TH-CENTURY BOY.
T
TEEN
AGE 13+
00 Noh Mi-Young, DAIWON C.I. Inc. All Rights Reserved.
04 TOKYOPOP Inc. All Rights Reserved.
www.TOKYOPOP.com

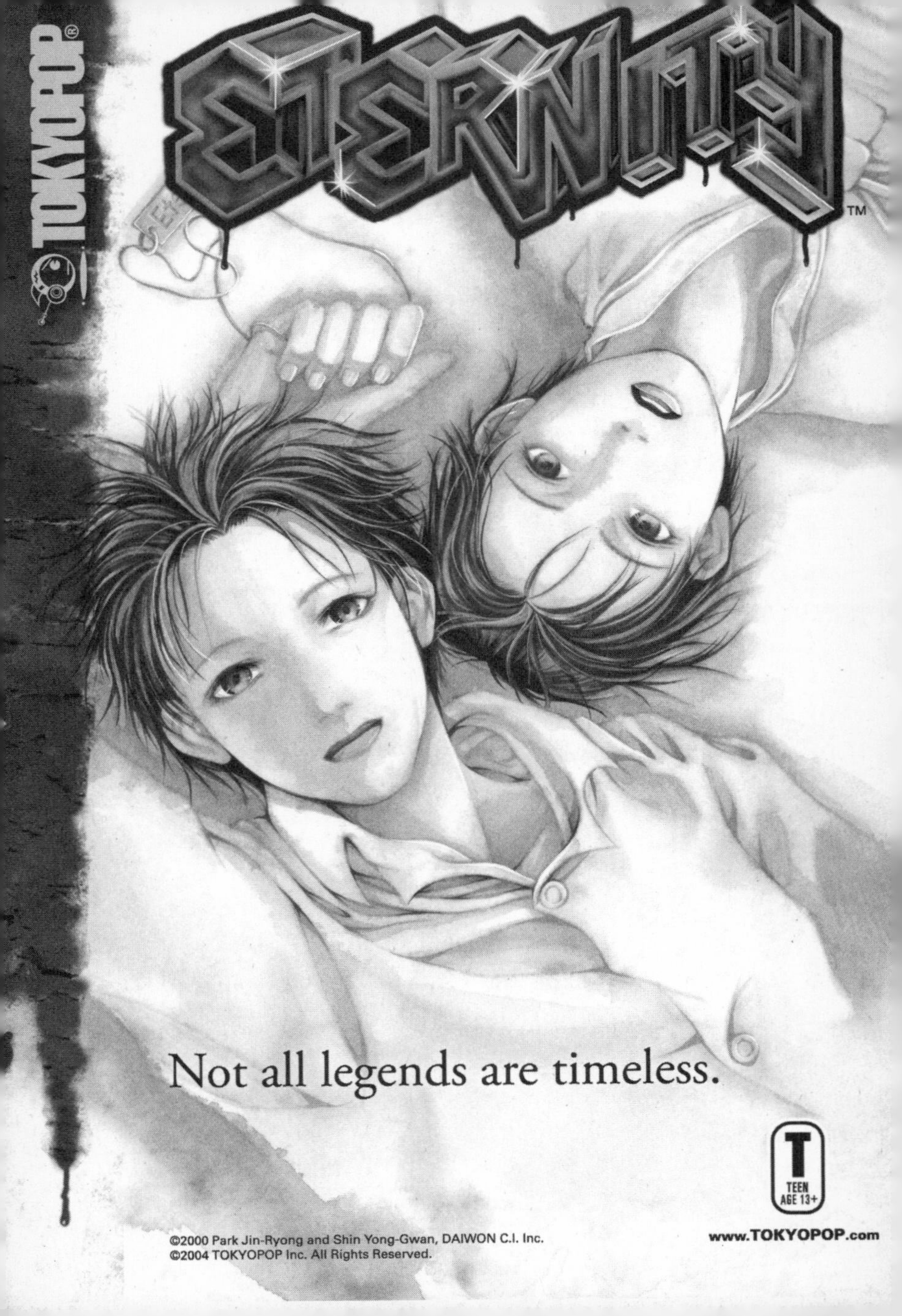

ALSO AVAILABLE FROM TOKYOPOP®

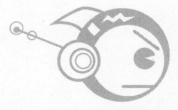

You want it? We got it!
A full range of TOKYOPOP
products are available now at:
www.TOKYOPOP.com/shop

09.21.04T

ALSO AVAILABLE FROM TOKYOPOP

MANGA

.HACK//LEGEND OF THE TWILIGHT
@LARGE
ABENOBASHI: MAGICAL SHOPPING ARCADE
A.I. LOVE YOU
AI YORI AOSHI
ALICHINO
ANGELIC LAYER
ARM OF KANNON
BABY BIRTH
BATTLE ROYALE
BATTLE VIXENS
BOYS BE...
BRAIN POWERED
BRIGADOON
B'TX
CANDIDATE FOR GODDESS, THE
CARDCAPTOR SAKURA
CARDCAPTOR SAKURA - MASTER OF THE CLOW
CHOBITS
CHRONICLES OF THE CURSED SWORD
CLAMP SCHOOL DETECTIVES
CLOVER
COMIC PARTY
CONFIDENTIAL CONFESSIONS
CORRECTOR YUI
COWBOY BEBOP
COWBOY BEBOP: SHOOTING STAR
CRAZY LOVE STORY
CRESCENT MOON
CROSS
CULDCEPT
CYBORG 009
D•N•ANGEL
DEARS
DEMON DIARY
DEMON ORORON, THE
DEUS VITAE
DIABOLO
DIGIMON
DIGIMON TAMERS
DIGIMON ZERO TWO
DOLL
DRAGON HUNTER
DRAGON KNIGHTS
DRAGON VOICE
DREAM SAGA
DUKLYON: CLAMP SCHOOL DEFENDERS
EERIE QUEERIE!
ERICA SAKURAZAWA: COLLECTED WORKS
ET CETERA
ETERNITY
EVIL'S RETURN
FAERIES' LANDING
FAKE
FLCL
FLOWER OF THE DEEP SLEEP
FORBIDDEN DANCE
FRUITS BASKET

G GUNDAM
GATEKEEPERS
GETBACKERS
GIRL GOT GAME
GRAVITATION
GTO
GUNDAM SEED ASTRAY
GUNDAM WING
GUNDAM WING: BATTLEFIELD OF PACIFISTS
GUNDAM WING: ENDLESS WALTZ
GUNDAM WING: THE LAST OUTPOST (G-UNIT)
HANDS OFF!
HAPPY MANIA
HARLEM BEAT
HYPER RUNE
I.N.V.U.
IMMORTAL RAIN
INITIAL D
INSTANT TEEN: JUST ADD NUTS
ISLAND
JING: KING OF BANDITS
JING: KING OF BANDITS - TWILIGHT TALES
JULINE
KARE KANO
KILL ME, KISS ME
KINDAICHI CASE FILES, THE
KING OF HELL
KODOCHA: SANA'S STAGE
LAMENT OF THE LAMB
LEGAL DRUG
LEGEND OF CHUN HYANG, THE
LES BIJOUX
LOVE HINA
LOVE OR MONEY
LUPIN III
LUPIN III: WORLD'S MOST WANTED
MAGIC KNIGHT RAYEARTH I
MAGIC KNIGHT RAYEARTH II
MAHOROMATIC: AUTOMATIC MAIDEN
MAN OF MANY FACES
MARMALADE BOY
MARS
MARS: HORSE WITH NO NAME
MINK
MIRACLE GIRLS
MIYUKI-CHAN IN WONDERLAND
MODEL
MOURYOU KIDEN: LEGEND OF THE NYMPH
NECK AND NECK
ONE
ONE I LOVE, THE
PARADISE KISS
PARASYTE
PASSION FRUIT
PEACH FUZZ
PEACH GIRL
PEACH GIRL: CHANGE OF HEART
PET SHOP OF HORRORS
PITA-TEN
PLANET LADDER

09.21.04T

W9-AGJ-330

STOP!

This is the back of the book.
You wouldn't want to spoil a great ending!

This book is printed "manga-style," in the authentic Japanese right-to-left format. Since none of the artwork has been flipped or altered, readers get to experience the story just as the creator intended. You've been asking for it, so TOKYOPOP® delivered: authentic, hot-off-the-press, and far more fun!

DIRECTIONS

If this is your first time reading manga-style, here's a quick guide to help you understand how it works.

It's easy... just start in the top right panel and follow the numbers. Have fun, and look for more 100% authentic manga from TOKYOPOP®!

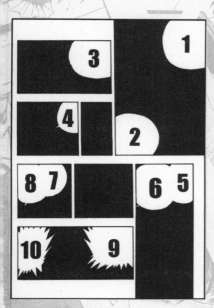

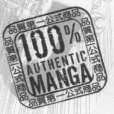